Mac Toys

12 Cool Projects for Home, Office, and Entertainment

John Rizzo

Scott Knaster

Wiley Publishing, Inc.

Dedicated to our moms.

Mac Toys: 12 Cool Projects for Home, Office, and Entertainment

Published by
Wiley Publishing, Inc.
10475 Crosspint Blvd.
Indianapolis, Indiana 46256
www.wiley.com

Wiley Publishing, Inc.

For general information on our other products and services please contact our Customer Care Department within the United States at (800) 762-2974, outside the United States at (317) 572-3993 or fax (317) 572-4002.

Trademarks: Wiley, the Wiley Publishing logo are trademarks or registered trademarks of John Wiley & Sons, Inc. and/or its affiliates. Mac is a registered trademark of Apple Computer, Inc. ExtremeTech and the ExtremeTech logo are trademarks of Ziff Davis Publishing Holdings, Inc. Used under license. All rights reserved. All other trademarks are the property of their respective owners. Wiley Publishing, Inc., is not associated with any product or vendor mentioned in this book.

Mac Toys is an independent (publication) and has not been authorized, sponsored, or otherwise approved by Apple Computer, Inc.

AirPort, Apple, DVD Studio Pro, Final Cut Pro, Finder, FireWire, iBook, iDVD, iLife iMac, iMovie, iPhoto, iPod, iTunes, Mac, Mac OS, Panther, PowerBook, Power Mac and QuickTime are trademarks or registered trademarks of Apple Computer, Inc.

Wiley also publishes its books in a variety of electronic formats. Some content that appears in print may not be available in electronic books.

Library of Congress Control Number: 2004100362

ISBN: 0-7645-4351-2

Printed in the United States of America

10 9 8 7 6 5 4 3 2 1

WILEY

Credits

Vice President and Executive Group Publisher:
Richard Swadley

Vice President and Executive Publisher:
Bob Ipsen

Vice President and Publisher:
Joseph B. Wikert

Executive Editorial Director:
Mary Bednarek

Executive Editor:
Chris Webb

Editorial Manager:
Kathryn A. Malm

Development Editor:
Emilie Herman

Production Editor:
Angela M. Smith

Media Development Specialist:
Jennifer Heleine
Kristin McMullan

Permissions Editor:
Carmen Krikorian

Text Design & Composition:
Wiley Composition Services

Cover Designer:
Anthony Bunyan

About the Authors

John Rizzo bought his first Mac in 1984, and soon began writing about them. A former staff editor for MacUser magazine, John now writes about Mac hardware and software for CNET.com and for Mac magazines. His books include the *How the Mac Works* series and *Macintosh Windows Integration*. John also publishes MacWindows.com, a web site devoted to helping Macs get along in a Windows world. John still has a T-shirt promoting Scott's famous Macintosh Programming Secrets.

Scott Knaster has been writing about Macs for as long as there have been Macs. Scott's books *How to Write Macintosh Software* and *Macintosh Programming Secrets* were required reading for Mac programmers for more than a decade. A regular speaker at Mac industry conferences, Scott has written books for non-programmers, too, including *Macworld Discover Internet Explorer* and *MSN the Everyday Web*. Scott has every issue of Mad magazine, which explains a lot about his philosophy of life.

Foreword

I believe Mac users not only think different, we are different. We like our Macs, thank you very much. We find ways to spend more time with our Macs because we like them so much. And we love to tinker with our Macs.

From the days of ResEdit, to the golden age of HyperCard, and into the AppleScript and Xcode era, Mac users have prided themselves on their ability to take their Mac and make it do something new or different. They turn their Macs into wireless jukeboxes; install neon lighting effects in 'em; use 'em to control robots, manage household appliances, and ever so much more. Heck, Andy Ihnatko uses some of the Macs in his extensive collection as "Original MacQuariums," complete with living fish.

Now I was fortunate to have been on the MacMania Geek Cruise to Hawaii last summer where Ihnatko presented a workshop on building a genuine MacQuarium from scratch. So I kind of know how to do that. But I've always wondered how to do some of the other cool Mac stuff I'm always hearing about...

What's the deal with controlling lights and appliances from your Mac? How hard is it to create your own Internet radio station? Classic arcade game emulators are supposed to let you relive old memories with old arcade favorites like Ms. Pac Man, Tempest, and Joust. But how does it work, and what do I need, and how do I set it up, and does it work in Mac OS X Panther, and...

You get the picture and the book you're holding in your hand is the answer. This book shows you how to do more than a dozen very cool things with your Mac. Want to run your own Internet radio station? Everything you need to know is right in Chapter 2. How about automating the lighting and appliances in your home? Piece of cake — read Chapter 1.

I'm deep into Chapter 8 myself, setting up an audio recording studio on my desktop, which is something I've always wanted. As soon as I recover from that (or, more precisely, as soon as my wallet recovers), I'm going automate the lighting in my office. And I'm thinking of maybe building a little robot...

I expect to spend a lot more quality time with *Mac Toys*; if you like to tinker with your Macs, you're going to love this book.

Bob "Dr. Mac" LeVitus

Winter, 2003

Acknowledgments

From John Rizzo:

John Calhoun and Keith Stattenfield deserve our thanks for their help on several of the topics in this book, and for their help in photographing their handiwork. (They also created some great Mac software.)

Thanks to Roger Evans' help on issues related to transferring film to digital format. Beside spending time explaining how his own invention worked, he pointed me in a number of directions that proved very helpful with the video-to-DVD chapter. Video and music guru Erik Holsinger also helped field my questions regarding these topics. Scott Sheppard was a helpful source of information on radio and recording technology.

While researching this book, I had the pleasure of speaking with numerous people at the companies that make the hardware and software described in *Mac Toys*. The folks at BIAS, Formac, and Live365 were very helpful, but many others were also key to our understanding of their products.

Editor Emilie Herman deserves a great deal of credit for the production of this book. Her suggestions and guidance were invaluable.

Finally, thanks to Scott Knaster shaping *Mac Toys* in its early stages, for producing some great work, and for bringing me on board. This has been one of the most enjoyable projects I've ever worked on.

From Scott Knaster:

Keith Stattenfield was a key contributor to this book. Without Keith's involvement, none of us would know how to make a digital picture frame. Keith helped in lots of ways, including brainstorming on several topics and connecting us with various experts.

Thanks to Lisa Lippincott and Steve Zellers for contributing their expertise. Although their work ultimately did not make into the book, the reasons were entirely beyond their control.

Leslie Evans provided answers to all the tough technical questions I had for her. Plus, Leslie is a terrific writer.

When I found myself looking for a book to write, super-agent Carole McClendon got me involved with this wonderful series. Working with Carole is always a joyful experience.

During the process of writing a book, things like life and health sometimes get in the way. When a family illness pulled me away from *Mac Toys*, my co-author and publisher could not have been more supportive. Chris Webb and Emilie Herman at Wiley were amazingly understanding, allowing me to put my family first when I really needed to. John Rizzo picked up the slack I created, doing all the work on the book that needed doing when I cut back. I will always be grateful for Chris, Emilie, and John's understanding and hard work.

I couldn't do anything without the support I get from my wife and kids. To Barbara, Jess, and Devi, thanks for giving me everything I need, including encouragement, love, sports news, and soup.

Special thanks from both authors to Chris Negus, author of *Linux Toys* and *Red Hat Bible*, for inspiring the Toys series of books for hardcore technology enthusiasts.

Introduction

"The Mac is a toy"—this was a common taunt we Mac users heard a lot from PC users in the mid-1980s. Back then, "real" computer users didn't need graphics or a mouse—typing commands at a dot prompt was the only way to do real work. Or so they said.

The Mac is now 20 years old, and time has proven the old naysayers wrong. The Mac turned out to be the model for every personal computer. Macs are powerful tools used to publish magazines and books, to produce professional music, and to create special effects on TV and in movies. Macs are also used for accounting and finance, marketing and sales, data management, and other important though less-than-exciting activities. In fact, time has also proven that it takes more power and sophistication to accomplish the more interesting tasks then it takes to do spreadsheets and programming. This is why that after using Macs for 20 years we came to this startling conclusion:

The Mac actually *is* a toy.

Apple tells you that you can watch a movie on PowerBook on an airplane flight, or listen to music using iTunes. But there are numerous hardware and software additions—*Mac Toys*—that you can add to your Mac to make it even more fun. You can use your Mac to create your own killer video, transfer your old LP collection to CDs, and to watch TV while skipping commercials. We teach you how to expand the functionality of the iPod, one of the most popular Mac toys around, and describe several home entertainment projects. You can also make your Mac *more* of a toy by turning it into a digital picture frame or a classic arcade game console.

The aim of this book is to help you get more fun out of your Mac. We've picked a dozen project areas that will help you use your Mac as a tool for hobbies that you may be working on or considering. This book will also introduce you to some new areas you might not have considered. Many of the projects are simple and everyday; others are purposely over-the-top. All are fun.

Who This Book Is For

There are plenty of books that tell you how to use Mac OS X, but they don't tell you much about what to use it for. On the opposite end, you'll also find books that make you an expert in a particular piece of software. But what if you want to *do stuff* with your Mac without becoming an expert—and you want to do a bunch of different things?

This is where *Mac Toys* comes in. This book is not just about Apple technology. It gives you the information you need to complete a project. We tell you about camera techniques to make better movies. You'll receive a background in audio technology that you'll need to even understand the difference between synthesizers, sequencers, and audio editors. Then we show you how to apply this knowledge using Mac software and hardware.

The Macintosh technology covered in this book focuses on what you need to know to complete your projects. Every piece of software has features you'll almost never use. These are not covered in *Mac Toys*. We feel that you don't have to be a master of every iMovie option to do great editing.

Given all this, we assume you've used a Mac for at least a few weeks. Mac power users will find lots of information here as well — some of the projects in this book are rarely if ever found published. We assume that you know how to surf the Internet, which you'll need to do to check out software and to follow the web addresses we provide for further information. We also assume you have some time to play with your Mac.

How This Book Is Organized

Each chapter is about a different project area. Some chapters focus on a single project, other chapters describe multiple projects in a related field. Most chapter start with description of what the project is and what you can do with it. You'll then find a brief description of the steps needed to complete the project to let you know what you're in for. There is usually a What You Need section that lists briefly the hardware and software that you'll need. (You can use this as a reference.) Some chapters provide an explanation of the technology being used, such as audio, video, or wireless communications.

Later on in the chapter, you'll find a more detailed description of the hardware and software needed, giving examples of what is available and providing cost ranges. These sections often evaluate the options of different price ranges and make recommendations as to what works well, and where to find the hardware and software.

After this, most chapters begin to describe the projects themselves, first in general terms, then more detailed, with step-by-step directions using specific software or hardware. In the cases where there are several projects, we start with the simpler projects, and end up with hard-core examples of what other people are doing. Several chapters include a Mac Toys Top Ten List, giving you our opinion of the best of the genre.

The chapters are arranged with simpler topics coming at the beginning, and more complex projects towards the end. The projects at the beginning don't take much skill or money. As the book goes on, we introduce projects that may take some practice on your part in order for you to get good at it.

We start the *Mac Toys* with a chapter on controlling your household appliances with your Mac. A step-by-step example is given, but you'll find suggestions for many different types of household automation projects. Home automation is fairly quick and easy to implement, inexpensive to start, and fairly low-tech. Still, home automation has a very high gee-whiz factor compared to the effort required. It's very cool.

Chapter 2 describes how you can set up your own Internet radio station, so that you can share your musical tastes with rest of the world. If you are not familiar with Internet radio, this chapter explains how you can be first a listener, then a broadcaster. It's actually much easier than you might think.

Chapter 3 moves to television — specifically, bringing TV to your Mac. We explore TV viewing on your Mac, and then recording TV on your Mac. Ever want to watch TV live while skipping commercials? This is the chapter for you.

In Chapter 4, we take a close look at Apple's iPod, a peripheral that lets you carry your entire music collection with you wherever you go. This is an ability that has won rave reviews and widespread popularity for the MP3 player, but you can extend your iPod's capabilities far beyond what it already can do.

Chapter 5 focuses on the Mac itself — specifically, a PowerBook or iBook that is no longer your main machine. We'll show you how to transfer it into a digital picture frame that you can hang on the wall, providing a constantly changing slide show of your favorite photos.

In Chapter 6, we describe how to cut the wires to your Mac and still have it communicate with the Internet and other Macs. This is wireless networking made simple.

With Chapter 7, we begin to move into some of the more meaty projects. Because there are some many different but related activities related to audio, we decide to put synthesizers, working with musical instruments, and audio recording all in this chapter. Where other chapters on music-related topics are focused on different ways to listen to, collect, or broadcast music, Chapter 7 covers how to create music using your Mac.

Chapter 8 will teach you how to turn your Mac into a classic video game machine. Star Wars, Robotron, and Frogger are part of gamming history but can be alive on your Mac. Your options range from installing some free software to building a Mac-powered video arcade game console.

Chapter 9 describes how you can convert your vinyl LP records to audio CDs, or even import them to your iPod. The can be a real money-saver if you have a large record collection, but needs to be done correctly in order to get good results. You might want to look at Chapter 7 first to get the basics about audio technology.

Chapter 10 is the sister chapter of 9 — how to convert your video or film collection to DVDs. The concept is the same as for digitized audio, but uses different hardware and software. We'll use iMovie to spruce up those old home movies.

Sticking with iMovie as a great video editor, Chapter 11 describes how to create your own home movies using your Mac and a digital camcorder. The goal here is not just to get images into your Mac, but the create an interesting video that people will want to watch — a killer video. Much of this chapter describes simple shooting and editing techniques that you can use to make your movies appealing and exciting.

We end the book with another, simpler project with a high gee-whiz factor — setting up a wireless jukebox in your house. With the Mac as the jukebox, of course.

What You Need To Use This Book

You'll need a Mac. You can do most of these projects with almost any recent version of Mac OS, but in our step-by-step directions, we're assuming you are running Mac OS X, version 10.2 or later. Panther (10.3) will work fine, but isn't required for any of these projects. In a few chapters, we mention some specific things that work with Mac OS 9 or earlier. These are projects that take an old Mac that is just sitting around and transforms it into something else.

The requirements for memory and hard disk space vary with the project. Controlling your appliances (Chapter 1) takes negligible system resources, while any of the projects involving digital video can require tens of gigabytes of free hard disk space and ample memory. Each chapter will go into details of what your Mac needs.

There may also be peripherals you need. For instance, if you're shooting a killer video you'll need a digital camcorder. If you're converting your LPs to CDs you need a phonograph turntable. In these chapters, you'll find recommendations for what to look for and where to look.

In terms of software, we try to stick with what comes with Mac OS X, such as iTunes and iMovie, or what is inexpensive. Yes, you can spend $1000 on professional video or audio editing software, but it just isn't necessary. Most of the commercial software that we use as examples is available as demonstration versions that let you try out the software before you buy it. Demo versions usually work for 10-to-30 days, or have some other limitations.

What's on the Companion Web Site

One of the exciting things about technology is the rapid pace at which it evolves. The advances in the newest wave of Macs, software, and peripherals are sometimes amazing, and almost always make our Mac Toys cooler than ever.

The flip side to this is that last year's hot computer wonder is next year's antiquated museum piece. This can be tough on buyers of computer gear, as well as on people who write about technology. For instance, just as we were putting this book to bed, Apple introduced some new products that would have been great to include. Fortunately, we can use technology itself to help us keep Mac Toys up-to-date: the Mac Toys Web site.

You can find the Mac Toys companion Web site at www.wiley.com/compbooks/extremetech.

You can use this site to check up on the latest tools for creating your Mac Toys projects. This includes advances in Apple products, as well as in the third-party tools we describe. If necessary, the Web site will revisit the recommendations we made in this book, so that if a better way comes along to build a Mac Toy, we'll let you know about it. From time to time, the Web site will also contain items not directly related to the projects in the book, but which we think you'd be interested in knowing about.

So, if you're interested in the latest and greatest in Mac Toys, check out the Mac Toys companion Web site.

Contents at a Glance

Contents

· ·

Control Your Lights and Appliances

L ights that go on and off, dim and brighten, all by themselves. Appliances that respond to the time of day and the presence or lack of daylight. Coffee makers that turn themselves on and off. You still can't order an "Earl Grey" (as *Star Trek's* Captain Picard does), but you can have your house obey voice commands.

This is the automated house, and your Mac is in control of it. Amazing as it sounds, the automated house isn't that difficult to create. It doesn't require ripping up anything in your house — there are no new wires. It just requires some simple, inexpensive modules plugged into your power outlets and some software on your Mac. For less than the cost of *Microsoft Office*, you can automate an entire home. This chapter looks at the scope of what's possible. How is any of this possible? Read on.

Home Automation and X10

Most of the home automation projects described in this chapter revolve around a technology called X10. You can find automation products that use infrared and radio frequency technologies, but they don't have low cost, ease of installing, and versatility of X10. With this technology, you don't have to build an infrastructure, so you can automate your rented apartment and take it all with you when you leave.

You can start with an initial investment of $40, and build little by little as you automate more functions. There are two basic steps to automating your home: putting in the X10 equipment (small devices that plug into AC outlets) and adding software to your Mac to control and respond to the devices. You can purchase X10 modules at RadioShack and other stores, and on the Internet.

First, a taste of what you can do with X10 technology.

Where X10 Came From

The name "X10" is unrelated to the Unix X-11 standard, and is much older than Apple's Mac OS X. The technology was invented by a small Scottish company, Pico Electronics Ltd. of Glenrothes Scotland in the late 1970s. For several years, Pico designed the first microprocessors for pocket calculators. The company worked on creating several other new products before they came up with the idea of digital signals over AC wires. They called their home automation technology "X10" simply because it was the tenth project they created. Pico soon formed a new company to create X10 devices, which is now called X10 Ltd.

In December 1997, the X10 patent expired and the technology became an open standard. The X10 company (www.X10.com) that Pico created is now just one of many companies that makes X10 hardware.

The Automated Home

The automated home makes events happen without you having to think about it — lights and appliances turn on and off, complicated TV and stereo systems become simple, and energy conservation saves you money. You can automatically open your drapes in the morning or shut off the coffee pot after you leave for work. You can also control items manually from anywhere in the house, and sometimes from outside of the house, from a phone or the Web. You can also set up the Mac to react to sensor readings and send out commands.

These are some of the main areas that you can automate:

- **Lighting.** Lights are the most common item automated and are probably where you will start your automation efforts. Lights will turn on just before you get home or just after you go to bed. Or, while you are out of town, have lights go on and off as if you were still in town. You also can dim lights. You can control individual lamps, as well as in-wall and ceiling-mounted lights. And because you can control lights from anywhere in the house, you can light a dark room before you step into it.

- **TV and stereo.** Complex home entertainment are, well, complex to use. You have TV, a satellite receiver, DVD player, VCR, stereo receiver/amplifier, and perhaps multiple speakers in different rooms. The automated house can simplify all of this. You can have a single button set to turn on multiple entertainment units, or have the house do it for you.

- **Security.** You can save a lot of money on traditional security services by creating your own with your automated home. You can connect door, window, and motion sensors, as well as cameras and alarms to the system. The automated home can call you or send you an email if some event is triggered, such as a smoke detector going off — this lets you call the fire department before the fire gets big enough for the neighbors to see it.

- **Water your yard only when it needs it.** You may have an automatic sprinkler system that turns on at certain times, whether you need it or not. In the automated house, your sprinklers will turn off when it starts raining. And if it has already rained, a sensor will detect if the ground is already soaked and prevent the sprinklers from starting.

- **Phone systems.** You can use a phone as a remote control from in your house or outside of it. You can use the keypads on the phone, or use voice recognition to issue voice commands. You can also screen calls so totally that the phone won't even ring if it's from someone not on your list. You can also have your home phone call you at different numbers to alert you to various conditions, including a flood in your basement, a fire, a house that's too hot, or maybe that your tropical fish tank heater is on the fritz.

- **Regulate temperature.** An automated house can regulate temperature in different ways. You can save on energy costs by keeping the heating or cooling systems to a minimum while you're out. They would only kick in 30 minutes before you got home, so you would walk into a comfortable climate. While you're away, you can have your house contact you if it gets too hot or too cold for your pets. You can then turn on the air conditioning or heating from your remote location. But temperature regulation isn't just a matter of controlling thermostats. The house can close the draperies at certain times of the day to block the sun.

Although there are wireless add-ons (both infrared and radio frequency), the bulk of this automation is accomplished through X10 technology. This chapter will tell you what you need to know to get started on any of these projects.

About X10 Technology

X10 is a standard for controlling home automation devices over your building's existing electrical wiring. X10 transmits low-power digital pulses (representing 1s and 0s) through a building's AC power lines. The information transmitted usually consists of simple commands telling a module to switch, off, or to dim.

X10 equipment is easy to install — you often just plug a module into an AC socket and then plug your lamp or appliance into the module. The modules are inexpensive, starting at just over $10. (There are also X10-enabled light switches and wall sockets, which we'll get into later in the section on lighting.)

The X10 modules can be receivers, transmitters, or both. (See Figure 1-1.) X10 receivers accept commands and respond by turning on or off. A lamp module could receive an "On" command through the AC power socket it is plugged into. The module contains a little switch, which opens when the On command is received, providing juice to the lamp and thus turning it on.

An X10 transmitter sends the command to the receiver connected to the lamp or appliance. A transmitter can be a hand-held keypad plugged into an AC outlet — you punch in a command, and a light goes on in another room. A transmitter can also be a sensor, such as thermostat or a motion detector.

Your Mac can also be an X10 transmitter, running X10 software and connected through a USB or serial port to an X10 interface box. Your Mac acts as a type of X10 transmitter called a controller, which means that you can program it with software. Some devices, including your Mac, can be both receivers and transmitters of X10 commands. These devices will respond to X10 commands by issuing other X10 commands.

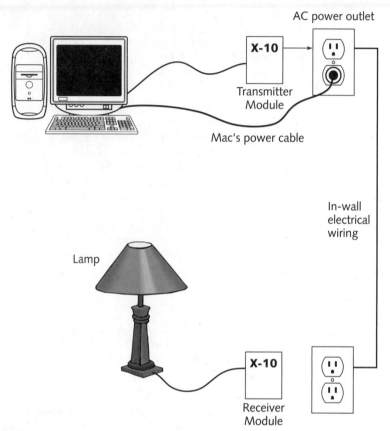

FIGURE 1-1: The basic X10 system consists of a transmitter and a receiver of commands.

Of course, you can have more than one transmitter and one receiver in your house. But when an X10 transmitter sends an On command, you don't have to have all of the lights and appliances in the house go on. The reason is that each X10 module has a unique address that identifies it as the recipient of a command. The address consists of a number from 1 through 16 and a letter from A through P (the first 16 letters of the alphabet). This gives you 16 times 16 addresses, or 256, in the form of 1A, 1B, 1C . . . 16N, 16O, 16P. Therefore, you can have a maximum of 256×10 devices in your house. The letters are called the house code; the numbers are the unit code.

For most X10 devices, you set the address manually. This is often in the form of two dials you can set with a screwdriver, one for the letter, one for the number (Figure 1-2).

FIGURE 1-2: Many X10 modules require that you set a unique address on two dials like these.

Image Courtesy of SMARTHOME, Inc. Copyright © 2003.

Because X10 signals depend on the electrical characteristics of your home's wiring, some houses can see problems with communications between devices. Fortunately, these problems (such as electrical interference) are well known and easily fixed by plugging in inexpensive devices into a wall socket. These are described in the "Troubleshooting" section later in the chapter.

What You Need

The great thing about home automation is that it is fairly simple and inexpensive. Unlike some of the other *Mac Toys* projects, you don't need a fast Mac or a lot of hard disk space or memory. The pieces are inexpensive and easy to find. Here's what you need:

- **A Mac.** You have a choice of running the software on the modern Mac you use every day or dedicating an old Mac to the task. To get the most out of home automation, you'll want to leave the Mac running all the time.

- **Software.** Beside the Mac itself, the software is the only Macintosh-specific item on this list, and probably your most important decision. You can choose from among five X10 automation applications.

- **Computer-to-X10 interface.** You can find these for as little as $35. However, check with your software first — each X10 application supports a certain set of specific interfaces. (See Figure 1-3.)

- **Cable converter.** If you're using a newer Mac and an X10 interface box with USB, you don't need a converter cable. You do need a converter if your interface box has the standard X10 serial connector. You also need a converter if your Mac is an older (pre-iMac) model without USB.

- **X10 modules and sensors.** These are the X10 receivers you'll use to control lights and appliances, and the thermometers, light sensors, motion detector, and other hardware you'll use to input data into the system.

- **X10 filters.** You may need between two and five noise filters for appliances that create electrical noise. These are small boxes that plug into the wall. (See the "Troubleshooting" section later in the chapter.)

- **X10 coupler.** You may need a phase coupler device to enable devices on opposite ends of the house to communicate. (See the "Troubleshooting" section later in the chapter.)

Where to Buy X10 Gadgets

You can find X10 hardware in certain retail stores. RadioShack is probably the biggest retailer carrying X10 hardware. The company carries products from several manufacturers, and has its own branded hardware. RadioShack's Web site (www.radioshack.com) has an online catalog in the Security & Home Automation section, but you may need to use Internet Explorer to access it, as Safari didn't work to well with the site at publishing time.

There are some great Web sites where you can buy X10 products. SmartHome (www.smarthome.com) is a large site that focuses on X10 and related home automation products. In addition to offering a lot of X10 hardware and two different Mac software applications, SmartHome.com has a good deal of information about X10 technology, as well as ideas for home automation projects. SmartHome.com also sells books and videos on home automation topics.

X10, Ltd. (www.X10.com), the company that started it all, doesn't offer much in the way of Mac software, but does have a large assortment of every type of X10 module and peripheral that you could think of.

Marrick Ltd. (www.marrickltd.com) is another manufacturer of X10 and other electronic equipment, which is available for sale at the company Web site as well as other places. Marrick doesn't sell Mac software, but has links to a few software sites. You'll also find X10 products at HomeAutomation (www.homeautomationnet.com).

A good way to get started is with one of the "starter kits" that most X10 vendors offer. These are bundles an X10 computer interface, some X10 appliance modules, and software. For instance, SmartHome offers several starter kits focused in different areas, such as lighting or security, as well as general-purpose kits. In addition to the convenience of getting everything you need to start, the starter kits are usually pretty good deals, offering a discount over the cost of buying everything separately. If you're paying for software as part of a bundle, just make sure you get Mac software. You can also buy software and software/hardware starter kits directly from some software manufacturers. (But before you do, read the section on X10 software for the Mac later in this chapter.)

Controller Hardware

We discuss the various X10 modules throughout this chapter, but first we want to describe the hardware that will be used to control the modules. These devices can issue the standard X10 commands: On, Off, Dim (for lights), Bright (the opposite of Dim), PreDim, All Lights ON, and All Units OFF.

First up is the X10-computer interface, followed by optional hand-manipulated X10 controllers. After that, some thoughts on the Mac itself, which will be the main controller in automated home.

X10-Computer Interfaces

The basic function of an X10-computer interface is to transmit and receive X10 commands and signals, and to accept and pass along commands from and to the Mac. There is nothing Mac-specific about any X10-computer interface — they will also work with PCs. The exact model of X10-computer interface you use depends on the Mac software you want to run. Each application will work with certain pieces of hardware.

SmartHome's PowerLinc USB ($35, www.smarthome.com/1132U.html) is the first X10-computer interface with a Universal Serial Bus (USB) port. (Figure 1-3 shows the USB port at bottom.) USB means you don't have to bother with converter cables, which can cost more than the PowerLinc. Another handy feature of the PowerLinc is that it preserves an AC outlet by providing an AC plug as a "pass-through," which you can use for any electrical device, including your Mac. The PowerLinc USB comes bundled with software for Windows — ignore it. If you want to buy the PowerLinc USB bundled with Mac software, try Perceptive Automation's Web site (www.perceptiveautomation.com/indigo/). This is the maker of Indigo, the only X10 software for Mac OS X that supported the PowerLinc USB at the time of publication. Perceptive Automation often offers discounts on the PowerLinc USB when you purchase it with Indigo.

At the time of publication, all other X10-computer interfaces used a serial connection. If you're using a Mac with a USB port, you will need *two* converter cables — one that converts USB to the old Mac 8-pin serial standard, and another to convert the Mac serial to a 9-pin X10 connector. The serial-to-serial cables are inexpensive (under $20), but the USB converters are not. One of the best USB-to-serial converters is the Keyspan USB Serial Adapter (www.keyspan.com), shown in Figure 1-4. While other USB-to-serial converter cables can be troublesome with Mac OS X, the Keyspan has some of the best Mac OS X drivers and is seamless to use. However, at $49 for the single-port model (USA-19HS), the converter costs more than the PowerLinc USB, and, you may need another converter cable to connect from the Keyspan to the serial port in the X10 interface. However, if you are using an older, pre-iMac model, you won't need a USB-serial converter.

FIGURE 1-3: SmartHome's PowerLinc USB is
the first X10-computer interface with USB.
Image Courtesy of SMARTHOME, Inc. Copyright © 2003.

Figure 1-4: You can use the Keyspan USB Serial
Adapter to connect USB to serial X10 interfaces.
Courtesy of Keyspan.

SmartHome offers several similarly priced, similar-looking PowerLinc models that have serial ports. X10 Ltd offers several models, including the CM-11 and the CP290, which are often included in a bundle with X10 modules and Windows software called ActiveHome. (MouseHouse's bundle of its software includes the CP290.) This is a unit that can accept downloading of commands, so you can turn the Mac off. Marrick's LynX-PLC ($100, www.marrickltd.com/lynx105.htm) is another X10-computer interface that works with some of the software packages.

When you are shopping for X10 equipment, you will also find bigger, more expensive inter- faces that are manually programmable. However, these devices are not necessary when you are using a Mac. They duplicate some of what the Mac's does, but don't give you the flexibility and capabilities that Mac X10 software can offer. However, even with a Mac, additional Hand-held controllers can sometimes be useful, as described next.

Hand-held Controllers

Your Mac doesn't have to be in charge of everything. You can use manual controllers to set cer- tain combinations of lighting or appliances to switch on with a single button. Wired controllers such as the SmartHome Mini Controller ($12, see Figure 1-5), which plug into an AC outlet, let you do things like turn all the lights on or off, dim lights, and start or stop appliances, all without getting out of bed.

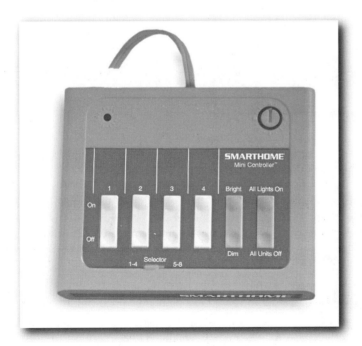

FIGURE 1-5: Manually operated X10 controllers (such as this SmartHome MiniController) plug into an AC outlet.

Image Courtesy of SMARTHOME, Inc. Copyright © 2003.

Other controllers are more sophisticated, with more buttons. The wall-mounted controller in Figure 1-6 lets you set combinations of lighting and dim settings for different occasions, such as morning, dinner, and watching TV. The SmartHome KeypadLinc 8 ($80) replaces an in-wall light switch or dimmer switch and is programmable.

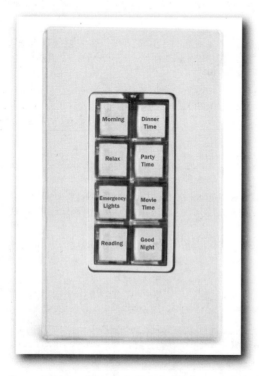

FIGURE 1-6: A wall-mounted controller lets you select combinations of settings with the press of a button.
Image Courtesy of SMARTHOME, Inc. Copyright © 2003.

You can also find X10-compatible hand-held wireless remotes, some small enough to put on your keychain. These are not strictly X10 devices, but are X10 compatible, in that they use infrared or radio frequency signals through the air to communicate to an X10-compatible receiver plugged into the house wiring. Leviton's Universal Remote Control gives you X10 commands, such as On, Off, Dim, and Bright.

Which Mac to Use

The question of which Mac to use comes down to a choice between using your regular Mac for X10 controlling or dedicating one for the purpose. Running X10 control software doesn't take a lot of processing power or hard disk space, making an old Mac a viable candidate, even if it is running Mac OS 7, 8, or 9. However, the lack of intensive hardware requirements means that you can run X10 software on your Mac OS X with your other applications without slowing anything down. Mac OS X gives you a slightly bigger list of software to choose from, in that one of the best X10 applications does not run on OS 8 or OS 9. (See the section on software a little later in this chapter.)

Another thing to keep in mind is that you'll get more automation from your Mac if it is running all the time. Some software lets you download the Mac's commands to a module, but with those kinds of commands, you don't really need a Mac at all — you could punch similar commands directly into a controller.

A drawback to older Macs is that they are more prone to hard drive failure; power supplies can also fail. The flip side to that argument is that you can also buy a used pre-iMac model for less than the cost of a new hard drive.

If you are going to use software designed to be on all the time, you might want to use a Mac model that is quiet. If your Mac has a separate monitor, you can usually turn off cathode ray tube monitors without affecting the Mac software. This will extend the life of the monitor and save on energy costs.

Prepping an Old Mac

If you're using a relatively modern Mac, there's nothing you need to do in terms of preparation — just install your X10 software, plug in a computer interface, and start setting up your automated house.

For an old Mac (one running Mac OS 9 or earlier), there are a few things you can do to it to prevent problems:

- Clean out the hard drive. Delete unnecessary files and folders or applications that you will never use. If the hard drive is close to being full, it will slow performance.

- Clean out the System folder. Use the Extensions Manager control pane to turn off extensions that you aren't using. An easy way to do this is to use the pop-up menu to select "Mac OS only." This will turn off any extensions that didn't come with the Mac.

- If you aren't using networking, turn off AppleTalk and File Sharing using the control panels. This will boost performance.

- Run one or more disk utilities, such as Apple's Disk First Aid (found on your Mac's system disk) or Norton Utilities. If the utility finds a problem, run it again. Keep running it until it doesn't find a problem.

- If you are having problems, reinstall the operating system from your system CD (or floppy disks).

You can upgrade the operating system on your old Mac to a later version, as long as you don't go too far — more advanced versions of Mac OS can bog down older Macs.

If your Mac is running System 7, don't upgrade it to Mac OS 8 unless your X10 software requires it. A Mac of this vintage will do better with System 7.5.5, which was a stable version. System 7.6 was also stable, but used more memory and doesn't work on all models. (Apple has a list of old models at that do and don't run on 7.6 at
http://docs.info.apple.com/article.html?artnum=8970).

If the Mac is running Mac OS 8, don't install Mac OS 9, which uses a lot more memory. If you have a pre-iMac (beige) Mac with a four-digit model number (such as Power Mac 7500), you can use Mac OS 8.6, which was a solid version. If your Mac is a pre-PowerPC Mac (with a three-digit model number, such as Quadra 700), then Mac OS 8.5 is the latest version you can use.

If you have Mac OS 9.0, the latest you should upgrade to is 9.0.4. Later versions were created to accommodate Mac OS X Classic mode.

Apple has some old system software updates at www.info.apple.com/. These are updates that were originally free updates, and not major updates.

X10 Software for Mac

The Mac X10 software you decide to use will determine which interface modules you can run, which Mac operating system you can use, and which computer interfaces you can use.

There are five X10 applications: In order of power and features, starting with the most powerful, there are Indigo, Thinking Home, Xtension, Mouse House, and CP290 Director, costing from $90 to $10. Three of these, XTension, Mouse House, and CP290 Director, are only available for Mac OS 8 and 9 or earlier, though XTension and Mouse House will run in Mac OS X Classic.

Thinking Home, MouseHouse, and CP290 Director let you download commands to an X10 interface, the C11 or the CP290 from X10, Ltd. However, these interfaces are mere schedulers — you can do much more with Mac as controller, such as generate X10 commands in real time, have the system contact you when events occur, and let you control your system remotely through the Mac. The real power is in programs like Indigo and Xtension, which require you to keep the Mac on all the time.

Indigo

Indigo from Perceptive Automation (www.perceptiveautomation.com/indigo/) is the newest — and the most powerful — of the X10 applications. It is easy to use and is flexible, with features going beyond simple timed events. Indigo can send you email when certain events occur (such as a power failure), and you can control the system with email. You can also set Indigo to start heating your hot tub just by sending it an email message. Indigo also lets you control your X10 system using a Bluetooth-equipped Sony Ericsson phone. Indigo supports AppleScripts, but there is much you can do in the way of scripting using menus and buttons that you don't have to write any AppleScript code to come up with some advanced triggering and control mechanisms.

Launched in 2003, Indigo was written specifically for Mac OS X — there is no Classic version, which means that you can't run it on an old Mac. At the time of publication, Indigo was the only X10 application that supported the PowerLinc USB computer interface from SmartHome, which means it doesn't need a USB-to-serial converter cable. It also supports SmartHome's

PowerLinc 1132A, a serial version that does require the converter. It also supports CM-11 (sometimes branded as ActiveHome) from X10 Ltd, and Marrick's LynX-PLC. Indigo does not download commands to the CM-11 interface module, but can do things that the module can't. For instance, you can have it automatically send you an email message when an event occurs. If you have an interface module that Indigo supports, X10-computer interfaces, you can try a fully functional copy of Indigo free for 30 days.

Indigo uses a simple user interface to create complex control situations. On the left side of the main window (see Figure 1-7) are four buttons labeled Devices, Trigger Actions, Time/Date Actions, and Group Action. With Devices selected, you see a list of X10-controlled devices, such as lamps and appliances, and X10 sensors, such as motion detectors or thermostats. Indigo gives you some samples (shown in the figure), but you can add your own with the New button. Double-click a device to enter its X10 address and other settings. To manually control a device, click once to select it and use the controls at the bottom. In Figure 1-7, we dimmed a light.

Click the second button down, and you get a list of *trigger actions* — actions that are responses to events. Instead of writing scripts, you choose items from pop-up menus. When you first install Indigo, you'll see a list of sample trigger actions, including "power failure email," "office light on," and "aquarium motion." Double-click an action, and you get a dialog with three tabs: Trigger, Condition, and Action (see Figure 1-8). The Trigger tab lets you define what causes the action. The Type pop-up menu lets you select triggers such as an X10 command, the change in a device's state, a received email, an application starting up, a power failure, and others. For each of these you select the circumstances in which the trigger is activated.

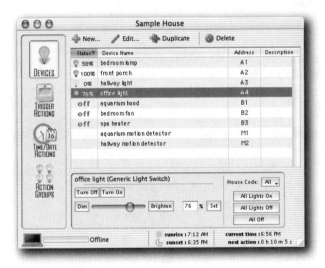

FIGURE 1-7: Indigo lets you send X10 commands manually through the Devices pane. Here, we are dimming a light.

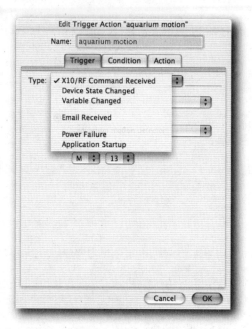

FIGURE 1-8: Editing a trigger action in Indigo lets you specify exactly what causes the trigger to fire and what will happen as a result.

The Condition tab puts further limitations on the trigger by letting you assign a time of day and specify whether various variables are true, false, greater than or less than, or follow other Booleans. Under the Action tab, you'll tell Indigo what to do in response to the trigger. The Type pop-up menu (shown in Figure 1-8) lets you select various types of actions, which you will specify after you select it from the menu. Included in this menu are send email, a way to notify yourself when something happens, and AppleScripts, which let you further customize your system.

Back in the main Indigo window, the third button is called Time/Date Actions and lists items that you can schedule for regular occurrence, such as turning lights on and off and dimming them. However, you can set conditions on these, so that they will or won't occur if certain actions are performed or certain sensors get a specific reading. For example, you can tell Indigo to start your sprinklers at 3 P.M. unless your outdoor rain sensors tell Indigo that it is raining.

Tip One of the powerful features of Indigo is that instead of setting an action to occur at a specific time, you can set it to occur at sunrise and sunset.

The last of the four buttons, Action Groups, lets you create settings for a combination of devices. You might create an action group called "Dinner Party" that has certain lights in multiple rooms turned on and dimmed to preset levels, with some of your other automatic actions disabled.

Another interesting Indigo feature is the ability to use a Bluetooth-enabled Sony Ericsson mobile phone as a remote control. To accomplish this, Indigo uses the Salling Clicker application from Salling Software (http://homepage.mac.com/jonassalling/Shareware/Clicker/index.html). Salling Clicker lets you run your Mac from the phone or a Palm hand-held. With Indigo's scripts, you can also use the phone to control Indigo, and therefore your house.

Indigo comes with extensive documentation in the Help menu. Perceptive Automation also has a helpful user forum at its Web site (www.perceptiveautomation.com/phpBB2/index.php), where you can post questions and read tips.

Thinking Home

Thinking Home ($39, www.alwaysthinking.com) from Always Thinking is now Mac OS X native. There are also versions available for earlier versions of Mac OS. Thinking Home doesn't measure up to Indigo in several ways. For one, the interface is a bit old, requiring a lot of typing, such as when you have to type to enter times to turn devices on. And unlike Indigo, you can't see the status of your devices all at once. More importantly, Thinking Home doesn't generate X10 commands based on input from devices. It only schedules events, such as turning appliances on and off, and dimming lights. The upside to being simpler is that Thinking Home can download these simple commands into an X10-computer interface, letting you shut off the Mac. If your X10 needs are very simple, Thinking Home might work for you (Figure 1-9).

While the Mac (and Thinking Home) is running, you can expand the functionality a bit by running a macro, a sequence of commands that is enacted by a single command. This enables you to set multiple devices at once. You can activate this command by voice if you have Apple's PlainTalk installed and turned on. (PlainTalk is included on the Thinking Home CD.) However, some of the supported X10-computer interfaces, such as the CP290 and the FireCracker, don't support macros.

Thinking Home has no USB support, so you will have to buy a USB converter such as the Keyspan device described earlier. Thinking home does support a number of different X10-computer interfaces from X10, Ltd. This includes the CM-11 and CM-12 (both called ActiveHome), and the IBM Home Director versions, called HD-11 and HD-12. Thinking Home also supports the CP10, CM-10, CM-17, CP290, as well as the FireCracker, a small wireless X10-computer interface that sends radio signals to a transceiver that plugs into the wall. If you have a choice, Always Thinking recommends the CP290 as the most reliable interface to use with Thinking Home.

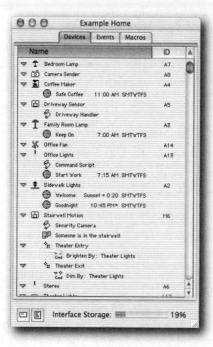

FIGURE 1-9: Thinking Home can do basic
scheduling of X10 events.

XTension

XTension ($90) from Sand Hill Engineering (www.shed.com) was once the top-rated X10 software for Mac. Readers who are familiar with X10 will argue that XTension's capabilities are closer to Indigo than Thinking Home, and therefore deserves to be ranked ahead of Thinking Home. However, at the time of publication, there was no Mac OS X version, and the developer had not committed to creating one. XTension didn't support USB X10-computer interfaces, but did support the CM11 (also called ActiveHome), three different models of Marrick's LynX, and an older interface called the Home Intelligence Corporation Two-Way.

Like Indigo, XTension does not download information to an interface, but it can generate X10 commands based on input from sensors and other X10 devices — again, one of the reasons to use a Mac instead of a manually operated programmable X10 controller. However, setting up XTension to generate X10 commands is quite a bit more difficult than doing so with Indigo, because XTension requires you to create scripts using AppleScript syntax and special AppleScript verbs from XTension. You don't exactly need to be a programmer, though it's more trouble than choosing items from menus, as in Indigo. If you want to generate X10 commands on Mac OS 7.1 through 9.x, XTension is the most capable tool.

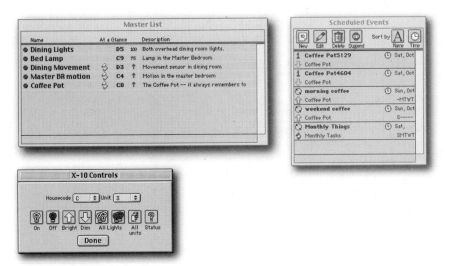

FIGURE 1-10: If you are running your X10 automated home on Mac OS 8 or 9, XTension is a good choice.

XTension's interface starts with a Master List of devices (Figure 1-10) that you can directly control with a separate X-Controls dialog. Like Indigo, XTension's Master List displays the current status of devices, including how much a light is dimmed. It also shows whether there is a script attached to it. The Scheduled Events window is where you configure a schedule for a device and attach a script to it.

Another interesting feature is that you can import a PICT graphic that is representation of your house. (You have to draw your own map in a drawing program.) Once it has been imported, you can drag items from the Master List to the map drawing. Icons appear on the map, which you can use to control the devices. For example, double-clicking on a lamp icon turns it on or off.

XTension comes with a detailed electronic manual, and the Sand Hill Web site is worth a look for all of its information on X10.

MouseHouse

At $34 MouseHouse (www.mousehouse.net, Figure 1-11) is an inexpensive application that will run in System 7 or 8. MouseHouse runs with the ActiveHome or CP290 computer interface. Although it hasn't been updated for more recent Mac operating systems, MouseHouse is similar in some ways to Thinking Home. It can download commands to the computer interface and thus let you turn off the Mac. And like Thinking Home, MouseHouse doesn't generate X10 commands on the fly, but does let you create macros.

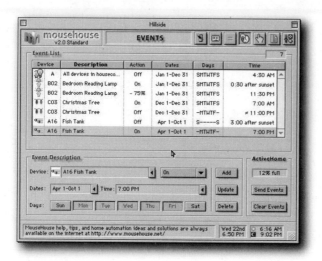

FIGURE 1-11: MouseHouse can schedule events in this window.

The MouseHouse Web site offers several starter kits for sale bundled with the software. The site also has some good information about X10 and X10 devices.

CP290 Director

If you have a really old Mac—such as one running System 7—and a CP290 X10 computer interface, and you want some really cheap software to experiment with, you might give a try to CP290 Director (http://thewoodwards.us/sw/CP290Director/index.shtml). This $10 shareware application runs only on System 7 through Mac OS 8.6. Because it isn't completely compatible with Mac OS 9, it's not a good idea to run it in Mac OS X Classic. The other limitation is that it works with only one X10 interface, the CP290 from X10, Ltd.

Home Automation Projects

There is almost no limit as to what you can automate with a Mac and X10 equipment. This section will give you a taste of what some of the possibilities are and a look at some of the hardware. This includes X10 receivers for controlling appliances and lights, sensors for recording the environment, and peripherals that can add to your X10 system. We start with lighting, which make up the most popular types of X10 projects.

Lighting

Lighting is a good way to start automating your house. It's easy, fast, and inexpensive to set up and get immediate results. There is also a lot you can do with automated lighting. If you wake before dawn, you can have lights come on in the morning in different parts of the house, then have them go off at different times during the day and at night. If you have fancy in-wall lights, you can control them, too, by having a particular combination of lights switch on with a single push of a controller button.

If you think creatively, there are other types of lighting you can control. For instance, by automating the lamp on your fish tank, you can give your fish the same amount of light every day. You can turn your Christmas tree lights on and off at a specific time or have them turn on when a motion sensor in the hallway detects that you've come home. And since your Mac knows what time it is, and the software knows when the sun will set today, so you can have lights go on at sunset, or shut off after sunrise.

For your lighting projects, you can use X10 lamp modules that plug into wall sockets, as well as special X10 switches and wall sockets. Each of these lighting devices is rated for a certain power level, typically 300 to 400 watts. You should be sure to stay within these levels. However, X10 devices for lighting should *not* be used for appliances. The reason is dimming.

Dimming

The basic X10 lamp modules that plug into wall sockets are different from those used by appliances in one important feature — they support dimming. When an X10 module is told to dim, it reduces the power delivered to incandescent bulbs. The standard lamp module will allow you to set the brightness between 0 and 100 percent. Assigning a number of 75 to a 100-watt bulb will get you approximately the brightness of a 75-watt bulb. By setting lighting levels differently for different times of the day or for different purposes, you can dramatically increase the versatility of your home's lighting.

Using your Mac software or a hand-held X10 controller, you can dim an incandescent light downwards from full brightness — that is, go from 100 to 50. You can also increase the brightness from another lever — say, from 40 to 75. The only thing you can't do is start from the off position and gradually get brighter. That's because X10 will first turn a light on at full brightness and then dim it. This means that you can't have the light wake you up by gradually getting brighter without going to full brightness first.

However, it is important to note that X10 dimming works *only* with incandescent bulbs — it won't work with fluorescent lighting. In fact, if the lamp has its own transformer, as do many compact fluorescents and halogen lights, the X10 dimming function could damage the lamp and the X10 receiver module. Similarly, appliances with transformers or motors (which is most appliances) can also be damaged by the X10 dimming function. You should never use lamp modules on fluorescent or halogen lights or on any kind of appliance.

Note You should be able to use an X10 module to dim halogen lights that do not have a transformer. However, since there are many different types of halogen lights, and it isn't obvious if they do or don't contain a transformer, it's safest to just avoid using X10 lamp modules with halogen lighting.

You can still use X10 appliance modules to turn standard fluorescent and halogen lights on and off. There is no problem if the lamp already has a built-in (non-X10) dimmer — when the X10 appliance module is switched "on," the built-in (non-X10) dimmer will work. However, X10 appliance modules may not work with compact fluorescent bulbs. In this case, there is no potential for damage, but the appliance module may sense a current flow that it interprets as an On command, which means that it might keep turning the light on.

Tip No space for an X10 lamp module at your AC socket? Try using an X10 light module that screws into a socket, such as X10's SocketRocket ($20, `www.x10.com/products/x10_lm15a.htm`).

X10 Wall-switches

If you have a lamp or a ceiling or wall-mounted light that is turned on and off by a wall switch, a plug-in lamp module isn't going to work. Ideally, what you would want is a situation where your Mac can turn the light on and off, but you can still use the wall switch when you walk into the room. Yes, you *could* have a completely automatic house, where motion sensors in every room turned on the light when you walked into it, but if the wall switch was in the off position, it wouldn't matter what your motion detectors saw.

Unless, that is, you were using an X10 wall-switch in place of your standard wall switch. This is a wall switch (like that shown in Figure 1-12) that looks and acts like your old switch, but also responds to X10 commands. These cost more than ordinary wall switches, but still start at under $10. There are several types of X10 switches for different wiring situations, such as two-way or three-way, and for different dimming situations. Some switches let you turn the lights on and off, but let your Mac do the dimming. Others will let you manually dim the lights at the switch, as well as let the controller dim it.

You may remember from the previous section that X10 dimming is a problem for fluorescent and halogen lamps and for appliances. You don't want to plug a vacuum cleaner into an AC outlet that is controlled by a dimming switch. For these situations, you can get X10 wall switches that don't dim — they just turn on and off, and don't respond to X10 dimming commands. These are the equivalent of plug-in appliance modules.

With X10 wall switches, you'll need to take care that you don't exceed the maximum power level for the switch. This is typically 500 or 600 watts.

X10 Wall Outlets

If you just don't like the look of an X10 module plugged into your wall socket, there is another way to go — replace the wall socket with an X10-controlled wall socket. You can find ones that are the equivalent of lamp modules (that is, they dim) and ones that are equivalent to appliance modules (they don't respond to X10 dimming commands).

You can also find "split" wall sockets — the top outlet is X10-controlled, while the bottom socket is a standard (always on) socket. This is handy for plugging in your vacuum cleaner or appliances that you don't want your Mac to control.

Replacing a wall switch with an X10 switch is a do-it-yourself task. If you've replaced a light switch before, X10 is no different. Be sure to shut off the circuit breaker that controls the circuit. If you can't figure it out, shut off the power to your home. Pull the original switch out, and note how it is wired—which colored wires go to which connectors. Then look at the directions that come with the X10 switch. The wiring differs depending on whether the room is wired in a one-way switch or two-way configuration. A book on basic home wiring from your local hardware store should help. SmartHome has wiring diagrams at its Web site for different configurations. (For instance, see www.smarthome.com/2383.html.)

Example: Motion-Triggered Porch Light

As an example, lets look at how you would set up a light to turn on when motion is detected. There are many uses for this, from lighting your backyard for security to having the lights go on automatically when you enter a room.

We'll use Indigo to set the conditions of when this will happen. Since we don't need the light to turn on in the daytime, we'll set the software to only turn on the light after sunset. Since this is a hallway light at the entryway of the house, we'll also set the light to go off 10 minutes after the last motion is detected.

FIGURE 1-12: X10 wall switches (such as this SmartHome SwitchLinc) respond to your Mac and let you manually turn the lights on and off.
Image Courtesy of SMARTHOME, Inc. Copyright © 2003.

First, install the motion detector in the hall. These are usually mounted on the wall or ceiling or in a corner. Next, enable that light to be X10-controlled with a plug-in lamp module, X10 switch, or other device. Make sure that you set an X10 address for both devices. (For the motion detector, you usually set the X10 address on the transceiver that plugs into an AC outlet.)

Now launch Indigo and configure the motion detector and the light:

1. Click the Devices button at the top left of Indigo's main window.

2. Click the New button at the top.

3. In the Create New Device dialog that appears, provide a name for the motion detector.

4. In the Type pop-up menu, choose Motion Detector.

5. Set the X10 address. The dialog should look like Figure 1-13.

6. Click the OK button. You'll now see the motion detector in the device list.

7. Click the New button to create a device for the light.

8. In the Create New Device dialog that appears, provide a name for the hallway light.

9. In the Type pop-up menu, choose the type of X10 control method. The pop-up menu lists several types of plug-in lamp modules and the Socket Rocket screw-in module. We'll select Generic Light Switch to indicate an X10-controlled wall switch.

10. Set the X10 address.

11. Click the OK button.

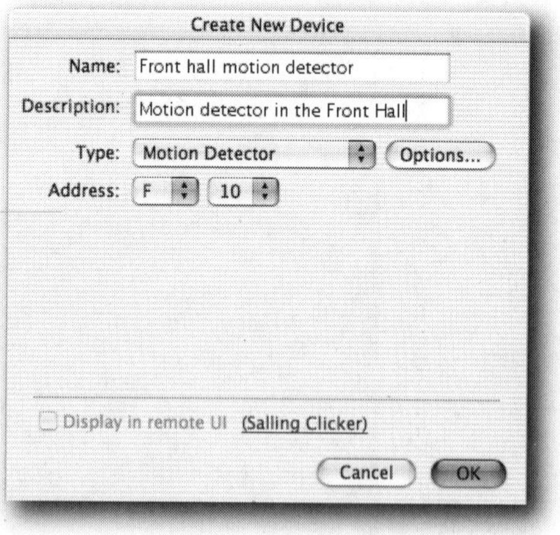

FIGURE 1-13: Setting up Indigo for a motion detector.

Next, you'll need to define a trigger action. This will tell Indigo to turn on the light when motion is detected. First, you define the trigger (receiving input from the motion detector). Next you set the Condition (after dark). Finally, you set the action (turn on the light). Here's how:

1. Click the Trigger Actions button at the left of Indigo's main window.

2. Click the New button at the top.

3. In the Create New Trigger Action dialog that appears, give a name for the trigger action, such as "Hall motion detected."

4. In the Type pop-up menu, choose X10/RF Command Received. (This refers to the X10 command received from the motion detector.)

5. In the Received pop-up menu, choose "On." (This refers to the "On" X10 command that will be received from the motion detector.)

6. Click Device button to select it. From the pop-up menu, select the name you gave to the motion detector. (The dialog will look like the one in Figure 1-14.)

7. Set the conditions under which Indigo will turn the light on. Click the Condition tab.

8. Select the button next to "If dark, after sunset." (Indigo knows what time the sun sets each day.) This will prevent the light coming on during the day.

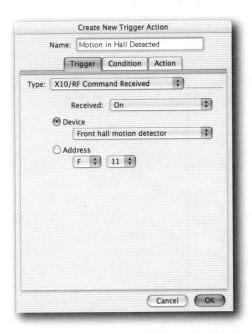

FIGURE 1-14: Creating a new Trigger Action begins by telling Indigo what will trigger the event.

9. Click the Action tab to tell Indigo what to do when it hears from the motion detector.

10. From the Type pop-up menu, choose Send Device Action.

11. From the Action pop-up menu, choose Turn On.

12. From the Device pop-up menu, choose the name you gave to the light (Front Hall Light in our example).

13. Finally, tell Indigo to shut the light off after a time. Click the check box next to "Auto-off after" and type 10 in the Minutes box.

That's it. If you want to have your Mac say something at the time of the action, you can type a phrase in the Speak field. (See Figure 1-15.)

Click OK when you're finished.

Security

You can use your Mac and X10 to make your home more secure in a lot of ways. The previous example of using motion sensors to turn on lights could be used for security. An outdoor motion sensor can pick up a person moving near a door or window and turn on lights on the outside and inside. You can also use your X10 system to make your home look and sound occupied while you are out for the day or for the week. This section presents some ideas of what is possible.

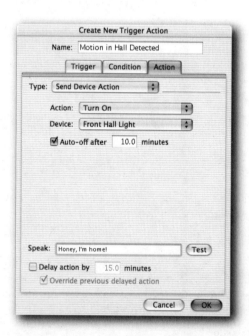

FIGURE 1-15: Defining the action in Indigo.

Sensors for Security

There are several types of sensors that you can use as your eyes and ears when you aren't around. They cost more than the X10 appliance and lighting modules previously described, but will be a lot less than having a security company come in and install a full-fledged security system.

Motion Detectors

Most consumer motion detectors use infrared technology to look for heat moving across its field of view. You'll want to make sure you get an X10 motion detector — one that responds to motion by sending out an X10 signal. (For instance, there's the SmartHome Version II Wireless X10 Motion Sensor, www.smarthome.com/4086.html.) Usually, a motion detector sends a wireless signal to a transceiver plugged into a wall socket. The transceiver sends the X10 signal to your Mac.

There are indoor motion detectors and more expensive outdoor models built to withstand the weather. If you have a cat wandering around the house all day, you can also find "pet-immune" motion detectors that ignore objects that are the size of a cat or a dog.

Open Door/Window Sensors

These are sensors that consist of two parts, one on the door and one on the door jam. When the door opens, the two parts separate, and the sensor sends out an X10 signal. You can use this signal to send you an email, turn on a surveillance camera, or turn on a light. Using Indigo, you can have an open door activate an action group doing all of these things.

Not all sensors are related to security. For instance, you can get rain-and-snow detectors to tell your Mac when not to water your lawn.

While You're Away

There are simple things you can do it enhance security while you are out of the house. On the idea that thieves would much rather burgle an empty house, the object is to make it look like someone is home.

If you're going on a trip, it's easy to set your Mac to turn on some lights at sunset. This should include lights at the front door and several windows. You can also add sound via a radio, or with a TV, which also adds the flickering light — a nice touch of realism if the glow of your TV is visible from the outside. For later in the evening, set your Mac to turn off the TV and lights in different rooms at different times, as you might do when you are at home.

You can also use motion sensors to give the impression that someone is home. For instance, you can have an outdoor motion sensor activate a series of events, turning on lights in a sequence to make it appear that you are moving toward the front door. Backyard sensors can activate outdoor floodlights.

If someone does break in, you can use motion detectors to trigger events to further give the impression that someone is in the building. Turn lights on when doors are opened, or start cameras rolling. You can even attach an alarm to an X10 appliance module to try to scare an intruder away. If you do, you should have it set to turn off after a while.

Video Surveillance

Video surveillance can be a part of your X10 system. The handy part about this is that you don't really need 24-hour per day surveillance (if you do, you should contact security professionals). With your do-it-yourself Mac-controlled system, you can set a motion detector or open-door detector to start one or more cameras rolling when someone comes to the door.

X10, Ltd. offers cameras that work well for this purpose. For instance, the Xcam2 (www.x10.com/products/x10_vk45a.htm) is a small, wireless camera that transmits its video to a video receiver that is connected to your VCR. The system uses X10's VCR Commander interface with your VCR, to start recording, and to stop recording after the motion detector stops detecting motion for 5 minutes.

Troubleshooting

The X10 system operates as a guest on your building's AC power lines. As such, it is subject to the electrical characteristics of your electrical system. There are several common problems you can easily overcome by adding special X10 modules. If your devices are not responding to commands, you may have one of these problems.

Interference and Attenuation

If you're having problems with devices not turning on or off when they are supposed to, or working intermittently, you may have one of two problems caused by appliances — noise and device attenuation. Fortunately, both problems have the same fix.

Interference occurs when an appliance adds electrical noise on the line. This noise can confuse X10 receivers. Noise-inducing appliances include refrigerators, devices with motors (such as plug-in fans, hair drivers blenders, or vacuum cleaners), and some fluorescent lights.

The fix is to add a signal filter to the noisy appliance, but first you have to find out which appliance is causing the problem. You can do this by turning off appliances one at a time while the X10 system is running. It's helpful here to setup a script on the Mac to continually act, such as turn a light or a radio on and off while you are doing this. If you have more than one noisy appliance (such as those mentioned in the preceding paragraph), you may want to turn them all off to start with. When you locate a noisy appliance, plug it into a device called a signal filter and plug the noise filter into the wall. Signal filters tend to run between $30 and $50 each.

Attenuation occurs when an appliance filters out your X10 signals because it thinks the signals are noise. The effect is the same as a noise-producing appliance in that the X10 receivers stop responding or respond intermittently. Appliances that can attenuate X10 signals include some big-screen televisions, cable and satellite receivers, and some stereo equipment. Equipment related to your Mac can also attenuate X10 signals. These include printers, power supplies for notebook computers and cell phones, universal power supplies, surge protectors, and higher-end power strips. (Cheaper power strips don't attenuate X10 signals.)

Troubleshooting for attenuation is a bit more complicated, because it is not enough to turn the devices off — you'll have to unplug them to remove their effect on the power system. Plugging offending devices into a noise filter can fix the problem because it isolates the device from the system.

Two-phase Problems

Another common problem with X10 systems occurs in houses wired as a two-phase 220- (or 240-) volt system. The symptoms are that X10 devices in one section of the house don't seem to respond to devices in another section. Within the two halves, everything seems fine. When this occurs, you are probably seeing a lack of communication between devices on the two separate phases of a two-phase 220- (or 240-) volt system. Each phase is 110 (or 120) volts.

The fix here is a device called a phase coupler (sometimes called a coupling capacitor or a signal bridge). It joins the two phases, allowing X10 signals to cross between them.

One way to test for this problem is to look for a 220-volt appliance, such as an electric oven, range, stovetop, or an electric dryer (not a gas a drier) — basically, appliances that use a lot of juice. Now, turn on your 220-volt appliance. If your X10 system suddenly works, then you need a phase coupler. Turning on a 220-volt appliance effectively joins the two phases, accomplishing the same thing as a phase coupler.

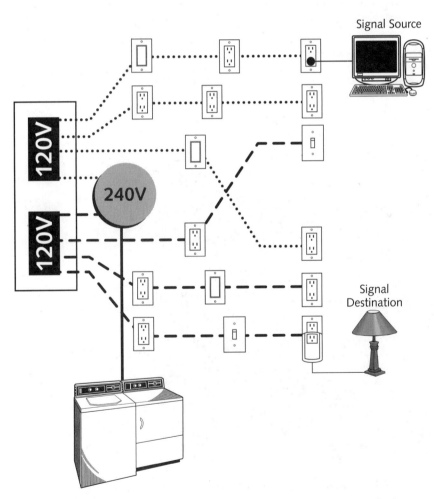

FIGURE 1-16: When a 220- (or 240-) volt appliance is turned on, it acts as a bridge between the two 110 volt phases. A phase coupler can do the same thing.

There are two types of phase couplers — one that plugs into the 220- (or 240-) volt socket that your electric drier or oven is plugged into. (SmartHome's SignaLinc, shown in Figure 1-17, is such a device.) This type of coupler is a pass-through device, letting you plug your appliance into it. You can tell a 220 (or 240) volt socket because of its size, which is bigger than a standard three-pronged outlet, as you can see from Figure 1-17.

If you don't have a 220-volt outlet in your house (perhaps because your major appliances run on natural gas), you can use a hardware phase coupler. This type of coupler sits just outside your homes' breaker box, and is connected to two circuit breakers in the breaker box. If you've ever wired circuit breakers before, it's not too difficult to install. If not, get an electrician to install it for you.

Weak Signals in Big Houses

If you've tried the "oven test" and still can't get X10 transmitters and receivers at opposite sides of a house to communicate, you may have another problem — the house is too big for the X10 signals to travel from one end to another. That is, the X10 signals degrade over the distance. You can solve this problem with an X10 signal amplifier, which boosts the signals that X10 transmitters are sending. As with other X10 devices, you plug a signal amplifier into a power outlet.

FIGURE 1-17: A phase coupler such as SmartHome's SignaLinc can get X10 devices on two sides of your home to communicate with each other.

Image Courtesy of SMARTHOME, Inc. Copyright © 2003.

"Wireless" Intercoms and X10

Many of the home automation Web sites sell "wireless" intercoms for homes that actually work on a principle to similar to X10 devices. That is, they use your home's in-wall electrical wiring to transmit voice. There also some baby monitors that use in-wall wiring. However, these types of devices are not compatible with X10 automation devices. In fact, they will interfere with and block X10 signals while in use.

Fortunately, when the intercom isn't being used, the X10 transmitters and receivers will function normally. To make sure that these intercom or baby monitors don't block your X10 system all the time, don't leave such a device in a permanent transmit mode.

Communications systems that are truly wireless—that is, they communicate through the air—don't affect X10 equipment.

Modules Turn on When They Shouldn't

A particular light turns on the same time every day, even though you don't have it set that is way. This problem is the opposite of the previous problem, in that X10 signals are traveling too far—in fact, your neighbor's X10 transmitters are sending signals to your receivers. The solution is to change the house code (that's the letter code) of your controllers and the modules. If the problem persists, there are so-called house-blocking filters you can install.

However, this problem is pretty rare, because the chances that you have a close neighbor running X10 are slim to begin with. The neighbor also has to have one of the 16 house codes set to the same one that you're using. In addition, the neighbor has to be fairly close to you and on the same pole transformer, a possibility in an apartment or condo building, but less likely in detached houses.

There are also one-time events—voltage spikes and dips—that can trigger standalone X-10 controllers into sending commands. However, this doesn't happen when your Mac is the controller.

Summary

You can make your Mac the controller of a home automation system to control lights and appliances around the house. The most common way to do this is through the X10 system, which transmits commands through your home's electrical wiring. Here are the key things you should remember about Macs and X10:

- Think about the software you want to get along with the X10-computer interface. Each software package only supports certain interfaces.
- If you're using a fairly modern Mac, using a USB interface can save you some money.
- Indigo from Perceptive Automation is the best software for Mac OS X.

- If you have an old Mac running Mac OS 7, 8, or 9 lying around, it can work just fine for controlling your X10 system. XTension is your best bet for software on a pre-OS X Mac.

- The X10 dimming command should only be used on incandescent lighting. Don't use X10 lamp modules for appliances or fluorescent or halogen lights.

- Plug appliances into appliance modules in order to control them.

- There are some common communications problems with X10 that can be solved by plugging in a few devices into AC outlets.

Broadcast Your Own Radio Show

When listening to the radio, you may wonder why they keep playing that same annoying song. Why don't they ever play the fourth track on Frank Zappa's *Hot Rats* instead? If you enjoy sharing your musical discoveries by making party mix tapes and CDs, you may have thought about what it would be like running your own radio station. Now you can share the music you love with the world, via the growing phenomenon of Internet radio.

It's not hard to be a digital DJ, to broadcast your own Internet radio station. It takes a little time and money and the knowledge of the tunes you want to play. You can create a prerecorded station, or you can do a live show. It's up to you and your Mac.

An Internet Radio Primer

Internet radio comes at a time when the diversity of traditional radio is shrinking. Across the country and within cities, more and more radio stations are becoming the property of fewer and fewer owners, causing more and more stations to sound alike. Disappearing are the quirks of localities and differing points of view. Fortunately, traditional radio isn't the only player in the game anymore.

Internet radio is changing the shape of the music business. You still need AM and FM radio if you want to listen while you drive around (at least for now). But when you're near a computer with an Internet connection, you no longer have to listen to what the record companies want you to hear. Listeners have hundreds of choices of Internet radio stations playing dozens of categories and subcategories of music and news. Tune into one, and chances are very good that you will hear music that you never heard before. In addition to stations that are Internet only, Internet radio offers feeds of broadcast stations from around the world, including news and talk as well as music.

The technology of Internet radio is a bit different from the Internet music file-sharing services. The record industry fought hard to get Napster and other file-sharing services shut down, claiming the industry owned the digital files that people were trading away. Internet radio, on the other hand, is a *streaming* technology. Instead of a file, you're sent bits in real time, as you listen to them. Once you listen to (or watch) a stream, it's gone — you don't have a file on your hard disk. Just like FM radio.

Still, the record industry fought Internet radio. The main issue was broadcast rights to copy-righted music. Internet radio industry began as a wild and wooly beast, broadcasting whatever it wanted, whenever it wanted, and without paying the royalties that traditional over-the-air radio stations have paid to record companies for decades. There were no rules for playing music over the Internet.

The Recording Industry Association of America (RIAA) was already fighting Internet file sharing when it came out against Internet radio. RIAA lobbied Congress to regulate Internet radio, resulting in the passage of the Digital Millennium Copyright Act of 2000. The intent of the Act is to make it more difficult for listeners to record music collections from Internet radio broadcasts. (There is more on these rules later in this chapter.) The Act also required that Internet broadcasters pay royalties for the right to play music, but did not set a fee structure. Two years later, the U.S. Copyright Office proposed a set of fees based on recorded industry recommendations. The fledging Internet radio industry complained that the proposed fees would drive them out of business. This was just after the dot-com bubble had burst, with hun-dreds of Internet companies still in their bankruptcy procedures. On May 1, 2002, many Internet radio networks protested with a day of silence.

Negotiations on the issue of royalties continued for another year. Then, in April 2003, record companies came to an agreement with the big Internet radio broadcasters on the royalties to be paid. RIAA reached another agreement with noncommercial college and university radio sta-tions in June 2003. The debate isn't over; both sides still complain about their industry being given the raw end of the deal. But the issue of *whether* Internet radio will be allowed to exist has been settled.

So, what does all this have to do with you and your own Internet radio station? The answer is that these rules of broadcasting and royalties created by the Act also apply to you. You don't have to be an expert in copyright law, but there are a few things you do need to know. We'll have more on copyright law a little later in the chapter. Right now, let's take a look at the state of Internet radio.

What's on Internet Radio

Internet radio includes a wide variety of professional and amateur stations. One type of profes-sional station feeds on-air broadcasts — AM and FM radio stations — over the Internet. This is handy if you move to a different city and still want to hear your favorite station. You can usu-ally find links to an Internet stream at the Web sites for the radio station. If you don't know the Web site for the station, there are several Web sites that will find them for you. Radio Locator (www.radio-locator.com/) will give the Web page and audio stream links to stations that you search for. Just type in the station's call letters (such as KALW) and get the URL, as well as the street address and phone number. RadioTower (www.radiotower.com) offers station feeds from overseas as well as from the United States.

You will also find professional Internet-only radio stations. These are dramatically different from over-the-air stations. There is more music, fewer commercials, and less formatting than on-air radio. There is also a greater variety of music offered on Internet-only stations.

But there are also thousands of amateurs with Internet radio stations. These can be the most interesting to listen to, because they are produced by people whose only motivation is the love of a particular type of music — much of which you won't hear anywhere else.

For a description of some of the best, see the list of *Mac Toys* Top Ten Internet Radio Stations at the end of this chapter.

Listening to Internet Radio

If you haven't heard Internet radio before, you should check it out before designing your own station. Listening to other Internet-only stations can give you an idea of what you want to emulate and avoid.

There are many Web sites that offer streams to Internet radio stations, both pro and amateur. But to listen to them, you'll need software called a streaming audio player, sometimes referred to as an MP3 player. Often video players have streaming MP3 functionality built into them. The most common for Mac users today are iTunes, RealOne Player, and Microsoft's Windows Media Player. QuickTime Player also has MP3 streaming functionality. The following sections compare and contrast the players to help you choose the right one.

Some Web sites use Web-based players — little Web pages with controls that use RealOne or QuickTime as a plug-in. For these, the "player" is a small Web page that pops up with some basic controls, and you never see the RealOne or QuickTime Player.

iTunes as an Internet Radio Player

iTunes is the most convenient Internet radio player, because it lets you look through lists of dozens of Internet radio stations without opening a Web browser, and with fewer clicks, less waiting, and no banner ads (see Figure 2-1). In the Source column at the left, click Radio. On the right, you'll see a couple dozen categories. Click one to see a list of stations. You'll notice that some stations appear two or three times with different bit rates (in kilobits per second). The higher the bit rate, the higher the quality of sound. However, higher bit rates will also use up more of the bandwidth of your Internet connection. This means that if you are surfing the Web or downloading files at the same time you are listening, a higher bandwidth station could cause your other Internet activities to slow down.

Apple chooses stations hosted by several Internet radio station services, such as Live365, as well as feeds for the Internet feeds of on-air stations. However, you can also use iTunes to play Internet radio stations that are not on the list:

1. Type in the URL (the Internet address) of the broadcast.

2. Go to the Advanced menu and select Open Stream.

3. Type the URL in the window that opens (see Figure 2-2).

FIGURE 2-1: iTunes lets you browse for dozens of Internet radio stations.

FIGURE 2-2: iTunes lets you go directly to an Internet
radio station not in the list, if you know the URL.

You can also use iTunes as the player used when accessing Internet radio stations from Web
sites. You do this by setting iTunes to be the helper application from your Web browser preferences. At this point, Internet Explorer is the best Web browser to do this with, because Safari
and Camino have no way to set helper applications.

The main drawback to using iTunes is that it doesn't display the name of the song currently
being played or the performer, as do some of the Web sites. This can be a fairly substantial
drawback, for if you like a song and wish to run out and buy the CD, you're out of luck.

The RealOne Player

You may have already used the RealOne Player to watch Internet news feeds or other content. RealOne Player can also play Internet radio stations. If you don't have a copy, you can download one at www.real.com. The big links are to the paid version, but there is also a free version if you are diligent enough to find it. (Try the bottom of the page.)

As with iTunes, you can type in a URL for a specific radio station. Go to the File Menu and select Open Location (see Figure 2-3).

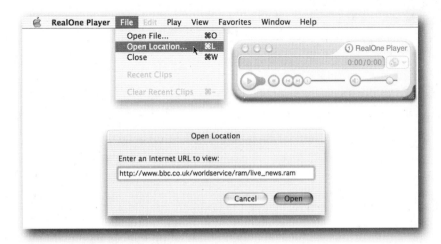

Figure 2-3: RealOne Player can play Internet radio stations, but you can't browse for stations as you can with iTunes.

Unlike iTunes, the free version of RealOne Player does not let you browse for or select a station from the player. The Radio command in the View menu will launch your Web browser and take you to the RealOne Web site, where you can select a radio station to play.

QuickTime Player

Like RealOne Player, QuickTime Player doesn't offer browsing for radio stations, but does let you type in an address. Go to the File menu and select "Open URL in New Player."

QuickTime Player comes with Mac OS X, sitting in your Applications folder. There are a few reasons to use QuickTime Player rather than iTunes: it takes fewer system resources, memory and CPU time, which means that if you have a lot of applications open, QuickTime Player is less likely to slow down your Mac.

QuickTime Player has another feature that iTunes and RealOne don't have: the ability to go back and listen to songs that already have been played during a session. You do this the way you would with a QuickTime movie, by dragging the progress indicator, which is the black triangle to the right of the time (see Figure 2-4). The time indicator will change as you drag the triangle right or left. You can drag it anywhere in the area of the solid lines — this indicates the amount of the radio program that has loaded. The dotted lines indicate that portion not yet loaded. When you drag the triangle back to listen to previously played material, the program continues to load, so you can move the triangle back to the right to hear it.

FIGURE 2-4: QuickTime Player progress indicator (black triangle) lets you go back and hear songs (or speech) that you've already heard.

Windows Media Player

Some Mac fans may think it strange to run something with "Windows" in the name, but Windows Media Player is another free tool for playing Internet Radio available for Mac OS X. It's not usually a first choice, because versions of Windows Media Player can be more troublesome than RealOne Player. Still, you may run into a Web site with Internet audio or video content that requires Windows Media Player, either as a plug-in or a standalone player.

To get Windows Media Player for Mac OS X, go to www.windowsmedia.com/download.

To play a specific Radio station, select Open URL from the File menu. To get to Internet radio, select Internet Radio from the Favorites menu. This will take you to the Radio page of Microsoft's Windows Media Web site (windowsmedia.com).

Okay, enough about listening to Internet radio — let's get on to creating your own station.

Note Windows Media Player has a darker side — a reputation for being "spyware," collecting information about where you go and who you are for marketing purposes or "to prevent unlicensed use." (Just what constitutes "unlicensed use" of free software is another issue.) The truth is that the Mac version doesn't add anything to the operating system, as does the Windows version, and the Mac license agreement doesn't have you agreeing to be spied upon.

Starting Your Own Station

In some ways, creating an Internet radio station is like creating a Web site. You can host content yourself, on your own computer, or you can pay someone to host it for you. Just as a Web site service might provide technologies that you would need to work with a Web site for a monthly fee, there are companies that specialize in providing what you need to host an Internet radio station. Or, you can run your own Mac server, or have your server hosted somewhere, the way ISPs offer to host your Web server.

Internet radio is a bit more complicated than the Web, however, because there are other issues involving copyrights and audio technology. A good way to start is to consider your options.

Your Broadcast Options

There is a continuum of Internet radio broadcast options ranging from paying someone to do everything to doing everything yourself. These can be boiled down to three categories:

- **Paid service, soup to nuts** — At this point, Live365 (`www.live365.com`) is the only Mac-friendly service offering everything you need to have a legal Internet radio station. You provide the music files and a modest monthly fee, and Live365 does the rest. This is the easiest method to reach a large number of people, particularly if you are setting up a prerecorded radio station that operates 24 hours a day, 7 days a week.

- **Live broadcast from your Mac to a broadcast server** — This is where you act as a DJ, talking in between the songs, reading the news, reciting poetry, or whatever you want to say. Obviously, you can't broadcast live 24×7, but you can do a regularly scheduled show or broadcast your own band live from a gig.

  In this scenario, you use your Mac to play the music and to accept your spoken words. This is sent to a broadcast server somewhere. Again, Live365 offers the easiest way to do this. You can also use SHOUTcast (`www.shoutcast.com`), though it is much more difficult to do with a Mac.

- **Your Mac as a server (live or prerecorded)** — There are many ways to run your own server, from using iTunes in order to broadcast to one or two people, to using a high-bandwidth, high-end machine to broadcast to the world. If you already have your own Mac running Mac OS X Server software, a radio station could be another service you're adding. You may want to create your own server in conjunction with a Web site you already run or if you are establishing special programs for your business or organization.

Setting Up Your Station

There's more detail on these steps later in the chapter, but here's an overview of the main tasks involved with setting up an Internet radio station:

1. **Decide on show: prerecorded or live (or both).** Most Internet radio shows are prerecorded, as are a large number of AM and FM shows. One aspect of a live show that is easier is that you don't have to upload and transcode your files ahead of time.

2. **Collect or create content.** Content includes music files imported from CDs, voice files, and any station identification spots. This is probably the most enjoyable aspect of putting together a radio station, but don't underestimate the time it takes to get your content together.

3. **Install or configure your server (if you're rolling your own).** The first step here is to identify various pieces of server software you're going to use and the Internet link. You then install all the server software you need.

4. **Upload files to host (for prerecorded shows).** This involves transcoding (converting) the MP3 files to a specific bit rate and frequency. CD-quality files are often 160 Kbps and 44 KHz. For radio broadcasts, you may want lower quality for smaller files.

5. **Pay royalties.** One of the most important benefits of Live365 is that they pay the royalties that keep your radio station legal. They keep track of how many times a song is played and how many people listen to it, and pay the record companies accordingly. If you are creating an Internet radio station on your own, you are responsible for paying royalties to the owners of the rights of the music you're broadcasting.

Rules of Internet Broadcasting

Regardless of how you decide to broadcast, you need to follow the federal broadcasting rules as set by the Digital Millennium Copyright Act. These rules are designed to protect the copyrights of the artists and record companies.

To start with, you have to legally own the music files you want to broadcast. That is, you need to own the CDs or your vinyl LPs that the music came from. (See Chapter 10 to learn how to digitize your vinyl collection.) Songs obtained with file-sharing tools — Napster, Limewire, Acquisition, or Kazaa — are not supposed to be broadcast.

There are also rules that restrict you from making it convenient for people to record collections based on your broadcasts. Although Internet radio doesn't deliver music in the form of files, there are programs that do let people capture the audio stream and turn it into a file. (For instance, there's Audio Hijack, www.rogueamoeba.com.) Because of this, you are prohibited from broadcasting an entire album — this would make it easy for someone to record the entire album. You also can't broadcast more than three tracks from a single album in any 3-hour period and no more than two tracks in a row. If you are broadcasting items from a boxed set, this is extended to four tracks (three in a row) within 3 hours.

It's worth noting that classical music is hampered by these rules. For instance, you couldn't broadcast a performance of Beethoven's Fifth Symphony — that would be four tracks in a row within 3 hours — unless the recording was from a boxed set.

Similarly, you can't create a broadcast that consists solely of one performer. So, if your dream is to create All-Beatles Radio, forget it. You could, however, mix in the post-Beatles material of the members and covers by other artists. You could create an All-Beethoven Radio, however, as long as you have performances by different artists.

There are also rules to prevent the predictability of radio content. For instance, you can't publish a list of songs that describe when particular titles will be played and in what order. If you are repeating a particular program, you are restricted to rebroadcasting a show of less than an hour to three times in 2 weeks. If the show is longer than an hour, you can rebroadcast it four times in 2 weeks. If it's 3 hours or longer, you can continually rebroadcast it.

These rules pertain to music that other people have created. If *you* are the artist — that is, if you want to broadcast your own performances or that of your band — then you can broadcast as often as you'd like and broadcast a show with only you or your group. The bottom line is that if you own the copyright to the music, you don't have to follow the Digital Millennium Copyright Act rules. However, the Internet radio host may require a letter from you verifying that you are the copyright holder.

Another exception is if you want to create a radio station featuring your friend's band or someone you work for. In that case, an Internet radio host will ask you to provide them with written consent from the copyright holder (your friend's band) to let you do this. Keep in mind that even with your own music, an Internet radio service may have additional rules that you may have to follow.

Soup-to-Nuts Service: Live365

There are several Internet radio hosts, offering varying degrees of service. One of the biggest, most complete, and most Mac-friendly is Live365. You've probably heard of Live365 if you've ever used iTunes to listen to Internet radio. Live365 is a good choice for Mac users, because it offers a handy Mac OS X utility, Studio365, that gives you an easy drag-and-drop method way to upload music files. Live365 also offers free music for your broadcast. Overall, Live365 provides you with more services than any other radio host, making it the easiest way to get an Internet radio station up and running.

Live365 works like a service that hosts Web sites. You pay a monthly fee and provide the content files. Live365 stores the files on a server computer and delivers music to listeners in the form of MP3 music streams. Live365 keeps track of and pays the required royalties — you never have to deal with the issue — and automatically creates a Web page that describes your radio station. They also offer other services, and if you buy a professional package (discussed in Step 2), you can run your own advertising on the station.

The basic procedure for creating a Live365 station is:

1. Create a free account.
2. Sign up for a paid broadcasting plan.
3. Convert your music to MP3 files.
4. Upload and transcode your files with Studio365.
5. Create a Promo spot (optional, but free).
6. Add content to your station's Web page (optional, but free).
7. Start the Broadcast.
8. Edit your station Web page.

Step 1: Create a Free Account

Start by signing up for a free listener account at Live365.com, which allows you to search for and listen to the hundreds of radio stations at the Live365 Web site. You have to be a registered user before you can become a broadcaster. To sign up, do the following:

1. Go to www.live365.com, and click the Sign Up link in the upper-right corner.

Note At this point, Safari had some problems with Live365.com. The Camino and Internet Explorer browsers don't have these problems.

2. A New Member form appears (see Figure 2-5) asking for some basic information, including a user name and password. Choose the user name carefully, because this is what will appear to people when they listen to your radio station.

3. After completing this form, click the Next button at the bottom. A screen will appear telling you that you will get an email message.

4. When you receive your "Welcome from Live365.com" message, go to the link in the message to activate your account.

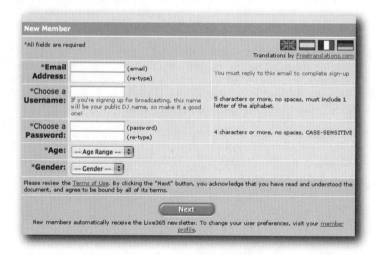

FIGURE 2-5: Live365's sign-up form gives you a free listener account.

You're now ready to select a broadcast plan.

Step 2: Choose a Broadcaster Plan

At the bottom of the Welcome message is a link to a page where you can purchase a broadcast tab. You can also go to www.live365.com, log in with your name and password, and go to the Broadcast tab.

Live365 offers over half a dozen broadcaster plans at different monthly rates. The more you pay, the more storage space you get for your music files and the more simultaneous listeners are allowed. Live365 starts at $10 per month, and even less if you commit to 6-month or 12-

month periods. This gets you 100 MB of storage space for your music and up to 25 simultaneous listeners. If you need more storage or listeners, you can always upgrade your plan. Live365 also offers so-called professional plans, which not only have a lot of storage space, but also let you sell your own advertising on your radio station. You should definitely get some experience under your belt with a basic user plan before considering a professional plan.

To choose a plan, it's useful to calculate the amount of storage space you'll need. First, there are two things you'll need to decide:

- The number of hours of music (or talk) you'll like to broadcast. The more hours of music you store, the more disk space you'll use.

- The quality of sound in terms of *bit rate*, measured in kilobits per second (Kbps). The higher the bit rate, the higher the quality of sound, but the more disk space you'll use.

If you know the bit rate of your files, you can calculate the amount of storage space needed and the length in time of your radio broadcast. For instance:

- At 128 Kbps, an MP3 file takes up roughly 1 MB of storage per minute of song length. Thus, 100 MB of storage will get you 1 hour and 40 minutes.

- At 64 Kbps, the file size is half that—0.5 MB per minute, or 1 MB for 2 minutes of music. Thus, your 100 MB of storage can hold 200 minutes, or 3 hours and 20 minutes. At 64 Kbps, you may hear some artifacts, a kind of swishing sound. This is lower than you would want for your personal collection on your Mac or iPod, but might be acceptable for Internet radio.

- For older music of poorer sound quality (such as that recorded before 1950), or for talk (such as comedy or news), you can go lower—to 32 Kbps or even 16 Kbps. This will give you 4 minutes and 8 minutes of broadcast per megabyte.

Set the bit rate with the Studio365 application, which we'll get into a little later.

One other consideration is whether you can do live broadcasting. On all accounts except the most basic, Live365 gives you the option to do live broadcasting from your Mac's iTunes playlists. If you want to do live broadcasting, the lowest-cost plan won't work. However, you can upgrade your plan at any time.

Once you choose a plan at the Live365 Web site, you'll be asked to create a name and a one-sentence description of your station. The description tells a prospective audience why they should listen to your station. This is not critical at this point, because you can go back and change the station's name and description later.

Step 3: Convert Your Music to MP3

You're now ready to assemble the music files you'll be uploading to the music service. If you are creating a standard (prerecorded) station, Live365 requires the files you upload to it to be in MP3 format. For a live broadcast, your files can be MP3, AAC, or any other format supported by iTunes.

This section will describe how to use iTunes to import music in MP3 format, how you can tell if your current music files are MP3 or AAC, and how to use iTunes to convert AAC files to MP3 format.

Import Music as MP3

To import songs from a CD in MP3 format to use for a prerecorded Live365 radio station, you need to make sure that iTunes Preferences is set up to do so.

First, tell iTunes what format you will be converting files to:

1. Go to the iTunes menu and select Preferences.

2. Click the Importing button in the toolbar.

3. Click the Import Using pop-up, and select MP3 Encoder (as shown in Figure 2-6).

4. Set bit rate. You'll want to import the music at a high bit rate so that the sound quality is good when you listen on your Mac or iPod. (The Studio365 application will automatically convert the data to a lower bit rate when you upload the files.) A bit rate 160 Kbps should be sufficient.

5. Click OK.

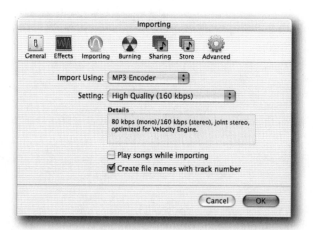

FIGURE 2-6: Setting iTunes Preferences to import from CDs using MP3. You can use a high bit rate, because the Studio365 will convert it to a lower bit rate when uploading.

Now, you can import your files. Insert your CD. In the Song Name column, uncheck the boxes next to the tracks you don't want to import, and press the Import button.

Music Already in iTunes: How to Tell MP3 from AAC

If you want to broadcast files that you've already imported using iTunes, you may have been importing them in AAC format (short for MPEG 4 Advanced Audio Codec). How can you tell an AAC file from an MP3 file? One way is to look at the file name in the Finder. MP3 files end in .mp3. The AAC files that you create yourself from CDs end in .m4a. The copy-protected AAC files you buy from the iTunes Music Store end in .m4p.

Fortunately, you don't have to go digging through the subfolders of the Music folder to find out what format a Music file is — iTunes can tell you. Select a song in iTunes and press the Command-I keys (or select Get Info from the File menu). Under the Summary tab, the first item will be "Kind" (see Figure 2-7). This will tell you the format. At the bottom of this window next to Where, you'll see the path, ending with the file. The listings you'll most likely see are:

- **MPEG audio file (.mp3)** — This is the format you need to upload to Live365.

- **AAC audio file. (.m4a)** — These are files you imported with iTunes. You will need to convert these to MP3 before uploading.

- **Protected AAC audio file (.m4p)** — This is a file you purchased from the iTunes Music Store. These are copy protected and cannot be converted to MP3.

iTunes can also import files in a few other formats, two of which can be converted to MP3:

- **AIFF audio file** — This is a high-quality, uncompressed format. If you are importing music from vinyl LPs (as described in Chapter 10), you may have AIFF files.

- **WAV audio file** — This is a Windows uncompressed sound format.

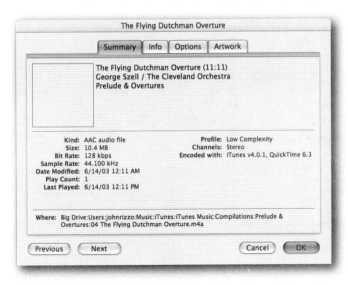

FIGURE 2-7: The Get Info dialog for a song in iTunes. This file is an AAC audio file imported with iTunes.

For more on the differences between digital audio file formats, see Chapter 7.

Converting AAC to MP3

If you have AAC or AIFF files that you want to use in your radio station, you can use iTunes to convert them to MP3 format. The files don't have to be in the iTunes library—you can use iTunes to convert files that reside in a folder or a disk. Converting keeps the original file in the original format and creates a new file in the MP3 format.

 Unfortunately, you won't be able to use music purchased from Apple's iTunes Music Store for prerecorded radio shows. These files use a special copy-protected version of AAC that prevents you from converting them to MP3 format. (This is to prevent these files from being traded in music file-sharing systems.) The AAC files that you create yourself don't have the copy protection. However, you can play the copy-protected files in a live broadcast, as is described later.

To convert files, open iTunes and do the following:

1. Tell iTunes what format you will be converting files to by setting iTunes Preferences to import to MP3, as previously described, and shown in Figure 2-6.

2. For songs in the iTunes library, select one or more songs to convert. To select multiple songs, hold the Command key down while you click on the song titles (see Figure 2-8).

3. If the song files have not been imported to the iTunes library, hold down the Option key while you open the Advanced menu and select Convert Selection to MP3. You'll now be able to browse for the folder containing your files.

You're now ready to transcode and upload your files to Live365.

FIGURE 2-8: After setting Preferences for MP3, iTunes can convert your selection to MP3 with this menu command.

Step 4: Transcode and Upload Your Files

The next step in creating a prerecorded Live365 radio station is to transcode and upload your MP3 files. Live365 offers the handy Studio365 for Mac OS X application, which you can download at www.live365.com/download. (There is also a Studio365Live application, which is not the application you need here. Studio365Live is used for producing live radio shows.) Studio365 not only uploads your MP3 files to Live365, but also does the transcoding for you, transparently in the background. It is a slow process, however, so set aside plenty of time.

Transcoding is a process of changing some characteristics of the file to make them more appropriate for radio broadcast. This is a *very* important step — with the wrong transcoding settings in Studio365, your files won't be able to be played, and you will have to waste a lot of time uploading your files again.

The main thing to remember is that *every* MP3 file in your Live365 library must have the exact same encoding characteristics. There are three settings:

- Bit rate
- Frequency
- Stereo mode (the Joint Stereo setting is best)

You should never mix tracks encoded at different bit rates, frequencies, or mode in a playlist. This can cause the tracks not to play, and Live365 says they can even make listeners' MP3 players crash.

Another important thing to remember about Studio365: Make sure that you use manual settings. Do not use Automatic mode. At publishing time, automatic mode was buggy in the versions we looked at.

You configure these settings in Studio365's Preferences dialog, which you can access in the Studio365 menu. Use the Encoder tab (see Figure 2-9). Here are some rules to guarantee success:

- The Automatically Determine Bitrate check box should always be unchecked.
- Each of the three pop-ups has an Auto setting. *Never use this.*
- The Stereo Mode pop-up lets you specify mono or stereo. You can cut down on the file size by using mono for older music that is not in stereo (such as music from the mid-1950s and earlier or comedy or other talk). For stereo files, *always* use Joint Stereo (not the plain Stereo setting).

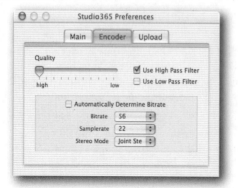

FIGURE 2-9: Always use manual settings in Studio365.

Furthermore, there are some combinations of settings that work best. Live365 recommends using only one of the following combinations of encoding settings:

- 56 Kbps / 44 KHz / Mono
- 56 Kbps / 22 KHz / Joint Stereo
- 32 Kbps / 22 KHz / Joint Stereo
- 32 Kbps / 22 KHz / Mono
- 32 Kbps / 11 KHz / Joint Stereo
- 24 Kbps / 22 KHz / Mono
- 24 Kbps / 11 KHz / Joint Stereo
- 16 Kbps / 16 KHz / Mono
- 16 Kbps / 11 KHz / Mono
- 8 Kbps / 12 KHz / Mono
- 8 Kbps / 11 KHz / Mono
- 8 Kbps / 8 KHz / Mono

All sorts of strange things can happen if you don't use one of these combinations. For instance, when using 56 Kbps / 44 KHz / Stereo, we found the song playing back at twice the speed it should have!

If you remember from earlier discussions, the higher the bit rate, the higher the quality — and the bigger the file size. Also, if you use 56 Kbps, you will rule out listeners connecting to the Internet via a modem. To hear a 56-Kbps broadcast, listeners will need a DSL or cable modem connection to the Internet.

Remember, whichever group of settings you pick, make sure that all of the files you upload use the same settings. Once the files are uploaded, you can check these settings at the Live365 Web site.

Uploading with Studio365

With the settings correctly made, you can now use Studio365 to transcode and upload your files to Live365's services. When you launch the application, a logon window appears, as shown in Figure 2-10. Type your Live365 name and password, and click the Connect button.

FIGURE 2-10: The logon screen of Studio365.

You can now select a file to transcode and upload — this is done in one step. One way to do this is to go to Studio365's File menu and select the Upload command. This brings up a browser window, as shown in Figure 2-10. If you've been using iTunes to manage your music, you'll find your MP3 files in the iTunes Music folder. The total path is:

```
[Your home folder]/Music/iTunes/iTunes Music/[Artist]/[Album]/[Song.mp3]
```

To follow this path, you can negotiate the columns of the file browser window that appears (see Figure 2-11). When you get to your MP3 file, select it and click Open to start the transcode/upload process. You can also type a path in the Go To field.

Another way to upload files is to drag them from the Finder to the Studio365 Dock icon. You can also drag MP3 files to a Finder toolbar icon, which you create by dragging the Studio365 icon from the Applications folder up to the Finder toolbar. Unfortunately, you can't drag music files from iTunes to the Studio365 Dock icon or Finder toolbar icon (at least, not as of the time of publication). You must drag files from a Finder window or use Studio365's Upload menu command.

When you've selected a file, Studio365 will first transcode it, then upload it. Fortunately, the Studio365 app lets you upload multiple files at the same time. You can keep adding files to upload while it is working on the first file. Studio365 can transcode one file at the same time it uploads another. Its status window (shown in Figure 2-12) shows which files are being transcoded and uploaded, and how many files are left to process.

FIGURE 2-11: This is where you'll find iTunes music files in Studio365 after you select the Upload command.

FIGURE 2-12: Studio365 can transcode and upload multiple files simultaneously.

The process is slow, but the connections are solid. Under normal circumstances, you won't find yourself having to reconnect or resend your files (unless your own Internet link is unstable, of course).

Sideloading: Free Songs for Your Live365 Broadcast

Live365 offers songs stored on its servers that you can add to your broadcast for free. Live365 calls this *sideloading*. There's no downloading involved, because the music files are never transferred to your Mac. Sideloading is much easier and quicker than uploading, because you don't do any transcoding and you're not actually moving any files. It simply adds the songs you choose to your list of songs.

To sideload a song, log into Live365.com and go to the Music Library section. Search for a song or artist or scroll through the list of featured artists. To sideload a track, click the orange arrow next to the play button to the left of the album cover picture, as shown below:

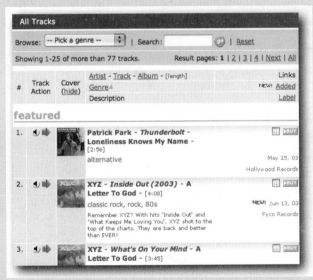

Click the arrow to sideload a song from Live365's Music Library to your radio station track list.

The song will appear in the list of tracks for your radio station.

Check Your Uploaded Files

It's a good idea to check your files at Live365 to make sure that you used the correct settings and to make sure that you didn't upload some songs with different settings.

1. In your Web browser, go to www.live365.com and log in with your user name and password.

2. Click the Broadcast tab.

3. Just under the tab, click the word Edit. A new set of tabs will appear below the first set.

4. In the lower set of tabs, click the Tracks tab (see Figure 2-13).

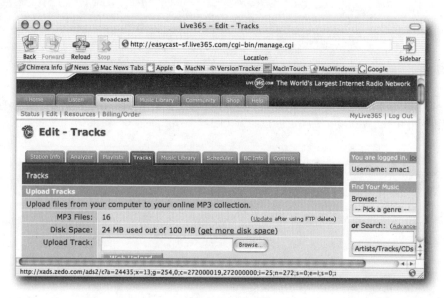

FIGURE 2-13: View your list of songs by scrolling down.

5. Scroll down to the list of songs (see Figure 2-14). You'll notice a column to the right called "BR/FR/ST." This stands for bit rate, frequency, and stereo mode. You'll notice in Figure 2-14 that to the right of each song, it says "56/22/JS" for 56 Kbps, 22 KHz, and joint stereo. If any of the tracks differ from this, you'll need to delete them here and upload them again.

FIGURE 2-14: Use the Live365 Tracks list to check if your file was uploaded correctly.

Create Your Live365 Playlist

Once your files are uploaded (or sideloaded) and checked, create one or more playlists for your broadcast at the Live365 Web site.

1. In your Web browser, go to www.live365.com, and log in with your user name and password.

2. At the Web site, click the Broadcast tab.

3. Just under the tab, click the word Edit. A new set of tabs will appear below the first set.

4. In the lower set of tabs, click the Playlists tab.

5. Scroll down, and you'll see two white fields. The left field shows your list of tracks. The right is your playlist, which starts out blank, but will fill up with your tracks (as shown in Figure 2-15).

6. Select a track on the left, and click the Add button. This will make it appear on the right. Continue to add as may tracks as you need.

7. You can now arrange your songs in the list by selecting one and using the up and down buttons to move it. If you want the songs to play in random order, click the Shuffle Play check box.

8. When you are finished, scroll down some more, and click the Save Playlist button.

9. Just below Save Playlist is a section called Check Playlist for Errors. Click the Playlist Analyzer button.

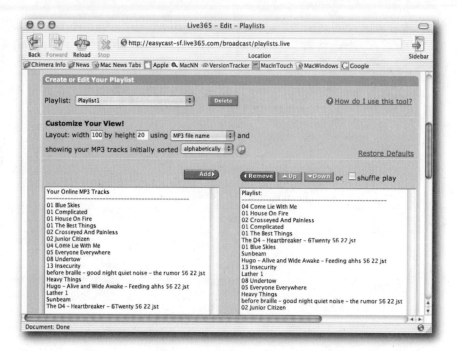

FIGURE 2-15: Create your playlist (on the right) by moving songs over from the left and arranging their order.

Remember, your playlist must conform to the rules of Internet radio broadcasting, as described earlier in the chapter.

Step 5: Start the Broadcast

You are now ready to start the broadcast. On the same Playlist Web page described in the previous step, scroll down to the Start or Cue Playlist section (see Figure 2-16). If you've created more than one playlist, select the correct one from the Playlist pop-up.

Click the Start Broadcast button, and your radio station starts.

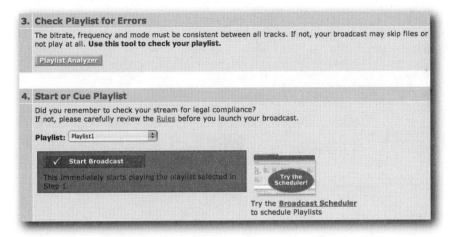

FIGURE 2-16: Press the Start Broadcast button, and your radio station will start as well.

Now you might want to listen to your station. At the top of the Web page, just under the Broadcast tab at left, click the word Status. Your station's Status page will appear. Near the top is a line called Title. Click the Speaker icon to play your station. (Note: this does not work with the Safari Web browser. Use Camino or Internet Explorer.) This launches your default MP3 player, which is iTunes for Mac OS X by default.

Step 6: Edit Your Station's Web Page

The Status page for your site is also the place were you can change the name and short description of your radio station. Just click on the Edit link next to the item you want to edit.

The Status page also lets you add some more descriptive information to the Web page that Live365 automatically creates to describe your radio station. The Status page will give you the address of this Web page. Scroll down to the line called Station Page. The address for your station's Web page will look something like this:

```
http://www.live365.com/stations/304172
```

except that the last part will be different. (Figure 2-17 shows a typical Web page for a station at Live365.) On this page, visitors can click on the play button (with the speaker icon) to start playing your station.

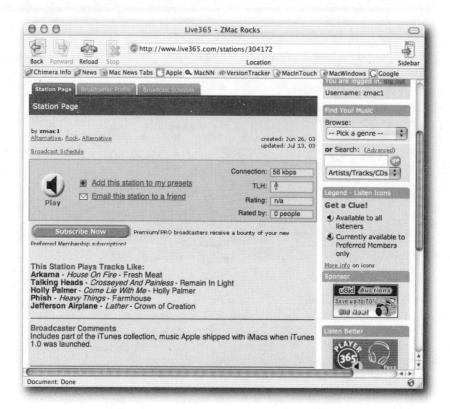

FIGURE 2-17: Live365 automatically creates a Web page describing your radio station.

 Tip   Want to know the direct play address for your station — that is, the address people can type into their streaming MP3 player? It's the same as the URL for your Web site, except that the word "play" is used instead of "stations." For instance, the address to play the station mentioned above would be:

```
http://www.live365.com/play/304172
```

Step 7: Create a Promo Spot

When listeners connect to an Internet radio station, one of the first things they hear is a promo spot — a short spot that identifies the station. Live365 lets you upload a 20-second station identification promotional spot. This is typically some music with a voice-over describing the station name and sometimes a short slogan.

To create such a promo spot, you need software that can mix music and voice and save it as an MP3 file. You also need 20 seconds worth of music. For the software, any audio software supporting two or more tracks will work. A nice one to use is Apple's iMovie — and it's a free download if you don't already have it.

As for music, you can't just pick 20 seconds of your favorite group. You need music that you have permission to use and music that is free from royalties. If you are a musician, you can write and perform your own jingle. Or, use a piece of royalty-free music, written for commercial purposes such as your radio station promo spot.

There are places on the Internet where you can buy royalty-free music — www.royalty freemusic.com/, for instance. To find more, go to Google.com and search for "royalty-free music." Apple's Soundtrack software also comes with thousands of royalty-free clips that can be used. (See Chapter 8 for more on Soundtrack.)

If you have an Apple .Mac account, you can get royalty-free music for free, and you won't even need to edit it. The .Mac iDisk contains a library of royalty-free music in a wide range of musical styles that you can use for your promo spot (see Figure 2-18). Not only that, but it offers each piece in multiple lengths (from 10 seconds to several minutes), each with a clear start, middle, and clean ending. You could use the 20-second version and talk on top, or use a shorter version and talk when the music ends.

To find the royalty-free music in iDisk, go to the FreePlay Music folder located here (no, it is not in the Music folder):

```
Software/Extras/FreePlay Music/
```

FIGURE 2-18: The FreePlay Music folder in iDisk offers royalty-free music files in a range of styles and lengths.

Here's how you create the promo in iMovie:

1. Launch iMovie, and create a new project from the File menu.

2. Click the clock icon at the bottom left to show the timing mode.

3. Import your audio clip from the File menu. It will appear at the bottom of the iMovie screen as an audio track.

4. Record your speech with your Mac's built-in microphone (if it has one) or with a mic connected to the sound in port. You do this by clicking the Audio button on the lower right. The round Record button to the right of the Microphone volume indicator starts and stops the recording.

5. Your voice track will appear on the bottom as another audio track. You can move it into position relative to the music clip by dragging it right or left.

6. Adjust the volume levels of each track. First make sure that the Edit Volume check box is selected. Now drag the volume indicator lines on top of each track up or down at the appropriate times.

7. Press the play button to hear what you've created. Adjust the two clips to your satisfaction.

8. Choose Export from the File menu. In the Export dialog, choose To QuickTime in the top pop-up. In the Formats pop-up that appears underneath, choose Expert settings (see Figure 2-19). Click OK.

FIGURE 2-19: Export your promo spot from iMovie as a QuickTime movie with Expert settings.

9. In the new dialog that appears, select MPEG-4 from the Export menu (see Figure 2-20).

10. Click the Options button. A new dialog appears (see Figure 2-21). Under the General tab, select None from the Video pop-up.

11. Click Okay and then Save.

12. You now have an MPEG-4 AAC file that you'll need to convert to MP3. You can use iTunes to do this. Make sure that iTunes Preferences are set to Import as MP3, as described earlier in the chapter.

13. Drag your MP4 file into iTunes, select it, and choose Convert Selection to MP3 in the Advanced menu.

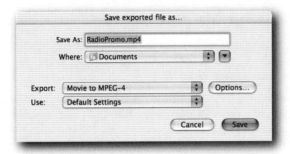

FIGURE 2-20: Select MPEG-4 as the format in the second Export dialog.

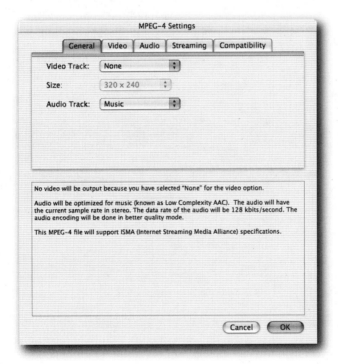

FIGURE 2-21: When you click the Options button, this dialog for MPEG-4 settings lets you specify Audio-only.

You can now upload your station identification spot to your Live365 playlist.

Live Broadcasting with a Service

There are several ways to do live broadcasting—playing music in real time and talking to your audience—from your Mac. With live broadcasting, the digital audio files stay on your Mac, and you feed the audio *stream* to an Internet service.

Several services offer live broadcasts, including Live365 and SHOUTcast. For Mac users, Live365 is the way to go. Live365 provides a great Mac OS X application, Studio365Live, which you use as your virtual console for your live broadcast (see Figure 2-22). Studio365Live offers drag-and-drop integration with iTunes. SHOUTcast is a free service, but is focused on Windows. There is a way to do live broadcasting with a Mac, but it isn't easy.

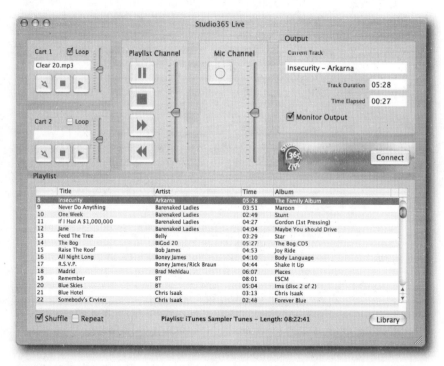

FIGURE 2-22: Studio365Live is a console you can use to broadcast live directly from your Mac to Live365.

Live broadcasting with Live365 works with any account except the lowest-cost account. At the time of publication, you needed at least the $15 monthly package. As with a prerecorded show, Live365 handles the licensing and royalties. You can also schedule a live broadcast as a part of prerecorded radio show—that is, for most of the time your station runs by itself, but for an hour a week (or whatever time you want to put into it) you can be a live DJ. You can promote your show not only by telling your friends about it, but by listing it at your Live365 Web page.

If you've ever wanted to do a live radio show, you will find Studio365Live an exceedingly fun piece of software, giving you the same kind of controls that old-fashioned radio DJs had.

Getting Ready

First, download Studio365Live, which is *not* the same application as Studio365. You can find it at www.live365.com/downloads/studio365live-mac/index.html. You'll need Mac OS X or later.

One of the nice things about a live broadcast is that you don't have to transcode or upload your music files. The files can be at any bit rate and don't even have to be MP3 files. You can play the AAC files that you've imported from iTunes. You can't, however, broadcast the AAC files you purchased from the Apple iTunes Music store.

You do have to set the bit rate and frequency of the stream in Preferences dialog, Stream tab (see Figure 2-23). Unlike when you upload files, you can set your stream for a high bit rate, such as 160 Kbps, 192 Kbps — all the way up to 320 Kbps, which is probably more than you need. Keep in mind that your listeners will need a DSL, cable modem, or other high-speed Internet connection to hear your broadcast if it is set at 56 Kbps or higher. (As with uploads, the Joint Stereo setting is recommended.)

FIGURE 2-23: Set the bit rate and frequency of the stream in Studio365Live Preferences.

A setting that you might want to experiment with is the Latency setting under the Advanced tab. It presents you with a slider bar from Low to High Latency. *Latency* is the delay in time between when you talk into a mic and when the audio is uploaded into the stream. A setting of low latency (low delay or nearly instant broadcast) uses a lot of your Mac's processing power. If you have a brand-new Power Mac G5, go ahead and move the slider down to Low Latency. With an older Mac, you may find your Mac choking on a low latency setting.

Create a Playlist

Creating a playlist in Studio365Live is a snap and is easier than uploading files with the Studio365 upload. That's because the live version is integrated with iTunes. Click the Library button, and a window appears displaying your iTunes music collection (see Figure 2-24). The Preview button in the Music Library window opens a drawer that lets you listen to any song in the list. You can drag songs from the Music Library window to the Playlist pane of the main Studio365Live window to add them to your playlist. However, an even easier method is to select an iTunes playlist in the pop-up at the top left. Then, click the Set Playlist button. The songs of the iTunes playlist are now listed in your Studio365Live playlist.

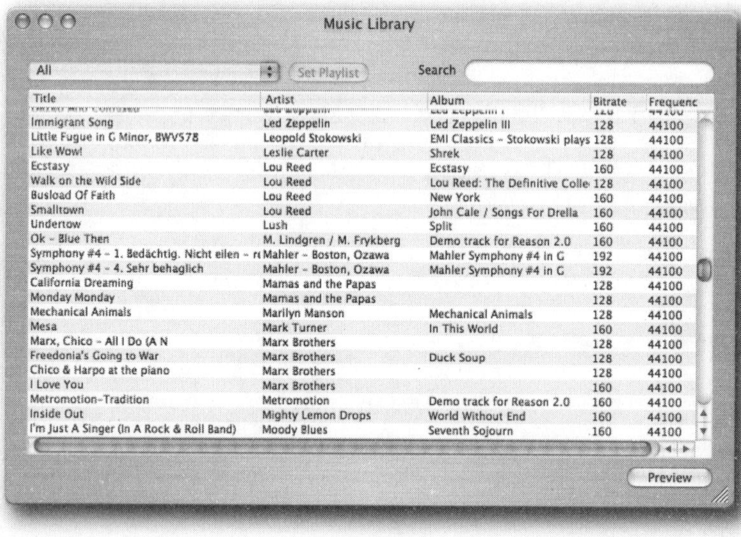

FIGURE 2-24: Your iTunes music library appears in the Studio365Live Library window. Your iTunes playlists appear in the pop-up.

If you're not using iTunes, you can drag-and-drop audio files from the Finder into the Playlist window of Studio365Live. To rearrange the order of the songs, drag them up and down. (Again, the "songs" don't have to be music — they can be recorded speech in MP3 or AAC files.)

The Connect button starts your live program by establishing a line with your Live365 radio station. The triangle button under Playlist Channel starts the music playing.

The Mic Channel

The Mic Channel panel (see Figure 2-23) controls the microphone connected to your Mac. Click the square button to turn the mic on — the button will show a red circle when the mic is live.

If you want to talk between your songs, you might want to temporarily stop the playlist between songs with the stop button in the Playlist Channel. If you want to talk over music, use the sliders to lower the volume of music.

Carts

If you've ever worked in a college radio station, you may recognize the Carts section in the upper left of the Studio365Live. The term *cart* is short for tape cartridges — short loops of tape similar to the old 8-track tape cartridges of the 1970s. Radio stations traditionally have used carts for short spots, such as prerecorded announcements or commercials.

In Studio365Live, carts are short audio files (such as MP3) that contain prerecorded announcements, your station identification, funny sounds, or whatever you wish. You use the arrow button to add the audio file to the cart. The triangular button plays the file.

A Note about SHOUTcast

SHOUTcast is a popular Internet radio portal that provides free streaming of MP3s. The problem for you is that it focuses on Windows PCs and WinAmp software. At the time of publication, there was SHOUTcast software for broadcasting live that you could run on Mac OS X, but it was pure Unix software — a command-line program that runs on the Terminal environment. SHOUTcast describes the software as being for "advanced users," which means anyone who knows their way around a Unix shell.

If this is you, and you want to try it out, download the SHOUTcast DSP plug-in at www.shoutcast.com/download/broadcast.phtml.

Roll Your Own Server

Running your own radio server on your Mac is a lot like running a Web site on your own Mac. You need a good Internet connection, preferably broadband. Listeners connect directly to your Mac by typing a URL into their audio players. The Mac could be in your home or office, or you could pay an ISP to collocate it.

However, don't assume that having your own server is less expensive than a Live365 solution. If you are broadcasting prerecorded music, you still may need to pay royalties. However, doing your own server makes sense if you are *not* broadcasting someone else's copyrighted material. For instance, if you're broadcasting a speech, business event, presentation, or a live performance of your own band, there are probably no royalties involved.

If you are planning to have thousands of listeners, the economics of running your own server may be more attractive. However, you don't need a large audience to justify broadcasting right from your Mac. You have a range of solutions, starting with a small radio broadcast with only one audience member — you — and moving up toward professional radio.

But first, we need to once more visit the all-important issues of digital copyrights.

Digital Copyright Issues

Running your own server doesn't release you from the rules of broadcasting set out by the Digital Millennium Copyright Act. If you don't own the publishing rights to a song, you're supposed to pay royalties when you broadcast it to other people. It doesn't matter if your station is noncommercial—Webcast licenses are required in order to broadcast music *legally*. There are two licenses typically associated with a recording, one for the songwriter and one for the performers of the music. Royalties are typically paid to one of three music industry groups that represents songwriters and artists: ASCAP, BMI, or SESAC. Which group the fees go to depends on the specific recording. Live365 has worked out contracts with the industry groups; anyone with a Live365 account is covered by these agreements.

With your own Internet broadcast server, you are responsible for obtaining licenses and keeping track of digital copyright payments for royalties. Several of these groups have forms at their Web sites. You can find out more about specific licensing agreements and current rates for royalties at the following:

- ASCAP (American Society of Composers, Authors and Publishers), `www.ascap.com/weblicense/webintro.html`

- BMI (Broadcast Music, Inc.), `www.bmi.com/licensing/webcaster/index.asp`

- SESAC, `www.sesac.com/licensing/internet_licensing1.asp`

- RIAA (Recording Industry Association of America), `www.riaa.com/issues/music/webcasting.asp`

- The U.S. Copyright Office, `http://lcweb.loc.gov/copyright/`

You'll also need to follow the rules of broadcasting laid out in the Digital Millennium Copyright Act, as described earlier in the chapter.

Tip

If, instead of music, you're broadcasting a speech or event, it's a good idea to have written permission.

Radio for One

You may find it handy to set up a radio station that only you will listen to. This is a matter of convenience—you may have a large collection of music on one Mac, and you want to listen to it on another computer. You can use iTunes 4 or later to create your own private radio station. With you as the owner listening to your own music, you can broadcast anything you like without paying royalties, of course. Unfortunately, the record industry forced Apple to remove a very useful aspect of iTunes—broadcasting over the Internet.

Currently, iTunes 4 and later has a Music Sharing feature that lets other Macs on a local network tune in. Given the abundance of Internet radio software for all kinds of computers, including Apple's own free QuickTime Streaming Server, you wouldn't think that this little feature of iTunes would create much controversy. That's where you'd be wrong.

When Apple first released iTunes 4 in April 2003, the iTunes Music Sharing feature worked over the Internet. The idea was to let you listen to the music collection on your home Mac while you were at work. A nice idea, but the recording industry howled in protest, just when Apple was trying to get its iTunes music store off the ground. Just a few weeks after announcing the sharing feature in iTunes 4, Apple removed the ability for iTunes to broadcast over the Internet. Apple did this through the iTunes 4.0.1 update, which limits streaming to local networks. Fortunately, there is at least one way to work around this, which is described later.

Some of the negative reaction from the music industry may be due to the fact that the Music Sharing feature is misnamed—it *never* let users do file sharing, as with the Kazaa and Napster services. It always produced an audio stream—a network radio broadcast.

Using iTunes Music Sharing

You can still use iTunes to listen to your collection over a local network. To turn it on, go to Preferences in the iTunes menu and select the Sharing pane (see Figure 2-25). Click the Share My Music check box. Other check boxes let you broadcast everything in the iTunes library or just selected playlists.

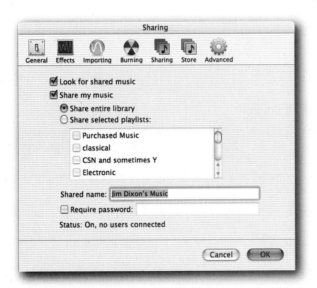

FIGURE 2-25: The Sharing pane in iTunes Preferences enables iTunes to broadcast the library to other Macs on a local network.

Other Macs on the network running Mac OS X 10.2 and later will automatically find your copy of iTunes (this is accomplished through Apple's Rendezvous technology). On another Mac, open iTunes and click the Sharing icon in the left column. The Mac running iTunes Music Sharing will appear as a music source in the left column of iTunes.

You can see that iTunes Music Sharing is by far *the* easiest way to create a radio station. This is what scared the Music industry. Still, iTunes stream is pretty small potatoes — it can only have five listeners. By comparison, Apple's free QuickTime Streaming Server can have 4,000 simultaneous listeners. If that's more your league, skip ahead to the "QuickTime Streaming Server" section. If you want to enable iTunes sharing to work over the Internet, read on.

(For more on iTunes sharing, see Chapter 12, Set up a Wireless Jukebox.)

Enabling iTunes to Broadcast over the Internet

There is at least one hack that enables iTunes 4.0.1 or later to broadcast over the Internet. It's a free utility called iCommune 401(ok) (`http://icommune.sourceforge.net/401ok/`), written by programmer James Speth.

The Readme file admits that "this software is inefficient, ugly, and poorly written." However, it does work. To enable it, turn on Music Sharing in the host Mac. Then launch iCommune 401(ok).

To access this Mac over the Internet, open iTunes on the remote Mac, choose Open Stream from the Advanced menu, and type the following:

```
daap://[IPaddress]:4689
```

`[IPaddress]` is the IP address of the host Mac. It takes a few seconds to get going, during which time you may get an error message, but have patience. Eventually, you will see the Shared Music icon in the iTunes source list.

QuickTime Streaming Server

QuickTime Streaming Server (QTSS) is free Apple software that you can download. Apple recommends that you run it with Mac OS X Server, because it is designed to work with the Server's administration tools. Running on a dedicated server Mac with Mac OS X Server, QTSS can support up to 4,000 simultaneous streams. However, QTSS does work with the desktop (nonserver) version of Mac OS X.

QuickTime Streaming Server supports streaming of prerecorded audio and movie files. It can also broadcast live, if you are also running QuickTime Broadcaster (described later in the chapter). QTSS can stream MP3 audio files via industry-standard icecast protocols.

Installing and Configuring QTSS

You can download QTSS at www.apple.com/downloads/macosx/apple/quicktimestreamingserver.html or by searching for "QuickTime Streaming Server" at Apple's support page (www.info.apple.com).

After downloading the program, just run the installer program to get started. You're now ready to configure QTSS.

1. Apple uses an html interface for configuring QTSS. In your Applications folder, double-click a file called QTSSAdminUrl. This will open a Web browser with a Web-based setup assistant.

2. The first two windows ask for a new user name and password. One is for a QTSS administrator, the next is for an MP3 broadcast user. (You can use the same name and password in each window.) Enter them, and click Next.

3. A third window appears asking if you want an SSL connection. Usually, you don't need to enable SSL.

4. The next screen (see Figure 2-26) asks where you want to store your QuickTime movies, and offers a default directory in the Library folder. If you already have a music collection, you may want to change this location to your iTunes Music folder. If so, type this in the Media Folder field: **~/Music/iTunes/iTunes Music**.

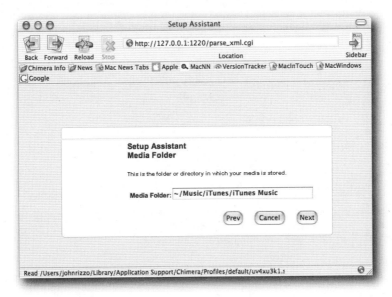

FIGURE 2-26: The QTSS setup assistant runs in a Web browser. Here, we changed the location of the media files to the iTunes Music folder.

5. The next screen asks you if you want to do streaming on Port 80, which allows you to broadcast audio through firewalls. Port 80 is used for Web communications, which means that it is not blocked by firewalls, and anyone should be able to receive your broadcast. This setting could interfere with Web servers running on your Mac, however. Click the check box to use Port 80, and click the Finish button.

The browser will now take you to the QTSS status screen, shown in Figure 2-27. You can now get to this page at anytime by double-clicking the QTSSAdminUrl icon in the Applications folder.

You'll notice that the server is now running. You can shut off the server with the Stop Server button in the upper left. Once stopped, the button changes to Start Server. The circled question mark in the lower left brings up a help screen.

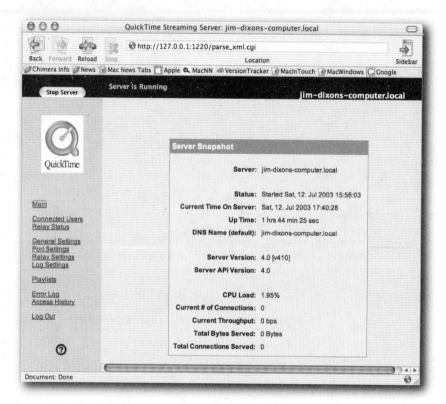

FIGURE 2-27: The QuickTime Streaming Server status screen.

Configuring QTSS

With QuickTime Streaming Server installed, you can now enter some basic settings through the same Web interface described in the last section:

1. If the main status screen (see Figure 2-27) isn't already open, open it by double-clicking the QTSSAdminUrl icon in the Applications folder.

2. Click the General Settings link at the left. This brings up a new screen, shown in Figure 2-28.

3. You can now change some of the settings. At the top is the location of your music folder, which in this example is the QuickTime Music folder.

4. The maximum number of connections is the number of users (too many simultaneous users will slow your Mac down). You can calculate the maximum throughput by multiplying the maximum number of connections by the maximum bit rate of your music (such as 160 Kbps).

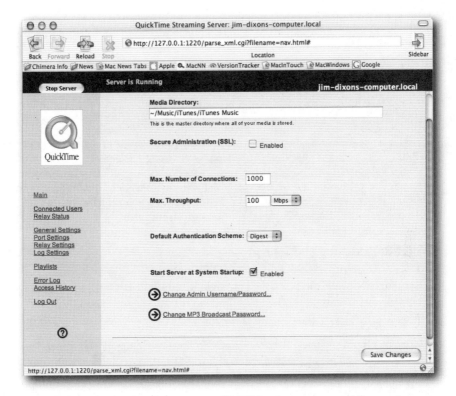

FIGURE 2-28: The General Settings screen of QTSS is where you can set the maximum number of users.

5. If you want the streaming server to start when you start up the Mac, click the check box called Start Server at System Startup.

6. Click Save Changes in the lower right to save your settings.

Create a QTSS Playlist

Before creating a playlist, make sure that all audio files in the playlist use the same encoding (such as MP3), sampling rate, compression, and bit rate (in Kbps). You can use iTunes to convert files that differ from the majority, as described earlier in the chapter.

To create a playlist, continue using the QuickTime Streaming Server playlist Web interface.

1. Click the Playlist link on the left side.

2. In the screen that appears, click New MP3 Playlist.

3. A new screen called MP3 Playlist Details appears. Give the playlist a name.

4. Give the playlist a "mount point," which is the last part of the URL that users will use to get to your radio station. If you had different playlists, each with a different mount point, then users could tune into each playlist individually.

5. Drag MP3 files from the left side to the right to create a playlist. To order the songs on the right side, drag them up or down.

6. Click the Save Changes button to create the playlist.

Tip Why build new playlists when you've got perfectly good playlists in iTunes? You can move your iTunes plays over the QuickTime Streaming Server using inexpensive shareware utility called iTunes Publishers (www.macalester.edu/~jaas/itunespub.htmls) by developer Josh Aas. To use it, Launch iTunes Publishers, select your iTunes playlist from the Playlist pop-up, and select QT Streaming Server as the format. When you save, you get a file that ends in ".playlist." Put this file in the /Library/QuicktTimeStreaming/Playlists folder.

Start Broadcasting and Tune In

To start the playlist, make sure that the QTSS administration Web pages say "Server is Running" at the top, then click the Playlist link at the left. Select your playlist under Available Playlists, and click the triangle to start playing it.

To hear how the broadcast sounds, launch iTunes:

Open up iTunes and select Advanced →Open Stream (Command-U). Enter your IP address or URL followed by the port number and finally the mount point. It should look something like 192.168.2.9:8000/oreilly (where the IP address or URL is your own). If everything goes well, you should hear some tunes blasting from your speakers.

To have listeners hear your broadcasts, tell them to type in the appropriate URL. You can also use this address yourself in iTunes (Open Stream from the Advanced menu). The basic form is:

```
[IPaddress]:[portnumber]/mountpoint
```

So, if you chose port 80, such a URL could be:

```
192.168.13.238:80/classics
```

Sometimes adding http:// at the beginning works:

```
http://192.168.13.238:80/classics
```

You can also sometimes use a "554" for the port number:

```
http://192.168.13.238:554/classics
```

QuickTime Broadcaster

For live events, you'll need one more piece of software, Apple's QuickTime Broadcaster (available for free download at www.apple.com/quicktime/download/broadcaster/). It will capture your live audio (or video) from most types of input. QuickTime Broadcaster then does real-time encoding of audio or video using one of several CODECs. It sends a single stream to QuickTime Streaming Server, or to another streaming server or a service, which will provide multiple streams to multiple users. QuickTime Broadcaster also gives you tools for managing the broadcast while it occurs.

A Look at a Pro: Inside Mac News Radio

Mac OS X broadcasting tools aren't just for amateur Internet radio. Macs are behind some of the professional radio you may already listen to. One such show, Inside Mac Radio, is not only produced and broadcast using Macs, but is all about Macs. Executive producer and host Scott Sheppard presents news, reviews, and interviews, and helps callers with their Mac problems. (Sheppard also runs the popular Mac Web site, OSXFAQ.com.) Inside Mac Radio is nationally syndicated on AM radio by the Universal Talk Network (UTN). It's broadcast live once a week from San Francisco on Saturdays from 1 P.M. to 2 P.M. PST. Sheppard also makes the show available on the Internet at www.insidemacradio.com, where you can hear any show at any time, or subscribe to it at Audible.com.

Let's take a look at how Inside Mac Radio works, and at some advice Scott has for would-radio broadcasters.

Production

Although the show is live, Sheppard starts working on a Power Mac G4 before the show goes on the air to create the show elements, the short "canned pieces." These include the "in music and out music," short jingles used to transition between the show and the commercials, and music/voice pieces that are used to transition to features — all staples of AM talk radio. These are all short — well under 30 seconds.

The main tools here are multitrack audio mixing editing software and the hardware needed to import the audio. Sheppard uses ProTools LE software from Digidesign (www.digidesign.com) along with ProTools audio hardware from Digidesign to create these pieces. (See Chapter 7 for more on audio editing software and hardware.) Sheppard uses 20 tracks in ProTools LE.

Once he's created the canned pieces, he moves them to a PowerBook that he uses during the live broadcast.

Using Macs during the Broadcast

"Since we do the live show, there's no editing — you just do it," said Sheppard. However, a Mac still has a role. "The PowerBook is the cart machine and the recording device." You may remember from earlier in the chapter, that traditional radio stations used tape cartridges, or *carts,* to play short transition pieces over the air. Sheppard uses virtual cart software called Sound Byte from Black Cat Systems (www.blackcatsystems.com/software/soundbyte.html). The $24 version of Sound Byte Lite holds up to 75 clips — more expensive versions hold hundreds. You can arrange your clips in playlists, in order to play them in a particular order. You can assign a hot button for each particular recording. You an even play multiple recordings at the same time. Sound Byte supports audio files in MP3, AIFF, WAV, or any format that QuickTime supports. At the radio studio, Sheppard plugs his PowerBook into a mixing board — the Mac feeds the audio clips directly into the board. This is the same mixing board that the studio's microphones are connected to.

Sheppard also uses the PowerBook to record Inside Mac Radio while it is being broadcast. The software he uses is Peak from Berkley Integrated Audio Software (BIAS), a powerful audio recording and editing package. (There's more about Peak in Chapters 7 and 9). The digital audio file is stored on digital audio tape (DAT) via a tape drive connected to the PowerBook. A line-out port from the studio's mixing board is connected to the PowerBook's audio-in port. Sheppard likes the degree of control a mixing board gives you.

"You could adjust the gain with Mac OS X software, but you're better off going through a mixing board," said Sheppard. Although his studio uses a $10,000 mixing board, Sheppard says you can go with much less. "You can get a mixing board for $75 — you don't have to have a really expensive board for voice radio." Scott likes the $60 EuroRack UB502 (www.behringer.com/02_products/prodindex_ub.cfm?id=UB802&lang=eng). "With this and a RadioShack microphone, you're in business."

You could also use a mixing board with audio-to-digital conversion, such as the TASCAM US-428 USB Audio/MIDI Computer Interface & Control Surface ($625, www.tascam.com).

As the show is being broadcast over the airwaves and recorded by the PowerBook, there is also a live Internet feed. The show goes directly from the studio's mixing board to another Mac running QuickTime Broadcaster, which encodes the audio and produces a 20 Kbps stream. This may sound low compared to the bit rates described earlier for your own shows, but this is AM radio, which only generates 8-bit-quality audio to begin with. From QuickTime Broadcaster, the show goes to a professional Internet streaming provider.

For later Internet broadcast at www.insidemacradio.com, Sheppard does some more processing on the recorded show.

Processing for Internet Broadcasting

To process the show for the Internet archive, Scott first uses iTunes to convert the big uncompressed AIFF digital audio file to MP3. He then uses Peak to edit out the commercials. (Yes, you get a commercial-free version at insidemacradio.com.) Peak has editing tools that give you precise cuts. Scott uses the complete MP3 file for the archives at his Web site.

Audible.com, requires another format, WAV. Sheppard uses QuickTime Pro to convert the show to WAV, at 16 Kbit per channel mono. This is still better quality than is needed for AM radio.

Mac Toys Top 10 Internet Radio Stations

With thousands of Internet radio stations available, it's nearly impossible to sample more than a fraction of them, let alone to pick the best. So we've picked a sampling of 10 stations that stand out as representing the best of what you can find on Internet radio and that demonstrate the variety available. In alphabetical order:

Alternative Nation

This station offers up new rock from that nebulous category of "alternative rock." The variety is good, with many songs on the hard side, but with breaks by slower or softer material. Alternative Nation is one of Live365's "preferred stations," which means that it occasionally becomes unavailable to listeners with free accounts.

Type this address in iTunes or other MP3 players: **www.live365.com/play/293643**.

The Live365 Web page is www.live365.com/stations/jtava.

American Mavericks

An ambitious project by Michael Tilson Thomas, Director of the San Francisco Symphony, American Mavericks highlights the achievements of American twentieth-century classical composers, such as Charles Ives, Lou Harrison, Steve Reich, John Cage, and Aaron Copland, and jazz crossover composers such as George Gershwin and Duke Ellington.

American Mavericks is a unique Web site, in that it offers four different ways to listen to and learn about the music:

- Performances of dozens of individual works by the San Francisco Symphony. Unlike most Internet radio stations, you get to choose the works to listen to.

- Two Internet-only radio streams of twentieth-century American classical music: the Smooth Channel (for more ambient-sounding or nature-inspired sounds) and the Chunky Channel (more dissonance). At one point the Smooth Channel fell silent, not because of a technical difficulty, but because it was "playing John Cage's 1952 work 4'33, which consists entirely of 4 and a half minutes of silence.

- Thirteen hour-long public-radio programs hosted by Suzanne Vega, in which the various twentieth-century styles and trends are discussed and compared with music samples and interviews.

- Dozens of interviews with composers and musicians.

You'll find all of these links at www.musicmavericks.org/listening/index.html.

BBC World Service

For a truly international news perspective in English, it's tough to beat the BBC World Service. The World Service provides news, currents events, and human interest features about the world to the world. You'll hear news you might not hear elsewhere. Also interesting are the man-on-the-street interviews, where reporters ask the opinions of ordinary people — people living in places like Nigeria, Thailand, and Bangladesh. Sports news includes events such as the Tour de France and soccer scores from every continent.

Type the following RealOne Player (File menu, Open Location): **www.bbc.co.uk/worldservice/ ram/live_news.ram**.

You can also listen to news summaries at http://news.bbc.co.uk/.

Harry Shearer's Le Show

Political satire from the multitalented Harry Shearer, Le Show continues a tradition of radio pioneered by the likes of Bob and Ray (with prepared sketches) and Jean Sheppard (with monologues directed at the audience). Harry Shearer also is a master of voices. If you've ever watched The Simpsons, you've heard Shearer do the voices of most of the non-Simpsons characters, including Ned Flanders, Mr. Burns, Smithers, Principle Skinner, and McBain. On Le Show, Shearer does the best Bill Clinton, George W. Bush, and Ronald Reagan anywhere. Shearer, who played Dirk in the Spinal Tap movies, also writes and performs original musical satirical pieces on Le Show.

The 1-hour Le Show program originates from Santa Monica's KCRW and can be found on some National Public Radio stations. However, many NPR stations won't carry Le Show because Shearer mixes in an eclectic mix of old and new music, including rock and jazz, and often steers toward controversial topics.

You can listen to individual episodes of Le Show by going to the Le Show Web site (www.harryshearer.com/leshow/) and selecting a show date.

MacVooty Radio

This station features the music of Slim Gaillard, the hep-cat singer, pianist, and guitarist who was a popular novelty jazz performer in the 1930s, 1940s, and 1950s. He had several hits, including Laughin' in Rhythm and Flat Foot Floogie, and appeared in movies and on TV in the 1950s and 1960s. Gaillard is known for the jive-talk language he called "Vout Oreenie," which he used often to comic effect. Phrases like "very groovy, very mellow-roonie, very solid o-routie" pepper his songs and song introductions. In fact, Gaillard claimed to have invented the term "groovy." You can judge for yourself at MacVooty Radio.

Tune into MacVooty Radio in iTunes Radio, listed under Jazz. Or, type this into your MP3 player: **www.live365.com/play/62006**.

The show's Web page is www.pocreations.com/slim.html.

PoCreations.COMedy

This station presents comedy from the 1950s to the present from a variety of comedians, often of a subversive nature with graphic language. It arranges comedy bits, and even snippets of bits, in categories. For instance, you're likely to hear 10 minutes of routines on sex, followed by another 10 on death, religion, drugs, or even noncontroversial subjects like football. The cuts can be as short as 10 seconds or as long at 22 minutes, as when the station played the entire side of a 1960s Firesign Theater album. (It was a single track, so technically didn't violate the Webcasting rules.)

To tune in, type **www.live365.com/play/26694** into iTunes or another MP3 player.

RadioStorm Hip Hop/R&B

As one of the most popular genres of popular music, hip hop can be found in a lot of places on the Internet and on the airwaves. One of the best 24-hour-a-day Internet stations is RadioStorm Hip Hop/R&B, which has the capacity to handle tens of thousands of simultaneous listeners.

You can access this station in several ways. You'll find it in iTunes Radio listed under Urban. You can go directly to it by entering `http://64.236.34.141:80/stream/1013` into an MP3 player. You'll also find it listed at SHOUTcast.com.

Retro Rock Adventures

As with broadcast radio, there are lots of places on the Internet to hear oldies. Retro Rock Adventures is one of the best broadcasters of 1960s and 1970s Rock. The station offers a variety of styles including progressive rock, experimental rock, folk rock, art rock, and classical Rock, all arranged in playlists that make sense. At the time, this music was sometimes known as "not commercial," even though many of the songs were hits. You'll also hear cuts that weren't hits, and artists that didn't make the top 40. Another thing that makes RetroRock Adventures stand out is that its playlists are huge — sometimes over 1,000 songs, which will go on for 3 days. You won't hear the same song twice.

To tune in, type **www.live365.com/play/191936** into iTunes or another MP3 player. You can also hear it at its Web page at Musical Sojourn (`http://musicsojourn.com/Cat/Prog/Streams/CRS1.htm`), where you can see what playlist is current being broadcast and what song is currently being played.

The Spirit of Jazz

For 35 years, San Francisco's KJAZ FM was a favorite West Coast station of jazz lovers and musicians. In 1959, the pioneering KJAZ was the first commercial jazz station in the country, though it always maintained a noncommercial sense of what jazz is. Dizzy Gillespie once called KJAZ "The greatest jazz station in the world." When the station ceased operation in 1994, victim of the homogenization of FM radio, Bay Area listeners raised $1.3 million in an effort to save the station — the owners had to refund the money. The owners then tried to get KJAZ onto satellite distribution, an effort that failed in 1995. However, with the rise of Internet radio, the spirit of KJAZ is back. Three former KJAZ DJs and staffers put together an Internet-only version of the old station using their own personal music collections.

In iTunes Radio, look under Jazz.

WFMU

There's nothing like a good, old-fashioned free-form radio station with a disk jockey playing whatever comes to mind at the time. These make particularly good listening late at night, when there aren't any scheduled programs. There are a few such stations scattered around the country. One of the oldest and still the best is WFMU from East Orange, New Jersey, not far from

Manhattan. A station termed "free-form" resists any kind of categorization, but we once heard an accurate rendition of the old King Crimson song, Larks Tongue in Aspic, by a completely acappella singing group.

To hear a live feed, look for WFMU in iTunes Radio listed under Public.

Summary

Internet radio is a big place, far bigger and more varied than broadcast radio. With your Mac, you can become a part of Internet radio. The easiest way is to subscribe to Live365.com, a Mac-friendly Internet-radio-hosting service. A big benefit is that Live365 takes care of paying any royalties due for your broadcasting. You'll use Live365's software to transcode your digital Music files to make them smaller, and upload them to the servers. (Just remember to use the same transcoding settings for *all* of the music files you upload.) Using a Web interface, you can create playlists and schedules. You can also do a live radio show right from your Mac. If you're the do-it-yourself type, there is ample opportunity to run your own broadcasting outfit with tools like QuickTime Streaming Server.

If you are looking to enlarge the source of music for your radio station, you might consider your vinyl LP and cassette tape collections. Chapter 9 will show you how to bring those collections on to your Mac. If you're interested in using your Mac to create your own music, check out Chapter 7.

Watch, Record, and Edit TV on Your Mac

Why would you want to watch and record TV on your Mac? Just "think different" for a second. Think of stopping the TV action and replaying it. Think of fast forwarding through commercials. Think TiVo, but without the monthly fee.

If you don't know TiVo, it's a cable TV service that puts a box in your living room that they call a digital video recorder (DVR). The term *DVR* is a bit misleading, though. The technology gives you more than the term implies, going well beyond what you can do with a VCR. (This is perhaps why DVRs are sometimes referred to as *personal video recorders*, or PVRs, though this term isn't particularly descriptive either.) By putting TiVo-like functionality on your Mac, you get even more capabilities, such as integration with iMovie and the ability to put TV shows on DVDs. If this doesn't appeal to you, you may just want to watch TV on your Mac — this is also possible, and for a lower cost.

This chapter shows you several ways to get TV functionality on your Mac, and what you can do with it. It could change the way you watch TV.

TV Features for Your Mac

The idea of marrying TV and Macs has been an appealing one for many years. The rumor mills once thought that Apple would be releasing a hand-held TV Mac — instead, Apple released the iPod. Apple briefly flirted with the TV-in-a-Mac idea in 1994, when it shipped 10,000 units of a unit called Mac TV, a black Performa LC 520 with a TV tuner card. After that, Apple sold TV tuners as an option in the several old Performa models, which had 32-MHz processors. With today's Macs running 50 times or more faster, there are now several new television features you can put on your Mac, including those of a DVR.

TiVo's DVR is basically a small computer with a hard drive and a TV tuner. It digitizes incoming video signals and can store them on its hard drive. This gives you the digital video recorder functionality:

- **Pause live TV.** A handy feature when the phone rings — pause, and you don't have to miss a minute of your show. When you do this, the DVR records the incoming TV signals to a hard drive. In the case of TiVo, this hard disk is in the DVR box. When you turn your Mac into a DVR, the hard disk is in your Mac.

- **Replay live TV.** With the content being cached to a hard drive, you can replay a segment over again — a handy feature for sports, or when you've missed a bit of dialog.

- **Record TV, instantly or scheduled.** Unlike a VCR, you don't need to load media (a tape). The hard disk is there, as long as it has free space.

- **Skip commercials.** Enough said.

- **Use an Internet-based service for content.** A DVR system lets you search for a show or browse for it.

There are a few things that you can do by putting TV on your Mac that you can't do with TiVo:

- **Watch TV on your Mac.** This can be full screen or in a small window to monitor some event as you use your Mac. If this doesn't go far enough, some systems let you output the video to your TV. (See Figure 3-1.)

- **View and edit TV content in iMovie.** For TV content that you want to keep, why fast forward through the commercials every time you watch it? With iMovie, just delete the commercials. You can also use iMovie to create a video containing your favorite music videos for a party or a video cookbook with your favorite recipes.

- **Output to DVD.** Just as you now record VHS tapes, you can record to DVDs, which take up a lot less room.

- **Analog-to-digital conversion.** Some of the Mac-based DVR systems let you convert your videotapes to digital format and to DVDs, a topic that is the subject of Chapter 10.

There are several different ways to get all or some of the features, depending on how much money you want to spend. However, even the most complete, most expensive DVR box for your Mac costs about as much as an iPod.

FIGURE 3-1: Watching TV on your Mac is just the beginning.
Courtesy of ESPN.

What You'll Need

In order to get television or digital video recorder functionality on your Mac, you will need the following components, either in an all-in-one package, or separately.

- **TV tuner.** This accepts input from your TV cable or antenna and can distinguish among the channels.

- **Analog-to-digital converter.** Usually hardware, this converts the standard TV signals into a digital format your Mac can work with.

- **Digital-to-analog converter.** This is optional, but allows you to view the results on your TV or output them to a VCR. Specifically, the analog output needs to be NTSC for television in North America.

- **Program guide.** Usually Internet based, the program guide lets you search for and find TV shows that you might want to view or record.

- **Software.** The software lets you control the system, change channels, pause, and do everything else you need to. All of the hardware packages come with software, but often the software differs as much or more than the hardware.

- **Your Mac.** Your television equipment will work best if your Mac's G3 or G4 processor is 500 MHz or above. With slower Macs, you may see some slowing down or skipping of the video if you are running other processor-intensive software, including iTunes. A PowerBook or iBook will give you the flexibility to keep any DVR equipment in your living room with your big-screen TV, and move your Mac into the room when you need it.

This chapter looks at four different TV solutions for your Mac, spanning in cost from $150 to $400. We'll start with two TV tuners: the Televio for a Power Mac's PCI slot, and the MyTV for any Mac's USB port. These two don't have DVR functionality—they just bring TV to your Mac.

Next, we'll look at two full-fledged DVR systems that include TV tuners. The first is a box that connects to your Mac's USB port, EyeTV from Elgato Systems. The second is the Formac Studio TVR, a FireWire box that is the most complete DVR solution, and a solution that you can also use for several other video projects.

After the hardware and the software that work with them is a discussion of online program guides.

TV Tuners for Your Mac

Buying a TV Tuner for your Mac can cost about the same as buying a TV. Unlike a TV, you have the ability to capture some of the video for later viewing. This capture is not as versatile or as high-quality as the DVR boxes, however. These TV tuners can support up to 125 cable and antenna stations, which you can watch in a resizable window or on the full screen. You can also tune into FM radio.

MyTV

MyTV from Eskape Labs (www.eskapelabs.com/mytv.html) is a product line of several different USB TV tuners. At under $100, MyTV-to-Go is the least expensive way to get TV on your Mac. It's also the smallest TV box. MyTV-to-Go doesn't offer any video capturing—for that, you can go to the standard MyTV box (see Figure 3-2), which is also a bigger box. For a slightly higher cost, Eskape offers versions of both MyTV modes that includes an FM radio tuner. MyTV is powered by the USB port, so it doesn't need a separate power cable.

FIGURE 3-2: The full version of MyTV offers a TV tuner for your Mac's USB port and video capture. It doesn't capture audio, however.
Courtesy of Eskape Labs.

MyTV can capture video as QuickTime movies in Motion JPEG format, a compressed format. It captures at about 30 frames per second (29.97 to be exact), the standard of NTSC television. This video can be from the TV signal, to let you record and watch a show later. However, there is no scheduling function as with the digital video recorder devices. There are also S-Video and composite video input ports into which you can connect an analog video camera or VCR. The MyTV software records video to the Movies folder in your home folder.

MyTV's capture feature is useful, but it isn't the best for converting your old analog videotapes to DVDs (as is described in Chapter 10). iMovie and other video editors use the uncompressed DV (digital video) format. You can convert the Motion JPEG that MyTV creates to DV using QuickTime Pro (www.apple.com/quicktime/upgrade/), Apple's $30 upgrade to the Mac's QuickTime software. (Open the captured video file with QuickTime Player, and choose Export from the File menu.) The problem with this approach is that you will lose picture quality.

MyTV does not digitize audio. To get the TV's sound to your Mac, you connect the analog sound-out port on the MyTV box into the analog audio-in port (the microphone port) of your Mac. However, many Mac models don't have an analog audio-in port. For these Macs, you'll need a USB audio capture device, such as those described in Chapter 7. The least expensive is the $35 Griffin iMac (www.griffintechnology.com/).

The Televio for Power Macs

If you have a Power Mac, you can get a TV tuner on an internal PCI card, such as the Televio ($150, www.televio.com/meilenstein_en/2_Televio/1/content) by Meilenstein. The Televio product offers some hardware and software features not found in other products, including the higher-priced DVR boxes. There's an infrared remote control with a numeric keypad (see Figure 3-3), which you can use to change channels and control other functions. You can also use the remote to control other Mac applications.

FIGURE 3-3: This remote control comes with the Televio TV tuner, a PCI card for Power Macs.
Courtesy of Meilenstein Software GmbH.

Another unique feature is in software. The Channel Preview gives you still thumbnails of multiple TV stations in one window, so you can see what's on without flipping through the channels. The thumbnails are updated at intervals. To watch a channel, double-click a thumbnail to launch a TV window. Another interesting feature is the ability to play a TV in the software's Dock icon. Of course, that's too small to enjoy a TV show, but it does let you keep an eye on it while you wait for a show or segment to come on. (Meilenstein also sells it's software separately for use with other PCI TV tuner cards.)

The Televio accepts input from a coaxial cable or a TV antenna. For a digital satellite signal, you need a digital Sat-receiver or a set-top box to translate the signal into a standard NTSC signal. The card also has another connector for an FM radio antenna. There are S-Video and composite video connectors for inputting video from a VCR or analog video camera. The Televio digitizes the audio as well as the video, from the TV signal and from your VCR or analog video camera.

There's also a video capture feature for TV and video that you input. This feature can capture the input in a variety of compressed QuickTime formats, such as MPEG-4 video compression or Motion-JPEG compression. However, if you also want to use your TV box to digitize old video for porting to DVDs (as described in Chapter 10), the Formac Studio DVR will give you higher quality conversion.

Display Options

If you are using your Mac to watch TV on a regular basis, you might consider using a large monitor on your Mac, particularly if your Mac is a PowerBook or iBook. You can use any brand of display as long as it is the right connector for your Mac. For instance, a PowerBook G4 with a DVI port and a Power Mac has an ADC port. Apple's Cinema Displays uses an ADC connector, but Apple offers a DVI-to-ADC adapter for the PowerBook. Apple sets the standards for displays in terms of quality and size. If you're going for size, it's tough to find a bigger flat screen than Apple's 23" Cinema Display.

Formac (www.formac.com) is another maker of top-quality displays. The Gallery line is similar to Apple's in design and look, and rivals Apple's in image quality. They also can cost 30 percent less.

Another thing to consider is the display's aspect ratio, the ratio of the width to the length. Apple's displays are wide, close to aspect ratio of movies (hence the name *Cinema* Display). If you are watching a lot of DVDs, you will see a bigger picture on Apple's displays. However, if you are watching TV, you'll get some wasted space on the sides. The Formac displays are squarer, more like a television monitor. For instance, the 20" Formac Gallery has a 4:3 aspect ratio, the same as standard TV. Apple's 20" is about 5:3. Because of this, when watching TV on the 20" Formac, you'll get a much better image than on Apple's 20", approaching the size of a TV image on Apple's 23" display.

Flat panel displays are certainly crisper and brighter than traditional cathode ray tube monitors, but have some drawbacks when it comes to TV viewing. One is that the color and brightness fade as the viewing angle departs from directly in front. Another problem is that they are sometimes too sharp for TV viewing in that you can see the pixilated edge of an object on screen — CRTs are naturally fuzzier. However, CRTs have problems, too. The biggest one is size — CRTs are huge, especially when you get up to the 21" size.

DVR Solutions

Moving from TV tuners to digital video recorders, you start getting real integration of television and the computer. Here's were you put your Mac to work with some of the really cool features, such as pausing live TV and scheduling recordings. The software will indeed put your Mac to work, as does any application that works with video. With slower Macs, you may find yourself having to quit other applications to get the video to run smoothly.

The two most Mac-friendly DVR units are the EyeTV and Formac Studio DVR. Both work well. Both are integrated with Internet-based program guides — search for a show, click a button, and the information downloads directly into the DVR software's recording schedulers.

The Formac Studio TVR costs more than EyeTV, but has more powerful hardware, better image quality, and more input and output options.

EyeTV

EyeTV from Elgato Systems ($200, www.elgato.com) is similar to MyTV in some respects, but goes farther. It's a USB-connected box containing a 124-channel cable tuner and hardware video capturing. It displays TV at different sizes or at full screen. It has a coaxial connector for your TV cable or antenna, and input jacks for analog video from a VCR or camera. (See Figure 3-4.) Unlike the MyTV tuner, EyeTV digitizes audio and sends it through the USB port.

Instant Replay, Scheduling with EyeTV

EyeTV also includes DVR software that not only lets you play and record, but lets you pause the TV action, jump ahead, and schedule recordings with some nice integration with online program guides. The on-screen controls come in the form of a floating palette referred as a "remote" (see Figure 3-5).

The EyeTV makes it ease to skip commercials. Just press the Jump button to skip 30 seconds ahead at a time. EyeTV also has an Instant Replay button that takes you back 7 seconds, so you can watch the bit one more time. Like the Formac Studio TVR, the EyeTV can do this because it records a buffer of what you are watching on the Mac's hard drive. The default setting is for 30 minutes worth — that is, it will hold the past 30 minutes of what you've been watching. You can make this longer if you have the hard disk space. EyeTV takes up 650 MB for an hour of TV at the standard setting, or 1.3 GB at the high setting. The high setting uses less disk space than the Formac Studio TVR uses, but the quality isn't as good. EyeTV's resolution is 352 × 240 pixels; Formac's resolution is 640 × 480 pixels.

Still, the EyeTV has a few things going for it in software. As was mentioned earlier, both the EyeTV and Formac Studio TVR software integrate an Internet program guide — click on a show at a certain time and date in the future, and it is added to your recording schedule. Both units work with TitanTV.com, but the EyeTV also works with several other Internet television guides, including Karelia's Watson and TVTV (www.tvtv.com), if you have EyeTV software version 1.3 or later. These guides are described later in the chapter.

A unique feature (if you have Mac OS X 10.2 or later) is that EyeTV 1.3 or later will start up your Mac in order to record a show you've scheduled. The Formac Studio TVR will wake up your Mac from sleep (as can EyeTV), but won't start it up for you. This means that you can set EyeTV to record shows at 3 A.M. without having to keep your Mac turned on.

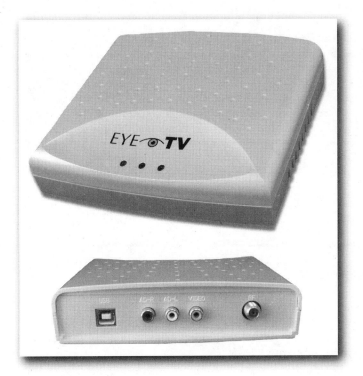

FIGURE 3-4: EyeTV connects to your Mac's USB port. (The rear is shown on the bottom.)
Courtesy of Elgato Systems LLC.

I/O and Video Capture

At $200, EyeTV is half the cost of the Formac Studio TVR. However, there are a few things it doesn't have that the Formac box does. For instance, because it uses USB instead of FireWire, it can be slower with some functions, such as changing channels. The EyeTV also doesn't have the video outputs of the Formac, so you can't connect EyeTV to your television screen or output to a VHS machine.

You also don't get native DV format media. EyeTV captures TV and input video as MPEG 1 video. This means that if you want to use it in iMovie, you'll have to convert it to DV using QuickTime Pro or another video utility. In addition to not getting the image quality you get with Formac's native DV format, there is a problem with the audio in this conversion — QuickTime will lose it. Elgato recommends first separating the audio track from the MPEG-1 file with a free utility called bbDEMUX (http://prdownloads.sourceforge.net/macbbdemux/). Then, you can convert the MPEG-1 audio into AIFF, which you can import into iMovie. For this conversion, Elgato recommends MAD (www.biermann.org/philipp/mad/), another free utility.

However, if it's just TV shows that you are interested in, EyeTV now lets you edit your recordings to strip out commercials, or save your favorite clips as QuickTime movies.

FIGURE 3-5: EyeTV's software controls are in this floating palette.
Courtesy of Elgato Systems LLC.

Remoteless DVR

Neither the EyeTV nor the Formac Studio TVR comes with a remote control, which would be handy for channel surfing from your couch. Both do work with Keyspan's $49 Digital Media Remote (www.keyspan.com). The receiver plugs into the Mac's USB port, and the credit-card-sized remote works from up to 35 feet away. Unfortunately, the Keyspan Remote doesn't have a numeric keypad, which means that you have to click through each of 125 channels to get to the one you want.

Formac Studio TVR

Formac Studio TVR ($400, www.formac.com) takes the everything-in-one-box approach. It is the most full-featured way to bring DVR functionality to your Mac, and is the most versatile TV device. The Studio TVR is the only DVR unit that also doubles as a full-fledged video capture device for converting your analog videotapes to digital (see Chapter 10). It imports video from a cable, antenna, or satellite, or from your analog video camera or VCR, and converts it to DV format — the same format used by iMovie. As a result, the images are crisp and sharp, even when displayed at full screen.

Because the DV format video involves a large amount of data, the Studio TVR connects to your Mac via FireWire. It also includes an extra FireWire port for connection to another FireWire device, such as a digital camcorder. The Studio TVR works with antenna, cable, or satellite. The box itself, shown in Figure 3-6, looks like the Formac Studio DV mentioned in Chapter 10. However, the DV model doesn't have the television tuner and is strictly a video capture device.

The Studio TVR software gives you complete flexibility as to the size of the TV window. You can resize the image to full screen or to predetermined sizes, and you can drag it to any size you wish. When you minimize the window, the video will play in the Dock icon, with sound.

Like EyeTV, the Formac Studio TVR software keeps a buffer of a TV feed. It's called the TimeShift Buffer. You have to turn it on using the Pause button. You can then press the Backward button to replay items. The Forward button will let you skip commercials. You can set the size of the TimeShift Buffer in the Preferences dialog. The default setting is 15 minutes, which means that after 15 minutes, the early video gets erased. You can change this setting to as long as you want, provided that you have the disk space (approximately 13 GB per hour).

You can also record shows on the fly or via a schedule. When you record a show, it is stored in a clips drawer. Here, you can play it or edit it to crop out commercials or anything else you don't want.

The Studio TVR software lets you export recorded shows as a QuickTime file. If you want to put the TV show on DVD, you can export it as MPEG-2, the format used on standard DVD players. (You can even add chapter markers.) The Export to Studio button will feed the video through the Studio TVR's output ports, either RCA (Composite) or S-Video, to let you view it on a television or record it on a VCR.

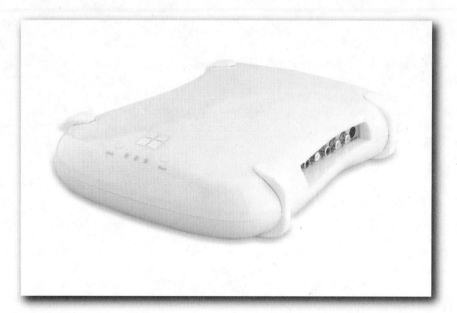

FIGURE 3-6: The Formac Studio TVR is the most complete DVR solution for a Mac.
Courtesy of Formac.

You also do a lot of this with iMovie, because the Studio DVR software is integrated with Apple's video editor. The Studio TVR software includes an add-on to iMovie called the iMovie Remote Control, which allows you to select TV channels and video sources directly in iMovie, where you can watch, record, and edit TV directly. If you want to use iMovie without having Formac's Remote Control palette appear, you can shut it off in Studio TVR's Preference dialog.

Note   The Studio TVR is Formac's second-generation DVR box, which replaces the older Studio DV/TV. The older unit didn't have all of the features of the current box.

Using TV on Your Mac

This section shows you how to set up and use your TV tuner and digital video recorder. We use the Formac Studio TVR, but most instructions are common to both the Formac and the EyeTV, and to the TV tuners described earlier.

Hardware Setup

The Studio TVR is unique in the number of ports it supplies, so it's worth going over them. The Studio TVR, shown in Figure 3-7, is connected for bringing TV to the Mac. On the right side are the main connections — a coaxial cable from the cable TV provider coming in and

FireWire to the Mac. There is an extra FireWire port not in use, which you could connect a digital camcorder or some other FireWire peripheral completely unrelated to video — the port is there as a pass-through FireWire port.

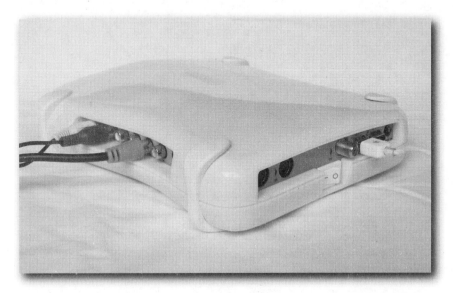

FIGURE 3-7: The Formac Studio TVR with FireWire connected (right), and video and audio out (left).
Courtesy of Formac.

On the left side of Figure 3-7 are auxiliary connections. There's an analog video camera connected to the Composite Video In port and two Audio In ports. The Composite Video Out and Audio Out ports can be connected to a television. All of these ports could be connected to a VCR as well. There are also S-Video In and Out ports on the right, which are unused in the figure.

There is no power cable connected to the Studio DVR — the unit is completely powered by the Mac through the FireWire cable. However, there is a Power Out plug, which you can use to power another FireWire device connected to the box.

Software Setup

After you connect the box to your Mac and your TV cable, you can set up the software. Most of this is automatic and deals with configuring the TV tuner for channels. When you first launch the software, you're usually asked if you want to scan for channels (see Figure 3-8). Usually, you'll say yes. Just as when you fire up a new TV for the first time, the TV Tuner software will scan available stations and build a station list (see Figure 3-9).

FIGURE 3-8: When you first launch your TV tuner or DVR
software, it will ask you if you want to scan for channels.

FIGURE 3-9: The Formac Studio TVR setup software is scanning for channels.

You can now start watching TV, channel surfing, and playing with the screen size.

Watch TV, Change Channels

Many of the TV tuner products start playing TV in a window when you launch the software. The manner of changing channels differs with different TV tuner software package. Formac gives you several ways to change channels. At the top left of Figure 3-10, you can use the arrows to advance the TV channel one at a time. On the right side is Formac's channel shelf, which lets you click on a channel to select it. (You open and close the shelf by clicking the heart icon.) If you click the channel number in the upper left, a pop-up appears (see Figure 3-11) that also lets you select a channel.

FIGURE 3-10: Formac's channel shelf lets you click on a channel to go to it.

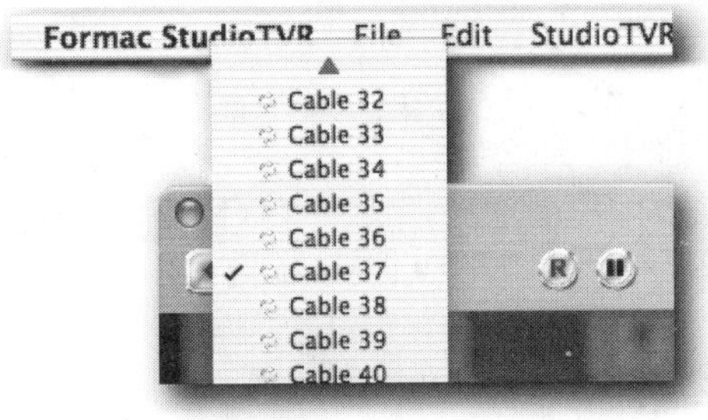

FIGURE 3-11: Formac's pop-up is a good way to go to a channel.

Tip If you are running Formac Studio TVR on an older Mac slower than 500 MHz, and the TV image is skipping frames or stuttering, that's a sure sign that the software isn't getting enough processor power. First, try quitting other applications and stopping Classic in System Preferences. If that doesn't work, you can lower the picture quality in the Studio TVR software's Preferences dialog, under Formac Studio Options. Try a Medium or Low setting instead of High.

Pause Live TV, Replay, and Skip Ahead

The first step beyond the TV tuner features is pausing live TV. In Formac Studio TVR, you do this by clicking the Pause button. When you press the Pause button, a small palette called TimeShift Buffer springs out of the bottom of the window (see Figure 3-12). This starts the buffer rolling — that is, the software is recording and retaining the last 15 or 30 minutes of your TV show.

FIGURE 3-12: When you click the Pause button, the picture freezes and the TimeShift Buffer control palette appears at the bottom.

Click Play to start the action. You'll remain in the buffer mode until you press the Live TV button, which will end the buffer mode. While you are watching TV in buffer mode, you can replay a portion of the action you just saw. In Studio TVR, the left double arrow will take you back a few sections. The left arrow and line puts you back at the beginning of where you started buffering. You can also drag the slider back.

If you think about it, a DVR isn't a time machine—you can't skip ahead of what hasn't yet come into your TV tuner. So, if you want to skip ahead of commercials, you'll have to buffer some of the incoming TV show first. A good way to skip commercials it is to start the buffer at the beginning of a show and leave it paused for about 10 minutes. Go make a phone call, open the mail, or feed the dog. Come back and start playing the show. With 10 minutes of buffer, you have enough time saved up to skip ahead of all of the commercials in a half-hour show.

While in Pause mode, you can't change the size of the window or minimize it. Studio TVR also won't let you open the Preferences dialog. Neither can you record a show for future viewing. To leave Pause mode, click the Live TV button (TV icon).

Record and Edit TV

To record a show that is currently being displayed, click the Record button (the R button in Formac Studio DVR). Both EyeTV and Studio TVR have preferences settings as to the format, but Studio DVR gives you the higher-quality option of DV format. Studio TVR shows a recording dialog with a hard disk free space indicator while it is playing (see Figure 3-13).

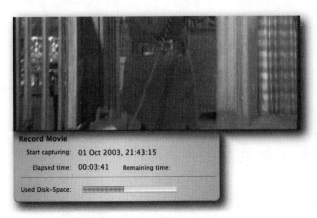

FIGURE 3-13: Studio TVR lets you know that it is recording with this dialog.

To play back recorded material in Studio DVR, click the Clips button at the top. A tray will slide out showing previously recorded shows. Click one, and click the Play button at the bottom of the window to play it.

To edit out commercials, you'll use the Edit palette at the bottom of the screen (see Figure 3-14). Move the slider at the bottom of the screen to the beginning of the section you want to cut, and click the Select Start button. Now move to the end of the section you want to cut, and click the Select End button. Now click the Clear button

You can also use iMovie to play and edit shows recorded with Studio TVR. (See Chapter 11 for information on editing in iMovie.)

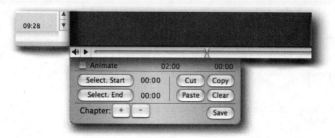

FIGURE 3-14: Use this palette in Studio TVR to cut out commercials in recorded TV shows.

Schedule a Recoding

In both EyeTV and Formac Studio TVR, you can manually schedule a recording in advance or have an Internet program guide schedule the recording of a show automatically. To manually schedule an item in Studio TVR, click the Scheduler button (clock icon). A new window opens, showing a calendar. Go to a date and double-click a time slot. A dialog will appear where you can set a time, select a channel, and provide a name for the recording (see Figure 3-15).

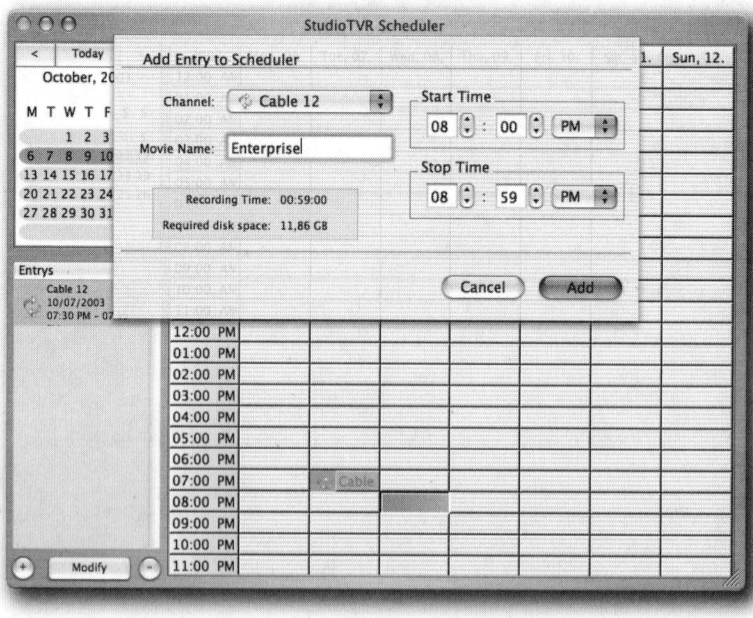

FIGURE 3-15: Manually scheduling a recording in Studio TVR.

If you've already signed up with TitanTV.com (a free service), you can automatically schedule a recording from the TitanTV schedule. (The next section covers how to sign up for and configure TitanTV). Here's how you use the schedule guide from Studio TVR:

1. Click the Online Service button (the book icon). This will open your Web browser to a specific page at Formac's Web site.

2. Click the link to "Titan TV's online program guide."

3. TitanTV will open to a TV listings page for your area at the current date and time.

4. Scroll through the current listings or search for a show or other criteria.

5. When you find a show you want to schedule, click the red dot next to the name.

The information will be downloaded to your software and entered into the scheduler. You'll notice in Figure 3-16 that not only has TitanTV filled in the date and time, but it has also added a description of the particular episode.

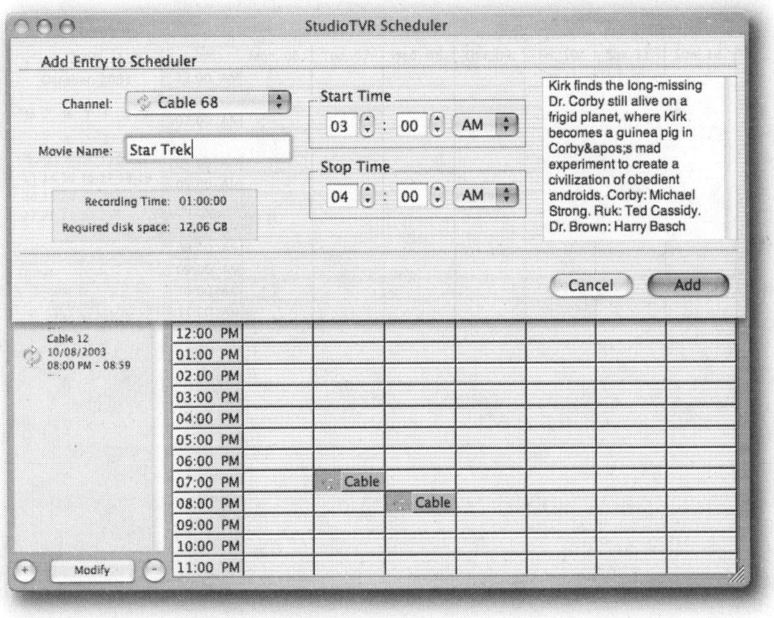

FIGURE 3-16: The scheduled recording that TitanTV has downloaded includes a description of the episode.

For a closer look at TitanTV and other online program guides, read on.

Online Program Guides

Internet-based television program guides such as TitanTV are integrated with DVR software, but you can also use them manually with TV tuners to search by show, channel, actor, or other attributes. You need to specify where you are, who your cable provider is (or if you're using an antenna), and what your plan is. You can view schedules for basic cable, digital cable, satellite, or old-fashioned over-the-air TV. You can also read about an episode of a show.

You view most Internet TV program guides with a Web browser. This includes TitanTV (shown in Figure 3-17), TVTV.com, TVGuide.com, and Yahoo TV. One service, Watson, is a Sherlock-like Internet tool that doesn't use a Web browser. We'll take a look at two of the best, TitanTV and Watson.

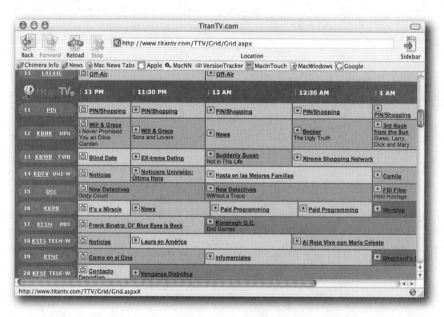

FIGURE 3-17: An Internet program guide such as TitanTV is customized to your TV service.

TitanTV

TitanTV (www.titantv.com) from Decisionmark Corp. works with a large number of computer and standalone DVRs and tuners, and can be used for simple browsing. TitanTV is a free service, but you do have to sign up for an account. You will need to have cookies turned on in your Web browser in order to sign up for and use the services. (The cookies are what enables TitanTV to bring up the current TV schedule for your system whenever you go to the Web site.) However, a TitanTV account is not highly personal—you don't even have to add your last name or your email address. You do need to add your mailing address.

At one point during the setup process, a screen will ask you to choose your PVR and your TV tuner (see Figure 3-18). If you have EyeTV or Formac Studio TVR, you can select them from the pop-up. Notice that for the Formac, it lists "DV/TV." This refers to the older model of the Formac Studio TVR, but you can use this setting for your TVR.

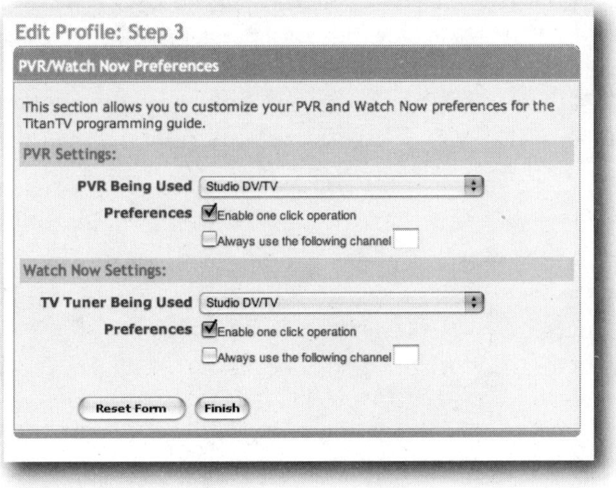

FIGURE 3-18: This step in TitanTV's setup process asks you for your Mac's TV hardware.

Once you have an account, you can go and see what's on the tube. TitanTV also lets you configure a favorites table where you can keep a few of your favorite channels, so you don't have to scroll through listings of dozens of channels you never watch.

Of course, you don't always want to see what's on right now. Flexible searching lets you search for a name of a show or type of a show, an actor, and the time the show will air, or a combination of these factors.

TitanTV is designed with Internet Explorer in mind. At the time of publishing, Safari did not work well, but the open source Camino browser (www.mozilla.org/projects/camino/) did function. However, the browser that you use to sign up for TitanTV is the browser you will need to access it.

Watson

Watson from Karelia (www.karelia.com/watson/) is an Internet services utility that inspired Apple to recreate Sherlock a few years ago as Sherlock 3. Like Sherlock, Watson offers a set of different search channels to let you search to look up a type of data from multiple different Internet-based databases, without a Web browser. One of the Watson's channels is a TV listings channel that you can use from within EyeTV or by itself. Karelia doesn't provide the program guide service itself, but instead searches TVGuide.com, run by the people who own the famous magazine of the same name. Not only is Watson faster and easier to use than the TVGuide.com Web site (which uses multiple windows), but it is integrated with EyeTV — the Web site is not.

Watson's TV Listings channel will bring you the program grid for your locality for up to 2 weeks in the future (see Figure 3-19). Watson displays a description of a program in a drawer at the bottom. On the right side of the drawer is an area called "More airings," which tells you the next time this specific episode will be on TV.

FIGURE 3-19: Watson is a Sherlock-like tool for browsing Internet services, including a TV program guide.

Another useful feature of Watson is its ability to store TV show information in the Apple iCal application. If you're not using your Mac to record shows, you can set iCal to remind you to watch the show or to record it on your VCR.

Watson's non-TV search channels are also very useful. These include searching for zip codes, tracking shipped packages, browsing a recipe database, and tracking eBay auctions.

Summary

If adding TV to your Mac combines two of your favorite toys, then you're in luck. You don't have to spend a lot of money or commit to a monthly fee to get TV in your Mac. How much you spend will determine what features you get. A basic TV tuner will let you watch television on your Mac. TV tuners are available as boxes that plug into your USB port or as a PCI card for your Power Mac.

If you want to go further, you can add digital video recorder (DVR) technology to your Mac to get features you can only find with a subscriber system such as TiVo. This includes pausing live TV, replaying segments, and scheduling automatic recording, which are standard with DVR solutions for your Mac.

EyeTV is an easy-to-use DVR box that costs just a little more than a good TV tuner. If you think you're also interested in digitizing your VHS home movies, the beefier Formac Studio TVR is a good option for you. (To find out how to use it for this purpose, be sure to read Chapter 10.)

Online program guides complete the Mac-TV experience by letting you search for shows and actors. With a single mouse click, you can tell the program guide to automatically set your DVR software to schedule the show for recording. It's much easier than getting your VCR to stop blinking 12:00.

Enhance Your iPod

The iPod lets you take your music collection to places you never could take it before — the subway, skiing, and flying over the Rockies in an airplane. With a few enhancements, you can also take your music collection even further — backpacking, on a sailing trip, or on a cross-country bike trip. You can extend your battery life, charge from new sources, and connect your iPod to stereos at home and in your car.

The iPod isn't limited to musical functions. It works as a hard drive, and can carry your calendar and contacts list. With a few enhancements, you can extend the iPod's nonmusical functions. And, if you really want to get hardcore, you can even run the Linux operating system on it.

Most of these enhancements come in the form of inexpensive hardware gadgets and software, some of it free. This chapter will guide you through the best of the iPod enhancers, and show you what to look for. In some cases, you may find what you need for less money in a general electronics store.

iPod Model Differences

The iPod's evolution over time has left a trail of different models with different capabilities. Because of this, iPod accessories often come in different versions for different iPod models. You should be aware of which iPod you have when shopping for iPod accessories. You don't want to buy something that only works with the iPod that came after — or before — the one you hold in your hand.

At the time of publication, there were three generations of iPod. However, because of their similarity, the first two generations are often referred to as "original" iPods by manufacturers. The third generation is referred to as the docking iPod. (Apple's official designation is "iPod with Dock Connector.")

The first and second generations have a circular scroll wheel surrounded by a circle of four buttons. A button in the center acts as the select button. The main difference between the first and second generations is that in the first, the scroll wheel was a mechanical spinning wheel. In the second, the wheel is a touch sensitive area with no moving parts. Both the first and second generation connect to the Mac with a FireWire port at the top.

FIGURE 4-1: First and second generation
iPods (often referred to collectively as the
"original iPods") featured buttons arranged
in a circle around the scroll wheel.
Courtesy of Apple.

The third generation iPod did away with the circular button ring and placed the four buttons above the scroll wheel (see Figure 4-2). It also:

- Has a docking port on the bottom, which is a 30-pin connector
- Comes with a docking stand for recharging and communicating with the Mac

In addition to FireWire, the third generation includes USB 2, mostly for PC users, though more Mac models are also including the port. One drawback to the newer generation is a slightly shorter battery life — 8 hours, instead of the 10 hours of previous models.

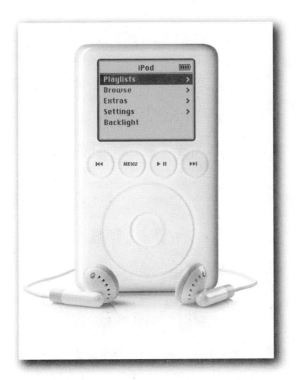

FIGURE 4-2: The third-generation iPods have a docking port
at the bottom, and the buttons located a row above the scroll wheel.
Courtesy of Apple.

Because of the differences in the placement of the ports, manufacturers of iPod gadgets usually
have one version for the first two generations and another version for the docking iPods.
Third-party iPod software often works with any iPod, though you should check with the developer. Some software may require a specific iPod system software version (described in the
"Care and Maintenance section" that follows).

Although each new iPod generation gets smaller in physical size, iPod storage has been
increasing. Because of this, you'll sometimes see models identified by their storage capacity, in
terms of gigabytes (GB). , Storage size won't always tell you which model you have, since each
generation of iPod has come in several capacities.

Tip

If you don't remember the storage capacity of your iPod, look on the back of the unit. Near the
bottom you'll see the capacity, and in very small print, the serial number.

When in doubt about which version of a device works with your iPod, check the manufacturer's Web site for pictures. Look for a picture of the gadget on your iPod, and note what they
are calling your iPod.

Inside iPod

The iPod is sometimes described as a FireWire hard drive with buttons. But if music is coming off spinning platters, why doesn't the iPod skip the way a portable CD player does when it's bumped? The answer is that there is more to the iPod than a hard drive — it's actually a hand-held computer, though simpler than a Palm or Pocket PC device, since you don't enter data directly into iPod.

Inside the iPod case is a sandwich of three layers: a hard drive, a thin battery, and a circuit board. On the circuit board are the electronics that make iPod a hand-held computer. The "brain" of the iPod is the PortalPlayer PP5002 chip, which contains an ARM processor core and the circuitry for decoding MP3, AAC, and other music files. There's also a mini operating system, stored in 1 MB of permanent flash RAM. A chip from Texas Instruments runs the FireWire interface and handles battery charging, and a digital-to-analog audio chip from Wolfson drives the headphones.

So why doesn't music skip when you bump the iPod? Like any computer, the iPod has RAM (the first iPods had 32 MB). In your Mac, when you launch an application, it loads from the hard drive into the faster RAM memory. In the iPod, music is loaded from the hard drive into solid-state RAM memory. In fact, the iPod can preload up to 25 minutes of music in its cache at once. So, when you listen to a song, you are hearing it from solid-state memory, not the hard drive. This is why the iPod doesn't skip when you bump it — there are no moving parts in RAM.

Care and Feeding

Though the iPod doesn't require a lot of maintenance, there are a few things you can do to keep it happy. You can update the iPod software when Apple offers a new version, and always keep the iPod in a case when you carry it around. The iPod is generally a very robust little device, but can freeze if things go wrong. If this happens to you and you can't get it going again, there are procedures you can use to bring it around.

Updating iPod Software

The iPod has two sets of software — there's one set running on the Mac, enabling it to recognize and communicate with the iPod when you connect it to the Mac. Another set of software runs on the iPod itself. Apple doesn't distinguish between the two, but does offer upgrades for both. These upgrades are often helpful, because they can fix problems, or improve iPod functionality. However, if your iPod is older, you may not need an update intended for newer models.

If you have your iPod software properly installed on your Mac, the Mac OS X Software Update feature will alert you when Apple creates a new version of iPod software. If you don't have Software Update set to automatically check Apple's servers over the Internet, you can do a manual check. Go to System Preferences, and click on the Software Update icon. Then, click the Update Now button.

When Software Update finds newer iPod software, it will present it in a list of Mac OS X updates available. Click on the iPod item in the list, and Software Update will present a description. In Figure 4-3, Software Update is describing an upgrade for newer models of iPods. If you had an older model, you could safely hit Cancel and not install the upgrade.

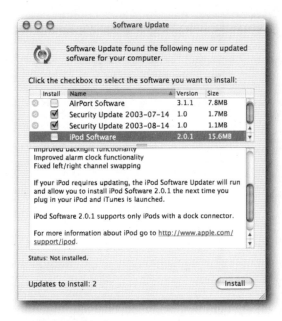

FIGURE 4-3: When Software Update finds a newer version of iPod software, click on it to read about it.
Courtesy of Apple.

To check the version of the software that your iPod is currently running, go to the iPod's main menu, click Settings, and then About. You'll see a line labeled Version, with the version number to the right.

Use a Case

There are several good reasons to keep your iPod in some sort of case when you are using it, and when you aren't. Although it's designed to resist shocks, the iPod does have mechanical parts moving very close to each other. A case can further protect it from shocks, prevent dents that might impair the iPod, and prevent the screen from getting scratched.

There are all kinds of fancy cases you can buy for the iPod, but the case that Apple shipped with some models does offer some basic protection — stiff, thick covering for the front and back to prevent dents and scratches, and a rounded bottom. When you drop the iPod on the bottom, it absorbs the shock by bending into the gap of air between it and the iPod, and rolls to the side (see Figure 4-4).

FIGURE 4-4: The round bottom of the Apple iPod
case can help absorb a shock if you drop the unit.
Courtesy of Apple.

What the Apple case does not give you is protection for the screen when you take it out of the case. One way to take care of that is to add clear plastic static-cling window decals, which you can pick up in an office supply store. For instance, Office Depot carries the Hammermill Inkjet Static-Cling Window Labels ($10). The label is meant to be put in a printer, so it is thick enough to provide scratch protection for iPod, but is optically clear, so it won't blur your screen. When it gets beat up, pull it off and cut yourself another piece. It will stick flat against your screen, and will also fit on top of your buttons if you want to protect those.

Still, removing the Apple iPod from its case can present a problem if you have your hands full. That's why some cases are designed to let you operate the iPod while keeping it in the case. One approach is the completely transparent or translucent case, such as the iSkin ($30, www.iskin4ipod.com) and the iPod Skin ($19, www.speckproducts.com). This type of case lets you use the iPod while enjoying its unique design. The best of these usually is made of a silicone or rubberish material to keep it from slipping from your hands.

Clear plastic cases don't offer this stiff project from dents that the Apple case does. There is another type of case that lets you operate the iPod while it's in the case, covers the screen, and gives you a stiffer, thicker wall. These are leather or composite cases with transparent areas over the screen, and often have a cover that flips up or to the side. Some of these covers have slots for holding credit cards and other items. XtremeMac has several in the $15 to $30 range (www.xtrememac.com). The Belkin iPod Organizer ($30) also has a place to put the iPod's earbuds. At the top of this category are the I-Volution cases from Vaja (www.vajacases .com), which run in the $55 to $90 range. These are padded leather cases that provide good protection from bumps, coverage of the screen, and attractive designs.

A lot of cases open up on the bottom to let you slip the iPod into its charging dock. However, this is not a good idea—charging the iPod while in the case can cause it to overheat. The best practice when charging is to remove the iPod from the case.

Resetting and Restoring iPod

We mentioned earlier that the iPod is a hand-held computer that is either running or in sleep mode—you can't really turn it off. On rare occasions, the iPod can freeze up on you, and not respond. To fix it, you can *reset* the iPod, which is sort of like rebooting your hand-held computer. If that doesn't work, you can *restore* the iPod, which erases the hard disk and reinstalls the operating system.

Reset Your iPod

Before you reset your iPod, double-check to see if the Hold switch is set to Hold. (Remember, the remote also has it's own Hold switch.) If it is, move it to the other position and try using the iPod.

If your iPod really is frozen, you can reset it. Resetting won't erase your music or any data files, and shouldn't change your preferences. To reset, connect the iPod to power (either the Mac or the AC adapter.) Now, press the Menu and Play/Pause buttons together and hold for 10 seconds. After the iPod is reset, the Apple logo should appear on the screen. If it doesn't, try letting the iPod sit unconnected for 24 hours and try again.

Restore Your iPod

If you still have a problem, you may need to restore your iPod. (For instance, you might see the iPod trying to reset itself over and over.) Unlike resetting, the restore procedure erases everything on the iPod—you will have to run the iPod Software updater to reinstall its system software. After that, iTunes will move all of your music and playlists back to the iPod. To restore your iPod, do the following:

1. Reset the iPod as described above (hold Menu and Play/Pause for 10 seconds) with the iPod connected to your Mac.

2. As soon as the Apple logo appears, let go of the Menu and Play/Pause buttons and press the Previous and Next buttons. Hold these until you see the "Do Not Disconnect" message on the screen. This command forces the iPod to mount on the Mac's desktop.

3. The iPod appears on the desktop. If you've previously stored any data files on the iPod and want to save them, you should now copy them from the iPod to your hard drive. If you don't see the "Do Not Disconnect" message or if the iPod is not mounted on the desktop, repeat Steps 1 and 2.

4. Run the iPod Software Updater on the Mac to reinstall the iPod's system software. (This is the step that erases everything on the iPod.) You can download this software from www.apple.com/swupdates. (You don't want to download iPod Software for Mac OS X.)

5. In the iPod Software Updater, click Restore. The installation begins.

6. If you have iPod software before version 2.0, after the installation is complete, you have to unplug the FireWire cable from the iPod and replug it when the iPod asks you to. iTunes will open. (If you have 2.0 or later, go to the next step.)

7. Type a name for the iPod in the iTunes Setup Assistant window.

8. You'll see an option called "Automatically update my iPod" set. If you leave this set, iTunes will copy your music to the iPod after you click the Done button.

9. When iTunes says the update is complete, Quit iTunes.

10. Unplug the iPod from the Mac. The iPod will ask you to pick a Language.

You're done. The iPod should be working just fine. If the iPod wouldn't let you complete the restore procedure, it may be in need of repair.

Note If you treat the iPod with a hard drive utility, such as Mac OS X's Disk Utility, you will disable its music playing capabilities. The damage is not irreversible, though. You can fix it by restoring the iPod's software, as was just described.

Power Options

One of the amazing things about the iPod is the long battery life — 8 hours on the docking models and 10 hours on older models. But this isn't always enough. Even 10 hours can pose a limitation if you are on a long trip, such as a drive across the country. Ten hours doesn't cut it on a trip away from AC power outlets, such as a backpacking trip or an intercontinental flight.

And there is one more limitation — the iPod's battery won't hold a charge for more than a few weeks. Without recharging it every few days, you're likely to find yourself looking at the empty battery icon in the iPod window.

Fortunately, there are ways to enhance and extend the iPod's powered-up status, to keep it running when you need it. This includes using the Apple's charging equipment, some alternative charging methods, external batteries, and replacing the iPod's internal battery. This section starts by exploring everything that Apple gives you to manage and enhance power, including tips for conserving power. We'll then move on to other ways to power the iPod using inexpensive third-party products.

Keeping Charged

One way to keep the iPod fully charged and ready to go is to always plug it into your Mac when you're not using the iPod. Plop the iPod in its dock, or for older iPod's, leave the white FireWire cable that came with it plugged into your Mac. The Mac needs to be turned on in order to charge the iPod.

If your Mac goes into full sleep mode, the iPod won't charge. However, you can have your Mac's display set to sleep separately, and the iPod will charge. Change your Mac's sleep settings in the Energy Saver area of System Preferences.

If you are traveling in civilization — staying in hotels, at friends' houses, or anywhere with an AC Power outlet — you should carry around Apple's recharging module. The retractable AC prongs make it easy to fit anywhere in your luggage. (If you don't have one, you can buy it from the Apple Store, www.apple.com/store for $50. Third-party models aren't the classy white, but are half the price.) However, don't forget to take the white FireWire cable with you — It's no ordinary FireWire cable, and you'll need it to work with the Apple AC adapter.

When using the Apple AC adapter, the iPod will display a large animation of a battery with a lightening bolt in the center of the screen. If you don't see this animation, check that the cable's firmly seated and that the AC outlet is working. If still nothing check to see if you need to throw a light switch to turn the outlet on.

Did you know that you can play your iPod while it is charging via the Apple AC adapter? Just plug in your headphones and use the controls as you ordinarily would.

A handy feature of the iPod is that you can quickly charge most of it in an hour, filling up 80 percent of the battery to provide you with 6 to 8 hours of music. To fully charge the iPod, however, it takes about 3 hours. There is no penalty for partially charging the iPod. Your iPod's lithium-ion polymer battery is immune to the "memory effect" of ni-cad batteries, which means that you can charge it as frequently as you like, for as along as you like, without ill effects on the battery. In fact, it is better for the health of the iPod battery to do more frequent charges than to let the iPod battery completely drain of power.

There's another reason for frequent charging. The iPod is actually always on, using power. When you shut it off, it goes into a sleep mode. Like your Mac in sleep mode, iPod's sleep mode uses a small amount of power, which means that the battery will drain even when you aren't using it. Apple says that a fully charged iPod will lose all of its power within 2 to 4 weeks. A partially charged iPod can empty much quicker than that.

Docks for Nondocking iPods

In order to get in the habit of connecting your iPod to your Mac, it helps to have some place to keep it while on your desk. The more recent docking iPods give you a dock. If you have an older iPod, the answer is to buy a desk stand for it. There are plenty available. On the executive end, there's the nickel-plated solid aluminum DVBase ($60) from MacMice (formerly DVForge) (www.macmice.com), which includes a metal polishing kit. This stand doesn't move when you press the iPod's buttons. You can also find more casual plastic stands, such as the simple, clear acrylic $16 PodHolder from PodShop (www.podshop.com), or the Habitat ($25 www.bubbledesign.com), which gives you a place to put the FireWire cable and earbuds when not in use.

Giving your iPod a place to live on your desk (such as the DVBase) is a good way to get in the habit of plugging it into your Mac and keeping it fully charged.
Courtesy of DVBase

Tips for Conserving Power

If you are away from power and are trying to stretch the iPod's battery life to the max, there are a few things you can do. First, get in the habit of sliding the Hold switch on the top to the Hold position. This is the best way to prevent wasting power. When the iPod is not on hold, a small bump against the controls can turn iPod on, letting it play when you aren't listening to it. Remember, the iPod isn't set to Hold if you don't see the little lock icon in the top left of the screen.

You can also use some of iPod's own settings to help you conserve power. One way to stretch the juice is avoid using the backlight — it will burn battery power faster than playing music. If that's not possible, consider setting the backlight to automatically turn off after a few seconds. This will turn the backlight off sooner than if you have to fumble around trying to turn it off in the dark. To set the automatic backlight, go to the iPod's Settings menu, select Backlight Timer, and select a time from 1 to 10 seconds.

It's probably obvious that the backlighting feature is a big power drain, but did you know that the Equalizer feature can shorten the battery life? If you need to extend the battery's charge, go to the Settings menu, select EQ, and then Off.

Another power-saving measure is to avoid using the Previous/Rewind or Next/Fast Forward buttons to change songs. The iPod plays music directly from its solid state memory, which doesn't take a lot of power. When you use the Previous or Next button to change a song, the iPod has to start the hard drive spinning, which uses more battery power.

This solid state memory works best when song files are smaller than 9 MB. Files bigger than this will cause iPod to access the hard drive more often, and will use more battery power. Getting files below this size is easy to do when you use compressed audio formats, such as AAC and MP3. But uncompressed AIFF files can get much bigger. This means that using uncompressed AIFF files not only takes up a lot more room on the iPod hard disk — it also consumes a lot more battery power. If you have AIFF files on your iPod, use iTunes to convert them to AAC.

iPodding through Foreign Lands

Apple's AC adapter is great for traveling through North America, but if you are iPodding through Europe, Asia, or Australia, you'll need AC connectors that fit into the various types of sockets found in different countries. You can use any converter that you would find in a travel store to charge your iPod with the Apple AC adapter while traveling.

For a multicountry trip, check out Apple's iPod World Travel Adapter Kit ($40). It comes with a set of six adapter converters (in iPod white, of course) that will work in North America, Continental Europe, the United Kingdom, China, Korea, Japan, Hong Kong, and Australia. You can find it at the Apple Store (www.apple.com/store) as well as on other Internet sites.

Car-powered iPods

A car's DC power outlet (known to those of a certain age as the *cigarette lighter*) can be a source of power for your iPod. You can buy automobile power adapters for the iPod from a variety of electronics stores and Web sites. Auto adapters plug into the car's cigarette lighter and into the iPod's 30-pin docking port, or, on older iPods, the FireWire port. When shopping, you will need to make sure you are buying the correct model for your iPod.

Since the iPod has such a long battery life, auto power adapters aren't always necessary. But they can be handy when you jump in the car and discover that you forgot to charge your iPod. Auto power adapters are also a good way to keep the iPod charged on very long rides, and on trips where you don't have access to an AC outlet, such as camping vacations. You can also listen to your iPod while it is plugged in and charging. (You can also *play* your iPod through your car stereo, but with a different piece of equipment. These solutions are described later in the "Road Trips" section.)

The main problem with auto power adapters is that the cords can get tangled with your car's gearshift. They can also get tangled with the cords used for a cassette tape player adapter (described later in this chapter), leaving you with a bit of an untangling job at the end of your trip. A solution to this is to choose an iPod car charger with a *coiled* cord, like the XtremeMac Premium iPod Car Charger (www.xtrememac.com), shown in Figure 4-5. Coiled-cord auto adapters are also more compact and won't fill your entire glove compartment.

The XtremeMac Car Charger has some other useful features, including a replaceable fuse to protect the iPod from a voltage surge. It also has a power LED indicator light to tell you if it is plugged in correctly.

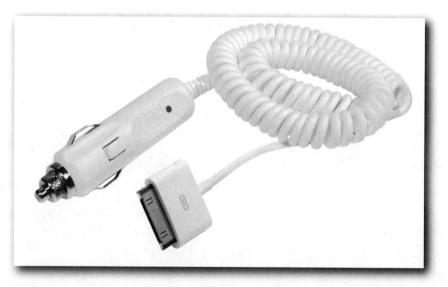

FIGURE 4-5: A car power adapter with a coiled cord won't tangle and is easier to store and carry. This is XtremeMac's Premium iPod Car Charger.
Courtesy of XtremeMac.

Add External Batteries

Some trips just don't give you much time near a power source — a backpacking trip to the mountains, a long journey involving multiple airplane legs, or just a really long day of skiing. A good option for these kinds of trips is to power your iPod wirelessly — with standard AA batteries, the kind you can buy anywhere. You can do this with an external battery pack that can charge your iPod after the internal battery drains. By simply carrying enough AA batteries (or stopping off and buying them when you need them), you can keep your iPod playing indefinitely. And, unlike the iPod's built-in battery, AA batteries will hold a charge for a long time when not in use.

The Belkin Battery Pack for iPod ($60, www.belkin.com) becomes part of the iPod by attaching to the back of the iPod with suction cups (see Figure 4-6). Four AA batteries can more than double the battery-operating time of the iPod, adding 12 to 15 hours of battery life. Of course, when those batteries are used up, all you have to do is add four more. The unit also includes its own charge-level indicator to let you know when your AA batteries are getting close to needing replacement.

FIGURE 4-6: The Belkin Battery Pack for iPod powers your iPod with AA batteries, for times when you can't get near a power source.
Courtesy of Belkin Corp.

Replace the Battery

Anyone who has owned a lot of notebook computers knows that rechargeable batteries don't last forever. This is also true of the lithium-ion polymer battery of the iPod. It's tough to say how long any individual battery will hold up, but eventually, it may start holding a charge for shorter and shorter periods. If your iPod will play when connected to your AC adapter, but won't make a sound when you unplug it, the battery is probably dead.

If your warranty has expired, then you can save some money by replacing the battery yourself. You can find replacement batteries for about $60 at Laptops for Less (www.ipodbattery .com) and at PDA Smart (www.pdasmart.com/ipodpartscenter.htm). The battery for the first and second-generation iPods (see Figure 4-7) is about the size of the iPod, but very thin. The battery for the docking iPod is smaller. When you order, be sure that you get the right battery for your model iPod.

FIGURE 4-7: The battery for a first- or second-generation iPod is about the size of the iPod.

There's no obvious way to open an iPod, so both vendors offer instructions. Laptops for Less has instructions with photographs posted at its ipodbattery.com Web site. PDAsMart sends you directions with the battery. If you're squeamish about prodding open your iPod, PDAsMart offers a mail-in replacement service for an additional $10 plus shipping.

If your iPod is still under warranty, don't replace the battery yourself. You'll void the warranty so that anything that goes wrong becomes your fault, whether you caused it or not. If your iPod is still under warranty and you think you're having battery problems, contact Apple. The standard iPod warranty is 1 year. If you bought an Apple Care plan, this could be extended to 3 years.

Expanding iPod's Musical Horizons

One iPod, one set of headphones. Well, who says it has to be that way? You can share your iPod with another listener, or with a room full of people. All you need are the right cables. The iPod is a great piece of portable stereo gear. Bring it and your cable to a party, and you can impress everyone with your killer playlist. Or, use it on your own home stereo, complete with wireless remote. (Don't worry, we're not leaving out car stereos. Those solutions are covered in the later section on road trips.)

Finally, does the iPod remind you of an old transistor radio — except for the fact that it can't receive radio stations? Not anymore. All you need to do is add a tiny radio receiver — designed for iPod, of course.

Sharing Your iPod with Another Listener

Can two people with headphones listen to your iPod at the same time? Yes, and it's cheap and easy. Just go down to RadioShack or your local hardware store and get a ⅛" mini-stereo splitter — a small piece of plastic and metal less than an inch long (see Figure 4-8). On one end is a ⅛" mini-stereo connector that plugs into the iPod headphone jack. On the other end are two female ⅛" mini-stereo receptacles. (Make sure that it's a stereo-to-stereo splitter, not stereo to mono.) When you carry it, just leave it connected to the earbuds or your second pair of headphones.

You can also find iPod accessory Web sites offering white splitter cables at two to four times the price that do exactly the same thing. Cables are also more susceptible to breaking than a solid splitter connector, and are bulkier to carry.

Connect iPod to Your Home Stereo

Connecting your iPod to your stereo opens up a whole new way to listen to music. Your iPod becomes another stereo component, like your tape deck or CD player, except that the music is already inside.

For most stereos, you'll need a standard Y-cable that includes a male ⅛" mini-stereo plug on one end and two RCA plugs on the other end (see Figure 4-9). The mini-stereo plugs into the iPod's headphone jack, and the RCA connectors plug into the left and right channels of any input port on your receiver/amplifier. The input ports can be auxiliary (Aux) ports, an extra tape-in port, or an extra CD-in port. You *should not* connect the iPod to phono input ports made for turntables, however.

At Mac-related stores and Web sites, you'll often see expensive Y-cables marketed for the iPod. The only thing special about these products is the color — iPod white. If you don't care about color, you'll find cheaper mini-stereo-to-RCA Y-cables in hardware stores and in electronic stores such as RadioShack.

FIGURE 4-8: An inexpensive stereo splitter will let you connect two sets of headphones to your iPod, and is easier to carry than a splitter cable.

In stereo stores, you'll often find high-end, thick, shielded cables, from companies such as Monster Cable. Although in Chapter 9, we'll recommend high-quality cables for connecting your stereo to your Mac in order to record your vinyl records, expensive cables just aren't necessary to connect iPod to your stereo.

When you connect your iPod to your home stereo, turn up the iPod's volume to about $^4/_5$ of maximum loudness, and use your stereo to control volume. When the iPod's volume is too low, you may hear noise if you have to turn up the stereo's volume too high.

If you don't have a home stereo, there's no need to buy one—iPod can function as the center of a new system. All you need are self-powered speakers—the kind that connect to computer systems.

Speakers that connect to stereo systems are often not powered. The amplifier in the stereo does all of the signal-boosting functions needed. Self-powered speakers used for computers plug into an AC outlet and include amplifier circuitry, usually in one of the speakers.

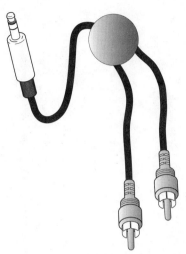

FIGURE 4-9: A cable with RCA connectors on one end and a mini-stereo connector on the other will let you hook your iPod to your home stereo.

Remote Control for Your Home Stereo iPod

iPod lacks one thing that the other components of your stereo does—a wireless remote control. You can easily fix this with TEN Technology's naviPod ($50, www.tentechnology .com), an infrared remote system that lets you change the song or the volume from the couch across the room. The naviPod plugs into the top of the iPod and includes a stand to hold the iPod in view of the remote (see Figure 4-10). It includes an infrared receiver and audio out port to connect to your stereo.

The naviPod also comes with a five-button remote to control the volume, move to the next or previous song, and to fast forward or rewind. If you don't want to add another remote unit to your collection, the NaviPod also works with universal "learning remotes," which can pick up on the infrared codes used by the NaviPod receiver. A universal remote will let you use one remote to control your CD player, amplifier, DVD player, and now, your naviPod-connected iPod. The naviPod comes in several models for different generations of iPod.

Add a Radio

Ever walk around town with the earbuds in your ears, wishing you could pick up the afternoon news? You can with the right iPod and Griffin Technology's iFM ($35, www.griffin technology.com). iFM lets you scan for stations, and lets you set up to six stations that will be retained after you turn iFM off.

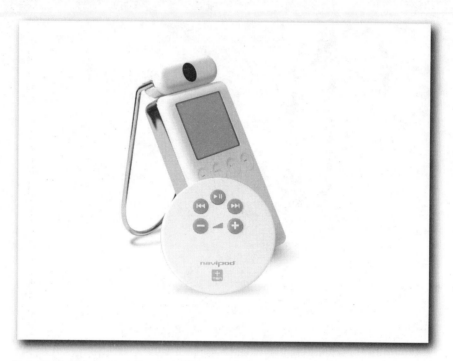

FIGURE 4-10: The naviPod is a wireless remote control for the iPod.
Courtesy of TEN Technology.

The iFM design is clever, in that it is actually an iPod case (see Figure 4-11) with a belt clip, so that you have a single unit to carry. You insert the iPod and connect iFM to the iPod's headphone jack. Also inside iFM is the iPod's remote, which controls the radio. Plug the headphones into the remote. When you turn iFM on, the iPod's music controls are disabled — use the iPod remote to tune to a station or preset, to set presets, and to control volume. iFM uses beeps as feedback to help you create presets. To listen to iPod music, just turn iFM off. iFM runs from the iPod's battery.

You may not be able to use iFM with your iPod. First, the use of Apple's remote is required. If your iPod is a 5-GB model, it didn't come with the remote. You can purchase one from Apple ($40, including an extra set of headphones). Also, at press time Griffin only had an iFM for the older, nondocking iPods.

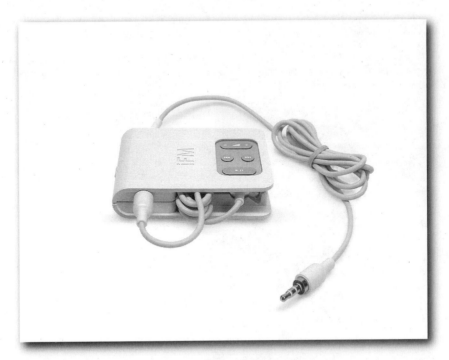

FIGURE 4-11: Griffin's iFM turns your iPod into an FM receiver. Insert your iPod and its remote, and you can choose to listen to the radio or iPod's tunes.
Courtesy of Griffin Technology, Inc.

Road Trips: Traveling with iPod

The iPod makes a great traveling companion. Whether you're traveling by car, train, or plane, iPod makes it easy to prepare your music for a trip. No more carrying around a box of tapes or pulling your CDs out of their jewel cases to pack them into a CD wallet. Just carry your music collection in your pocket.

The iPod and the automobile were made for each other. Volkswagen knew this in 2003 when it was including an iPod with every new Beetle it sold. (Apple listed the Beetle as an iPod accessory on its Web site.) The problem is, using headphones while driving a car is a bad idea, because it can prevent you from hearing car horns, sirens, and other important sounds. Driving with headphones also is illegal in many states. It's also antisocial if others are in the car with you. Fortunately, it doesn't take much to connect your iPod to your car stereo. There are several different types of solutions that work in your car, in any rental car, and your friends' cars. If you keep your iPod fully charged, you often don't need extra power in the car. In fact, power is also an issue when traveling by plane or train, and traveling overseas. If you do need a power boost, see the earlier section called "Power Options."

Most of these "iPod Toys" are hardware devices, but there is also some handy software that can extend iPod's usefulness on a trip.

At the end of this section, we'll discuss one more type of trip where iPod shines—skiing or snowboarding. Because cold weather is not a friend to iPod, there are some special considerations you should know about.

FIGURE 4-12: The iPod is a great companion on trips. Professional snowboarder Keir Dillon takes his onto the slopes.
Courtesy of Burton Snowboards.

Wired to Your Car Stereo

The most popular way of connecting an iPod to a car stereo is the same way you connect a hand-held CD player—through the car's tape player. In fact, you use the same cassette tape player adapters that are sold for portable CD players, such as the Sony Car Connecting Pack. Cassette adapters are available for $20 and under. There are units sold as iPod cassette adapters, but they're no different from those made for CD players.

On one end, you have what looks like a cassette tape, with a wire coming out to plug into the iPod's headphone port. On closer inspection, you'll see that in place of magnetic tape in the cassette is a magnetic head that transmits magnetic signals to the tape player's read head. You insert the cassette into the car's tape player and turn on your iPod. Turn the iPod's volume up fairly high, about ⁴⁄₅ of maximum. Then, use the car's tape player volume controls. If the iPod volume is too low, you may get a buzz from the car stereo.

When you are shopping, beware of cassette converters that are *too* cheap. If the cable is too thin, the stranded wire inside the cable can break after a few bends, and you may find one or both of the speakers going quiet. If you go to a store and are confronted with several brands, trust the one with the thicker wire.

Tip

If you are driving at night listening to iPod, it might be handy to have the backlight stay on all the time. You can do this in the Settings menu at the top level of iPod's menus. Under Settings, select Backlight Timer. Scroll to the bottom of the list and click on Always On. To shut it off, you'll have to go back to this menu and choose Off at the top of the list. If you have backlighting set at always on and are on a long trip, you might want to have the iPod plugged into the car's DC power outlet (as described in the earlier section called "Car-Powered iMacs").

Of course, many cars no longer have cassette tapes, which are going the way of the 8-track of the 1970s. If this is your situation, you'll need to go wireless.

Connect Wirelessly to Your Car Stereo

The most convenient way to play your iPod over your car stereo is to go wireless with one of several iPod gadgets designed for this purpose. The first, and still one of the best, is Griffin Technology's iTrip ($35), which lets you hear your iPod music from your car speakers while keeping the iPod in the glove compartment. iTrip is a tiny radio transmitter that sits on top of your iPod (see Figure 4-13), transmitting to your car's FM radio. It will actually work with *any* radio, including the clock radio in your hotel room.

The iTrip tends to produce better sound than similar products, but the sound quality is limited to that of FM radio. This means that it doesn't broadcast the very high frequencies. iTrip (and other products) have an upper limitation of 15 KHz frequency. The iTrip gives you sound equivalent to that of an FM radio. A cassette adapter may sound better in a car with a high-end stereo in the car, but in other cars, you may not notice the difference.

The iTrip is an ingenious and convenient device. It plugs into the iPod's headphone port. It is powered by the iPod, so it doesn't need a separate power source. You never need to turn iTrip off, since iTrip automatically turns itself off if no music is playing for 60 seconds. iTrip comes with software that installs on the iPod. This gives you a screen to let you choose the FM frequency you'd like the iPod to broadcast on. You then tune your radio to that station and listen to the iPod on your car stereo. Griffin offers two models, one for the docking iPods and one for earlier iPods.

There are other radio transmitters available, such as the Belkin Tunecast Mobile FM Transmitter ($30). However, it does not attach to the iPod as the iFM does. iFM is also the only product that lets you tune into *any* radio frequency on the dial.

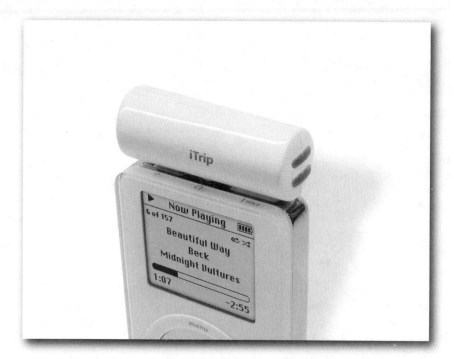

FIGURE 4-13: iTrip adds a tiny radio transmitter to let you play music through your car stereo without wires.
Courtesy of Griffin Technology, Inc.

iPod Holders for Your Car

The iPod is small enough to fit in any number of places in your car: a cupholder, the small cubbies that some cars have in front of the stick shift, or the space between seats.If you'd like to mount the iPod firmly in place while you drive, you can do that too. Several companies make iPod stands that sit in cupholders. For instance, there's the Belkin TuneDok ($30) and Akron's pad iPod Car Mount ($25, www.welovemacs.com/001cm330.html).

However, the ultimate car iPod holder at this point has to be the TransPod from Netalog (about $80, www.netalog.com). Not only does it hold the iPod, but it powers it as well. Instead of mounting in the cupholder, a bracket plugs into the DC power adapter. The TransPod also connects to your car stereo. It comes bundled with either a radio transmitter or a cassette adapter. The later features a handy coiled cord, which is not common in cassette adapters. A model for the newer docking iPods, the TransPod FM ($100, shown in Figure 4-14) comes with the FM transmitter built in.

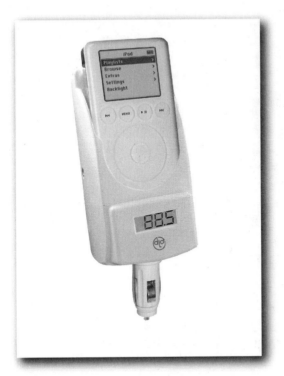

FIGURE 4-14: The TransPod mounts the iPod in the cigarette lighter, so it powers it as well. It also comes with a connection to your car stereo.
Courtesy of Digital Lifestyle Outfitters (www.everythingipod.com)

Add Driving Directions

If you're going to have your iPod mounted in your car, you might as well do something useful with it. Sure, changing playlists is useful, but how about having the iPod display driving directions? With the newer docking iPods, the directions will end up in the Notes menu of the Extras menu. In older iPods, the driving directions will be in the Contacts menu. There are several freeware or shareware applications that move Internet-based driving directions into one of these iPod locations.

MibaSoft's PodQuest ($10, `www.mibasoft.dk/podquest.html`) is shareware that that grabs driving directions from MapQuest on the Internet and delivers them to your iPod. When you double-click the PodQuest icon, the program adds a menu in the upper right of the Mac OS X menu bar. (See the top of Figure 4-15.) From this menu, you select Directions in North America. PodQuest launches your Web browser to the MapQuest.com. In your Web browser, you type your starting point and destination, and click Get Directions. When your Web browser returns with the directions, go to the PodQuest menu and select Download Directions To iPod. A window appears asking you to name the directions. This is the title you will see on your iPod.

FIGURE 4-15: The PodQuest menu takes you to the MapQuest Web site. Once you get them, the Download Directions command gets the text and installs it on your iPod.
Courtesy of Mibasoft.

PodQuest will now install the directions on your connected iPod, either in the Notes menu for newer iPods or in the Contents menu. PodQuest will unmount the iPod from the desktop, letting you disconnect it and take a look at the directions.

The directions are installed in the form of a VCF file. To delete a set of directions, connect the iPod to the Mac again, and double-click the iPod icon on the desktop. Go to the Notes (or Contacts) folder, and drag the appropriate VCF file to the trash.

iPod on the Slopes

For skiers and snowboarders who like music, the iPod is the greatest invention since metal edges. It's small, able to deliver tons of tunes, and has a battery that can last all day. However, the iPod battery doesn't like the cold, so there area few things you should do to keep the tunes flowing.

First, keep your iPod inside of your clothing. An inside pocket is much better than an outside pocket or belt. The iPod battery operates most efficiently at room temperatures, and won't perform well (or at all) when it is below 50°F. If your iPod is too cold, the battery will poop out long before you do. An inside breast pocket is a warm place, and a safe one as well.

Don't Leave Your iPod in the Car

You've heard this about your dog and your kids, but it also applies to your iPod: don't leave your iPod in the car on sunny summer days. The temperature inside of a car parked in the sun with the windows rolled up can approach 150°F—much too hot for iPod. Apple says you should never store your iPod anywhere it gets above 45°C (133°F). Doing so could permanently damage the battery, the display, and other components.

If you get into a hot car with your iPod, you might want to let the air conditioner run for a minute or two before you crank up the tunes. You also shouldn't play the iPod when it's 95°F or hotter.

The summer isn't the only time you have to worry about. If you live in a cold climate, you shouldn't leave the iPod in your car in the winter, either. Apple warns that you should not store iPod below −20°C (−4°F).

Rule of thumb: Always take your iPod with you when you leave your car.

There's a better chance that your battery will last all day if you start off with your iPod fully charged. If you are using it in the car on the way to the slopes, use a DC power adapter (see the "Power Options" section earlier in this chapter). At night, keep it plugged into the AC power adapter. If you just can't keep your iPod warm enough to keep the juice running all day, add a battery pack, like the Belkin unit described earlier in "Power Options" section. This will let you run your iPod on AA batteries when the internal battery gives out.

Another challenge is controlling the iPod with gloves on. In addition to the technical skill it requires, pulling the iPod out of your jacket and exposing it to the cold every 40 minutes will affect the battery life. You also don't want to get iPod wet if it's snowing. Fortunately, there are several strategies you can use to deal with this.

- **Use the Apple wired remote control.** Keep your iPod safe, warm, and dry while you pause and start, change the volume, and skip to the next or previous song. (Try to lay off the skip buttons, though, because they use battery power.) The 1.5-inch remote (see Figure 4-16) clips onto to outside of your jacket. The small controls are still a challenge to use with gloves, but in using it, you don't risk tossing your iPod into the snow.

  The remote comes with many of the more expensive iPod configurations. If you have a lower-cost iPod configuration, you'll have to buy a remote. Apple sells it with an extra set of the earbud headphones for $40.

  Plug the remote into the iPod's headphone port, then plug the headphones into the remote. Be sure that you move the iPod's switch to the Hold position.

Tip If the Apple remote controls aren't working, check to see that the remote is plugged in all the way — if you can see any chrome in between the iPod and the white cable, you haven't pushed it in far enough. Also, the remote has its own Hold switch — check to see that it is off.

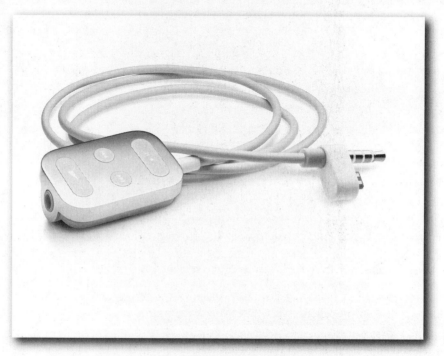

FIGURE 4-16: If the Apple wired remote makes sense anywhere, it's on the slopes.
Courtesy of Apple.

- **Create long playlists.** Long playlists will reduce the number of times you'll have to browse for a new playlist or album. This will conserve battery power and, if you aren't using a remote, reduce iPod's exposure to the cold.

- **Use no playlists — set the iPod on random.** If you're willing to listen to anything on your iPod, you can ski all day and never choose a playlist or album. Go to the Settings menu, select Shuffle, and then Songs. To start iPod playing from everything it has (as opposed to a playlist), go to the Browser menu, then Songs, and start the first song. The iPod will randomly play music from the entire collection. If something comes up you're not in the mood for, just hit the Next button on your remote.

The iPod Snow Jacket

Jacket design can help you enjoy your iPod on the slopes. Desirable features include easily accessible protected interior pockets, a good place for the remote, and a hood and body that didn't get in the way of the wires. But what if you could put the remote on your sleeve, make the buttons father apart, and have the headphones pop out of the hood?

That's what Burton Snowboards thought when it released its limited edition Burton Amp Jacket in early 2003. You start by slipping your iPod into a padded pocket (see Figure 4-17), accessible via a three-layer flap. The jacket is wired for iPod — plug the iPod into the jacket, and you can listen to it with the earphones that pop out of the high collar. The coolest part was straight out of a James Bond movie — iPod controls integrated into the fabric of the lower-left sleeve (see Figure 4-18). The controls are big enough to handle with your gloves on. And, oh yes, the jacket is has a GORE-TEX covering for keeping wetness out.

FIGURE 4-17: The Burton Amp iPod jacket (modeled here by pro snowboarder Keir Dillon) keeps the iPod warm in its own interior padded pocket, but gives you easy access to it.
Courtesy of Burton Snowboards.

FIGURE 4-18: The Burton iPod jackets also feature iPod controls built into the sleeve.
Courtesy of Burton Snowboards.

The problem with the Burton Amp Jacket is that it was a limited edition, and it cost $500, not including the iPod. Fortunately, the jacket was such a hit that Burton released production-run versions called the 2L iPod Jacket. The men's is called Ronin; the women's model is the Radar. The 2L iPod Jacket is very similar to the original, but with a bit lighter color, and a better price — about $349.

Tip If you have the original 2003 Burton Amp Jacket, but have replaced your older iPod with a newer docking iPod, Dr. Bott (www.drbott.com) has a $25 converter that will let you plug the new iPods into the Amp jacket.

Other Uses for iPod

No one's going to argue that the iPod is the world's greatest PDA. You can't enter information directly into it, and the screen can't display the kind of graphics that a Palm device can. Music is the main reason for owning an iPod, and music is what the iPod does better than just about any other hand-held device. Still, you can add calendars and contact info to your iPod, and other useful pieces of information. With the help of some third-party software, there are other uses for iPod as well. Since you're carrying it around anyway, why not let your iPod help you?

The first new use discussed in this section is related to indirectly related music—a method of safeguarding your music files. The other uses have to do with making the iPod a better PDA.

iPod as Backup for iTunes

The iTunes folder on your Mac may have tens of gigabytes of music stored in files. Have you ever thought about what would it take to replace your digital music collection if your hard drive failed? Fortunately, you already have a duplicate of this music—locked in your iPod. The only problem is, Apple doesn't provide any way of moving your music back to your Mac if you ever need to restore your music collection, or move your collection to a second Mac. iTunes only moves music files one way, towards the iPod. If you mount the iPod on the desktop, you won't see the music files. Apple has purposely hidden them so that you can't copy data from iPod to a Mac.

You can't really blame Apple for this (at least, not too much). The record companies are pressuring Apple to do all it can to dissuade illegal music trading. Apple's advertising slogan, "Burn it, Rip it, Share it" sounded like a call for music piracy to some in the music industry.

Still, as a user, why back up the gigabytes of data in your iTunes folder when you already have a backup in your iPod? This is what independent software developers thought, which is why there are now a number of utilities that let you move your iPod music back to your Mac. If you have more than one Mac, you can use this software and your iPod to copy your tunes to all of your Macs. It's all freeware or inexpensive shareware.

How inexpensive? Well, PodWorks by Buzz Anderson, goes for a whopping $8 (http://scifihifi.com/podworks/). You'll have to shell out $10 for iPod Access (www.drewfindley.com/findleydesigns/ipodaccess/). And iPod.iTunes (www.crispsofties.com/i.i/index.html) will set you back $35. These are some of the best of the field.

PodWorks sports a simple interface (see Figure 4-19) and is one of the fastest of the iPod-to-Mac utilities, partly due to its ability to directly read the iPod's database of songs and the related information. iPod Access also reads the iPod's database, but isn't as fast or responsive. Many other programs read song information from every music file in the iPod, which is a slow process. If your iPod is connected to your Mac and mounted on the desktop, the list of songs and playlists appear almost instantaneously when you launch PodWorks. And because it reads the iPod's database, PodWorks can display a lot more data than just the song title, including "Date Added" and "Play Count."

PodWorks may be the nicest of these utilities to use, but it lacks some features that the others have. PodWorks doesn't display the Composer field, which is useful when selecting classical music. iPod Access and iPod.iTunes do display the Composer field. PodWorks also doesn't integrate with iTunes. You have to drag the music files from PodWorks to a Mac folder, then drag them to the iTunes Library. This creates another set of files and folders inside the music folder, so you have to delete the first set you copied to your hard drive.

This biggest drawback to PodWorks is that it doesn't recreate playlists in iTunes. Fortunately, you can fix this deficiency with free utility, iPod Playlist Cloner (http://homepage.mac.com/beweis/b_itunes.html), which will copy a playlist from iPod to your hard drive, and create the playlist in iTunes.

FIGURE 4-19: PodWorks lets you copy your music from your iPod back to your Macs, and it keeps, but won't recreate, playlists in iTunes.

iPod.iTunes is probably the most complete utility for restoring both the music files and your playlists back into iTunes. Its interface is a bit on the confusing side, however.

Tip   It's a good idea to store your iPod-to-Mac music transfer software on your iPod—when iPod is mounted on your desktop, drag it to the iPod. Then, if your hard disk fails and you need to restore your music files, you'll have a copy of your restoration software.

Tips for using an iPod as a PDA

You can move several types of PDA information from your Mac to your iPad. For instance, you can move your contacts from Apple Address Book contacts and your iCal calendar to iPod using iSync (see Figure 4-21). Connect your iPod to your Mac, open iSync, and choose Add Device from the Devices menu. Double-click iPod, and it gets added to the iSync window (see Figure 4-20). Now, click the iPod button in the iSync window, click the Sync button, and you're done.

FIGURE 4-20: Apple provides iSync to move Address
Book contacts and iCal calendars to the iPod.
Courtesy of Apple.

To view your calendar on iPod, go to the iPod's Extras menu, and select the Calendar menu. You'll see a calendar, as in Figure 4-21. You can use the scroll wheel to go to another date and month. The dates with little squares on them have appointments. To see the appointments for a day, just click on the day.

FIGURE 4-21: The iPod calendar display. Use the
scroll wheel to change the date and month.
Courtesy of Apple.

Address Book and iCal are not the last word in PIMs (personal information managers), however. There are some other excellent calendar and contact applications, including Palm Desktop and Microsoft Entourage, that can easily move data to your iPod. For iPods, there is nothing special about iSync — it moves data from the Mac to the iPod, a fairly simple task. The iPod can accept contact and calendar data in vCard and vCal formats, an industry-standard supported by many PIMs available for the Mac.

Moving Palm Desktop Data to iPod

It's easy to move calendars and contacts from Palm Desktop on to your iPod. Palm Desktop is also a great Mac OS X PIM, superior in many ways to Address Book and iCal. And, it's free. (If you don't have it, you can download Palm Desktop for Mac OS X at the downloads page of www.palm.com.) Palm Desktop is easy to use, has a powerful set of features, and lets you print out just about anything in any form, including a wide array of paper date books.

To move your Palm Desktop calendar to iPod, do the following:

1. Make sure that the iPod is mounted on the Desktop. (If iPod normally doesn't appear on the desktop, you can change this in iTunes. Click the iPod in the Sources column at left, then click the iTunes button at the bottom right of the iTunes windows. Click the check box labeled Enable FireWire Disk Use.

2. With Palm Desktop opens, go to the File menu and select Export. A dialog appears (see Figure 4-22).

3. Choose Calendar from the top pop-up menu.

4. In the bottom pop-up menu, select vCal. This is important — if you forget this step, iPod won't recognize your calendar.

5. From the file browser, choose the Calendar folder on the iPod. (If you've done this before, Mac OS X will have iPod's Calendar folder already selected.)

6. Click Save. Palm Desktop will ask for a name. Give it a simple name, like "calendar."

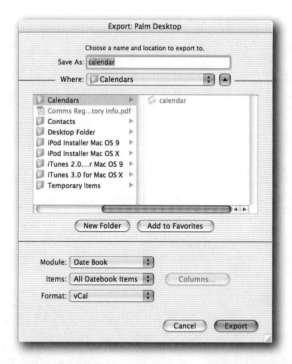

FIGURE 4-22: To move your Palm Desktop calendar to iPod, Choose Export from the File menu. Be sure you choose the vCal format from the bottom pop-up.

The next time you want to update iPod's calendar, just export it again using the same name for the calendar file. Palm Desktop will warn you that a file already exists with that name — you should continue saving.

Exporting your contacts from Palm Desktop uses the same procedure, except that you'll choose Contacts in Step 2 and place the file in iPod's Contact folder.

Moving Entourage Contacts to iPod

Microsoft Entourage is another great PIM and email program, one that is in wide use. However, it isn't as easy to get your contacts and calendar onto your iPod with Entourage as it is with Palm Desktop. The good news is that you export your contacts in vCard format, though it isn't as straightforward as in Palm Desktop. The bad news is that to move calendars, you'll need another piece of software.

To export your Entourage addresses to iPod you can't use the Export can't use the Export command — it only supports text, not VCF format. Instead, you'll begin to forward the contacts via email, but you don't actually have to send mail. With your iPod mounted on your Mac desktop, do the following:

1. Open your Entourage address book.

2. Select all contacts by clicking on your list of addresses near the top of the window, and pressing the Command-A keys.

3. Go to the Contact menu and choose Forward as vCard. An email window will open with each contact as a separate VCF file. Entourage has created temporary VCF files, which can now be moved to iPod.

4. Open the Attachments field in the email window. Open your iPod icon on the desktop. Now, select all of the VCF files in Entourage' Attachments field, and drag them to the iPod's Contacts folder. (See Figure 4-23.)

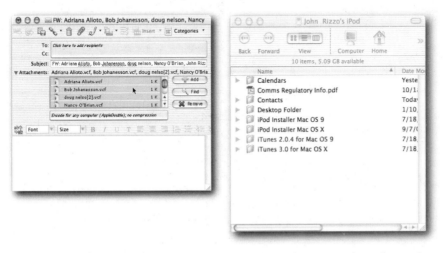

FIGURE 4-23: Choose *Forward as vCard* command and drag the contacts from the email window to your iPod's Contacts folder.

The only problem with having individual files for each contact (instead of a single file) is that you will have one extra menu to negotiate on the iPod. If you want to create a single file, you can use the Mac OS X Address Book application to do this. In this case, copy your Entourage-created VCF files to a folder on the Mac hard drive. If you are using Entourage, you're probably not using OS X's Address Book — so it's okay to delete any address you had in Address Book first. Then, go to Address Book's File menu and select Import vCards. Import the cards you just moved from Entourage to a folder.

With the vCards in Mac OS X Address Book, you can now use iSync to move the addresses to iPod (as previously described) or Export the addresses as a single VCF file to your iPod's Contacts folder by selecting Export vCard from the File menu.

Moving Entourage Calendars to iPod

Unfortunately, there is no direct way to move your entire Entourage calendar to the iPod without using another piece of software. You can drag individual events to the iPod's Calendar folder — Entourage will create an iCalander-format file ending in .ics — but this isn't an efficient way to get your whole calendar to your iPod.

One way to move your entire Entourage calendar to iPod is to use Apple's free iCal (www.apple.com/ical/). Open iCal, go to the File menu, and select Import. In the screen that comes up (see Figure 4-24) Select Import Entourage data. Then, Click the Import button. iCal will locate the data and import it. You can now use the Export command to export a single .ICS file to your iPod's Calendar folder. You could also use iSync to synchronize iCal (and Address Book) with your iPod, as described earlier.

FIGURE 4-24: You can import your Entourage calendar into Apple's iCal, which you can use to move it to your iPod.

Another way to move your Entourage Calendar to your iPod is with a shareware utility called iPod It ($15, www.zapptek.com/ipod-it/), a synchronizing utility designed for iPod. The advantage of using iPod It is that you can also move your Entourage address book entries and a bunch of other Entourage data to your iPod, all at the same time in one step. You can move all or subsets of your Entourage data, including email, contacts, notes, and tasks, as well as data from some of Apple's applications.

To move your Entourage calendar to an iPod, plug in and mount your iPod on the desktop. Launch iPod It. Click the Events icon to set which events that you want to move — either all of them or those between a certain date. Click okay. Now click the Sync button in the lower left of the iPod It screen (see Figure 4-25).

iPod It can do even more, as described in the next section.

FIGURE 4-25: iPod It is the easiest way to copy an Entourage calendar to iPod.

Expanding iPod's PDA Functions

For many iPod fans, the ability to carry calendar and contact information is a big plus. Why carry a Palm if you already have an iPod? Well, because there are some things that a Palm does that iPod doesn't. But there is software that brings iPod closer to a Palm device, perhaps enough to make the iPod the only hand-held you need to carry. The good thing is that compared to music, text takes very little storage space. Which means that your iPod has a lot of room for extras.

A lot of the information that you can add to iPod comes from the Internet. You may recall that in the section on travel earlier in this chapter described PodQuest, a utility that downloads driving directions from the Internet and moves them to your iPod, all with the click of a mouse button. There are several utilities that do this for all kinds of other Internet-based data.

For instance, consider the iPod It utility described in the previous section. As you might guess from Figure 4-25, it isn't limited to moving Entourage data to your iPod. The first row of items lists Entourage data, and the second row lists Apple applications that you can get information from, including email from the Mail application. The third row lists two Internet resources, news and weather from the Internet — iPod It will download this information and move it to your iPod, so that you can read it while on the train to work.

Click the News button in iPod It to see the screen in Figure 4-26. You can select different types of news stories to download. The Export Now button will download the selected info from the Internet and install it on your iPod. The Okay button will save the settings, and will download the information when you click the Sync button — that's the button that will move everything you've set. The text will end up in your iPod's Notes menu, or, if you have an older iPod, in the Contacts menu. A setting in iPod It's Preferences dialog lets you choose to remove older news items whenever you do a new sync.

FIGURE 4-26: This screen comes up when you click the News button in iPod It. Export Now will download the selected info from the Internet and install it on your iPod.

If you're not interested in reading anything on the iPod screen, how about listening to your data? iSpeakIt ($10, www.zapptek.com/ispeak-it/) takes any document or Web page, reads it using the Mac's built-in computer voices, and creates an AIFF file. You can then move this file to iTunes, convert it to an MP3 or AAC file, and have it automatically moved to the iPod the next time you plug it in.

Tip If you want to listen to commercial books on your iPod, go to Audible.com to purchase electronic files of actors reading books that will play on your iPod.

Want to read books on our iPod? Book2iPod (free at www.tomsci.com/book2pod/) is for docking iPods that have the Notes menu. Book2iPod gets around the iPods limits of 4 KB per note and 1,000 notes, to place entire books on your iPod. The books have to already be in text format. One place to get classic, public domain books for free is Project Gutenberg (http://gutenberg.net/). Moby Dick, Paradise Lost, and Hamlet are all up there, as well as less weighty material.

An Alternate OS — Linux for Your iPod

As a hand-held computer, the iPod runs a small operating system that manages memory, provides a user interface, and executes your commands. It turns out Apple's iPod operating system isn't the only choice you have. Developer Bernard Leach has created a version of Linux that runs on the iPod. The Linux on iPod project is still in the development stage, but Leach does have enough code running to be a development platform for programmers who want to build Linux applications to run on iPod hardware.

When *Mac Toys* asked why he would port Linux to the iPod, Leach's first answer is "because it's there." This sounds like the desire of Linux advocates to port to every available computer platform. However, Leach didn't start out trying to replace the iPod's operating system. He just wanted to modify the existing iPod software for his own amusement. "What it ran wasn't so important as being able to get it to run something!" said Leach.

This was a bit difficult, because iPod is officially a closed platform — Apple doesn't give out the specifications of the hardware or the software. Leach was able to figure out the iPod hardware, but the software proved trickier. "Once I actually got the hardware and starting looking at how it worked I realized that things were a little complicated," said Leach. "At one point during this work of reverse-engineering the hardware details I realized I probably had enough to get Linux up and running." He then ported Linux to the iPod and posted it on the open source development Web site, SourceForge.net. "Once I had a real OS there I figured that people might be interested in writing applications for it."

Leach does see potential benefits to running Linux on iPod. For instance, a Linux music player might be able to enable iPod to play more audio file formats, and playlist editing could be enhanced over what is available in the docking iPods. Leach also thinks that running Linux could enable iPod to connect to peripherals such as readers of flash memory used in digital cameras. Leach said "This would be great on longer trips as a secondary storage/backup for the digital photos." You'd have space for thousands of photos, and all you would need to carry on a trip would be the camera, a flash card reader, and your iPod.

Even for developers, running Linux on iPod is a bit different from running Linux on a PC or a Mac. For one, the iPod has no keyboard. You communicate with Linux running on the iPod via the Telnet commands typed on a personal computer over Ethernet to a Mac or PC connected to the iPod's FireWire cable. The iPod's processor is not robust enough to run one of the X11 graphics user interfaces that are common on Linux.

If you know your way around Linux installations and are interested in checking out Linux on your iPod or writing some software, go to `http://ipodlinux.sourceforge.net/`. Linux for iPod is a free download.

Summary

As you can see, expanding your iPod's functionality doesn't have to cost much. Except for the Burton iPod ski jacket, all of the iPod gadgets described in this chapter cost under $100. Most are well under $50, and many are under $25. Most of the software is under $20, and some of it is free. The key points to remember are these:

- Whenever you get a new piece of hardware or software for your iPod, make sure that you get a version that works with your iPod model. The different models generally fall into two categories — those with a docking connector on the bottom, and the older one without it.

- The iPod itself doesn't need much in the way of maintenance. Keeping it up-to-date with the latest Apple software is a good idea. If you get into trouble, you can reset the iPod, or restore its software if you get into real trouble. You can replace the battery if it stops holding a charge, but don't do it yourself unless your warranty has expired.

- There are lots of options available for powering your iPod when you aren't at your Mac, including chargers for your car and external battery packs. There are also things you can do to stretch your battery life.

- iPod makes a great component in a home stereo. It just takes a few cables. If you want a remote control, they're available.

- The iPod is a great traveling companion. You can find lots of add-ons to make the iPod a better traveler. If you're on the slopes, keep your iPod warm.

- There are lots of things you can do with your iPod besides listen to music. Sure, music is what iPod does best, but there's no harm in getting the most out of your iPod by adding new functions.

If you are looking for sources of music to put on your iPod, check out Chapter 9, which will tell you how to get your old vinyl LP collection onto your iPod and CDs. Chapter 7 describes how to use your Mac to create your own music.

Make a Digital Picture Frame

O ne of the reasons why personal computers are so popular is their
   amazing flexibility, which we're exploring throughout this book as
   we look at all sorts of Mac toys. By using some clever software or
adding the right hardware, you can have your Mac perform many roles.
With more radical modifications, you can transform your Mac into something completely different from Apple's original vision.

Even by the usual broad standards of computing flexibility, this chapter's
project is unusual. Inspired by the efforts of Apple Engineer Keith
Stattenfield, we're going to describe how to give an underused portable
Mac—in this case, an iBook—new life as a digital picture frame that mag-
ically changes the photos it shows. We're going to follow the same blueprint
that Keith used to create his picture frame.

Once you put your digital picture frame together, it will be a conversation
starter for houseguests, an attention-getter at parties, and a Mac toy for all
your computer-savvy friends to envy. Of course, it will also be a picture
frame.

FIGURE 5-1: An iBook *before* you start tearing it apart to convert it into a digital picture frame.
Courtesy of Apple.

Explaining Keith

Keith Stattenfield has been writing system software at Apple since the dawn of time, and way before the advent of Mac OS X. In fact, don't tell anybody, but Keith still has a fondness for his days as technical lead on Mac OS 9 (his car's license plate reads MAC OS 9), although he now regularly reminds anyone who asks that the venerable operating system is "still dead." In addition to his Apple duties, Keith is the owner and operator of Keith Explains!, a media conglomerate consisting of a cable-access TV show and a Web site, including a merchandise shop. To find out more, visit www.keithexplains.com.

FIGURE 5-2: A digital picture frame displaying a nice family scene.

Overview

Turning your iBook into a digital picture frame is a surprisingly straightforward process. Keith says he completed the task over a weekend. Strictly speaking, it doesn't even have to be an iBook. Almost any old portable Mac will do, as long as it's thin enough to suit your desired frame. The only software you have to run is a screen saver, which is available for all portable Macs. So, to be clear: our project uses an iBook running Mac OS X, but you can create a similar picture frame using any PowerBook or iBook, whether it runs OS X or an earlier OS. Here is a brief overview of the raw materials you'll need for the project:

- Any iBook or PowerBook, running a screen saver and any version of Max OS
- Extra-thick "shadow box" picture frame (available at most art supply stores)
- Mat (decorative cardboard frame that surrounds the picture, available at most art supply stores)
- Felt backing and small piece of mirror
- An external keyboard and mouse; this can be wireless (infrared, Bluetooth, RF) or wired (USB)

FIGURE 5-3: Items needed for this project (in addition to the iBook itself).

You can find where to get these parts later in this chapter. You'll also need the following tools:

- Assorted screwdrivers, including small Phillips head for taking the case apart
- Glue gun
- Drill press or hand drill
- Coping saw

Basically, you'll take the iBook apart, reassemble and glue down the necessary pieces in the shadow box, reconnect the cables, and enjoy your cool picture frame. Following are the steps:

1. Set up the screen saver software with images you want.

2. Remove the iBook case and interior parts. Arrange the parts on a cloth or towel for easy access. Just take the parts out — don't try to open the disk, disassemble the logic board, or do anything else radical.

3. Drill holes in the case for ventilation, power, and access to connectors.

4. Reassemble and glue the pieces you need in the shadow box that will form the picture frame. Glue the screen into the top of the box, surrounded by the frame.

5. Hang it on the wall or set it up on a desk. Enjoy!

The Importance of Accessorizing

One of the most important choices you'll have to make when creating your digital picture frame is an extremely nontechnical one: What do you want it to look like? After all, you're creating an item of furniture here, and once you discard that nifty case, you no longer have the world-renowned Apple design team on your side. You'll find a good selection of choices by visiting an art supply store and looking at shadow boxes, which are simply extra-thick picture frames. For best results, look for one that's just a little bigger than your screen. Your frame will look coolest if it's as thin as possible while still holding all the parts. You should be able to fit everything into a frame just a bit thinner than the iBook or PowerBook case itself. To see a selection of frames online, check out www.frameplace.com/xshdboxs.htm.

You should also select a framing mat to go around the screen when you mount it inside the top of the box. This is the piece that will be visible around the screen when you hang it on your wall or place it on your desk. These are available at art supply stores in a wide variety of colors and patterns.

Setting Up the Software

Before you start taking the computer apart, it's a good idea to make sure that all the software you need is installed, because the process is more convenient now than it will be after it's been transformed into a picture frame. Because you're going to use a standard screen saver to show the pictures, this is a simple process. The instructions listed are for the built-in screen saver in Mac OS X, but you can use OS 9 with any third-party screen saver that switches among a set of images, such as Setting Sun, available at www.versiontracker.com/dyn/moreinfo/mac/3968.

Here's how to set it up if you're using the built-in screen saver in OS X:

1. You might want to start by performing a clean OS install and running a disk diagnostic program, such as Norton Utilities or DiskWarrior, on the picture-frame-to-be. Although this isn't strictly necessary, it can help eliminate any problems that might be caused by crusty old software on the computer.

2. Make sure that the pictures you want to display are on the iBook's hard disk. If they aren't, you can copy them using an external disk or network connection. If you're using a third-party screen saver, be sure to install it, too.

3. Create a new folder and put the pictures into that folder. If you want to be able to switch between various sets of pictures, make a folder for each set. The folders can be anywhere on the disk.

4. Click the Apple menu, and choose System Preferences.

5. Click Screen Effects. (If you don't see Screen Effects, click Show All at the upper left, then click Screen Effects.)

6. Click Pictures Folder in the list on the left, then click Configure.

7. Click Slide Folder to choose the folder of pictures you want to use. Click OK when you're done.

8. Click the Activation tab and make sure that the slider is all the way to the left (5 min).

9. On the toolbar, click Show All, then click Energy Saver. If you have a Show Details button, click it.

10. Set the first slider ("Put the computer to sleep when it is inactive for:") to Never (all the way on the right). Make sure that the check box for the second slider ("Use separate time to put the display to sleep.") is unchecked.

11. You can now Quit System Preferences.

That's it! If you forget to do something or need to make a change, don't worry. Your picture frame will still be a fully functioning computer.

Taking Apart Your iBook

This project begins by locating and taking apart an iBook or other Mac portable. If you've been a dedicated Mac geek for a long time, you might have an old, unused iBook or PowerBook around that you want to dedicate to this purpose. In particular, if you have access to an iBook with a dead CD or DVD drive, you can use it for this project, because the optical drive isn't part of the finished picture frame. Another source of cheap old computers is eBay or local computer stores. The instructions in this section are specifically for taking apart a dual USB iBook, but if you're working with something different, you can generally find take-apart instructions on the Web, such as the "Wall Street" PowerBook instructions at http://homepage .mac.com/sysop/PhotoAlbum3.html, or the take-apart manuals available for sale at www.powerbookmedic.com.

Before you start, here's a word of warning: be careful! You're about to open a product that has high voltages inside and do unauthorized things to it. Please be sure that you know what you're doing before you start.

Power Play

Depending on how you use your picture frame, you're likely to want it powered on all the time, so it will have to be connected to AC power, which means that you really don't need a battery. If you want your picture frame to be able to run on battery power, you'll probably need to remove the battery cells from the battery case so that they'll fit inside your shadow box.

Here are the steps to follow when you're ready to take apart your iBook:

1. Find a large surface to work on, such as a workbench or dining room table, cover it with a towel or cloth, and spread out your tools and the iBook.

2. Turn the iBook upside down. Remove the screws in the bottom, including the ones under the white rubber feet.

3. When you have removed all the screws, pry the bottom cover off the iBook and set it aside. It's now just a souvenir.

4. Turn the iBook over with the front side facing up. Remove the two screws at the top left and top center. Take the top cover off. You won't need it either, just the stuff inside.

5. Remove the four small screws that hold the screen onto the lid. Then, using your thumbs and forefingers, pop the lid free of the lid clips holding the screen in place. There are six clips: on the left and right sides at the top, center, and bottom. Once the screen is free of the lid, you can detach the cables and thread them through the hinge.

6. Move the following pieces to the picture frame: logic board, AirPort card, antenna, hard disk, battery cells, and speakers, to keep them handy.

Assembling the Picture Frame

Once you have all the pieces taken apart, you can start to reassemble them into the bottom section of the box. If you're going to use an infrared (IR) keyboard, you should also glue in the IR transceiver and a mirror to reflect the signal. The LCD screen is mounted in the top of the box, surrounded by the mat.

Following are the exact steps you should take:

1. Using a drill press or hand drill, make a hole in the top of the box to allow the fan to blow air away from the computer/picture frame. For improved ventilation, Keith also drilled several more holes in the top of the case to let air circulate.

2. Using the drill press or hand drill again, cut out a hole in the bottom of the box for the AC power cord. Figure 5-4 shows where the holes should go.

3. For easy access to the iBook's connectors (USB, Firewire, and so on), drill a hole in the bottom of the box that lets you connect to them easily. If you're using an infrared keyboard, make a hole for the IR transceiver.

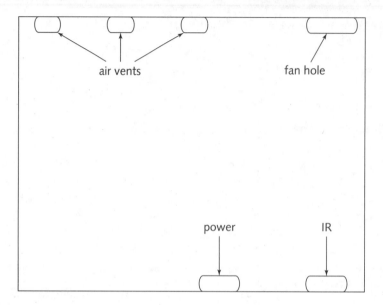

FIGURE 5-4: Where to drill holes in the frame.

4. Using a glue gun, glue the following items into the bottom of the shadow box:

   a. Logic board

   b. AirPort card

   c. Antenna

   d. Hard disk

   e. Battery cells

   f. Speakers

   The optical drive won't fit in the box. That's OK, because you won't have any use for it, and you won't use the keyboard or trackpad.

5. The only additional part is an infrared transceiver in the lower-right corner (g) to communicate with a Macally IR keyboard (see www.macally.com). Keith used a small piece of mirror and a cutout at the bottom of the box to accept and reflect input from the IR keyboard.

6. Glue the framing mat to the outside of the screen, and put the mat and screen inside the top of the shadow box.

7. Reassemble the top and bottom pieces of the shadow box.

Hanging It Up

Although your digital picture frame is anything but a standard picture, you should be able to hang it on the wall just as you would any moderately heavy picture (10 pounds or so). If your frame uses a wire for hanging, get a picture hook that's rated for 25 pounds—they're not expensive. If your frame has a sawtooth hanger, you might want to use a screw with an anchor to hold it in the wall. The choice can also vary depending on how your walls are constructed, so if you're not sure what to do, check with your local frame store or home improvement center.

Showing Pictures

Now that you've got everything put back together, it's time to take advantage of your picture frame. Even though you've done major surgery on your iBook, it's still a functioning Mac, so you should be able to run the screen saver software you set up earlier if you need to make any changes.

Once you start up your picture frame, the screen saver should kick in after 5 minutes and start showing your selected pictures. Use the wireless keyboard to change your settings (if you set one up) or just plug in a USB keyboard and mouse. (If your Mac dates from pre-USB days, either you'll need a wireless keyboard or you'll have to shut down, connect your keyboard, and reboot.)

Easier Way Out

What if you like the idea of a digital picture frame, but you don't have the desire (or the spare iBook) to do this chapter's project? Although it kind of violates the do-it-yourself spirit, you can simply buy a digital picture frame from various sources, such as Digi-Frame (www.digi-frame.com/home.html). Of course, then you won't have a full-on Mac hanging on your wall, just in case you ever need one.

Summary

If you're handy with taking apart electronics and putting them back together, you should be OK with the skill level required for this project. Basically, you're simply taking out the guts of a functioning iBook and placing them inside a picture frame so it looks nice in your house. There are a few ways you can customize your picture frame to make it uniquely yours:

- Pick a frame and mat you really like. You can even stain the frame to match the furniture, like Keith did.

- Instead of an IR or USB keyboard, you might want to use Bluetooth or UHF peripherals. There's no real advantage to using one as opposed to another — just use whichever is easiest for you to acquire.

Your digital picture frame is sure to be an object of beauty in your home, even though you had to abandon that award-winning Apple skin to create it.

Wireless Networking: Around the Room, around Your House

Apple has a well-deserved reputation for innovation; it thinks up and creates products that never seem to occur to others. But Apple-style innovation isn't simply invention. Sometimes Apple innovates by taking existing technologies that are unpolished or hard to figure out, simplifying and integrating them, and then delivering them to customers in a soft blanket of "ease of use."

One of the best examples of this technique is wireless networking. When Apple introduced AirPort technology in the iBook in 1999 (see Figure 6-1), it was the first time that a computer had been designed from the start with wireless network access built in. Apple didn't invent wireless networking — it teamed with Lucent, which was already working on products to take advantage of a new networking technology with the typically geeky name of 802.11b. But the iBook version was "Appleized." Instead of 802.11b, Apple called it AirPort. In place of tricky, confusing configuration tools, Apple provided easy-to-use software to do much of the heavy lifting. AirPort soon spread to the entire Apple product line (and 802.11b to the Windows world and beyond) and became immensely popular. In fact, wireless networking is one of the fastest growing areas of computing technology.

FIGURE **6-1: The original iBook was the first computer with wireless networking designed in, via an internal AirPort card and built-in antenna.**
Courtesy of Apple.

If you haven't yet taken the wireless plunge, you might be happy with your current network setup, but wireless networking is one of those things you didn't know you couldn't live without. Once you get a taste of hooking up to the Internet without having to plug in, you'll want more. It's easy to become addicted to carrying your laptop around the house and getting on the net. In this chapter, we'll discuss various ways you can beef up your wireless network so you can use it to surf the Web from your front porch, send email while you watch the baseball game in your living room, and extend your network so you can get on the net from even the most wireless-resistant parts of your home.

To create your wireless network, you'll need the following:

- Computers that you want to connect to the network
    - A base station (such as an AirPort Base Station) or wireless access point
    - A wireless card for every computer on the network (this is built into many recent Macs and other computers)
- An Internet connection, assuming that you want the computers on the network to be able to access the Internet

Ready for Takeoff

Although wireless networking seems like magic, it can be incredibly simple to set up. You don't even need to wave a wand, although antennas will help. In this section, we'll discuss the various bits and pieces of wireless networking.

Let's start with some fundamental terminology and technology. Apple refers to its wireless networking technologies as AirPort (www.apple.com/airport), while the rest of the world uses the name Wi-Fi (short for "wireless fidelity"), a play on the old term "Hi-Fi" (high fidelity) that described fancy stereo systems in the 1960s (ask your parents). You'll also see it called 802.11, which is the series of technical standards that the industry uses to describe various kinds of wireless networking. We will cover these standards later in this chapter.

Apple's AirPort technology and the 802.11 standard it's based on are flexible enough to enable a lot of flexibility when designing your network. Because 802.11 is not a proprietary Apple technology, you can even add Windows-based PCs to your wireless network.

Networking Cards

Every Apple computer made since 2000 includes a special slot inside for an AirPort card. If you have one of those and you want to join the wireless networking party, you just buy the AirPort card from Apple and install it. If your Mac is older than that, Apple doesn't make an AirPort card for you, but you can still play along by getting a wireless networking card from another vendor, such as Cisco or Lucent, and installing it in a PowerBook's PC or PCMCIA slot or a Power Mac's expansion slot. Installation is straightforward; just insert the card in the slot and install any accompanying driver. Check out www.penmachine.com/techie/airport1400.html for more info on adding wireless to an older computer.

Some of the newest Macs — the 17-inch iMac, Power Mac G5, and PowerBook models that started shipping in January 2003 — won't work with the original AirPort card. Instead, they need an AirPort Extreme card, which uses the faster 802.11g standard but is also compatible with older wireless networking equipment. As long as you have the right wireless card for each computer, you can freely mix and match Macs with original and "Extreme" AirPort capabilities.

Base Stations

You need a base station, such as the AirPort Extreme Base Station (used in this project), to broadcast the wireless signal to your computers. Hook the base station to the source of your Internet connection, such as a cable modem or a good old phone line. The base station then talks to your wireless-savvy computers through thin air. You can set the AirPort software to share your Internet connection among all your computers.

Apple currently offers two flavors of AirPort Extreme Base Stations. The more expensive, more communicative model (M8930LL/A) includes connectors for a modem (if you dial in to connect to the Internet) and an antenna (if you want to expand the range of your network). This one costs about $50 more than the version without the modem and antenna connectors, but the antenna capability gives you tremendous flexibility in making sure that your network covers your area. You can learn the details of the differences between the two base station models at www.apple.com/airport/specs.html.

PowerBook: Bad Reception

Apple's computers have built-in antennas that hook up to the AirPort card slot inside to provide a connection to other AirPort equipment in the vicinity. When Apple redesigned the PowerBook and introduced the 15-inch G4 Titanium model in 2001, users discovered that it had a terrible time talking to the base station, especially as compared to other iBooks and PowerBooks. Apple never fully acknowledged the problem, which reportedly was caused because the antenna was placed around the keyboard rather than alongside the screen, and because the titanium in the case weakened the signal. Later revisions of the Titanium PowerBook improved the problem, although the wireless performance was still worse than with other PowerBooks and iBooks.

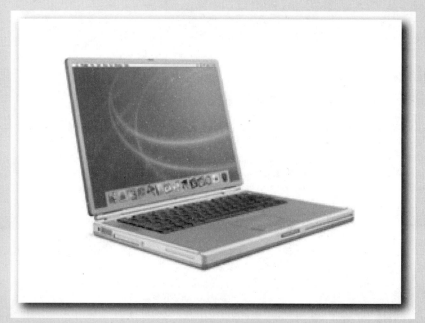

The PowerBook G4 suffers from poor AirPort reception due to its antenna placement and metal case.
Courtesy of Apple.

If you have a Titanium PowerBook, there are a couple of ways to improve wireless reception. One suggestion is to get an external wireless card that fits into the PowerBook's PC Card slot. Because the card brings the antenna outside the metal case, reception is much better. Another solution is to get a more powerful base station than the ones Apple sells or to add an antenna to your existing base station (discussed later in this chapter).

Before introducing the AirPort Extreme product line in January 2003, Apple went through a couple generations of base stations. The original models came in a silver case (Apple calls that "Graphite"), which was later replaced by a white model ("Snow"). These early versions suffered from a couple of problems. The earliest Graphite models included a poorly chosen resistor that was prone to failing after a less than a year of usage. If this happened to you—and it happened to almost everyone who owned one of these—your base station would simply stop working one day. If your base station was less than a year old, and therefore still under warranty, Apple would replace it for you, and the company eventually adopted a generous policy of replacing deceased base stations even if they managed to outlive their warranties.

If you have an old base station and it suddenly stops working, you might be eligible for a free replacement; check with Apple to find out how. AirPort Extreme models never suffered from this fatal flaw. For much more detail on the problem in the original base station and lots of technical info on all AirPort Base Station models, see www.vonwentzel.net/ABS/.

There are non-Apple alternatives as well. Most companies use the term "access point" instead of base station, and you can find many models that are compatible with Macs or cross-platform networks, often at cheaper prices. As usual, Apple really shines in making their stuff easy to use and well suited to working with Macs, as you'll see if you compare AirPort features with other access points, but you can save money if you're willing to work through a setup that's probably a little trickier than Apple's. If you're interested in this subject, you can find some great information at www.wireless-starter-kit.com/.

Software

AirPort hardware comes with a typically Apple-easy Setup Assistant that performs two roles. You use it to make sure your base station is alive and well, and it also gets your computer connected by filling in the right values for its wireless networking settings. Figure 6-2 shows the Setup Assistant.

Apple supplies AirPort Admin Utility for more advanced fooling around, such as setting up multiple base stations to extend a single network. We'll step through that procedure later in this chapter. In general, you won't have to use this utility very often.

When you have everything set up just the way you want, you might still need to tweak a few settings occasionally. For simple changes, such as whether to show the little AirPort signal indicator in the menu bar, you can use the Network panel in System Preferences, as shown in Figure 6-3.

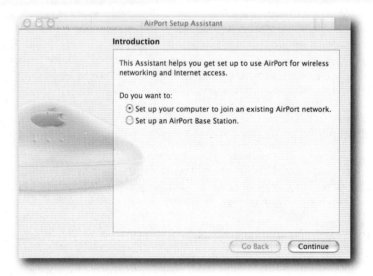

FIGURE 6-2: AirPort Setup Assistant.
Courtesy of Apple.

FIGURE 6-3: The Network panel in System Preferences lets you fine-tune your AirPort setup.
Courtesy of Apple.

Your Number Is Up

Where do all these wacky numbers like 802.11 come from? They're standards, sets of specifications created by the Institute of Electrical and Electronics Engineers, better known as the IEEE (pronounced eye-triple-ee, `http://ieee.org/portal/index.jsp`). This group gathers many smart folks together, has lots of really cool technical arguments, and decides on rules that everybody should follow in order for equipment from various manufacturers to get along well together. The IEEE then assigns numbers to these standards, like 802.11 for wireless networking.

There are actually several versions of the IEEE 802.11 standard for wireless networking (`http://grouper.ieee.org/groups/802/dots.html`). The original AirPort cards and base stations use 802.11b, which operates at 11 megabits per second (Mbps), while the newer AirPort Extreme equipment adopts 802.11g, pushing data through the air at speeds up to 54 Mbps. Because Apple always prefers friendly and fun names, such as AirPort, the company avoids using the geeky 802.11b and 802.11g terms in most of its ads and documents, although the technical specs point out that they're the standards being used.

Another flavor of the wireless networking standard is 802.11a. This version moves data at up to 54 Mbps, just as fast as the 802.11g standard that AirPort Extreme is based on. But 802.11a equipment can't run the older software, while 802.11g cards and base stations work fine with the original standard. When Steve Jobs introduced AirPort Extreme at his Macworld Expo keynote in January 2003, he cited this compatibility as a key reason why Apple chose to use 802.11g, and he said that 802.11a was "doomed to failure." That certainly sounds like a strong indication of which direction Apple is pursuing!

One more point about 802.11g: When Apple shipped the AirPort Extreme products in early 2003, it wasn't actually finished yet, although it was finalized and approved later in the year. Despite this seemingly important fact, Apple and many other manufacturers immediately began shipping hundreds of thousands of 802.11g devices. How is that possible? These devices supported an early version of 802.11g called a draft, on its way toward becoming a standard. Because the draft changed before it became final, Apple was able to update the software running on your computer and living inside your base station via the Software Update panel in System Preferences.

Continued

Continued

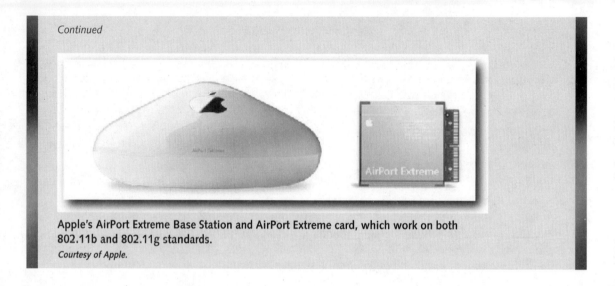

Apple's AirPort Extreme Base Station and AirPort Extreme card, which work on both 802.11b and 802.11g standards.
Courtesy of Apple.

On the Internet Runway

Once you have the hardware you need, you can get your wireless network going by putting everything together and setting it up. Apple provides excellent software for getting the base station set up and sharing an Internet connection. In this section, we'll describe how to accomplish these setup steps.

Setting Up the Base Station

Your base station has to be plugged into the source of your Internet connection and to a power outlet, so you should find a location for the base station that includes easy access to both of those. Although most AirPort networks share broadband connections, you can also use a dial-up connection as long as you have the base station model that includes a modem (M8930LL/A). When you've chosen a place to put your base station, connect the power adaptor and your source of Internet connection — usually DSL, a cable modem, or a standard phone line. When you plug in the base station's power, the three lights on the front will blink in various patterns as the base station starts up. After about 30 seconds, the light show will stop and the middle light stays on.

Setting Up the Connection

Once you have plugged in the base station to power and an Internet connection, you'll use the convenient AirPort Setup Assistant to get the base station connected to the Internet and get the Macs talking to the base station. First, run AirPort Setup Assistant to get the network set up. When you do this, the Internet settings on your computer are copied to the base station, setting it up for Internet access. The Setup Assistant is smart enough to detect whether the base station has been set up already, and it takes you through the appropriate screens for what it needs to find out.

Connection Details

The AirPort Base Station shares an Internet connection by means of a standard technology called Dynamic Host Configuration Protocol (DHCP). This scheme assigns a local Internet Protocol (IP) address to every computer on the wireless network and then directs traffic between the local computers and the Internet. If you want more control over how this works, including setting the range of local addresses, you can use the Network tab in AirPort Admin Utility.

To share the Internet connection with another computer, all you have to do is run AirPort Setup Assistant on that computer. Setup Assistant will ask if you want to join the existing AirPort network — just say yes!

Getting through AirPort Security

All those bits flying through the air recall Laurence Olivier's thoughtful question in *Marathon Man*: "Is it safe?" Security on wireless networks is an important issue, as it is with all computer networks.

AirPort and other Wi-Fi networks employ a technology called Wired Equivalent Privacy (WEP), which uses a key to scramble your data as it's moving through the network. The name comes from the idea that using this security was supposed to make your network as secure as if it were wired; in other words, someone intent on seeing your data would have to gain physical access to your network. It didn't work out that way. Unfortunately, not long after WEP was in wide use, smart folks discovered serious flaws in its technique. With the right software, snoopers can watch encrypted data on your network and, if they get to watch long enough, they can eventually figure out the key, leaving data open to unscrambling. In addition, every device on the network can see all the data due to the way that WEP keys work.

The better news is that although you can't be completely sure you're safe, most home networks don't generate enough data to provide spies with a key. For the best results, there are steps you can and should take to secure your network. The most basic of these is to make sure that you turn on WEP on your network. Even though it's vulnerable to prying software, it blocks casual viewing of your data.

The wireless industry knows that WEP isn't good enough, so there are a couple of new security standards under development. The first is called Wi-Fi Protected Access (WPA), and it should be available by the time you read this. However, this is just an interim solution. The long-term fix for security is yet another standard, known as 802.11i. Apple appears to be hedging its bets on these two technologies, possibly because it's not clear which one will catch on. Once one or the other emerges, Apple will likely provide software and firmware updates to support it in AirPort Extreme equipment.

Here's a summary of the steps you should take to make your wireless network as secure as possible:

1. **Turn on WEP security.** To do this, start AirPort Admin Utility and click *Name and Password*. Make sure that *Enable encryption (using WEP)* is checked and enter a password. The password dialog comes up with 128-bit as the default key length — make sure that you keep it at 128-bit. See Figure 6-4.

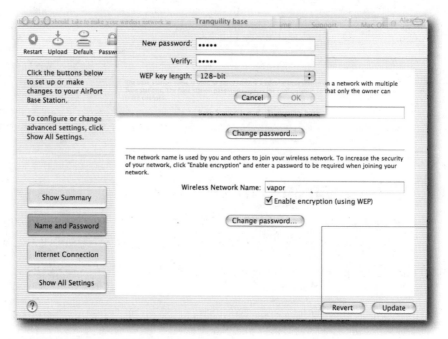

FIGURE 6-4: Be sure to turn on WEP encryption in AirPort Admin Utility to give your network some security protection.
Courtesy of Apple.

2. **Turn on access control.** This powerful feature allows you to limit AirPort access to only the computers you specifically admit. Any computers not on your access list will not be permitted to join the network. To set this up, click *Show All Settings* in AirPort Admin Utility, then click the Access Control tab. For every computer you want to allow on the network, click the Add button, then enter the computer's AirPort ID and a descriptive name. You can get a computer's AirPort ID from the Network panel in System Preferences. Look at Figure 6-5 to see what this looks like.

FIGURE 6-5: Setting up an access control list using AirPort Admin Utility.
Courtesy of Apple.

3. **Use strong passwords.** This is great advice for passwords in general, because it makes them harder to guess. Strong passwords are as long as possible; include a combination of letters, numbers, and special characters and don't contain names or words. In addition to using strong passwords, you can also change your network passwords frequently, although this is probably more trouble than it's worth for small networks.

For more information about wireless security issues, we recommend the following sites:

```
http://wifinetnews.com/archives/001034.html
www.giac.org/practical/gsec/Princy_Mehta_GSEC.pdf
```

Extending Your Trip

There are several techniques for extending the range of your network. In this section, we'll focus on two of the most popular ways to give your network greater reach: adding antennas and teaching base stations to talk to each other.

Add an Antenna

You can give your wireless signal a little extra oomph by adding an antenna. This is useful when you have pretty good coverage already, but you need to reach a dead spot or two. Connecting an antenna is very easy if you have an AirPort Extreme Base Station and a little trickier if you have an older base.

Apple makes two models of Extreme Base Stations. As discussed earlier, the more expensive (by about $50) model includes an antenna connector. All you have to do is find a compatible antenna and hook it up. The AirPort Setup Utility automatically notices the presence of the antenna for you, and you get the added range.

The only trick here is making sure you that get the right kind of antenna. There are two basic kinds of antennas for Extreme Base Stations: omnidirectional and unidirectional. The first sends the signal in all directions, while the second concentrates the signal in a narrow range.

If you're trying to reach a specific hard-to-get spot, go for the unidirectional antenna; otherwise, the omnidirectional model is best. Dr. Bott makes compatible antennas that Apple sells in its stores. See www.drbott.com for more about them or take a look at Figure 6-6. Note that there are lots of antennas in the world, but most of them aren't compatible with the AirPort Extreme equipment. Check the antenna's system requirements carefully to be sure.

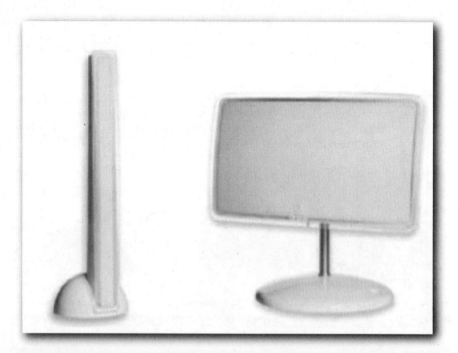

FIGURE 6-6: Omnidirectional and unidirectional antennas from Dr. Bott for AirPort Extreme Base Station
Courtesy of Dr. Bott.

If you want to add an antenna to an older (Graphite or Snow) base station, you'll need an antenna that connects to the Lucent card inside. To make this work, you'll have to do a little surgery. Open the base station by removing the three screws on the bottom. Once inside the base station, connect the antenna to the Lucent card. If you have a LAN or broadband connection and you're not using the modem in the base station, you can remove the modem connector from the back panel and run the antenna cable through the hole. If you still need the modem connector, use a Dremel or similar tool to carve out a hole in the back of the case.

Once you've connected the antenna, it will automatically boost the range of your base station. If you're unsure about installing the antenna yourself in your pre–Extreme Base Station, there are companies that will do it all for you, including selling you the antenna. One company that offers this service is Quickertech at www.technowarehousellc.com/quan.html.

Of course, if you really want fast and easy Wi-Fi access, you can always try Wi-Fi Speed Spray, available from the following site: www.j-walk.com/blog/docs/wifispray.htm. And if you want a really cheap antenna, start with an empty can of Pringle's Potato Chips, as shown here: www.oreillynet.com/cs/weblog/view/wlg/448. Note: When you check out these links, it helps if you have a sense of humor.

Wireless Bridging (WDS)

One of the cool new features of AirPort Extreme is the ability to connect multiple base stations together over the air and extend the length of your network. This feature, called wireless bridging or wireless distribution system (WDS), requires no additional cables or hardware, but you need two or more Extreme Base Stations — this trick won't work with earlier models of base stations.

To set up a wireless distribution system, designate one base station as the main and the others as satellites. In AirPort Admin Utility, click *Show All Settings* and make sure that *Extend wireless network (using WDS)* is checked (see Figure 6-7).

To set up the connection between base stations, you need the MAC address (also called the AirPort ID) of the remote station or stations. You can get the AirPort IDs of all your base stations from the main screen of AirPort Admin Utility, as shown in Figure 6-8.

When you click the *Configure WDS* button, a dialog pops up that gives you space to fill in the addresses of up to four remote base stations (see Figure 6-9). Carefully enter the values for the other base stations you want to add — if you get one wrong, your network won't work, and you'll have to figure out why.

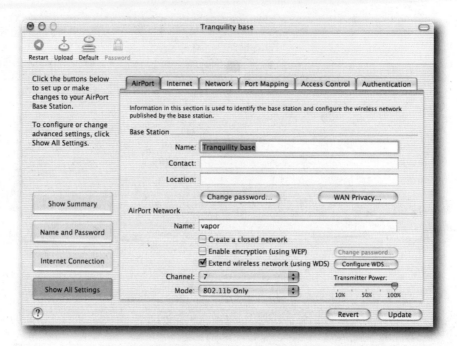

FIGURE 6-7: AirPort Admin Utility screen for setting up the main base station of two that use wireless distribution system (WDS).

Courtesy of Apple.

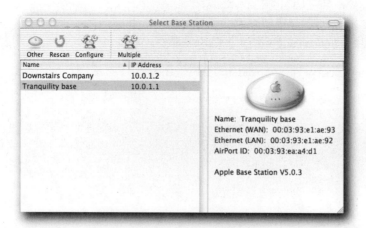

FIGURE 6-8: The main screen of AirPort Admin Utility includes the AirPort of ID of each base station in range.

Courtesy of Apple.

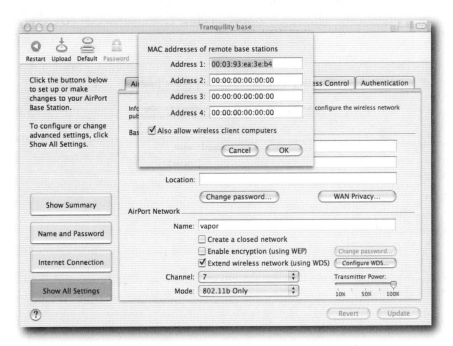

FIGURE 6-9: You must manually enter the addresses of up to four remote base stations for wireless bridging.
Courtesy of Apple.

Note

When setting up wireless bridging with AirPort Admin Utility, you have to fill in complicated 12-digit hexadecimal numbers by reading them off the screen from another part of the same program. That seems slightly broken to us, and not really exemplary of the Apple way. In a future version of the Admin utility, it would be really nice if the remote station IDs were discovered and filled in automatically, after you confirmed the ones you wanted, of course.

After you've set up the main base, it's time to configure the remote stations. Go back to the main window, the one that lists all base stations in range, and double-click the one you want to be a remote. As we did before, click *Show All Settings* on the lower left. This time, make sure *Extend wireless network (using WDS)* is NOT selected — that's only for the main base, not the remotes. Then, make sure the *Channel* pop-up is set to the same value as it was for the main station (see Figure 6-10). Click *Update*, repeat this process if you have any more remote stations, and your extended network is in business.

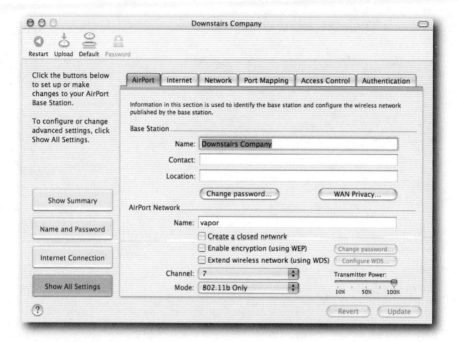

FIGURE 6-10: Make sure the remote base stations are tuned to the same channel as the main station and that the *Extend wireless network (using WDS) box* is NOT checked for the remote stations, only for the main one.

Courtesy of Apple.

Summary

Once you've created your wireless network, you're likely to become very fond of it. You'll find uses for your laptop in every room of the house once you can connect to the Internet from anywhere. Here are a few tips to remember as you create, maintain, and expand your network:

- If you stick to Apple equipment, such as AirPort Base Stations, you'll spend more and have less to figure out, because Apple makes things easier for you than other manufacturers do (as usual).

- If you get an AirPort Base Station, consider the more expensive model because it includes an antenna connector that can expand the range of your network or eliminate troublesome dead spots.

- You can freely mix computers that use 802.11b (the original AirPort) and 802.11g (AirPort Extreme).

Make and Mix Your Own Music: Synthesizers, MIDI, and Mix Software

Your Mac is a magical multipurpose music machine. You can make and modify music on your Mac, and add in tunes played on musical instruments. Technologies built into Mac OS X give you higher-quality audio than was possible with Mac OS 9, enabling you to plug in multiple musical devices and have them work with each other. The Mac OS X technologies, called Core Audio and Core MIDI, have also caused an explosion of available software for both professionals and hobbyists.

Musically speaking, you can now do everything on a Mac—turn it into a digital audio studio. You can also make the Mac the digital hub of your studio and plug in a variety of instruments, mixers, and output devices. Or, simply do one of a number of tasks for the hobbyist or pro.

Use the Mac to control a musical instrument or use the Mac *as* a musical instrument with software synthesizers. Use the Mac as a digital recording and device or use it as a mixer to produce your own songs, with you playing all the instruments. Use the Mac to create musical notation from what you play or use the Mac to arrange music and print out a score.

Mac OS X also has native support for MIDI, the Musical Instrument Digital Interface, for connecting to musical keyboards. Digital audio and MIDI both represent music digitally, but are very different entities. You can work with one or the other, or both. This chapter looks at tools that students and hobbyists can afford, as well as those used by the pros.

Digital Audio Basics

Digital audio has its own buzzwords and acronyms, just like most areas of computing. Digital audio is certainly more fun than, say, computer networking, so its tempting to blow off the bits and bytes terms and go right to the software. Trouble is, terms like "sampling rate" and "signal-to-noise ratio" will pop up all over digital audio software and hardware. A little knowledge of the differences between digital and analog audio go a long way in helping you choose the software and hardware you need.

Sampling Rate and Sample Size

Sound is inherently an analog phenomenon — air vibrating at continuously varying rates. In your Mac, sound (or audio) is digital, converted to discrete bits of data represented by 1s and 0s. A confusing aspect to computer audio is that both analog and digital audio have parameters measured in hertz (Hz) and kilohertz (KHz): frequency and sampling rates. Hertz basically means "times per second," while KHz means "thousands of times per second." Both frequency and sampling rates have to do in some way with the quality of sound.

With analog sound, frequency is measure of pitch. The higher the frequency, the higher the pitch. When speakers or headphones vibrate at 440 Hz, the musical pitch of A is produced. The highest notes you can hear are over 20 KHz. The more frequencies a piece of audio equipment can produce, the better quality music it can reproduce. For instance, the iPod can produce sounds from 20 to 20,000 Hz. If you use headphones that produce only 50 to 15,000 Hz, you'll miss some of the bass and some of the treble.

In digital audio, kilohertz refers not to frequency, but to the sampling rate. The process of converting analog sound to digital audio takes measurements, or *samples*, of the frequencies and volume at selected moments. The number of times per second that these measurements are taken is the sampling rate, measured in kilohertz. The higher the sampling rate, the more faithful reproduction of the original sound. As in digital photography, where higher resolutions produce more realistic photos, higher sampling rates produce better-quality sound.

The sampling rate of a standard audio CD is 44.1 KHz — that's 44,100 measurements per second (see Figure 7-1). When you're working with audio-editing software, you'll find that you have the ability to save sound at lower sampling rates, such as 22 KHz or 11 KHz. The reason you would even consider this is that a lower sampling rate produces fewer bits — and a smaller file, which is easier to store and to move over the Internet. You may remember from Chapter 2 that Internet radio uses sampling rates of 22 KHz. But audio CDs are by no means the top of the digital audio quality heap. A sampling rate of 96 KHz is a standard in professional-quality digital audio software and equipment. Higher rates can also be found. Another standard sampling rate, 48 KHz, is also commonly used in sequencing software, including Apple's Final Cut Pro.

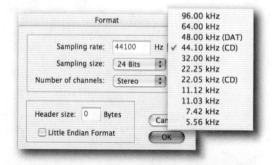

FIGURE 7-1: Audio recording software lets you choose the sampling rate and sample size when you import it. This dialog, from HairerSoft's Amadeus II, is typical.

Better Fidelity with DVD Audio

If you are old enough to remember the introduction of audio CDs in the 1980s you may remember the claims from audiophiles that vinyl records produced better sound than CDs. The computer geeks denied it—"digital is better" was the slogan. Twenty years later, even the technophiles agree that the audiophiles had it right. If you have a good enough stereo system, you *can* hear the superiority of vinyl records over CDs. The main reason is that the 16-bit sample size of CDs is not big enough to reproduce the entire dynamic range that the human ear can perceive. It turns out that a 24-bit sampling rate is big enough to record the entire human ear dynamic range.

So why did the definers of the CD standards go with 16-bit instead of 24-bit? The reason was purely commercial. Twenty-four-bit files are bigger than 16-bit files. A 650-MB CD can only hold about 40 minutes worth of 24-bit audio—less than many vinyl records already in the stores. With 16-bit digital audio, CD manufacturers could fit over an hour's worth of music onto a CD.

Of course, audiophiles represent a market, too. Thus, audio DVDs were born. An audio DVD can hold several times more data than a CD, enough to hold over an hour's worth of music using a full 24-bit sample size as well as a 96-KHz sampling rate.

There is one other number used to measure digital audio quality—sample size, measured in bits. You'll often see sample size and sampling rate presented together, as in "24-bit, 96 KHz digital audio." The higher the sample size, the more accurate each sample is. The sample size determines the dynamic range of the recording—that is, the range of volume from soft to loud. Audio CDs use a sample size of 16 bits. Professional-quality digital audio software and hardware often uses a 24-bit sample size, which is enough to reproduce the entire dynamic range of the human ear. As with sampling rates, a higher sample size results in a bigger file size.

Compression

To handle the large file sizes of high-quality audio, computers often use compression to create files. Compressed audio is automatically decompressed when played. Compression makes files smaller, but results in a certain amount of loss in audio quality. For this reason, audio CDs and DVDs use uncompressed audio, in the form of AIFF files. The Windows Audio format, or WAV, is also usually uncompressed. However, in audio-editing software, you will be able to compress AIFF and WAV formats if you want to.

Popular compressed digital audio file formats include MP3 (short for "MPEG 1 layer 3") and AAC (Advanced Audio Coding, part of the MPEG 4 standard), which iTunes began supporting in version 4. AAC has more efficient compression than MP3. So for the same file size, AAC can retain more data than MP3, and thus give you better sound quality.

Tip

When you are capturing and editing audio, keep your audio in uncompressed form until you really need to compress it, such as when you create the finished audio. This will prevent the loss of quality (and introduction of noise) during your editing process.

Audio recording software will offer a variety of audio compression codecs (short for compressor/decompressors, a term also used with digital video). Codecs are compression algorithms, some which are in the public domain, and others which must be licensed. The MPEG 1 layer 3 codec is a public domain technology that compresses from 10:1 to 12:1. Others yield less compression, such as IMA 4:1, which gives you a file about one-fourth of its original size. Mac OS X's QuickTime software supports over a dozen audio compression codecs, which is why you will see these options in freeware and shareware editors. You'll also see older compression formats, such as MACE and A-Law (also called AU). These are usually included for backward compatibility with old files. More expensive packages offer other options.

Noise

Noise is a relative thing. A lawnmower right outside your window on a quiet Sunday morning will drown out the string quartet playing on the radio. However, the same lawnmower at a football stadium rock concert would barely be noticed. The lawnmower didn't get any quieter, but the difference in volume between it and the music did.

This difference in volume is an audio phenomenon known as *signal-to-noise ratio*, which is the difference in volume between the background noise on a recording and your audio content. The bigger this difference — the bigger the signal-to-noise ratio — the less noticeable the noise will be. Signal-to-noise (S/N) ratio is usually measured in decibels (dB), which can be determined by a mathematical formula. For instance, consumer audio equipment typical produces sound at a S/N ratio of 50 dB and higher. Below 20 dB, the music becomes too noisy to listen to. However, there is no fixed number for what is acceptable and what is not, and often your software and equipment won't report a number. The point to remember is that you want to minimize the noise relative to your recording signal.

You can minimize noise in your recordings, but it's almost impossible to eliminate. Noise sources include the pops and clicks of a vinyl LP, the background activities during a live recording, or a hum produced by your own equipment. Cheap or damaged cables can also introduce noise. And the more steps in your audio production process, the more potential to introduce noise. The trick is to use techniques to maximize the signal-to-noise ratio.

One technique is to record "hot" — at high levels on your recording equipment or software. Lower volumes will be closer to the volume of noise. However, you also want "clean" recordings, without distortion or clipping that can occur if you push the recording levels too high.

Another way to keep a high signal-to-noise ration is to use digital equipment with the highest sample size, and sample down only at the end, for example, when you are creating files for a CD. This is another reason why higher-quality digital recording equipment and software uses 24-bit sampling instead of CD-quality 16-bit sampling.

If you do end up with noise in your recordings, you can use noise reduction filters built-into low-end products such as Felt Tip's Sound Studio (www.felttip.com) and Amadeus II from HairerSoft (www.hairersoft.com). Of course, noise reduction is also part of high-end audio production software, such as Logic Audio Platinum by Emagic (now owned by Apple, www.apple.com/software/pro/logic/) or Steinberg's Cubase (www.steinberg.net).

You can also find software that specializes in and only does noise reduction. SoundSoap (www.BIAS-inc.com) from Berkeley Integrated Audio Software (BIAS) is a $100 noise reduction application that offers multiple, very easy-to-use tools that remove different types of noise from digital audio files (see Figure 7-2). You can listen to the file with the filters on and off, relieving you from worrying if you've made a big mistake. You can buy SoundSoap as an individual application, or as a VST plug-in for higher-end digital audio applications, including those from BIAS, Inc.

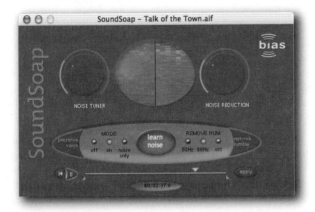

FIGURE 7-2: SoundSoap makes it easy to remove noise from digital audio files.

A more expensive noise reduction app is Ray Gun Pro X (www.arboretum.com) from Arboretum Systems, which isn't as easy to use as SoundSoap, but offers some sound enhancement tools in addition to noise reduction capabilities.

Inputting (Capturing) Audio

Now that you know something about audio, you're ready to bring it into your Mac. Inputting sound is also known as *capturing* sound. There are many different tools available for capturing sound, and many different types of sound input to capture. (Chapter 10 focuses in on one application of capturing analog audio — inputting the signals from vinyl records.)

One thing you can say about capturing sound with your Mac is that the sound will end up in digital form at some point. The source sound can be digital or analog. Digital sources include audio CDs, Internet streams, and other musical devices that can output audio. (MIDI is also digital, but it isn't audio. We'll get to MIDI a little later in the chapter.) Analog audio sources can include musical instruments, microphones, sound mixers, or your home stereo system. Capturing sound from these sources includes the additional step of converting analog signals to digital form, which requires some hardware.

Audio Capture Hardware

When choosing sound capture hardware, you can spend anywhere from nothing (by using the hardware already in your Mac) up to about $13,000. You can help make your choice by deciding on the features you need and sound quality you're aiming for. Most add-on capture hardware connects to your Mac's USB port. If you have a Power Mac, you have the option of putting an audio capture card in your PCI slot.

The Mac's Built-in A/D Hardware

Some Macs don't have a built-in audio-in port. But on those that do, using the analog-to-digital (A/D) circuits built into your Mac is the low-end approach in terms of sound quality and features. The options available vary with the Mac model. Many Macs have a built-in microphone, often located at or near the top of the display, which looks like a small hole. Many Mac models also have a line-in port (sometimes called a microphone port), with A/D conversion hardware on the motherboard. The line-in port is typically a single stereo $1/8$" miniconnector. You may need a converter cable to get to two inputs (for the left and right channels) of different sizes into the one port. Your local RadioShack is a good source of converter cables, as are stereo and music stores and even some hardware stores.

The Mac's built-in A/D hardware is certainly good enough for certain tasks, such as Internet voice communications using iChat AV or commenting on home movies with iMovie. But there are limitations. For instance, the built-in microphone is usually monaural, not stereo, and is not of a quality that could capture singing very well. The A/D conversion hardware of the line-in port is limited to a 16-bit sample size, which could lead to a low signal-to-noise ratio, and a sample rate of 44 KHz — not a great place to start for pro-quality production. And the Mac's internal A/D circuitry is not well shielded from the other electronics inside of the Mac, making the line-in port prone to producing noise.

As far as sound output, most Mac's audio out ports are also limited to 44 KHz, 16-bit (CD quality). This is fine for listening, but if you want to export audio for further audio processing, you may want hardware that can produce 96-KHz, 24-bit audio.

Adding Sound Capture Hardware

If your Mac doesn't have a sound-in port, or you want better quality and more features, then you'll have to shop for hardware. Both USB hardware and PCI cards usually come with both A/D conversion and D/A — outputting analog audio.

You don't have to spend a lot of money. For instance, $35 will get you Griffin Technology's iMic (www.griffintechnology.com), shown in Figure 7-3. Weighing only 2 ounces, iMic is a USB capture device that includes A/D and D/A circuitry. It produces digital audio with a 24-bit sample size and 48-KHz sampling rate, higher quality than a Mac's sound-in port. The iMic has two $1/8$" ports for input and output. To have the input port accept microphone-level input or line-level signals output by tape decks and CD players, you have to set a switch on the iMic.

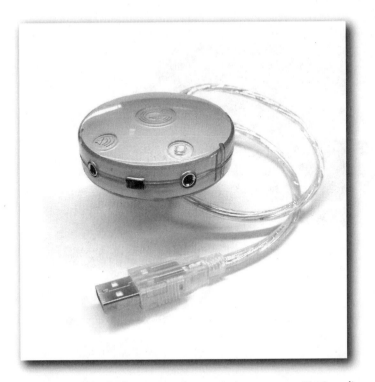

FIGURE 7-3: iMic is the least expensive way to improve your Mac's audio capture capabilities.
Courtesy of Griffin Techology, Inc.

At the $100 level, you're entering the midrange of audio capture devices, with features such as higher sampling rates and more connectors. Griffin's PowerWave is a 24-bit 48-KHz USB box that has audio RCA input and out jacks as well as the ⅛" miniports. It also includes a 20-watt per channel amplifier for connecting standard stereo speakers (not just speakers designed for computers). M-Audio's Transit (www.m-audio.com) is another $100 unit using ⅛" mini stereo connectors for analog audio in and out, but it supports higher-quality sound, 24 bit, 96 KHz, which is DVD quality. At higher prices, not only is 24-bit, 96-KHz sampling standard, but you get more types of ports. M-Audio's $150 Audiophile 2496 (Figure 7-4, www.m-audio .com/products/m-audio/audiophile.php) is a PCI card for Power Macs that includes digital S/PDIF ports and MIDI ports. S/PDIF (Sony/Philips Digital Interface) is a method of transferring digital audio between devices without having to covert it to analogy audio. S/PDIF connecters are usually coaxial jacks, the same used for analog audio.

An equivalent USB interface is the $180 Edirol UA-20 (www.edirol.com/products/ info/ua20.html), a 24-bit, 44-KHz capture device. You can plug an electric guitar directly into the audio in port, and it also has S/PDIF digital audio ports and MIDI in and out. The box also features a dial to adjust the input level. Hardware controls are another feature that become more prevalent as the price increases.

FIGURE 7-4: The Audiophile 2496 for PowerMacs provides both an audio digitizer and a MIDI interface.
Courtesy of M-Audio.

Professional devices begin in the $400 range and go up to thousands of dollars. Professional features include multiple channels for each of the different types of ports, FireWire for communicating with the Mac and other devices, and hardware controls such as sliders for mixers. You can also find rack-mounted units. Companies offering pro boxes include M-Audio, Edirol, eMagic (www.emagic.de), and Digidesign (www.digidesign.com), which has a wide range of produces going up to the very high end.

Configuring Inputs and Outputs

For basic configuration of input and output ports of various devices, Mac OS X 10.2 and later gives you two tools. For simple configuration, there's the Sound pane of System Preference. For more detailed control options or more complex setups there's the Audio MIDI Setup utility, which you will find in your Utilities folder, inside the Applications folder. You'll use the Audio tab shown in Figure 7-5. (We'll get to MIDI tab in the section on MIDI later in the chapter.)

You can select which hardware will be the default sound capture hardware using the Default Input pop-up menu. This can be the Mac's internal audio hardware or an external device. You can do the same with output devices. Most USB audio devices will appear in the pop-up menus in just a few seconds after you plug them in. (There is no need to restart the Mac.)

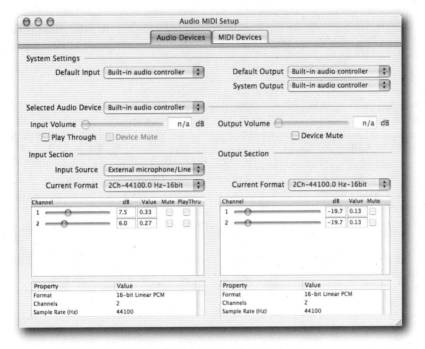

FIGURE 7-5: The Audio tab of Audio MIDI Setup lets you configure your audio devices.

After selecting the defaults, you can configure some settings of specific devices. You can use these controls, you can route the audio signals to different devices. For instance, you could set your system beeps and warnings (the System Output) to go through the Mac's built-in little speaker (the Built-in Audio Controller), while channeling your work through your USB or FireWire audio hardware.

If the device supports it, you can also set a sampling rate and sample size and set recording levels for individual channels. For devices that don't need drivers, you'll see either two channels (stereo), or a single monaural channel (as is the case with some microphones or Apple's iSight camera/microphone). The Audio MIDI Setup utility will show multiple channels for devices that support them and which have their own Mac OS X drivers.

Audio Capture Software

Yes, you can spend $1,000 on professional audio software, but you don't have to. The big professional packages often provide you with a complete digital studio, with all of the features described in this chapter and then some. There are also very inexpensive shareware solutions that can do basic recording as well as some editing tasks. At all levels, different packages tend to focus on different tasks, so there is quite a variety of software available.

This section will present a tour of what you can expect in digital audio software at different price ranges. It is not intended to be an exhaustive list of the dozens of packages available. A good source place to find out about other audio apps is the MacMusic Web site (www.macaudio.org).

What You'll Need

The first software you need to think about are device drivers — small files that enable the Mac to recognize your audio hardware. Mac OS X comes with its own driver software already installed, so you usually don't need drivers for the lower-end audio capture devices such as those from Griffin Technology. (This is also true for lower-end MIDI hardware described later in the chapter.) The Mac will recognize these simpler devices when you plug them in. Higher-end, more complex hardware might require that you install drivers or other software to make them work or to enable special features. You should always check with the manufacturers before you buy — their Web sites will often tell you if you require any software. Also check the "requirements" area. If Mac OS X is not listed, there's a good chance the device requires a driver that only exists for Windows.

There are dozens of Mac OS X applications you can use to stop and start recording, from free-ware and inexpensive shareware to professional packages. You can use just about any of them with most capture devices. However, some of the hardware capture devices come with their own recording and editing software. For instance, to work with its iMic and PowerWave USB capture interfaces, Griffin offers an app called Final Vinyl as a free download at its Web site (www.griffintechnology.com).

Other times, a company will sell software tailored to its own hardware. Digidesign (www.digidesign.com) sells a line of digital workstation applications called Pro Tools that work with the company's midrange to high-end hardware devices. The line starts with Pro Tools LE ($75) and goes up to several hundred dollars. All are multifunction digital audio workstations that include a plug-in architecture for using other specialty software, such as synthesizers and MIDI editing tools. You can also use other software with Digidesign's hardware.

There are also plenty of standalone software applications. We'll look at some of them next.

Low-cost Audio Software

If simple recording and editing is all you need, there are plenty of choices. If you're new to computer audio, it makes sense to cut your teeth on free or inexpensive applications first and grow into more complicated packages as you gain more understanding of the issues.

Audio In is a simple, free program that can record from any sound capture device or microphone connected to your Mac. (The Web site is http://home3.swipnet.se/ ~w-34826/soft.html. If that doesn't work, you can find it at www.versiontracker.com.) Audio In lets you schedule when to record, and lets you skip silent periods.

Earlier in the chapter, we mentioned Amadeus II from HairerSoft (www.hairersoft.com), $25 shareware that adds some sound-editing and -analyzing features to the basic recording capabilities. You can split up long recordings, or join shorter ones together. It supports 16- and 24-bit audio at varying sample rates up to 1,000 KHz. It supports many file formats, including AIFF, MP3, and WAV, MP3. There are also some effects, including fading and noise filters. It also supports VST plug-ins that let you add other effects. HairerSoft offers a set of free VST plug-ins, and others are available on the Internet. You can download a time-limited demo of Amadeus to check it out.

A similar audio app is Sound Studio from Felt Tip software ($50, www.felttip.com), which can record two channels with high-quality 24-bit, 96-KHz sampling. A feature called *resampling* lets you change the sampling rate and sample size. Like Amadeus II, Sound Studio also lets you do some basic editing, displaying the waveforms for your sound and letting you cut pieces out and fade out or in (see Figure 7-6). You can also do pitch shifting, raising or lowering the pitch of a section, and do some basic mixing of two channels into one. Sound Studio also comes with filters to clean up sound and add effects such as chorus and flange. You can try out Sound Studio for 14 days before purchasing it.

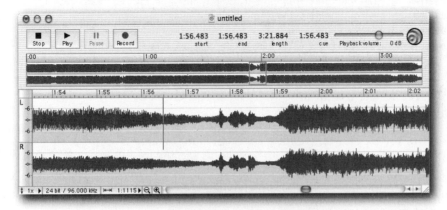

FIGURE 7-6: Sound Studio gives you some basic waveform editing tools. The top waveforms represent the entire piece; the large, bottom waveforms are the portion of the piece in the rectangle above.

For a taste of the pro apps, try Spark ME from TC Works (www.tcelectronic.com/SparkME), a free version of the $800 professional Spark XL. (You do have to enter your name and address, and phone number before downloading.) Spark ME is more sophisticated than Sound Studio, but is also more complex, and since it doesn't come with any help files or a manual, it is tougher for the beginner to figure out. If you have high-quality hardware, Spark ME supports sample rates of up to 192 KHz and a sample size of up to 32 bits — higher than even DVD audio. Spark ME supports VST plug-ins, a standard type of plug-in for adding new capabilities such as filters and effects. (There's more on VST plug-ins later in the Chapter, in the section on sequencers.) It even has a built-in file management feature, giving you easy access to files in your project. TC Works also offers a $50 version called Spark LE (www.tcelectronic.com/SparkLE), which adds more effects and can save directly to MP3 format.

You'll also find other manufacturers offering multiple versions of audio software. For instance, BIAS's Peak LE ($85) is the low-end version of the company's midrange Peak ($500) software. It includes a lot of the tools of the high-end version, but is limited to two-channels (stereo), which is typical with the low-end packages. (Chapter 9 describes how to use Peak LE to digitize your vinyl LP collection.) The full Peak program is described in the section on midrange packages later on.

Capturing Audio That Is Already Digital

Before we move on to the midrange audio-editing packages, there is another class of free or shareware programs that is worth mentioning. These record only sound that is already digital. You know that iTunes can import a file from a CD, but if you only want to import a portion of a song iTunes can't help. iTunes also can't capture audio from Internet streams, such as Internet radio broadcasts or the soundtracks of streaming video presentations. *Digital* audio capture is a feature found in big digital audio workstation applications, but you can also find inexpensive utilities that can do this for you.

The free WireTap application from Ambrosia Software (www.ambrosiasw.com/utilities/freebies/) will capture the audio from whatever Mac OS X application happens to by producing sound. Using WireTap is simple. First start playing your audio with any application, including RealPlayer, iChat AV, iTunes, DVD Player, or a Web broadcast—anything that can play sound will work. WireTap's small floating control pallet persists no matter what application is present. Click the red circle to record; click the square to stop recording.

WireTap can capture at 16 bit, 48 KHz, and lower settings are available for smaller files. You have a choice of codecs to use for compression, or you can have no compression. However, one drawback is that it only saves files in AIFF format, either compressed with one of the codecs supported by QuickTime, or uncompressed AIFF. You can choose which format in the Preferences dialog, shown in Figure 7-7. (You can use iTunes to convert an AIFF file to ACC or MP3, as described in Chapter 2.)

FIGURE 7-7: WireTap saves anything your Mac is playing. The small control pallet at the bottom right is available no matter what application is in the front.

If you'd like to record directly to MP3, you might try Rogue Amoeba's Audio Hijack Pro (www.rogueamoeba.com/), a $30 shareware utility. In addition to flexible output features, Audio Hijack Pro includes some filtering and editing features to help enhance the sound.

Midrange Audio Packages

When you move up to the midrange of audio software, you get a digital audio workstation with many different features related to the creation of music that you could use in your video work as well as for straight audio projects. You get high-quality sampling, support for many different file formats, including AAC and MP3, and plenty of effects. The ability to burn audio CDs is also common, and you start to get some integration with MIDI content. What you don't get in the midrange that you find in the high end is the complete integration of MIDI production, such as MIDI sequencing.

Berkeley Integrated Audio Software (or BIAS, at http://BIAS-inc.com/), dominates the midrange with two lines of audio applications, Peak and Deck. Peak 4 ($500) is a popular application that focuses on professional, intuitive waveform editing, processing, and mastering. But instead of working on one audio file, Peak lets you apply its advanced audio-processing tools to multiple files at the same time as a batch process, a feature that makes Peak a real audio-processing tool. It also comes with a parametric equalizer for boosting or reducing the volume of certain frequencies. Peak goes beyond 24-bit, 96-KHz sampling, offering up to 32-bit, 10-MHz (yes, megahertz, not kilohertz) sampling, as well as the ability to resample. There's also strong support for VST plug-ins. (VST is a standard audio/MIDI plug-in technology described later in this chapter.) There are several versions of Peak: the $500 version, the low-end Peak LE mentioned earlier, and a $200 Peak DV version aimed at creating soundtracks for digital video. The later two don't have the batch-processing ability and lack a lot of the effects of the full version of Peak.

BIAS's other product line, Deck ($400) is a midrange tool for audio production focusing on the recording, mixing, and mastering of music. Rather than waveform editing, Deck works like an old studio tape deck, letting you layer in and mix multiple tracks, and blending the levels together (see Figure 7-8). Where the low-end packages work with stereo, Deck can handle 64 simultaneous tracks for recording and playback. (The high-end packages cost twice as much can handle hundreds of tracks.) The interface features on-screen mixing consoles and other tools that look like their hardware counterparts. There are also features for editing soundtracks for video and sync up video sound effects. If you need to do wave editing, Deck is integrated with Peak and includes a copy of Peak LE. (BIAS also offers bundles of the full-fledged versions of Deck and Peak together.) BIAS also offers a lower-cost, pared-down Deck LE version.

Deck lets you import prerecorded MIDI tracks in sync with audio files, but it doesn't include the MIDI sequencing features of the high-end packages. Deck is also limited to 16-bit audio at sample rates of 44.1KHz or 48 KHz.

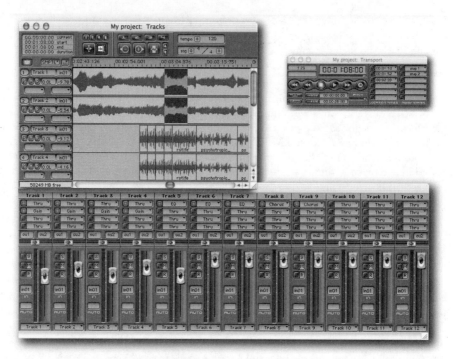

FIGURE 7-8: Deck can record and play back 64 tracks simultaneously, and gives you the tools to mix them.

Mix Master Mac

If you're mixing tunes instead of tracks, check out Fidelity Media's Megaseg (www.megaseg.com, $170) for professional DJ features. You can cross-fade between songs and beatmix between songs, just like a DJ at a nightclub—except that the songs are all stored on the Mac. Megaseg's support for multiple outputs lets you preview a song with headphones while you are playing another song over the speakers. Megaseg also catalogs up to 10,000 songs on your hard drive and lets you create playlists of that length as well. You can even schedule events within playlists, such as the playing of certain songs or messages. Megaseg's cataloging features blow iTunes away. For instance, MegaSeg lets you assign multiple categories to a song and lets you view multiple categories at once using Boolean search options. Searching for music is fast, even with thousands of songs. Megaseg supports AAC files purchased at Apple's Music Store, as well as most other audio formats. And running on Mac OS X, Megaseg is rock solid, enabling pro's to carry it around to gigs on an iBook or PowerBook.

Top-of-the-line Audio Software

At the top end of audio applications are full-feature digital audio workstation packages that can do almost anything that's required. This includes Emagic's Logic Platinum and Steinberg's Cubase. These pro packages offer hundreds of tracks, high-quality sampling, advanced plug-in architectures and file management features, and the ability to route an audio signal between different processing modules in a manner that you determine.

Like high-end audio hardware, high-end recording software blends with MIDI software. That is, the high-end audio packages and the high-end MIDI applications are the same. So, before describing these applications, the next sections will provide details on what MIDI actually is and what you can do with it.

MIDI and Your Mac

You may not realize it, but you encounter MIDI (the Musical Instrument Digital Interface) every day. The music for TV commercials and for many movie scores was created using MIDI instruments and computers. Computer games sometimes use MIDI tracks as background music. If your cell-phone's musical ring plays harmonies (instead of single-tone melodies), then it probably uses MIDI to store and produce the sound. With a MIDI-enabled musical keyboard, you can record a piece of music, move it to a your Mac, edit it, and have it play back with the sound of multiple instruments.

So what is MIDI? Well, it's not a type of digital audio. Although you can use MIDI to connect a Mac to an electronic piano, MIDI is much more than a type of communications port.

At its heart, MIDI is a set of electronic specifications — a *protocol* in computer lingo — that describes music. MIDI is not recorded sound, but a description of everything about a musical performance. MIDI describes the pitch of each note, the intervals between notes, the rhythms, the timing, and the harmonies, the tempos and the keys — and when used with synthesizers, the instrument sounds that play the parts. MIDI also lets you alter any of this, using software on your Mac. On computers, the MIDI information that describes a piece of music can be stored in a MIDI file. MIDI software can also convert this information into musical scores.

MIDI is also a way of communicating between devices that understand the MIDI protocol. This can include musical instruments, synthesizers, drum machines, audio production devices, and computers. Unlike most of these devices, the Mac doesn't have a built-in MIDI port. However, you can add MIDI ports with a box that plugs into your USB port.

You can also think of MIDI as an alternative to audio to use in your compositions. You can mix audio and MIDI content together using sequencing software. And although there is a great deal you can do to tweak digital audio, MIDI is far more editable. Mixing in some MIDI content and adding MIDI effects can add a lot to your music.

Mac OS X and MIDI

Mac OS X makes a Mac a versatile MIDI machine, offering a degree of MIDI integration that Mac OS 9 never had. Starting with version 10.2, Mac OS X includes built-in integration of audio and MIDI functions that were previously provided by multiple, third-party products. Apple refers to these functions inside of Mac OS X as Core Audio and Core MIDI. By having a single system inside the operating system instead of multiple software add-ons that might conflict with each other, Core Audio ensures compatibility between multiple devices and software, simplifies configuration, and provides services to applications. This last bit makes it easier for developers to create software that uses MIDI and audio, and has made possible a large number of low-cost MIDI shareware applications for Mac OS X. Similarly, a large number of hardware drivers are available to make MIDI hardware work with the Mac and be instantly recognized.

Core Audio and Core MIDI makes it easier for you to use different types of MIDI and audio interfaces and devices together. Mac OS X manages the communication between the various tools, and between MIDI and audio. This is the same system that enables Mac OS X's built-in synthesizer to take MIDI commands and output audio — which means that applications (including QuickTime Player) can let you to hear MIDI files or other MIDI data.

If you convert your MIDI data to audio with digital audio workstation software, Core Audio provides digital audio in full 24-bit, 96-KHz resolution, which is the professional audio standard. (Mac OS 9 supported only 16-bit, 44-KHz sampling). Core Audio also can convert files to lower resolutions for applications that need it. Mac OS X also supports multiple channels of audio (Mac OS 9 supported only two).

Core Audio and Core MIDI provide a single user interface to manage multiple MIDI devices connected to your Mac. This is the Audio MIDI Setup utility.

Making MIDI Connections

The standard MIDI connector is called a five-pin DIN connector (see Figure 7-9). You'll find it on electronic pianos, drum machines, and other musical and audio devices. The In and Out ports move MIDI information in and out of the instrument. If you are playing music on a keyboard, the signals go from the instrument to the Mac via the Out port. If you are sending MIDI signal generated on the Mac to be played on the instrument, they would go into the In port. A third port, the Thru port, takes exactly what is entering through the In port, and passes it out unchanged.

FIGURE 7-9: The standard MIDI connector has five pins. MIDI devices often have In and Out ports, and some also have a Thru port.

You may have already seen DIN 5 ports on electronic musical instruments. But if you've ever plugged in anything to your Mac, you know that you won't find a MIDI port there. Fortunately, adding a MIDI port is easy and not necessarily expensive. There are three methods of connecting MIDI devices to your Mac:

- Add a USB-to-MIDI interface connector or box. (FireWire is also available at the higher end.)

- Add a MIDI card to the PCI slot of a Power Mac.

- Use a *MIDI controller*—these are instruments (such as piano keyboards) that can plug directly into your USB port without the need for a MIDI interface box.

There is a wide range of USB-to-MIDI products available. For well under $100, you can get a simple connector with a USB connector on one end and one or two MIDI connectors on the other end (see Figure 7-10). As you go up in price to several hundred dollars, the size of the converter increases to a box, and the number of features grow to include audio in/out ports and manual controls. At the high end, MIDI converter boxes can have multiple audio and MIDI channels, both in and out, and ports for microphones. Sources for MIDI converters include USB Stuff (www.usbstuff.com/roland.html), M-Audio (www.midiman.com/products/midiman/usbmidi.php), and your local musical instrument store.

FIGURE 7-10: For the budget-minded, simple USB-to-MIDI converter cables like the Roland Edirol UM-1S USB to MIDI will do the job without breaking the bank.
Courtesy of Edirol Corporation.

MIDI interface cards for Power Macs are often combined with sound capture functionality—converting analog sound signals into digital audio. With MIDI being a fairly simple interface, the price of these cards usually goes up with the sample rate of the audio capture. Some of the vendors of interface cards include MOTU (www.motu.com) and ST Audio (www.staudio.com).

With a keyboard that is a MIDI controller, you often don't need a MIDI converter interface at all. That's because these keyboards have the MIDI interface built in. Strictly speaking, a MIDI controller doesn't have to generate audio at all—it could output only MIDI signals. However, these days, most MIDI controllers also output audio that could also be connected to a Mac.

These can be very economical, because controllers with small keyboards (such as with 25 keys) start at just over $100. MIDI controllers can also be guitars and other instruments. There are lots of MIDI controllers available, including those from M-Audio (www.midiman.com), Edirol (www.edirol.com), and Evolution (www.evolution.co.uk).

MIDI Drivers

Like other peripherals you can add to your Mac, when you shop for MIDI interface hardware or a MIDI controller, you should make sure that it is compatible with Mac OS X. Often, this means making sure that the vendor has Mac OS X drivers available. The Core Audio of Mac OS X 10.2 and later has made it easy for manufacturers to create MIDI drivers, as is evidenced by the large selection of hardware available to you. These drivers usually come with installer programs to make sure the files are put in the right place. If you are downloading drivers from manufacturers' Web sites, make sure that they are for Mac OS X — drivers for Mac OS 9 won't work.

In Mac OS X, Apple also provides "general class" drivers (stored in /System/Library/Extensions) for USB MIDI devices. This allows the Mac to recognize some MIDI devices without the need to add any drivers. It also enables the Mac to detect the presence of MIDI hardware, just as it does with a digital camera when you connect it to a USB port.

Configure MIDI Devices with the Audio MIDI Setup Utility

Earlier in the chapter, we used the Audio MIDI Setup utility to set the in and out ports of audio devices. You can use the same utility to set MIDI devices connected to your Mac. This time, you'll use the MIDI Devices tab (see Figure 7-11), which presents you with a visual image of the port connections and devices. Audio applications compatible with Mac OS X's Core Audio and Core MIDI will use these settings.

First, connect the MIDI interface to the Mac. Open the Audio MIDI Setup utility (in the /Applications/Utilities/ folder) and click the MIDI Devices tab. You'll see your device as an icon, which you can double-click to name and configure. When you add MIDI devices (such as musical instruments) to the MIDI interface, their icons will show up here. You can specify the connections to the MIDI interface by dragging the output and input tabs of the instrument to the MIDI interface icon.

Mac OS X will recognize when you connect another MIDI device. You can also add a device manually here by clicking the Add Device icon. To view or change settings, double-click a MIDI Device's icon. A new dialog slides down with settings for the device, including which of MIDI's 16 channels are used for transmitting and receiving. (You have to click the More Properties box to expand the dialog to see everything.) You may notice that the fields for Manufacturer and Model are empty (see the top of Figure 7-12). You can enter them here.

You can also change the device's icon in this dialog. Click the icon once, and the dialog changes to one shown in Figure 7-12. Here you can select a new icon for your device. (These images are kept in the file /Library/Audio/Midi Devices/.)

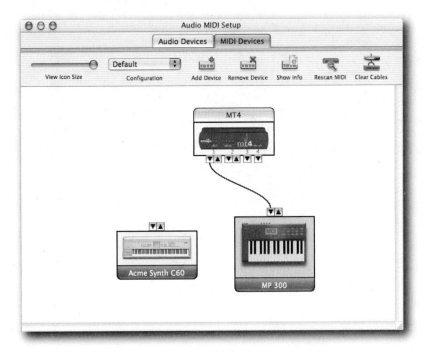

FIGURE 7-11: The MIDI Devices tab of the Audio MIDI Setup utility.

MIDI Files

When you record a performance on a MIDI instrument with your Mac, your MIDI software can save it as a MIDI file. When you play a MIDI file, you are not listening to a recording. You are listening to your Mac recreate the performance based on a set of instructions using a synthesizer. When you stop playing a MIDI file in the middle, the sound doesn't stop immediately — the last chord that was played fades away. Because MIDI files don't have to store digital audio, they are small in size. A 12-minute song can fit in a 72-Kbyte MIDI file. A digital recording of the same song as an MP3 file would take 12 MB.

MIDI files have many uses for musicians. In addition to being used for storing and trading performances, they are also great for practicing or performing when you don't happen to have a band to around to back you up. You can make your own MIDI files or use files created by others. You can find MIDI files on the Internet for free and for sale. Just do a Google search for "MIDI files" and you come up with Web sites such as MIDI Farm (`www.midifarm.com`) and Ifni MIDI (`www.ifni.com`). (For a good selection of J. S. Bach works as MIDI files, see `www.bachcentral.com/midiindex.html`.) Mac OS X's QuickTime can play MIDI files in Web browsers, in Finder previews, and in the QuickTime Player, using its own built-in synthesizer.

There is more about QuickTime's abilities in the section on synthesizers later in this chapter.

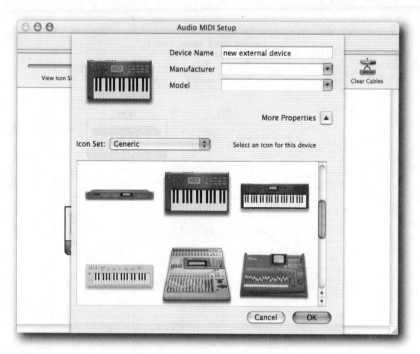

FIGURE 7-12: You can change the icon representing a MIDI device.

MIDI Sequencing

A MIDI *sequencer* is an application that you can use to record your performance of a MIDI keyboard, guitar, drum machine, or other instrument with a MIDI connection. These applications are called sequencers because the MIDI files they create are said to consist of sequences of pitches combined with information such as duration and rhythms and how loud or soft you played them. The sequencer acts like a tape recorder, except with MIDI instead of audio.

There are a variety of uses for sequencers, including composing music, editing soundtracks, and producing recordings. You can use sequencers for creating musical arrangements, experimenting by changing the instruments playing the different parts. You often have the ability to view the notes on a staff and print the chart. A sequencer can also be a practice tool for musicians. If you want to practice one section of a piece, you can have the section loop (repeat).

To recreate your performance (to turn it back into sound), a sequencer uses a synthesizer, either one built into the software or the QuickTime synthesizer of Mac OS X. You can also output the finished MIDI track to external MIDI hardware that has its own library of sounds to use.

A Brief Tour of MIDI Sequencer Software

As with audio software, there is a wide range of sequencers available. For $50, you can get Five12's Numerology (www.five12.com), a MIDI sequencer aimed at performing musicians. It uses modular approach similar to that of traditional analog sequencers. Numerology doesn't include it's own synthesizer, but works with a number of free and shareware synthesizers. A free demo is available at Five12's Web site.

In the midrange of products, Emagic's MicroLogic introduces users to some of the techniques of the pro packages, but for only $100. Master Tracks Pro ($100) from GVOX (www.gvox .com) is a solid MIDI sequencer that records up to 64 tracks. Each line in its track editor window (see Figure 7-13) represents a different MIDI instrument. Storm Music Studio from Arturia (www.arturia.com, $150) is a multifunction studio application that includes MIDI sequencing, though it focuses on synthesizer functions. Sagan Technology's Metro ($319) provides a full-featured MIDI sequencer at a midrange price.

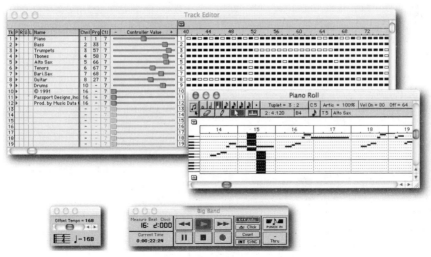

FIGURE 7-13: GVOX's Master Tracks Pro is an affordable MIDI sequencer.

At the professional level, there are the Big Three of sequencer software. These are packages that try to be complete digital audio workstation software, containing top-of-the-line digital audio mixing and production with MIDI sequencing functions. The high-end sequencers let you simultaneously record and play back multiple tracks of MIDI data and digital audio. One of the leaders is Emagic (www.emagic.de), which Apple acquired in 2002. Apple claims that more than half of the American and British top 10 hits are produced with Emagic products, including the Logic Audio product line, which ranges from $400 to $1,000. At the top of that range is the highly rated Logic Audio Platinum, which Apple now describes at its Web site (www.apple.com/software/pro/logic/).

Mark of the Unicorn's MOTU Digital Performer (www.motu.com, $800) is another popular integrated digital audio and MIDI sequencing production system for editing, arranging, mixing, processing, and mastering multitrack projects. The third of the Big Three is Steinberg's Cubase SX (www.steinberg.net, $800). The Big Three differ in their approach to interface, and you will find dedicated users of each.

The rest of this section takes a look at some of the common features of MIDI sequencing software.

MIDI Editing

MIDI enables you to alter the instructions that describe the music to a much greater degree than you can with digital audio. You can change the pitch of a note, the rhythm and duration, and the tempo of the piece. You can replace individual notes or move around entire sections of the piece, often with the standard Cut, Copy, and Paste commands. Transposing the song to a different key is also a standard ability of a sequencer.

You can also add effects, such as chorus and reverb, to specific portions of a piece, and to a higher degree of specificity than you can with digital audio. The more expensive packages have plug-in architectures that let you add effects.

Sequencers provide a method of editing called nondestructive processing, which doesn't make final changes to your tracks until you say so. You can listen to what the changes would sound like without having to first commit to them. This gives you the freedom to experiment with effects and other processing at will.

MIDI Recording Features

Most sequencing software supports MIDI recording in multiple tracks. Low-cost software will offer something on the order of 16 tracks — the professional suites can handle hundreds of tracks. You can use your MIDI instrument to add harmonies or rhythm tracks to previously recorded tracks. If you decide against a track or a portion of a track, a sequencer well let you mute it.

There are several types of MIDI recording. *Real-time recording* captures your performance as you play it. Remember, this isn't audio — your MIDI controller converts your performance to MIDI signals that are sent to your Mac. Real-time recording saves these MIDI signals live, as you generate them.

Another type of MIDI recording, *step recording*, lets you add the MIDI data with your instrument at a slower tempo, or even one note at a time. This is useful if you want to add a part that is too difficult for you to perform. In step recording, use the MIDI sequencer to assign values for the durations of the note. Step recording also works with chords.

If you've just entered a MIDI track through a musical instrument and are not happy with your performance, a feature called *quantizing* can tighten it up. Quantizing can move the start and stop times of notes closer to the beat. Quantizing can also make performances sound more mechanical, however, which is why most sequencers let you set the degree of quantizing. By using this adjustment, you can make a performance sound tighter without sounding stiff.

Digital Sequencing

The process of multitrack MIDI recording described above is traditional MIDI sequencing. Most MIDI sequencing applications include the ability to do another type of sequencing called *digital sequencing*, which records actual (digital) audio tracks along with the MIDI tracks. The source of the audio can include microphone input for vocals or acoustic instruments and audio signals from guitars. The ability for software to mix MIDI and audio is one reason why so many audio capture devices contain both audio and MIDI input.

While MIDI sequencing is often used for composing music, digital sequencing is often used as a production technique in digital audio workstation software. Digital sequencing can turn your Mac into a full recording studio. You aren't able to edit audio as extensively as you can with MIDI, but there is still a great deal you can do with a digital sequencers. For instance, you can tweak the pitch of a note that is a bit out of tune and adjust the timing of a note that came in too early. You can move sections around, as with MIDI, and loop sections. And as with MIDI, you can apply effects to digital audio.

Loop-based Sequencing

Some sequencers don't do traditional MIDI sequencing or editing, but focus on *loop-based sequencing*, also called *sample sequencing*. Loop-based sequencing is a combination of MIDI sequencing and digital sampling. Instead of manipulating individual notes, as with traditional MIDI sequencing and even with digital sequencing, loop-based sequencers work with prerecorded pieces of audio called audio loops or samples.

For instance, you would use several samples of drum and base lines to create the rhythm section, then add tracks with loops of horn sections and synthesizers. Loop sequencers let you match the tempo of the various loops so that you can fit it all together for your composition. You can also change the pitch to follow chord changes. Effects such as chorus and reverb are often available. You can also synch your loop sequencer to a MIDI sequencer or an audio multitrack recorder, or to tape machines. And, you can usually export the finished product as an audio file.

A good example of a loop-based sequencer is Apple's Soundtrack ($300, www.apple.com/ soundtrack). Soundtrack (shown in Figure 7-14) is a part of Apple's Final Cut Pro video suite, and was introduced as a separate package in the summer of 2003. Soundtrack comes with a library of some 4000 royalty-free samples (loops) of different instruments to start you off. (You can also import your own.) File management features let you keep track of your samples. Soundtrack also comes with effects from eMagic and Apple. Soundtrack supports 126 simultaneous tracks.

Another well-respected loop-based sequencer is Live ($400) from Ableton (www.ableton.com) distributed by M-Audio (www.m-audio.com/products/software/ableton/). Live has been around longer than Soundtrack, and its user interface is excellent. You can easily drag and drop loops into tracks and match the tempos, and it has features you can use in a live performance (as the product name implies), such as letting you trigger tracks via a MIDI instrument or the Mac mouse or keyboard.

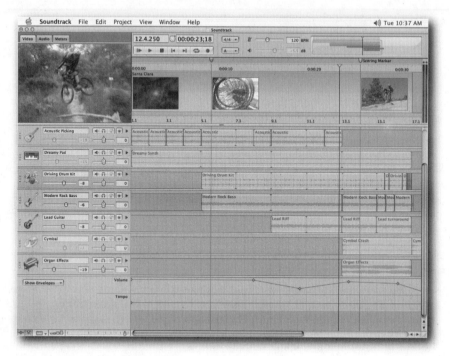

FIGURE 7-14: Apple's Soundtrack is a loop-based sequencer.

VST Plug-ins

Throughout this chapter, we've been referring to VST plug-ins, which is one way to add functionality to an audio or MIDI application. VST plug-ins let you add effects for digital audio and MIDI sounds. For MIDI sequencers, VST plug-ins are a way to add software synthesizers and drum machines to your collection, giving you more sounds to create your music.

VST is short for Virtual Studio Technology, a standard originally created by Steinberg, maker of the high-end Cubase digital workstation. Emagic's Logic Audio also supports VST plug-ins, as do many of the midrange and low-end applications previously mentioned in this chapter. The big exception is Mark of the Unicorn's Digital Performer, which doesn't support VST. Instead, it uses a the company's own standard, called MAS (MOTU Audio System).

Nevertheless, VST plug-in support has become widespread, and plug-ins are available not only from the audio/MIDI application vendors, but from third-party vendors as well. You'll also find free plug-ins available on the Internet. (For instance, DB Audioware, a seller of VST plug-ins, offers free plug-ins at www.db-audioware.com/vstfree.htm.) You may not be able to use every VST plug-in with every piece of software, so check with the manufacturer before purchasing an expensive plug-in.

Synthesizers and Digital Samplers

Since MIDI isn't audio, it doesn't make any noise. In order to hear the music that MIDI describes, your software uses synthesizers and digital samples to create the sound that eventually comes out of your speakers. We mentioned earlier that QuickTime includes a synthesizer, and there are synthesizers available as VTS plug-ins for other audio and MIDI software.

You can also turn your Mac into a powerful synthesizer for recording or performance with standalone synth software. Whether it's creating simple jingles, adding effects to performances, creating techno/dance music, or making symphonic arrangements that sound like movie scores, you can do it on your Mac. However, synthesizers are processor-intensive, so it's good to have a fast Mac.

Synthesizers and Digital Samples

Standalone synthesizer software often includes the ability to use digitized samples. However, technically, a synthesizer is not the same as a digital sampler. A synthesizer creates sounds from scratch. A digital sampler creates sound from recorded samples of a sound that have been digitized.

Synthesizers were originally analog electronic devices, creating sounds from combinations of different types of electronic waves produced by various electronic (analog) modules. Synthesizers are better at creating new sounds, those that you can't produce from nonelectronic musical instruments.

A digital sampler plays back digitized recordings of actual instruments, altered to play at different pitches. A digital sampler is better for recreating realistic sounds of actual musical instruments.

The first electric pianos created synthesized sounds. It was an interesting new sound, but electric piano doesn't really sound like an acoustic piano. Today's digital pianos, however, come much closer to sounding like real acoustic pianos. The number of samples reflects the accuracy of the sound a sampler can reproduce. For instance, one way to sample a trumpet is to take one recording of a trumpet playing middle C, and then digitally alter the note to get all the notes of the scale. However, it will sound more accurate if multiple samples of the instrument are taken at different ranges.

In synthesizer software, you will find both synthesized and digitized sounds, but the difference is worth noting. The higher-end synthesizer software has the ability to let you create your own sounds, while others will only let you modify the sounds that come with the software.

Digital samples can be stored as files, which you can buy and use with your synthesizer software. There are several formats for this, including the popular soundfonts format created by Creative Labs and Emu Systems. There are two formats of soundfont files: DLS files (downloadable sound) that end in the .dls extension, and SoundFont 2 files, which end in the .sf2 extension. Mac OS X's QuickTime supports both.

QuickTime Synthesizer Functions

Mac OS X's QuickTime technology has a basic synthesizer functionality called QuickTime Musical Instruments. It uses 120 instrument sounds licensed from Roland to play MIDI files and MIDI encoded soundtracks attached to QuickTime movies. (Using MIDI in a movie soundtrack instead of audio greatly reduces the file size.)

As is discussed later, there are inexpensive applications that give you access to QuickTime Musical Instruments, letting you play them. You can also add samples to QuickTime to expand its repertoire of synth sounds.

Adding Soundfonts to QuickTime

Since QuickTime 5, you've been able to add DSL and soundfont files to the Mac's built-in library of digital samples. Basically, you can add new sets of sounds and then select them to replace the Roland samples that comes with Mac OS X.

You can buy sets of soundfonts, and free soundfonts are readily available on the Internet. (Try www.Soundfonts.com, www.sseyo.com/soundfonts.html, and www.audiomelody.com/SoundFonts.htm, for starters.)

Soundfonts (either SF2 or DLS files) are bundled as a single package file for a set of instruments, called a *bank*. After you download and decompress the file, place it in this folder in your home folder:

~/Library/Audio/Sounds/Banks

Again, that's in your home folder, not the Library folder at the root level of your hard drive.

Next open System Preferences, click the QuickTime icon, and click the Music tab (as shown in Figure 7-15). Your new soundfont bank will appear in the list. Click one to select it, and click the Make Default button. QuickTime will now use the new soundfont bank of instruments when playing MIDI files.

As is explored in the next section, you can change the individual instruments of this bank or the original Roland samples using QuickTime Pro.

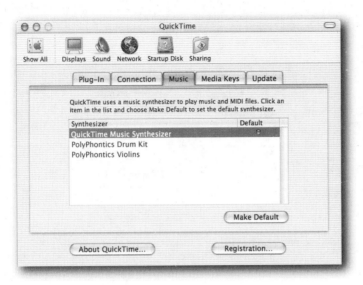

Figure 7-15: After adding several SF2 files, you can select one in
System Preferences.

Changing an Instrument with QuickTime Pro

If you happen to have QuickTime Pro, Apple's $30 upgrade to standard QuickTime
(www.quicktime.com), you can change the instruments that play the parts of a song in a
MIDI file or a movie that has a MIDI soundtrack. Of course, there are much more powerful
MIDI tools than QuickTime Pro, but it does provide an easy way to tweak a MIDI file.
Here's how:

1. With QuickTime Pro installed, open a MIDI file with the QuickTime Player.

2. In the Movie menu select Get Movie Properties.

3. The Properties window has two pop-up menus at the top. In the left menu, select Music
   Track. In the right menu, select Instruments.

4. You then get a list of the synthesized instruments in the song (shown in the left window
   of Figure 7-16). Double-click an instrument, and a New Instrument dialog appears (the
   right window of Figure 7-16).

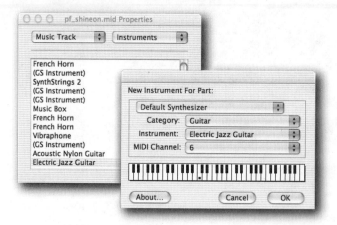

FIGURE 7-16: QuickTime Pro lets you change the instruments of a MIDI file.

5. You now have access to the dozens of instruments that come with QuickTime. The Category pop-up menu lists classes of instruments, such as strings, brass, and guitars. You can choose a new category or let the selected category remain.

6. From the Instrument pop-up, select a new instrument. The MIDI Channel pop-up channel lists which of 16 channels the instrument is assigned to.

7. To hear what the selected instrument sounds like, click on the piano keys at the bottom of the window.

8. Click OK when you're finished.

You can change as many instruments as you like. When you play the MIDI file with QuickTime Player, it will have a different sound.

Inexpensive Synthesizer Software

There's not a lot you can do with QuickTime as far as synthesizing goes. However, for little or no money, you can expand QuickTime's synth capabilities by accessing QuickTime synthesizer for purposes other than playing MIDI files.

SimpleSynth (http://pete.yandell.com/software/) is a free synthesizer program that lets you play QuickTime, DLS, and soundfont samples from a MIDI keyboard or other MIDI instrument connected to your Mac. SimpleSynth is simple to use—just plug in your MIDI interface and launch SimpleSynth. You can switch to a SF2 or DLS files by clicking the Open button and choosing your file. And you change individual instruments.

Melonsoft's PianistEnvy ($5, www.melonsoft.com/products/pianistenvy/) lets you play music via point and click or on your Mac keyboard using QuickTime's 120 instruments. You can manipulate notes with controls for press, duration, and octave. PianistEnvy also can record and play back your work.

A similar but far more sophisticated application is Cider Factor Software's iPiano ($25, www.machotshot.com/iPiano) also lets you play notes on the Mac keyboard using the QuickTime synthesizer. However, iPiano can also accept MIDI input from MIDI instruments and output MIDI to other music applications. It can also save MIDI, AIFF, and QuickTime files. Even better, iPiano can let you record pieces in up to 16 tracks and mix them. iPiano doesn't use the standard time-line display of a MIDI sequencer, but you can mix in real time. The interface is simple (shown in Figure 7-17), along the lines of iTunes and iMovie, and is a great starting place for the people to start playing with Mac synthesizers.

If you want to spend a little more money, you create your own individual sounds. For instance, PolyPhontics from Best Software Design ($60, www.bestsoftwaredesign.com) is a digital sample editor that lets you save samples in SF2 and DLS formats.

Midrange and Pro Synthesizer Software

As previously mentioned, there are synthesizer functions in the top digital audio workstation software, such as Cubase, Logic Audio Platinum, and Digital Performer. But for musicians who are serious about turning their Macs into musical instruments, there are serious standalone synthesizer applications. These applications also require some fast Macs, because they use a lot of processing power.

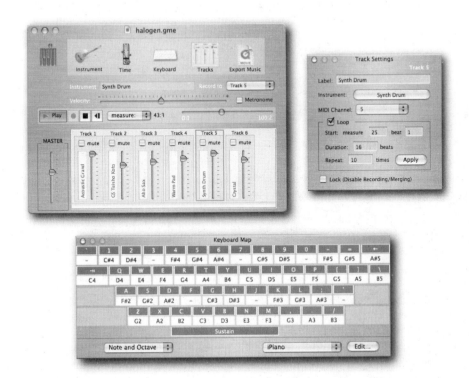

FIGURE 7-17: iPiano uses the Mac's built-in synthesizer sounds to do performance and multitrack recording.

Moving up to the midrange and above, the tools begin to cater more to professional musicians, using interfaces that replicate synthesizer hardware. They also go beyond playing digital samples, and can synthesize new sounds from scratch. Arturia Storm Music Studio ($150, www.arturia.com/en/storm2.lasso) is an affordable package that lets you drag together real-looking modules — synthesizers, drum machines, and a sequencer for recording. There are 23 modules in total. Storm produces excellent sound as well. It's not as flexible as the high-end packages, however. For instance, you can't save specific patches to use in different pieces. But for the price, Storm is a good value.

Native Instruments' Absynth ($300, www.native-instruments.com) uses a combination of sampling and synthesis to produce sounds, and lets you mix the techniques, enabling users to get a wide variety of sound out of the program. You can even create waveforms by hand. Absynth comes with over 800 presets to get composers started.

At the top of the heap is Reason from Propellerhead Software (www.propellerheads.se, $400) a professional software synthesizer package that produces sound equal to hardware synths. In fact, its interface resembles a rack full of equipment (Figure 7-18), except that you don't have to wire it all together. If you know your way around professional synth hardware, you can create any configuration you need — start with multiple synthesizers, digital samplers, and drum machines, then add some effects modules, a mixer, and others. Reason also includes a real-time sequencer. Reason displays the devices in a scrolling window, to which you can keep adding. The only limit is the speed of your Mac. There is also endless flexibility, allowing a pro musician to do just about anything. Professionals swear by Reason, because it actually enables a studio to replace a rack full of equipment with a PowerBook, and get the same results. The Propellerhead Web site offers a collection of MP3 files of professional electronic music created with Reason — reason enough to visit the site.

Classic Synth Simulators

Remember the Moog synthesizer on the cover of Switched on Bach? You can now reproduce the late-1960s Moog V synthesizer on your Mac's screen, right down to the patch cables between the modules and wood grain finish of the cabinet. And it works. Arturia created Moog Modular V ($330, www.arturia.com/en/moogmodular.lasso) with the help of Robert Moog, the famous synthesizer pioneer. Arturia's Moog Modular V isn't a set of digital samples of the sounds the famous Moog made, but a set of emulations of the old analog hardware modules, including oscillators, triggers, envelops, and filters. The modules work together to produce sound, just as in the original. Although you can patch together the modules yourself with on-screen patch cables, you don't have to, as the software comes with preset patches.

If you're interested in sounds of the 1980s, check out Propellerhead's ReBirth ($160, www. propellerheads.se/products/rebirth/), which emulates the classic Roland TB-303 bass machine and Roland TR-808 and TR-909 rhythm machines. The sampled sounds of these old analog workhorses are common enough, but the actual units are expensive collectors items. ReBirth emulates the actual Roland hardware as well as some other modules of the era. Which means ReBirth not only sounds like the real thing, but works like it.

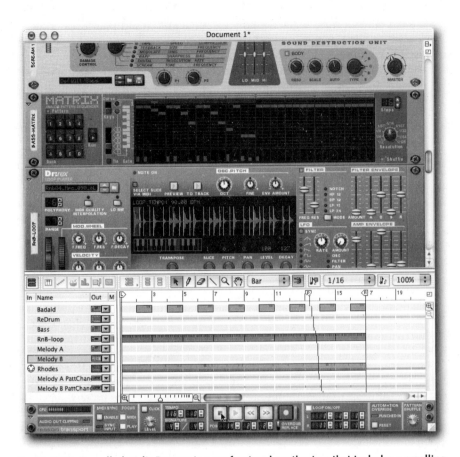

FIGURE 7-18: Propellerhead's Reason is a professional synthesizer that includes a scrolling rack of synthesizers and other equipment.

Musical Notation Software

Like synthesizers, musical notation is a feature of many sequencers. However, you can also find standalone applications specializing in creating musical scores. These packages are creative tools, helping you compose and arrange sheet music.

With Music notation software, MIDI input and output is standard. MIDI input lets you use musical notation software like a word processor, using your piano keyboard instead of the Mac keyboard to put notes on a page instead of words. In fact, notation software will often install fonts to use in representing the notes. You can also create and edit notation with the Mac keyboard and mouse, though the techniques to do this vary widely, and probably make up the biggest differences between the different packages. Most notation applications will also let you type in lyrics and have them match the rhythms on the page. And, of course, printing of your score is a standard feature. You can use MIDI output to play back an arrangement you've created, with the instrument sounds you're intending to use. Beethoven may have been able to compose without hearing his compositions, but for the rest of us, playback is a great feature.

To decide on software best for you, take a look at the features list of the major packages to see if it's missing anything you need. For instance, if you don't need more than eight voices per staff, Ars Nova's $95 SongWorks (www.ars-nova.com/songworks.html) is an economical way to go. It includes some helpful features, such as suggesting chords to go with your melodies, or vice versa.

NoteAbilityPro ($225, http://debussy.music.ubc.ca/~opus1/NoteAbility/NAwelcome.html) is unusual in that it isn't from a software company, but is a package created by Dr. Keith Hamel at the University of British Columbia. NoteAbilityPro has some unique features that you might not find in even higher-priced software, such as the ability to do MIDI steptime recording, and it does have unique interface. It is geared toward classical music, so adding guitar chords is not easily done.

Moving up towards the high end, Gvox' Encore ($400, www.gvox.com) supports up to 64 separate staves per score. Like other professional packages, Encore can transcribe to different keys. Unfortunately, Gvox does not offer a demo version to let you try it out.

The top staff of musical notation is Sibelius ($600, www.sibelius.com) from Sibelius Software, a tool written for composers and arrangers. A contender for the top spot is Finale ($600) from Coda Music (www.codamusic.com). At publishing time, there was still no Mac OS X-native version of Finale, though one was expected some time in 2004. Finale is not as easy to use, however. Sibelius (named after the nineteenth/twentieth-century Finnish composer Jean Sibelius) attempts to stay out of your way as you compose. There are a minimum of mouse clicks, navigating of menus, and selection of icons. As shown in Figure 7-19, the musical score takes up most of the screen and is what Sibelius focuses on.

Lyrics, At Last

Rogers had Hart, Sullivan had Gilbert, Jerry Garcia had Robert Hunter. If you are your own lyricist, you can have MasterWriter ($289, www.masterwriter.com). MasterWriter includes a full-function word processor with a big set off tools for crafting words. For instances, there are two rhyming dictionaries. One lets you find a rhyme for a word, when you specify the number of syllables you need. Another returns rhyming phrases—type in "shoes" and get phrases like "cultural taboos" and "enchanted by the muse." There's also a dictionary of common phrases that use your word of choice, and a dictionary of alliterations (remember nattering nabobs of negatism?). Here again, you can search by the number of syllables, as you can in the pop culture dictionary—dozens of categories of people, places, foods, and events, both real and fictional. MasterWriter also includes 33,000 sayings, clichés, and other word combinations.

The Songs module is where you actually type your lyrics, but you can do much more than that. The Audio subsections lets you lay down a basic drum track and record sound, for those times when you think you've got a melody fragment or two that you want to save. You also get a 1-year subscription to Songuard, an online song registration service.

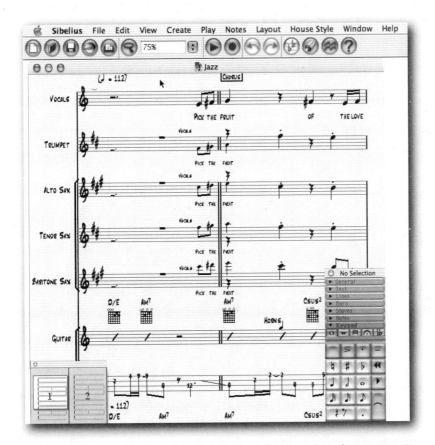

FIGURE 7-19: Sibelius provides a handy toolbar and floating palette for accessing its notation-editing features. It also offers several styles of notation, such as the jazz style shown here.

You can start a composition with a blank staff or choose one of several dozen of Sibelius's pre-set blank scores, including rock bands, jazz, vocal, and several types of orchestral scores. Enter notes from a MIDI instrument or with the mouse and Mac keyboard. Pop-up contextual menus and a floating palette make it easy. Sibelius also offers powerful tools that actually assist you in composing and arranging. For instance, an auto-arrange tool will let you take your piano part, copy it into an orchestral score, and then take a guess at the best arrangement for an orchestra. You can then edit it from there.

Sibelius supports several styles of notations that you can display and print, including traditional, avante garde, TAB, and jazz. Sibelius's MIDI playback is also easy and powerful, including several performance modes, such as espressivo and rubato, which vary the tempo of a performance, as in classical piano, or can give it a bit of a swing feel, useful in jazz. You can download a demo version from the Sibelius Web site.

The Ultimate Mac Recording Studio

What would an ultimate Mac-based home music studio look like? The fact that you *can* do everything on the Mac in software — create, record, mix, and produce music — doesn't mean you wouldn't want any hardware. The ultimate Mac-based recording studio would be connected to lots of other equipment. Since there is a lot of hardware available, an almost endless selection is possible. Figure 7-20 shows a generic studio configuration that could be expanded upon.

■ **The Mac.** In this configuration, the recording and mastering is being done on the Mac, with maybe a software synthesizer or two thrown in for fun. Because of this, you'll want the fastest Mac available, a top-of-the-line dual processor Power Mac G5 filled with memory. If it's a portable studio you're after, there's no reason you couldn't use a PowerBook instead. You may have to cut down a bit on the CPU-gobbling synthesizers, though, to avoid a latency problem — a delay between what you record and when you hear it.

Doing so much of these functions in software on a Mac can save tens of thousands of dollars or more over the hardware. And considering that renting professional studio time can cost $1,000 a day, the Mac and all the software can pay for themselves in a week or two. This is one of the reasons the audio software industry has been growing so rapidly since Mac OS X enabled high-quality audio and MIDI functions to work on a Mac.

■ **MIDI interface.** The MIDI interface provides the MIDI In and MIDI Out ports to various musical instruments and other MIDI devices. The MIDI interface in Figure 7-20 is USB, but there are also FireWire devices. As mentioned earlier, many MIDI interfaces also have audio. But you're going for separate MIDI and audio devices in this ultimate setup.

■ **Audio mixer.** The purpose is similar to the MIDI interface, but with audio signals. This mixer takes the various audio signals from instruments, a microphone, and from the Mac, and routes them to the Mac to the speakers, so that you can hear what you are recording. For the recording on the Mac, each audio source will be kept in a separate track. The audio connections could also be digital audio. Some mixers have slider controls for controlling levels, but this isn't a requirement. For instance, Digidesign's $10,000 ProTools HD Digital I/O (24 bit, 192 KHz) uses the software level mixers in the ProTools software running on the Mac. Of course, you don't need to spend near that much. The ProTools HD sends digital audio to the Mac via a PCI card.

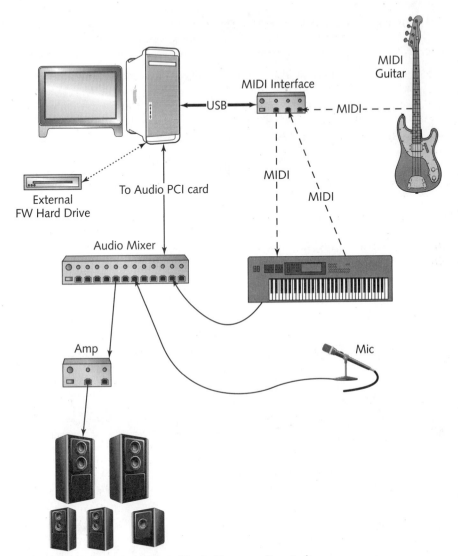

FIGURE 7-20: One version of the ultimate Mac recording studio.

- **Keyboard MIDI controller.** There are a number of connections here, but the most important is the MIDI out to the Mac. This lets you record what you're playing. You may want MIDI in from the Mac to be able to have the software trigger events on your keyboard. And you can have audio out to have the option of recording audio instead of MIDI.

- **MIDI guitar.** This only has a MIDI out port going to the Mac. Its output is mixed with audio signals in the sequencer software.

- **External FireWire hard drive.** Storing your work on an external hard drive dedicated to the task has several advantages. It keeps your work portable, enabling you to move it to other Macs. It's also a bit safer to have it on a drive separate from the operating system.

- **Microphone.** A good quality microphone and good placement is important for high-quality vocal recordings. With your sequencing software, you can lay down multiple vocal tracks yourself, and edit out and rerecord small parts where you might have hit the wrong note or sang the wrong word.

- **Other possibilities.** One or more hardware synthesizers or drum machines could be added. You might have MIDI out coming from the Mac to trigger events on the synthesizer, and then audio out from the synthesizer to the mixer. You could also add other MIDI instruments, including wind instruments, into the mix.

 Note Want to see how the pros are using Macs? At its Creative Professionals site (www.apple.com/creative/), Apple has stories on how rock stars and movie soundtrack composers are using Macs. The site describes their hardware and software configurations.

Summary

As you can see, the term "music software" can mean a lot of things. This chapter has been an introduction to these worlds. There are two big, different parts: digital audio and MIDI. Each has a set of techniques and software available for creation, recording, and editing. Mac OS X's built-in support for both high-quality digital audio and MIDI makes it easy to use various hardware and software tools together.

Much of the higher-priced software is geared toward professional musicians. For them, the user interfaces get easier as the price tag goes up. For the hobbyist, the user interfaces of the high-end software may seem baffling, and the lower-cost software may better meet their needs.

If you're looking for one place to download freeware and shareware, and demo versions of the more expensive software, go to this Apple page: www.apple.com/downloads/macosx/audio/

Here, you'll find much of the software mentioned in this chapter, plus more we couldn't get to.

Two other chapters in this book describe more focused audio projects. Chapter 2 shows you how to create your own Internet radio station, and Chapter 9covers converting vinyl LPs to audio CDs.

Turn Your Mac into a Classic Video Game Machine

A few years before the Mac rolled out of Cupertino another computer revolution hit game arcades, pool halls, and bars. Pinball machines were making way for a new type of arcade game with names like *Space Invaders*, *Pac-Man*, and *Donkey Kong*. They were called "video games" because you locked your gaze on what appeared to be a television screen. In fact, these were the first computer monitors that the general public saw.

The first video arcade game, Nolan Bushnell's Computer Space of 1971, was a commercial flop. Instead of giving up, Bushnell created Atari and released the first commercially successful game, *Pong*. By 1982, players were dropping $5 billion worth of quarters into video games each year.

The arcade games of the late 1970s and 1980s were primitive by today's technological standards (see Figure 8-1). They were at first black and white, then had a few colors and only small portions of the screen moving at any one time. This was a hardware limitation — at that time computers had less processing power than today's iPod.

Yet, there is still a certain appeal to the first video arcade games. The creators of these classic games came up with innovative designs that didn't depend on technology, but were captivating and engaging. They were based on simple, abstract concepts that were creative and fun.

You can play these very same classic games on your Mac. It takes some free software pulled together from different sources. The hardware you use is up to you. You can play with your standard Mac, or you can add some control hardware to make the games easier to play. Or, you can go all out and recreate the classic video game experience by recreating the hardware of 20 years ago. We'll take a look at some of the options.

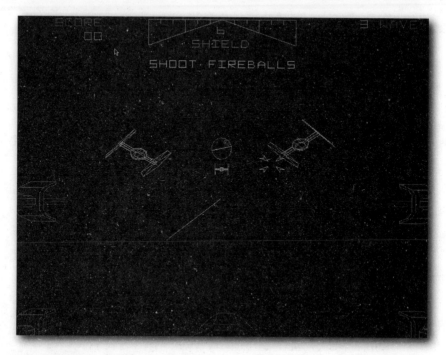

FIGURE 8-1: Atari *Star Wars* was a popular arcade game in 1983 that featured sound bites from the 1977 movie.

Not familiar with some of the classic arcade games? Check out our Top 10 Classic Games list at the end of this chapter.

Rescued from Extinction

Although you still occasionally see *Ms. Pac-Man* (the sequel to the less-successful original), classic arcade games have for the most part disappeared, a victim of advancing computer technology. In the 1990s, new games with full-motion, 3-D action and complex sound replaced games like *Frogger*, *Star Wars*, and *Tron* in the arcades. The old games were sold for scrap. Some went into private collections, and used replacement parts become rarer every year.

Classic arcade games would be historical footnotes, written about but never again experienced, were it not for dedicated fans who also happened to be software programmers. In the 1990s they bought old game cabinets and opened them up, curious as to what made the first generation of computer gaming tick. They extracted the software, analyzed the hardware, and began porting the games to personal computers.

The most notable contribution came from Italian programmer Nicola Salmoria. In 1996, he created several programs that let you play various classic arcade games on a PC running DOS.

The next year, he combined these into a single program he called the Multiple Arcade Machine Emulator, or MAME. Since then, dozens of programmers from around the world have contributed to the MAME project, making it the major software platform for preserving classic arcade games. Today, MAME supports more games than any other program of its type. At last count, 2,100 different games were partially or fully supported. MAME has been ported to many computer platforms, including Macintosh. The Mac version is called MacMAME, and it can run hundreds of different games (see Figure 8-2).

Both MAME and MacMAME are noncommercial, free, open source programs. The programmers who continue to create new versions of MAME are volunteers from all over the world. Their preservation and resurrection of dead arcade games formed the basis of today's computer gaming industry.

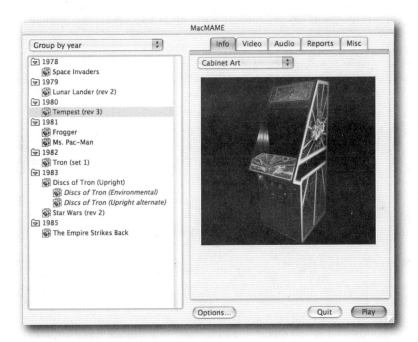

FIGURE 8-2: MacMAME lets you run multiple classic arcade games in Mac OS X or in Mac OS 9.

Jobs and Woz in Gaming

Mac ties to arcade games go back farther than MacMAME. In fact, Steve Jobs and Steve Wozniak were involved in the arcade game revolution right at the beginning. Woz helped Steve Jobs (who was then Atari employee number 40) write Breakout, one of the first popular arcade games, released in 1976. This might have something to with why Apple chose to include a version of Breakout on the iPod.

MAME is not your average application. Most software, including game software, is designed for specific hardware—you can't move a program around between different computers as you can a Word file. MAME is an *emulator*—a special piece of software that lets you take programs that were designed for one particular computer platform and run them on a completely different computer platform.

An emulator is a bit like the Matrix from the movies of the same name, in that it creates a false world in software. Living in this false world is the arcade game, which thinks it is residing inside of an arcade game box, running on the processor and interacting with the hardware subsystems it was designed for. This is, of course, a fiction—the game is actually running on your Mac and its PowerPC processor. The emulator provides the native stimulus and feedback that the game software needs, and accepts the output to display the graphics and sound.

As an emulator, MAME is similar in concept to Virtual PC (originally from Connectix, now owned by Microsoft). Virtual PC allows your Mac to run various versions of the Windows operating system and Windows software. Virtual PC emulates a Pentium processor and runs Windows, a large and complex operating system. MAME emulates multiple processors, each of which is far simpler and slower than a Pentium, running operating environments that are the fraction of size and complexity of Windows. So although PC games in Virtual PC appear sluggish on all but the very fastest Macs, games in MacMAME can run pretty much as fast and smooth as they did in the old arcades.

Whether you're running Windows in Virtual PC or *Donkey Kong* in MAME, the beauty of an emulator is that you don't have to make any changes to the original software. The emulator takes care of all the differences in hardware and operating systems. The same games will run on versions of MAME for Windows, Mac OS X, Linux, and other operating systems.

Homage in an Icon

MacMAME

The MacMAME icon depicts an original Mac turned into an arcade machine. On the screen is another icon, a space invader from the legendary 1978 game. *Space Invaders* was the first mainstream hit video game, the first to move outside of arcades and into shopping malls and diners. It was created by Taito, Inc. of Japan, and licensed by Bally/Midway, which also built cabinets. In 1980, Atari licensed *Space Invaders* for its home system. Since then, there have been many versions built for multiple platforms. The original black and white version runs on MacMAME.

Installing MacMAME

The MAME organization is headquartered at www.mame.com, the worldwide center of MAME activities for the programmers. That's where they post the core MAME code updates, seek volunteer programmers, and share information. However, MacMAME is maintained by another group at www.macmame.org. The MacMAME group takes the core MAME code updates and ports them to the Mac. (To make things more confusing, there is another site called www.macmame.net, which provides news and information, but does not offer MacMAME itself.)

To download MacMAME, go to www.macmame.org and click Downloads. On this page, you'll find versions of MacMAME for different languages (English, French, and Italian). MacMAME is a small download, about 4.1 MB in size for the Mac OS 9 version, 8.5 MB for the Mac OS X version.

On the MacMAME.org download page, you'll see a section of optional "plug-in" files. These have mostly to do with graphics acceleration. Most of them are for specific graphics cards. However, at the time of this writing, most of these had not yet been ported from Mac OS 8/9 to Mac OS X. These are labeled "Not compatible with Mac OS X." (If you don't know what graphics card is installed in your Mac, you can check with Apple System Profiler.) However, there is one file that every Mac OS X user should download, the OpenGL plug-in. This small (100 KB) file will help with performance games that use 3-D.

You can ignore the items labeled "source" unless you want to look at the source code of MacMAME and the plug-ins.

Installing MacMAME is simple. The downloaded file is a .sit archive that you can decompress with StuffIt Expander. (A double-click should do it.) Drag the decompressed MacMAME folder to your Applications folder.

Upgrading MacMAME

The MacMAME group doesn't provide updaters. If you are updating an older version of MacMAME, you'll have to do an update manually. Start by installing the new version on the desktop. Then move all of your needed configuration files from the old MacMAME folder into the new MacMAME folder. These files will reside in various subfolders, as described in the next section. (You can also move the older folders into the new MacMAME folder.) When you are finished, delete your old version and move the new MacMAME folder into our Applications folder. Be sure to check out the readme file that comes with the new version—if the new version is a major upgrade, there may be additional steps required.

Setting up MacMAME

Although MacMAME is fairly easy to get up and running, its setup is a bit different than most Mac applications. When you open the MacMAME folder, you'll see the MacMAME application, a readme file, and over a dozen folders (see Figure 8-3), most of which are empty to start with. The setup process is mostly a matter of dropping files into the appropriate folder. When you start using MacMAME, the emulator itself will create files in some of the MacMAME subfolders.

FIGURE 8-3: Inside the MacMAME folder.

First, put any of the graphics plug-in files you downloaded in the Plugins folders. The games aren't distributed with MacMAME — you have to get them yourself. When you do have them, the game files go into the folder called "Roms." (There's more about the games in the following sections.)

The Documentation folder comes with a lot of text and HTML files, user guides, and various readme files. It's good to take a look through the *User Guide*. Once again, at the time of this writing, much of the material in these files had not been updated for Mac OS X. This means that some of the information may not apply to your system.

Several MacMAME subfolders can contain graphics related to games — screenshots, photos of the original cabinets, and original promotional fliers from the game. These can often be found at the Web sites that offer games in the form of .png files (which you can view with a Web browser or Mac OS X's Preview application). When the art is in the appropriate folder, MacMAME will display it when you select the art Category. For instance, you'll notice in Figure 8-2 that Cabinet Art is selected in the pop-up menu at the right, and the original cabinet for *Tempest* is displayed. Figure 8-4 shows the screenshot item from the pop-up.

Tip

For photos of the original cabinets of many historically important games, see www.videotopia .com/games.htm.

Having screenshots installed in the Screenshots folder can be useful in helping you locate a game. With the pop-up menu at right to Screenshots, you can see what the different games look like as you click through the game list at left. If you don't have the art installed, MacMAME will display "None Found" on the right side.

MacMAME also lets you take your own screenshots of running games—just use the Command-G key combination. (The normal Mac Command-Shift-3 and –4 won't work when a game is playing.) This will create a .png file, which you can put in the Screenshots folder. Just be sure not to change the name of the screenshot.

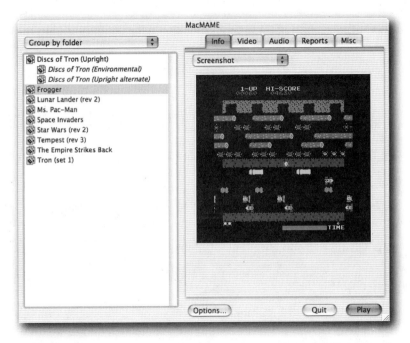

FIGURE 8-4: You can view any game screenshots that you have installed when the Screenshot item is selected in the right pop-up menu.

Installing Games in MacMAME

The classic arcade game files that run on MAME are called *ROMs*, short for read-only memory. The name comes from the sets of ROM chips inside the arcade game console that store the game software. Each game in the classic period typically contained a dozen or so ROM chips. The games were extracted from the ROM chips and put in personal computer files. All of the ROM code for any given game is contained in a single .zip file.

Before we describe installing game files in MacMAME, we need to discuss the important issue of digital rights.

ROMs and Copyright

Unlike the MAME emulator itself, the ROMs are not open source software, but are technically owned by the original manufacturers of the old arcade games. For many of the games, you have to already own the game console, or own the actual ROM chips, in order to avoid violation of copyright law when you run them.

The digital rights issue with arcade games is similar to that of music files. You can buy a CD and create your own MP3 files, and move them onto your iPod. However, if you post the files on the Internet, you are facilitating copyright infringement.

There is a difference, however. With digital music, it is easy to be in compliance with copyright law — usually, you can go buy the CD or the digital file from the iTunes Music Store or some other service. With classic arcade games, compliance is not easy, because most of the original manufacturers don't offer the ROM files or the old ROM chips for sale. You could buy an original motherboard on eBay or at other auctions, but many games aren't easy to find.

Does playing a 25-year old game that is no longer available constitute a breach of digital rights? Technically, yes. However, some copyright infringements are perhaps worse than others. For instance, some of the games that run in MAME are not so old, dating from the 1990s, while others are available as computer games or for home game systems. Playing these games can be said to directly affect the income of the holders of the licenses. (Newer games will also have more sophisticated graphics that will be more taxing on your Mac, and thus might not be as enjoyable to play, at least on slower Macs.)

However, the biggest no-no is attempting to sell ROM files. Even if you extract the ROM code yourself, selling these files is a clear act of software piracy that will bring the wrath of lawyers upon you. To sum up, let's just say that downloading ROMs is a murky area at best, and you should use your best judgment.

Locating ROMS

There is no copy protection in the ROM files to prevent you from running the game, just the knowledge that you are infringing on copyright — it's an honor system. Web sites that offer ROMs as a download will sometimes make you promise that you already have the ROMs for the files you download.

Because of the controversy and legal threats, it is not uncommon for sites to stop offering ROM downloads, and for new sites to appear. Here are some of the sites that offered ROMS at the time of writing:

- **www.mame.net/downmisc.html.**   The official MAME site (not the MacMAME site) offers three lesser-known games from the 1980s. The owners of the copyrights have given their permission for these ROM files to be distributed.

- **www.mame.dk.**   This site has seems to alternate from being available to not, but has a large database of classic arcade games with a handy search engine and the best repository of information about the games. You can even search by year. Each entry has a description of the game and lots of technical details. Mame.dk is also the best source for game ROM files. However, in order to download ROMS, you have to sign up for a free account and login. (If you don't login, you don't get a link to the ROM files.) You can also download .png files that contain pictures of the original cabinets, flyers, and the marquee.

- **www.classicgaming.com/vault/.**   This page doesn't have the information of mame.dk or the selection of ROMs, but it doesn't require a login. It also isn't updated as often as mame.dk, so it could contain ROMs that haven't been updated for more recent versions of MAME.

- **www.gamearchive.com/Video_Games/Manufacturers/.**   On this page, you see a list of four game manufacturers. Click one of these links to get to games.

When all else fails, search for MAME at google.com.

Installing ROMs in MacMAME

Once you download a game, you should have a .zip archive containing a set of files. Each file inside the archive represents a ROM chip in the original game. DO NOT decompress the .zip file — drop the entire .zip archive into the Roms folder inside the MacMAME folder. MacMAME works best when the games are kept as .zip archives.

With the ROM .zip file in the Roms folder, MacMAME will display the game in the game list on the left side. The pop-up menu on the left side lets you display the games by year, as shown in Figure 8-5, or as a simple list (By Folder), as shown in Figure 8-4, by Manufacturer, or by Genre (Maze, Shooter, and so forth).

We've seen some of the choices for the right pop-up menu earlier in this chapter that display cabinet art and screenshots. This menu also will display information about a game that is selected in the left column. One selection you should check after installing ROMs is Mini Audit, shown in Figure 8-5. This will tell you if your .zip archive for the selected game contains all of the ROMs. In Figure 8-5, it tells us that we are missing the last ROM file for the 1979 game *Lunar Lander*. It also tells us that there is no known version of the file. This tells us that the game won't operate properly. (In fact, *Lunar Lander* will launch, but won't let you burn thrusters to the right or to the left, a serious flaw indeed.)

What, No *Pong*?

You won't find ROM files for the original 1972 *Pong* at any Web site. Any *Pong* you find has been recreated. That's because *Pong* did not use ROM, so doesn't have ROM files. (ROM chips were first introduced in 1974's *Tank* from Atari.) *Pong* didn't need storage because it didn't have any graphics to speak of—just two white lines representing ping-pong paddles, and a white dot representing a ball. *Pong* also didn't use a microprocessor. Without a microprocessor to emulate or a ROM to extract code, there is nothing to run on MAME (or MacMAME).

By the way, although Pong is notable for being the game that launched the video gaming industry, it was not entirely created by Nolan Bushnell and Atari. Pong's roots go back to the 1958, when physicist Willy Higinbotham created a Pong-like game called Tennis for Two for the entertainment of engineers at Brookhaven National Laboratory. The game was displayed on oscilloscopes.

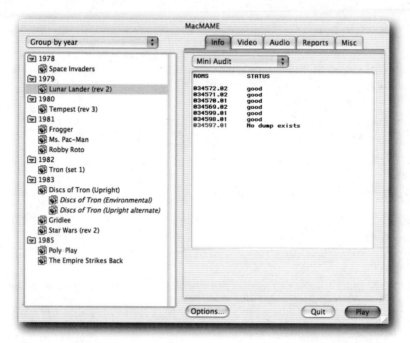

FIGURE 8-5: The Mini Audit view shows you the status of your ROM files.

Tip

If you upgrade Mac OS X after you install MacMAME, MacMAME may no longer see the ROMs. To fix this, go to MacMAME's "config" folder. Drag the "default.cfg" file to the Trash. Then throw away the MacMAME preference file. In Mac OS X, it's called "MacMAME Prefs" and is located in this folder: /Users/yourname/Library/Preferences/.

Configuring Game Sound

For some games, you may need to place additional sound files in the Sound Samples folder of the MacMAME folder. For these games, some or all of the sounds have not been emulated. These games use the additional digitally sampled files to play some of the game sounds.

If you are playing a game and you think it is missing some sounds for certain actions or between levels, chances are you need some sound files. You can get sound samples at the official MAME site (www.mame.net/downsamples.html). Not all games use sound files, however. If your game isn't listed on this page, then it doesn't need sound sample files.

MacMAME has a few sound settings in the Audio tab on the right side of its window (see Figure 8-6). These settings apply to all games, not just the selected games. You have a choice of three sample rates, 11025 Hz, 22050 Hz, and 44100 Hz. The last is the highest quality, but may slow down performance. If you are having performance problems with a game and quitting other applications or the Classic environment doesn't help, try lowering the sample rate.

You'll also find a setting called Emulate FM. This can improve sound for certain games by enabling MacMAME to emulate special FM sound chips. However, this setting can reduce performance.

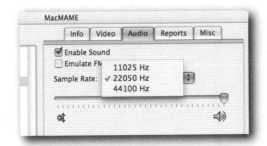

FIGURE 8-6: MacMAME's sound settings.

Video Settings

You may notice that some old games (such as *Pac Man*, *Frogger*, and *Tron*) appear in a tiny rectangle at the center of your screen. That's because these games were pixel-based (raster) games set as small as 256 × 256 pixels, the resolution of the displays in the late 1970s and early 1980s. The MacMAME Video tab gives you the option of enlarging these games, via the top pop-up menu (see Figure 8-7). Here, you have a choice of Actual Size, Double Size, and Triple Size. Double size draws 4 pixels for every one pixel of the original. Triple Size draws 9 pixels for every one original pixel. For a 256 × 256 pixel game, Triple Size fills the screen of a 15" (1024 × 768) display.

Vector games (such as *Star Wars* and *Lunar Lander*) are not based on a pixel width and will fill the entire screen regardless of what size you have set.

This top menu also gives you the options called "Double Size with Scan Lines" and "Triple Size with Scan Lines." These options remove every other line (or every third line) to simulate the low quality of the early-1980s arcade game monitors.

The lower of the two pop-up menus lets you change the bit depth of the color. For older games, 16-bit (or 64,000 colors) is more than enough. More modern games will need 32-bit (millions of colors), but this will slow things down.

The settings at the bottom half of the video tab apply to vector games. These settings work differently from the ones above them, in that you need to have vector game selected. Most of these exist to simulate the low-quality arcade monitors of the early 1980s. Anti-aliasing makes the lines fuzzier, but uses processing power, so it can slow down game play. Flicker adds, well, flicker, but also uses processing power. Moving the Beam Width slider to the right makes lines fatter.

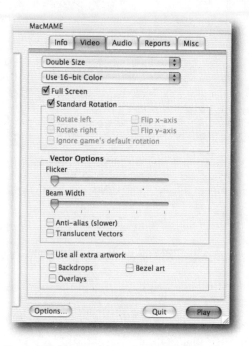

FIGURE 8-7: The most important of MacMAME's video settings is the top pop-up menu, which lets you enlarge games that appear small on screen.

Playing Games

To start a game, just double-click its name in the game list in the MacMAME window. Your screen goes black except for a box that tells you some facts about the game and its original hardware (see Figure 8-8). Pressing a key will bring up the game screen as you would have seen it in the arcade.

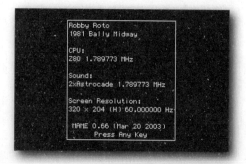

FIGURE 8-8: The first screen that comes up presents information about the game and the hardware it ran on.

Load the Game

There are some differences between playing games on an arcade cabinet and playing on your Mac. For one, your Mac doesn't have a place to insert quarters. Your Mac also doesn't have big red buttons to start the game, to tell the games how many players there are, or to shoot, hop, or perform whatever other acts you need to do in the game. MacMAME games think they're running in the original hardware and they still expect to receive quarters as well as input from big red buttons. MacMAME simulates these actions with keyboard commands. If you don't know the keyboard commands, you won't be able to start a game.

First, press the 5 key to drop a virtual quarter in the machine. While you're at it, pour in a bunch of quarters by pressing the 5 key several times. The next step is to "press the start button," which you accomplish by pressing the 1 key. In some games (such as *Star Wars*), you "pull the trigger" (press the mouse button) to start the game.

Some games support multiple players. To start the game for two players, press the 5 key followed by the 6 key. This deposits virtual quarters in different slots — or at least the game will think so. Then, to start the game, press 1 followed by 2. A few games support three and four players. To load the game for three players, press 5, 6, and 7 followed by 1, 2, and 3. For four players, it's 5, 6, 7, and 8 followed by 1, 2, 3, and 4.

When you need to pause, hit the Esc key. This will bring back the Mac menu bar and the Dock, if it was displayed. Command-W closes the game and takes you back to the Mac-MAME window. Command-Q will quit MacMAME.

Game Action Controls

If you're playing using your Mac's keyboard and mouse, MacMAME supplies a set of keyboard commands that produce the actions of various buttons, joysticks, and other controllers (see Table 8-1). Information on using actual joysticks and other add-on controls appears later in the chapter.

Moving the mouse in some games moves an object or character the way a wheel or joystick can. For example, you can use the mouse in *Star Wars* and in some of the *Tron* games. You can also use it in some games to simulate a dial or trackball, such as in Tempest, though it is not particularly easy to use this way.

The Arrow keys are the best tools to move the game object in maze games, such as *Pac Mac*, *Frogger*, and *Dig Dug*. The arrow keys often work in other types of games, though they may not be as easy to use as the mouse.

In shooting games, you can often use the mouse button or Shift key as the trigger. In others, it is the Control or Option keys on the left side of the keyboard. Control and Option are also assigned as Button 1 and Button 2, which often act as "shoot" and "bomb" in some games. If there is some game action that you don't know how to perform, there's a good chance either the left-side Control or Option key will do it. The Space Bar is assigned as Button 3 for games that need yet another button.

Tip

Avoid randomly pressing keys to find out what they do. Game play is almost entirely controlled by the mouse, arrow keys, the left-side Control or Option keys, the Space Bar, and occasionally the Shift key. There are other keys that can change settings, sometimes to your detriment. For instance, F10 throttles the speed, limiting the performance of game play. Hitting F10 a second time turns off speed throttling. These keys are listed in the MacMAME *User Guide* in the Documentation folder.

Table 8-1:   Common MacMAME Keyboard Commands for Game Control

Key	Action
5	Insert quarter (for additional players use 6, 7, 8)
1	Start (for additional players use 2, 3, 4)
Arrow keys	Move
Mouse	Move or steer
Mouse button	Shoot
Shift	Shoot
Control (left of keyboard)	Button 1 (shoot or other function)
Option (left of keyboard)	Button 2 (bomb or other function)
Spacebar	Button 3
Esc	Pause the game, display the menu bar and Dock
Command-G	Take a screenshot
Command-W	Close the game and return to the MacMAME window
Comman- Q	Quit MacMAME
Tab	Bring up key command configuration menu.

Changing Game Controls

MacMAME lets you change the keyboard controls listed in Table 8-1, as well as many others. After you launch any game, hitting the Tab key brings up MacMAME's main configuration menu, shown in Figure 8-9. Use the up and down arrow keys to move the screen arrows to a selection, then press Enter. The main choices are Input (general), Input (this game), and Analog controls, which refer to joystick actions.

FIGURE 8-9: Pressing Tab when a game is launched
brings up MacMAME's main configuration window.

Figure 8-10 shows the configuration menu that appears when you select Input (general). To change the key combination for a command, use the up or down arrows to move to an item, then type the new key you want. For items that have an "on" or "off" choice, use the right or left arrow keys to change the setting.

Note that at the top of the menu is the key command for bringing up the main configuration menu, the Tab key. If you accidentally type another key when this item is selected and fail to note what the new key is, you won't be able to get back into configuration mode. (This is another reason why you should not randomly type keys in MacMAME to see what they do.) However, don't fret if you totally mess up the control settings. Go into the MacMAME folder, open the Config folder, and delete the file called default.cfg.

To get out of the Input (general) menu, use the down arrow to scroll all the way to the bottom and select Return to Main menu. It's a long way down! If you are closer to the top of the menu, use the up arrow key. If you go above the first item, it brings you down to the bottom.

The Analog Controls item of the main configuration menu have to do with mouse actions and arrow keys set for joystick-type controls. For instance, in *Star Wars*, moving the mouse up moves the crosshairs down. You can change this by altering the setting for "AD Y Stick Reverse." (For real joysticks, MacMAME lets you configure joystick action directly without having to use these menus.)

Performance Tips

Slower Macs or more demanding games can cause performance problems. This includes steering that doesn't respond, slow shooting, or jumpy graphics and sound. If you're experiencing these problems, there are a few things you can do.

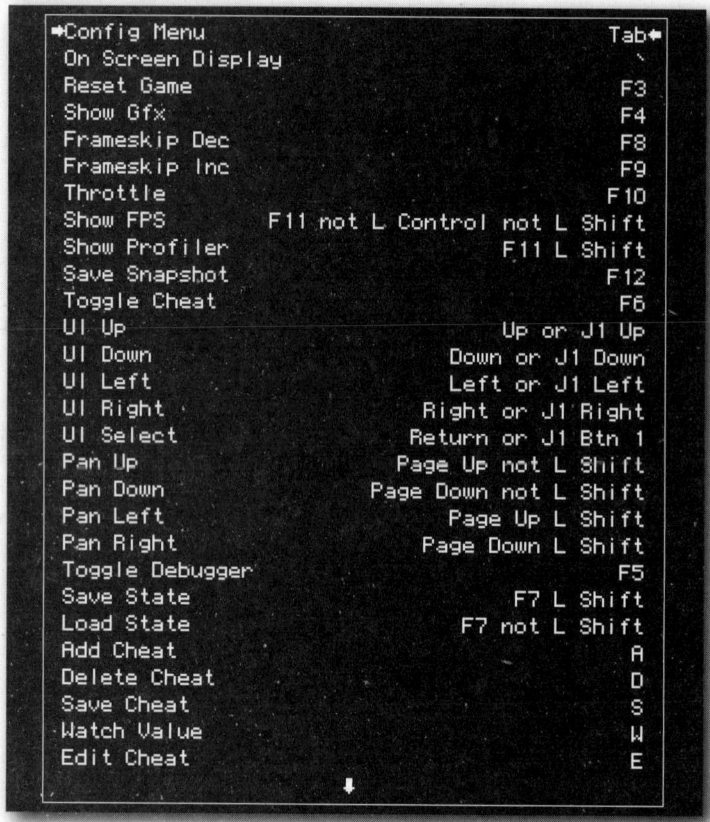

```
➡Config Menu                                        Tab⬅
 On Screen Display                                     ﹨
 Reset Game                                          F3
 Show Gfx                                            F4
 Frameskip Dec                                       F8
 Frameskip Inc                                       F9
 Throttle                                           F10
 Show FPS          F11 not L Control not L Shift
 Show Profiler                       F11 L Shift
 Save Snapshot                                      F12
 Toggle Cheat                                        F6
 UI Up                              Up or J1 Up
 UI Down                          Down or J1 Down
 UI Left                          Left or J1 Left
 UI Right                        Right or J1 Right
 UI Select                      Return or J1 Btn 1
 Pan Up                       Page Up not L Shift
 Pan Down                   Page Down not L Shift
 Pan Left                        Page Up L Shift
 Pan Right                     Page Down L Shift
 Toggle Debugger                                     F5
 Save State                           F7 L Shift
 Load State                       F7 not L Shift
 Add Cheat                                            A
 Delete Cheat                                         D
 Save Cheat                                           S
 Watch Value                                          W
 Edit Cheat                                           E
                         ⬇
```

FIGURE 8-10: This screen appears when you select Input (General) from the
main configuration window.

First, try quitting other Mac applications you have running. Turn off the Classic environment
if it's active. (Open System Preferences, Click the Classic icon, and press the Stop button.)
Simply turning off Classic often does the trick.

If you're still having problems, try adjusting the sound and video settings as described in the
sections "Configuring Game Sound" and "Video Settings" earlier in this chapter. Choose less
processor-intensive settings, such as lower sound quality, fewer colors, and fewer fancy graphics
settings.

Enhancing Your Mac with Hardware

The mouse isn't the best way to play games that were designed for big-bulbed joysticks, steering wheels, and flight controllers — it doesn't have the speed or accuracy of the original controllers, and it doesn't help get you the high scores you can rack up on the real thing. Even the arrow keys aren't good enough for hardcore fans of maze games. Fortunately, there is a whole range of cool devices that work with MacMAME and plug into your Mac's USB port.

When shopping for a device, make sure you don't accidentally pay extra for features that are not supported by MacMAME. For instance, some game controllers and joysticks provide a feature called *force feedback*, which vibrate when something crashes or goes kablooie in the game. However, because force feedback must be supported by the game itself, you probably won't be surprised to learn that 25-year-old classic arcade games don't support this relatively new technology.

Another thing to look for is compatibility with your operating system. If you have Mac OS 9, the device must be compatible with the Mac's Input Sprockets software. Mac OS X doesn't use Input Sprockets, and generally has better compatibility with input devices than Mac OS 9. Sometimes a manufacturer will include software that is Windows only, but the device will still work with Mac OS X. Check with the manufacturer before you buy.

Before we look at the different types of devices, here's some information about setting up joysticks in MacMAME.

Configuring Joystick Action in MacMAME

MacMAME for Mac OS X includes a simple dialog that you can use to make your joysticks work the way you want. Go to the Misc tab on the right side of the MacMAME window. Click the Configure Joysticks button at the bottom. You'll see a dialog like the one in Figure 8-11.

The top part of the Configure Joysticks dialog contains settings for digital joystick action; below that is the section for Analog joystick action. These represent two distinct kinds of joystick action. A digital joystick action controls only four directions: turning up, down, left, or right. An analog joystick action can go in any direction (not just the basic four) and also determines the position on screen. The same physical joystick or game controller can be used for digital and analog joystick actions.

The two Joystick pop-up menus indicate the player you are configuring — if you are the only player, select number 1 in these menus. The Button pop-up menu lets you select the button you are configuring. The rest of the buttons let you pick the device you're using for each setting.

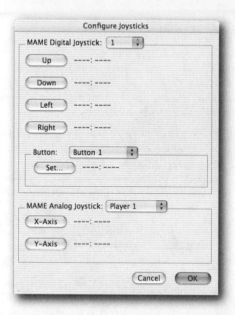

FIGURE 8-11: MacMAME for Mac OS X offers this
dialog to set joystick controls.

Game Controllers

The first upgrade from a mouse for playing classic arcade games consists of inexpensive game
controllers. These are two-handed devices with multiple buttons and other controls. Game
controllers start at just over $20 and can go for as much as $60. An example is the Macally
iShock 2 (available at www.macally.com for about $40), shown in Figure 8-12. Hand-held
game controllers work well for steering, shooting, and flight simulation. They can also function
as joysticks through the use of thumb-activated controllers, such as the two large round knobs
on the iShock 2. Many controllers support two players.

Hand-held USB game controllers for your Mac are similar to the ones that come with standalone gaming boxes such as Playstation or XBox. They can be more flexible than a plain
joystick, but they don't really replicate the classic arcade game experience for many games.

FIGURE 8-12: Macally's iShock is a hand-held game controller that works with many games in MacMAME.
Courtesy of Macally Peripherals.

Joysticks

You'll find more game controllers than joysticks for your Mac, which reflects the types of games being made for Macs and PCs. However, for most classic arcade games, a joystick provides a more authentic experience than a game controller. Resting on your desk, a joystick can give you a more solid feel than a hand-held game controller. There is a wide range of USB joysticks that work with MacMAME. Prices start at $20 and go up to several hundred dollars for real arcade-style gaming. As with hand-held game controllers, joysticks have features that aren't supported by MacMAME, which means that a $25 model, such as the Logitech Attack 3 (Figure 8-13), might work as well for you as a fancier set.

FIGURE 8-13: Many consumer joysticks, such as the
entry-level Logitech Attack 3, feature sculpted handles.
Courtesy of Logitech, Inc.

Most standalone joysticks are sculpted, so you should try to get your hands on one to see if it's right for you. The sculpting means that the sticks are not symmetrical, and they sometimes come in right-handed and left-handed versions. The buttons are typically located right on the stick.

For true fans of the arcade cabinets, the standalone, sculpted plastic consumer joysticks are no match for the good old big metal posts and half-dollar-sized buttons that you can pound on. If you want to get serious about joysticks, it's tough to beat the X-Arcade from Xgaming (available at www.xgaming.com/apple.shtml), shown in Figure 8-14. This arcade-grade piece of hardware is bigger than your Mac's keyboard, and plenty heavy, too, using the parts found on real arcade machines.

FIGURE 8-14: The X-Arcade two-player model offers real arcade-style game control for your Mac. It also comes in a single-player version.
Courtesy of Xgaming.

X-Arcade gives you the feel of an actual arcade game, letting you get aggressive when chasing those high scores — you can slam the joystick to one side or the other without having to worry about tipping it over. Similarly, the large buttons are designed to persistent, intense hammering. And there are a lot of them — eight for each player, which is more than enough for any game.

The X-Arcade goes for $130 for one player, and $180 for two, including the $30 USB adapter kit. X-Arcade is Mac compatible and doesn't require special software — plug it in and it works. Xgaming also offers adapters that enable X-Arcade to work with Xbox and other home gaming hardware.

A Dial for Tempest and Slider Games

There are some classic games where neither joystick nor hand-held game control works well. For instance, *Tempest*, the classic game from 1980, is one of the toughest games to play in MacMAME. Unlike most other arcade games, Tempest uses a dial as its main controller. Playing *Tempest* is very awkward with a mouse or arrow keys, and even a joystick is a struggle.

For *Tempest* and other "dial" games, the PowerMate from Griffin Technology (www.griffin technology.com) does the trick (see Figure 8-15). PowerMate is a big aluminum knob that plugs right into your USB port. PowerMate sits on a skid-free rubber pad that keeps it from sliding around your desk. (The pad also glows an electric blue.) It has a sturdy feel that gives you a high degree of control in *Tempest*. It also works well for the "side-to-side" games such as *Breakout* or the *Space Invaders*– inspired titles such as *Galaga*. At $45, the PowerMate is in the same price range as a joystick or game controller.

Griffin calls the PowerMate a "USB multimedia controller and input device." In fact, Griffin designed the PowerMate to be a volume control for audio and video editing, and it works great for that use. You can configure the PowerMate to control something different in every application — a sound volume control for iTunes or an effects adjustment for a paint program. But for our purposes, the PowerMate really shines for playing *Tempest*, where all other devices fail.

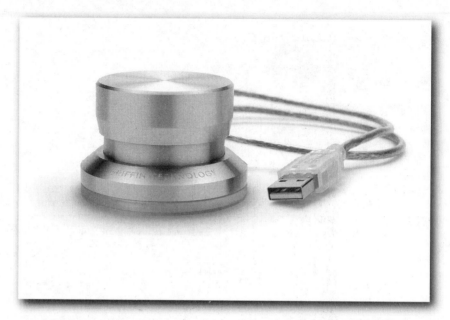

FIGURE 8-15: Griffin's unique PowerMate was designed to be an external volume control, but is well suited as the main game controller for playing *Tempest*.
Courtesy of Griffin Technology, Inc.

The Ultimate Mac Gaming Machine

For some classic gaming fans, sitting at a desk in front of a Mac just doesn't cut it. For them, recreating the arcade game experience means building an arcade-style cabinet powered by a Mac loaded with MacMAME. Unlike ordinary arcade games, a MacMAME cabinet can play a lot of different games.

Building a gaming cabinet is not something Norm Abram has demonstrated on the *New Yankee Workshop* on PBS, but it does take some carpentry skills and tools, as well as a little wiring. There is an economic incentive — fans have built an entire MacMAME cabinet for about the same cost of a X-Arcade double-joystick. But some gamers have spent two or three times this cost. Building a MacMAME cabinet is not about economics or practicality. You do it for love of classic arcade games.

There are two basic ways to go:

- Turn a Mac into a classic gaming machine. This is where the Mac — or Mac parts — live inside the cabinet. In this case, the Mac is dedicated to the task of powering an arcade machine. This is not a bad fate at all for an older Mac (although it shouldn't be too old).

- Build a classic gaming machine that works as a Mac peripheral. Here, you could plug in any Mac to the game machine, which lets you keep using the Mac for other purposes when you aren't gaming.

Keith Stattenfield and John Calhoun, software engineers at Apple, took the first approach with their homemade MacMAME cabinets. 8-Stattenfield transformed a Power Mac G4 and a 17-inch cathode-ray tube monitor into a MacMAME arcade machine (Figure 8-16), which he keeps in his office in Cupertino.

FIGURE 8-16: Keith Stattenfield's MacMAME gaming cabinet is powered by a 500-MHz Power Mac G4 motherboard and Mac OS X.

John Calhoun has built several MacMAME cabinets and Mac picture frames (Chapter 5) using LCD screens. (John Calhoun has his own spot in Macintosh gaming history, as the author of *Glider*, one of the first games for the Mac. Calhoun now offers various versions of *Glider* for free at `http://homepage.mac.com/calhoun/`.)

Let's take a look at some of the steps you need to take to transform a Mac into a classic arcade box.

Cabinet Carpentry

There are two common styles of gaming cabinets: cocktail and standup. Keith's is an example of a cocktail cabinet. "Cocktails are shorter than ordinary tables so that you are high enough to see what's happening on the screen," advises Keith. They're also less expensive to build than the standup variety. Keith spent about $80 on wood for his cocktail cabinet, which cost a total of about $200, not including the Mac. This was on ³/₈" plywood, but fiberboard will also work.

John Calhoun uses plywood with a more fine-grained veneer, which he sands and spray paints black. His cocktail cabinet (see Figure 8-17) isn't as deep as Keith's because he uses PowerBooks with flat screen displays

FIGURE 8-17: John Calhoun's cocktail-style MacMAME cabinet.

Full-sized standup cabinets — the kind you find in arcades — will cost more in wood, and also take up more room in a home or office. Calhoun came up with a table-top standup cabinet design that is smaller than those found in arcades, but still functions like one (see Figure 8-18). Again, this design is enabled by the use of a PowerBook LCD display. He downloaded the MAME logo from MAME.org, printed it out, and mounted it with a pair of small florescent lights behind it. The speakers are located under the MAME logo, facing down.

Cabinet builders usually start with a plan, either drawn up on paper or found on the Internet. John Calhoun creates his own designs and likes to make full-scale models of his MAME cabinets out of cardboard, which act as 3-D plans. (He has some photos of his cardboard models at his Web site.) When the builders are satisfied with the design, they then careful mark out the dimensions on the wood, trying to get as many sides to a piece of wood as possible for the sake of economy. The cabinets usually include a shelf to hold the monitor at the desired angle.

FIGURE **8-18: This mini-standup-cabinet is a transformed PowerBook.**

Many builders of MacMAME (or MAME) cabinets have documented the process of building the cabinet on the Web. You can see some of Calhoun's MacMAME projects, including some of the cardboard models, at his Web site, `http://homepage.mac.com/calhoun/pro-jects`. Another site with a great set of photos and descriptions of building a MAME cabinet is at `http://rtcw.no-ip.org/cabinet/part1.shtml`.

Install Mac Components in Cabinet

Full-sized standup cabinets can fit an entire Mac inside. For cocktail cabinets, builders remove the Mac components from their case and install them inside — the wood cabinet becomes the Mac case. Keith Stattenfield screwed down the Mac's motherboard to the bottom of his wooden cocktail cabinet. You can see John Calhoun's PowerBook motherboard in Figure 8-19, as well as the hard drive, which is necessary to boot the system and to store MacMAME.

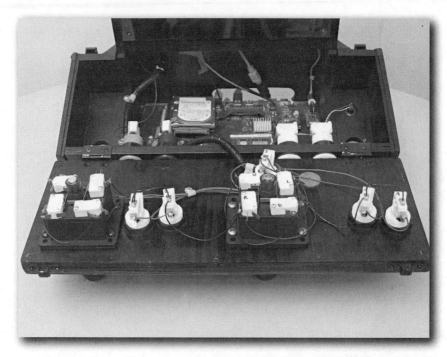

FIGURE 8-19: The back of this view shows the PowerBook motherboard with a hard drive. The front shows the wiring for the joysticks and buttons.

Keith's cabinet has a slot to access the Mac's CD drive (not visible in Figure 8-16), just in case you need to install some new software on it. However, a CD-ROM drive is optional for a MacMAME machine. Once you get your cabinet working, there isn't any reason to keep adding system updates. Some builders include Ethernet ports on the outside of the cabinet to use for adding new MacMAME games via ROM files.

The Mac's little built-in speaker usually doesn't produce enough sound to get through the wooden box, so cabinet builders usually cut one or more holes in the cabinet for external facing speakers connected to the Sound Out port on the Mac or Mac motherboard. In John Calhoun's cocktail cabinet (see Figure 8-17), he cut speaker holes in the front and placed chrome fan grills over the openings. His desktop cabinet has speakers pointing down from the "hood" over the screen.

Builders who aren't putting a Mac inside the cabinet have a few extra steps. They need to install connectors for USB and video on the outside of the cabinet. This lets you plug in any Mac to the cabinet. The USB connector leads to the USB-joystick interface described in the next section. The video connector goes to the monitor inside. However, with the Mac outside of the box, this setup doesn't need the speaker.

For the display in a MacMAME cabinet, an old CRT monitor works well. Keith Stattenfield mounted an old 17" monitor, a nice size for reproducing classic arcade games. John Calhoun uses the flat-panel displays from old notebook Macs, which enables him to build smaller cabinets.

Some MAMErs use television sets instead of computer monitors. Televisions can be less expensive than monitors and are closer to the low-quality monitors of the original early 1980s arcade games. However, they also cause the same kind of eye strain that the old monitors did. A better setup for your vision would be to use a computer monitor along with some of the low-res simulation features of MacMAME, described earlier in the chapter. If you do use a television, you'll probably have to reduce the screen resolution in System Preferences to make it work.

Wiring for a Joystick, Buttons, and a USB Interface

You can find parts for arcade-grade joysticks and buttons from several sources. One good source is Happ Controls of Elk Grove, Illinois (www.happcontrols.com—click on the Industrial link). Another is 9th Tee Enterprises (www.9thtee.com—click on the Arcade Parts link) of Hickory, North Carolina. Industrial-strength joysticks can be had for under $15. Buttons start at under $2.

Your task when building a cabinet, of course, is to wire the joystick and buttons together so that they all connect to the Mac. For this, you need a specially designed piece of interface hardware that enables the Mac to see the joystick and buttons as if they were part of a keyboard. This USB interface is a circuit board that gets mounted in the cabinet, with pins to attach wires and a USB port. Figure 8-20 shows all of the wires from the bottom of the joysticks and buttons connecting to pins on the USB interface board. Happ Controls sells such a board called USB Game Control Interface (UGCI). However, a USB interface that is popular with a lot of MAME cabinet builders is Ultimarc's I-PAC (www.ultimarc.com/, also available from 9th Tee), which stands for Interface for PC-to-Arcade Controller. Although the I-PAC USB board will work with Mac OS 9, Keith Stattenfield says that he had better results with Mac OS X.

In today's arcades, most of the professional cabinets have the same standard joystick and button configuration. This was not so in the classic arcade era: Many games had unique controls and different functions for buttons. To enable a MacMAME cabinet to play as many games as possible, builders often opt for a lot of buttons, usually 6 to 8 per player.

Configure Mac and MacMAME

The last step in turning a Mac into an arcade game is configuring the Mac's software. The basic difference between a standard Mac and a Mac-in-an-arcade- cabinet is that a game box doesn't normally have a keyboard or a mouse connected while you're using it. However, while you're setting up, it's handy to use a keyboard and mouse to change a few key settings.

First, set MacMAME to automatically launch when the Mac starts up. In Mac OS X, open System Preferences and click the Login Items icon. Then, click the Add button, select the MacMAME application, and click OK. Now scroll through the list and put a check mark next to MacMAME.

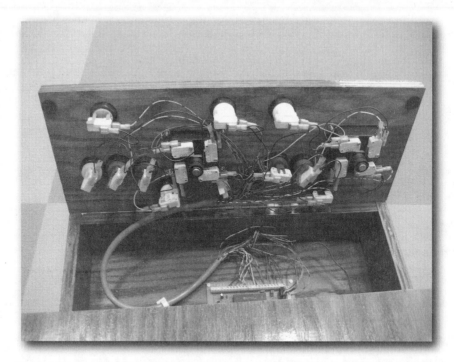

FIGURE 8-20: The wires from the joysticks and buttons connecting to a USB interface board.

The next batch of settings are in MacMAME's keyboard configuration mode, which, as described earlier in the chapter, let you assign keys to certain actions. Because each button connected to the I-PAC USB adapter acts like a key on the Mac keyboard, you can select certain actions to be mapped to keys, which in turn correspond to buttons.

When MacMAME is launched, you use the joystick to scroll up and down the games list to select a game. You then use a game button that functions as the mouse down button to start the game. Take aim and have fun!

Mac Toys' Top-10 Classic Arcade Games

If you're not old enough to have been in arcades during the classic era of gaming, roughly 1978–1985, you might not be familiar with many of the titles of the great video games of old. This list is meant as an introduction to some of the best arcade games you can play on MacMAME. The list is certainly not definitive, and it's missing many popular, creative, and notable games, including *Asteroids*, *Robotron 2084*, *Dig Dug*, and *Frogger*, but we had to stop somewhere. The games are not listed in any particular order.

Star Wars (Atari, 1983)

Star Wars used a flight controller that was part joystick, part steering wheel, and included firing buttons. Featuring voices from the movie urging you to "use the Force," *Star Wars* was one of the first successful attempts at 3-D gaming, though it isn't a true 3-D enviroment.

The game view for *Star Wars* is from inside the cockpit as you fire at TIE fighters, shoot at towers on the *Death Star*, and fly through the trench to blow up the *Death Star*. One cabinet type included a cockpit you climbed into. The images are all blue, red, and yellow wireframes on a black backgournd.

Star Wars can be tough with a mouse. Not only is it not as accurate as the original flight controller, but moving the mouse up moves the aimer down.

Want an extra points? "Use the Force" while in the trench by not firing any shots except one at the exhaust port.

The Empire Strikes Back (Atari, 1985)

The Empire Strikes Back, Atari's little-known sequel to *Star Wars*, is notable because it expands on the original, offering additional methods of scoring, more scenarios, and more action onscreen due to a faster processor (see Figure 8-21). *The Empire Strikes Back* keeps the TIE fighter dogfight of the original and adds three more scenes from the movie: fighting Probots, battling the camel-like Imperial Walkers, and navigating an asteroid field. In each scenario, the game sets goals for earning a letter towards becoming a Jedi knight, which means bonus points and extra abilities.

A year before *The Empire Strikes Back*, Atari released *Return of the Jedi*, which was a disappointment to many *Star Wars* fans. It completely abandoned the cockpit perspective, vector wireframe of the original, using third-person perspective in a raster screen. *The Empire Strikes Back* is a true sequel to *Star Wars*, using the same 3-D wireframe cockpit view. In fact, this game existed as a conversion kit for *Star Wars*. However, Atari did not produce many of the kits, and it is not as well known as the original.

Fly between the legs of Imperial Walkers to earn bonus points. You'll start with 5,000 points, and the bonus increases by 5,000 for each Walker you fly under.

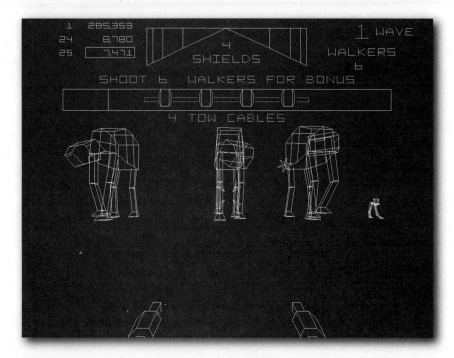

FIGURE 8-21: *The Empire Strikes Back* extends the original *Star Wars* arcade game. You can kill Imperial Walkers by launching tow cables (Option key) or shooting the view ports in the heads.

Courtesy of Lucasfilm Ltd. Copyright and Tradmark Notice: Star Wars © Lucasfilm Ltd. & TM. All rights reserved.
Used under authorization. Unauthorized duplication is a violation of applicable law.

Donkey Kong (Nintendo, 1981)

The game that launched Nintendo as a major player in the gaming industry, the original *Donkey Kong* innovated by creating a new kind of game play. The main character, now known as Mario, was named Jumpman in the original version. You maneuver him through various levels of girders, elevators, and conveyor belts, to try to save Pauline, held captive by Donkey Kong, a big red ape. You can gain extra points by gathering various items that belong to Pauline. The ape doesn't sit by idly, but hurls rolling barrels, fireballs, and bouncing rivets that Jumpman must dodge. Being a carpenter (later, Mario famously became a plumber), Jumpman can grab a hammer to fight some of the obstacles in his path. Donkey Kong is a classic not only because of the merits of the game itself, but because it became the archetype of many computer games for decades to come.

Tempest (Atari, 1980)

Tempest was a hit game in its day, and it still has legions of fans. *Tempest* is nominally set in space, but is mostly an abstract game without a story line. *Tempest* was Atari's first color vector game, producing a wireframe 3-D tunnel of varying shapes. You maneuver a "shooter" on the rim of the tube, firing down along lanes of the tube at various objects coming your way (see Figure 8-22). If any reach the rim, they crawl along the rim to get you out. Destroy all of the objects, and you move to the next tunnel, which has a different shape.

Tempest can be tough to play on a Mac, as it used a rotary dial not common in other games. However, the Griffin PowerMate dial works well with *Tempest*.

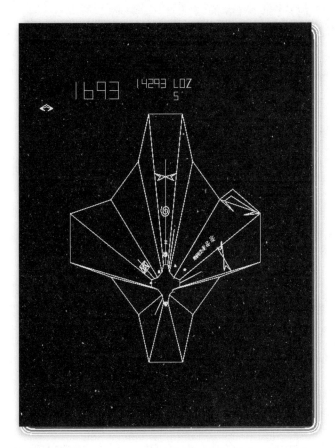

FIGURE 8-22: *Tempest* was a completely abstract shooter game that could be addictive.

Tron (Bally Midway, 1982)

Tron was created as a promotion for the Disney computer-animated movie of the same name. The game turned out to be more popular than the movie. *Tron* includes four games that you must complete in order to move to the next level. You can play them in any order. In *Grid Bugs*, your human figure has to shoot multiplying spider-like creatures while trying to get into a room. *MPC Cone* is a *Breakout*-like game in which the human shoots the bricks in a moving wall in order to move the figure through. *Tanks* is a maze populated by enemy tanks you must destroy. In *Lightcycles*, you try to surround the computer's cycle before he does it to you.

Tip   When playing *Lightcycles* in MacMAME, hold the Control key to increase your speed.

Discs of Tron (Bally Midway, 1983)

This sequel was meant to be part of the original *Tron*, but didn't make it in time for the release of the Disney movie. The gameplay involves having your *Tron* character throw discs of various types at Sark, your opponent, while dodging the discs he throws at you. Both of you stand on discs, and in upper levels, you can both jump between multiple discs. There was an "environmental version" of the *Discs of Tron* cabinet that you stepped into. You stood on a lighted disc, just like the character onscreen. Speakers all around produced the sound of Sark's discs flying past you.

Discs of Tron works pretty well with a mouse to aim and fire discs and the arrow keys to move the character in MacMAME.

Galaga (Namco, licensed to Bally Midway for the U.S. market, 1981)

Atari's *Space Invaders* of 1978 inspired an entire genre of slider games, where you slide a shooter (usually a spaceship) back and forth along the bottom of the screen, while shooting at objects trying to attack you. *Galaga* was one of the most popular, and it spawned several sequels, clones, and bootlegs. (*Galaga* itself was a sequel to Namco's 1979 *Galaxian*.) In *Galaga*, the alien spaceships break formation to attack you. Galagas are a special type of enemy that take two shots to destroy. They also have a tractor beam that can steal your ship — you then have the task of liberating the captured ship.

Defender (Williams Electronics, 1980)

One of the most popular video arcade games of all time, *Defender* was the first big video game hit for Williams, which is now one of the major forces in the arcade industry. *Defender's* plot line lead to several popular Williams' spin-offs, including *Stargate*, *Robotron: 2084*, and Blaster. Defender has a complex story, one in which events from outside of the screen view can influence play. The object is to defend a human population from alien invaders by shooting alien ships, which can capture the humans. You need to rescue captured humans, or they mutate to join the enemy against you. There are various types of alien ships and weapons you must fight, and you are aided by a long-range scanner at the top-center screen. The design of the planet is reminiscent of Atari's earlier *Lunar Lander*.

Joust (Williams Electronics, 1982)

As a knight riding a flying ostrich, your job is to joust with enemy knights on flying buzzards and battle pterodactyls (shown in Figure 8-23). When you knock a knight off his bird (aim for the head), he turns into an egg. Pick up the egg for extra points, or it hatches into another enemy character. After a few levels, parts of the floor begin to disappear to reveal a pool of deadly lava.

Joust becomes more interesting when played with two players. That's because you can sometimes compete against each other for points, joust directly with each other, or work cooperatively against the game. Each level (called a "wave") is different in this respect.

Tip

You can fly using the flap button. In MacMAME, this is the mouse button by default.

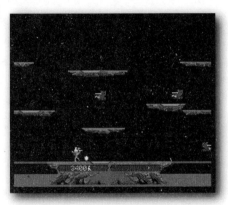

FIGURE 8-23: In *Joust,* your ostrich can fly to attack enemy knights and turn them into eggs.
Courtesy of Williams Electronics.

Ms. Pac-Man (Bally Midway, 1981)

No list of classic video games is complete without *Ms. Pac-Man,* the longest-lived popular game ever. The dot-and-fruit-eating circle (a smiley face in profile) is still found in arcades and restaurants throughout the world, either in it's original form or in one of several rereleases. *Ms. Pac-Man* was a sequel to the 1980 original. Where the original had a single maze, *Ms. Pac-Man* has four different mazes. *Ms. Pac-Man* also had the fruit (and a pretzel) move around the maze, instead of being stationary as in the original. *Ms. Pac-Man* ghosts are also better able to hone in on the *Pac-Man* character than in the original.

The classic appeal of *Ms. Pac-Man* lies in the simple design of the graphics, play that slowly increases in difficulty, a sense of humor, and catchy jingles. It's a formula that game manufacturers today could do well to emulate.

For more tips and information on playing these and other classic arcade games, see www.klov.com/.

Summary

Whether you are reliving past arcade glory or discovering the first generations of video games for the first time, you can bring back classic arcade games on your Mac using the open source MacMAME emulator.

Installation of MacMAME is not quite as automatic as commercial software. There are a few things to remember:

- Various types of files go into different folders within the main MacMAME folder.
- Don't decompress the SIT files.
- Video settings: Vector games will fill the entire screen. Raster games will vary in size depending on MacMAME's video settings.

What you use to control the game depends the game and on how authentic an experience you need. You can use the Mac's keyboard or mouse, or an inexpensive joystick. People who are serious about gaming don't mind spending a few hundred dollars on beefy, arcade-style controls. The ultimate experience is to build your own multipurpose gaming cabinet. Keep in mind that a lot of these early games did not used standardized controls, and for these games, it is difficult to recreate the original experience.

But for some people, playing the classic arcade games isn't the point. It's about preserving a bit of technological history that would have been forgotten were it not for the new technology of emulation.

Convert Your Old Vinyl LPs to CDs

The age of CDs and iPods has certainly done wonders for taking high-quality music out of the living room and injecting it into the rest of our lives. But what about your collection of vinyl LPs? Laying out $1,500 to buy CD versions of 100 of your favorite LPs probably isn't an exciting option, considering that you already paid for your albums once.

Maybe you've already discovered that not every LP in your collection is available on CD. Like the first album from Human Sexual Response — you know, the one with *Land of the Glass Pinecones* on it. If early 1980s New Wave was never your thing, how about that rare original copy of the Grateful Dead's 1968 *Anthem of the Sun*, before Warner Brothers remixed and rereleased it? Or maybe you have the rare 1954 recording of Fritz Reiner and the Chicago Symphony performing Strauss' *Also Sprach Zarathustra* — the one that RCA withdrew because the organ was slightly flat, even though it's one of most electrifying performances of the piece ever.

Whatever's in your LP and cassette tape collections, you can transfer them to CDs and copy them to your iPod using your Mac. PowerBooks and iBooks are particularly handy, since you can easily move them to your stereo system — but iMacs and Power Macs will work as well. This chapter covers everything you need for the conversion, and goes through the process in detail, from vinyl to the label for your CD. If you'd like a more general background in digital audio on the Mac, you might want to read Chapter 7 first. (For more on enjoying your LP collection on your iPod, see Chapter 4.)

The Conversion Process in a Nutshell

Converting analog vinyl to digital bits isn't all the complicated once you know what you're doing. It does take time, however. You've probably noticed that importing a CD with iTunes is much quicker than actually playing the CD. If iTunes displays a 10:1 speed ratio, a 60-minute CD will take 6 minutes to import. No such luck with LPs — the ratio is 1:1 during recording. After that, you'll spend some time cleaning up the recording and separating it into tracks.

Here's the bird's-eye view of the conversion process:

1. Set up your hardware and software.

2. Clean the album.

3. Do one or more short test recordings for volume levels.

4. Record your albums or cassette tapes.

5. Separate the album into tracks with your audio software.

6. Perform noise reduction with software, if desired.

7. Burn a CD.

If you want to move your files to an iPod, convert the songs to AAC format using iTunes and plug in your iPod.

Sounds simple, doesn't it? It generally is, but the devil is in the details. The results you get can vary depending on the condition of your LPs and your stereo equipment and what measures you take. (You can sometimes make things worse.) It may take some trial and error, and after converting a few albums, you may discover a technique that gives you better quality or a quicker conversion. And, if you're interested in not just CD-quality sound, but DVD-quality sound, there are a few things you should know.

Let's first take a look at what hardware and software you need to collect. We'll then move on to the techniques involved with conversion.

What You'll Need

You may already have everything you need if you've set up your Mac for recording and mixing, as described in Chapter 7. If not, you can spend under $100 to get everything you need to start converting, assuming that your stereo equipment is in working order. For $300, you can make the process easier and add noise reduction. There is also optional hardware and software you can use to improve the process. But even this cost is a bargain compared to the cost of buying new audio CDs to replace a large LP collection.

Remember that the LP-to-CD conversion process takes time and is more likely to be a long-term weekend hobby rather than a one-time session if you have a large vinyl collection. Given this, you may want to invest in software and hardware that can make the process easier.

Here's an overview of what you need:

■ **A phonograph turntable (or cassette deck) in working order.** The next section describes how you can tune up your turntable for better results.

■ **An amplifier for the turntable.** This can be a stereo receiver/amplifier, or a special phono amplifier.

■ **Sound capture hardware for your Mac.** This typically consists of USB devices of the type described in Chapter 7, which can be anything from the $35 iMic from Griffin Technologies to high-end audio devices.

■ **Cable.** This varies with your hardware, but typically, you'll have a cable using two RCA connectors for your stereo equipment and RCA or ⅛" mini-stereoconnector(s) in your sound capture hardware.

■ **Sound capture software.** You can use any software that can record from your audio capture device, as was described in Chapter 8. This ranges from freeware and shareware to high-end digital audio workstation software. For converting LPs, packages that cost around $100 are best suited for the purpose.

■ **Optional noise reduction software.** This software can remove the pops and clicks of LPs and noise created by the equipment. If you are transferring music from cassette tapes, then noise reduction software is more of a necessity than an option.

■ **A Mac with CD burning capability.** This includes most Macs built in the past few years. The optical drive can be a CD-R or CD-RW drive, a "combo" drive (CD read/write and DVD read-only), or a "superdrive (CD read/write and DVD read/write). If your Mac can't burn CDs, you can pick up a FireWire CD-RW drive for well under $200.

■ **10 GB or more of drive storage space.** How much space depends on how much recording you plan to do. You can use the hard drive space inside your Mac or use an external FireWire drive. Using a separate hard drive gives you the option of disconnecting it from your Mac and safely storing it when it's not in use, protecting it from any catastrophe that might occur with your Mac.

Figure 9-1 shows a typical setup for the conversion process, including a USB-to-audio converter. If your amplifier/receiver doesn't have a phono input, you can use a phono preamp in its place. The tape player can connect directly into the USB converter if you wish. The next section has specific recommendations for these items.

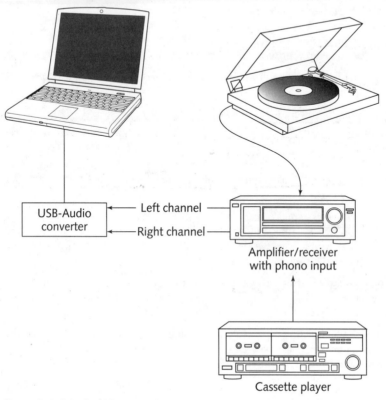

FIGURE 9-1: A typical LP conversion setup.

The Prep Work—Setting Up for Conversion

As with painting a house, the prep work for digitally recording LPs is very important to the quality of the final job. The prep work can be time-consuming, but there is good reason for it—you want your digitized recording to sound as close to your LP as possible, or at least, with a quality that is not annoying. Remember, the CDs you buy in the store were created either with direct digital recording, or were transferred from the analog master tape. The process of digitizing an LP has a number of steps that can introduce problems with a recording.

Tune Up Your Turntable

If you have an LP record collection, you probably have an older phonograph turntable that could use a tune-up. This is a matter finding a few easy-to-replace parts, and takes just a few minutes. If you no longer have a turntable, but are looking to buy one for this project, a used turntable could also need a tune-up. Regardless of whether you're picking up a used turntable or using a trusted old piece of equipment, consider replacing the belt and the stylus before starting your recording.

Replace Your Belt

First, consider the belt. Not all phonographs have a belt, but those that do are preferable (as well as more expensive). If you are buying a turntable, you're better off with a used belt-driven model than a new direct-drive turntable. Direct-drive turntables rotate the record platter using a shaft or gear connected directly to a motor. Unfortunately, the vibrations of the motor can produce noise in your recording. Belt-driven turntables separate the platter from the motor, which sits off the to the side, spinning the platter with a rubber belt. This physical separation produces little or no noise, resulting in a cleaner recording.

Typically, the belt in a belt-driven turntable needs to be replaced every five years or so. A replacement belt will probably run you between $10 and $25 and is well worth the cost. With age, the rubber can stretch and crack, which can result in uneven rotation of the platter. Instead of turning at a constant 33 rpm, the speed will vary slightly, slowing and then speeding back up during the course of play, thus affecting the pitch of the music. You might not even hear this variation at first, but might regret not replacing your belt after you listen to the recording a few times. If your turntable has a speed adjustment knob, you may notice that it frequently needs readjustment — a telltale sign of a stretched belt.

Another problem can occur if the turntable has been sitting unused for long periods of time. In this case, the belt can deform, producing a slight thumping that your recording might pick up on quieter sections of music.

Finding a replacement can be more difficult than actually installing it, because turntables are increasingly rare in home audio shops. If you can't find a belt for your turntable, try searching the Internet. You can start at the Web sites of the manufacturer of the turntable, which might sell replacement parts or list sources for part. You can also do an Internet a search of your turntable make and model. There are a few suppliers that have a wide variety of belts, including Elex Atelier (www.elexatelier.com), Turntable Basics (www.turntablebasics.com), and KAB Electro Acoustics (www.kabusa.com).

Sellers of turntable belts will often identify belts by the turntable model. If a Web site or supplier doesn't list your model of turntable, that doesn't necessarily mean they don't have the belt you need. You can identify your belt by its dimensions. First, note whether it has a round cross-section or is flat. Next, measure the width and the circumference. To measure the latter, hold the belt with a pencil point or pin and pull it so that the circle closes. Measure the length and double it to get the circumference. Keeping in mind that your old belt has probably stretched, subtract 3 to 5 percent. If you aren't sure, another method is to measure the amount of string it takes to run around the two pulleys on the turntable.

To replace the old belt, you can often lift off the platter to reveal the old belt strung between the two pulleys. If the platter doesn't come off easily, check your manual for alternate instructions. (If you don't have a manual, you can often find PDF versions on the Internet, even for old turntables.) Or, you may have a direct-drive turntable, which has no belt.

Replace Your Stylus

The stylus (or phonograph needle) is the first piece of equipment in the chain of events that produce sound out of the speakers. The stylus consists of a tiny diamond (sometimes a sapphire), a little strip of metal that holds the diamond in place, and small plastic connector that attaches to the phonograph cartridge, which is the at the end of the tone arm.

The diamond's job is to move back and forth in response to the shape of the continuous spiral groove in which it travels. The vibrations of the stylus are picked up by the phonograph cartridge and turned into electrical signals, sent on to your amplifier. The health of the stylus has a direct impact on the quality of the music produced by the turntable.

For instance, if the little strip of metal that holds the diamond is bent, the stylus can't accurately transmit the vibrations to the cartridge. The level of wear on the diamond can also affect audio accuracy. The diamond is shaped to enable it to bounce along optimally as it travels through the groove, picking up every microscopic curve. Although you can't see it with the naked eye, a stylus that is worn is misshapen and thus doesn't vibrate in the groove as intended. Such a stylus can miss some of the curves and introduce noise.

To find the right replacement stylus, you can use some of the same Internet sources that supply belts. However, it's not the make and model of the turntable that's important, but the make and model of the phonograph cartridge that you need to search for.

Replacing the stylus simple. Usually, grab it by its plastic connector and pull. The new stylus simply plugs into the place where you removed the old one from.

Adjust the Tone Arm

Another part of your tune-up is adjusting the balance of your tone arm, the long bar that holds the phonograph cartridge. The method of adjustment is usually described in the turntable manual and deals with the weights on the back end of the tone arm. If the cartridge end of the tone arm is too light, it can skip on slightly warped records or when it hits a bad scratch. In fact, if you have bad scratch on an LP, you can try setting your tone arm heavier temporarily. However, a tone arm that is too heavy can introduce noise and will add to the wear and tear of your record in the long term.

Phono Preamps

The signal coming from the phonograph cartridge is weaker than the standard audio signal coming from the back of a tape player or tuner/amplifier. In fact, the signal is too low to connect the turntable directly to your Mac's audio capture hardware, as you can with a cassette tape player. You need to first connect the turntable into your stereo amplifier, or into a separate phonograph preamp.

You'll need a separate preamp if your amplifier/receiver doesn't have a specific phono port. These ports used to be standard on stereo amplifiers, but most new models no longer include them. Phono preamps can be had for as little as $25. You can find them at a retail stores that sell turntables and at the web sites of some turntable manufacturers.

Sound Capture Hardware

As mentioned in Chapter 7, you can use the Sound-In port of your Mac (if your Mac has one), but the results may be less than desirable, as this port can introduce noise into the recording. You can remove noise with software, but that process will degrade the dynamic range of your recording to some degree. A better choice is to go with an audio capture device. You can find internal PCI cards for Power Macs, but most audio interfaces plug into your Mac's USB ports.

Chapter 7 describes the range of hardware from the $35 iMic to interfaces costing several hundred dollars. With increasing price you get higher-definition digital sound, full-sized RCA connectors (instead of ⅛" mini-stereoconnectors) and often MIDI ports. Although MIDI is not relevant to recording vinyl LPs, it would be useful if you wanted to connect a musical instrument to your Mac. Some hardware also comes with audio capture software.

Another converter is the Transit from M-Audio ($100, www.m-audio.com), shown in Figure 9-2. It only has ⅛" mini-stereo-connectors for audio in and out, but does support 24-bit, 96-KHz digital audio.

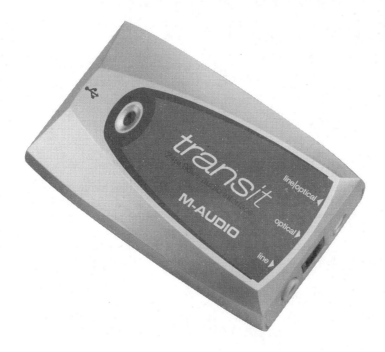

FIGURE 9-2: M-Audio's Transit converter.
Courtesy of M-Audio.

The higher-definition DVD sound is something you might want to consider. CD quality is 16 bit, 44.1 KHz, which is what the built-in Mac input port supports. (The higher-resolution 24 bit, 96 KHz is called "DVD-quality" audio because the increased definition results in bigger files, which means an album's worth of music won't fit on a CD, but will fit on a DVD disc.) Digital audio recorded at 24bit, 96 KHz will retain more of your vinyl record's dynamic range. This improved quality is most noticeable with recordings of acoustic instruments and of the human voice, as well as in music with a large dynamic range, such as classical music.

Note

For the scoop on what the bits and KHz really mean, see Chapter 7.

Some audio capture hardware that supports 24-bit, 96-KHz input also has audio output which you can use to t to connect your headphones or speakers or connect to an external audio tape recorder. You can also play audio DVDs on a DVD player connected to your stereo system — most audio CD players will not play 24-bit, 96-KHz audio DVDs.

The downsides to 24-bit, 96-KHz audio are:

- The iPod only runs 16-bit, 44.1-KHz audio. If you want to play your music on an iPod, you'll have to make 16-bit, 44.1-KHz copies of your music.

- DVD-quality audio files are 50 percent bigger than CD-quality ones. This means that you'll need more disk storage.

For cassette tapes, it's probably not worth the bother to record in high definition. Cassette tapes don't have the dynamic range of vinyl records and have much lower signal-to-noise ratios (which means more noise during quiet music). Reel-to-reel tapes, however, can be much higher quality than cassettes, and might take advantage of the increased definition that 24 bit, 96 KHz offers.

Cable Concerns

The type of cables you'll need depends on your equipment, so it's better to decide on the hardware you'll be using before you buy cables. The output ports of stereo equipment usually have two RCA connectors, one for the left channel, one for the right. Mac audio capture will either have two RCA connectors, or a single ⅛" mini-stereo-connector, like the headphone port on the iPod. If you have the latter type, you will need a Y-cable with a single mini-stereo-plug on one side, and two RCA plugs on the other.

The cables you use can also affect the quality of your recording. Poor-quality or old cables with oxidized connectors can introduce noise. The degree of quality is easy to spot — thicker cables are of higher quality than thinner cables, and gold-plated connectors are higher quality because they don't tarnish. Cables with dirty connectors can also be a source of noise, and can attenuate an audio signal, decreasing the volume.

It's also good to keep your cables short — less than 6 feet is good; shorter is better. Signals can degrade over a long cable, and since most stereo cables are unshielded, longer cables are more susceptible to picking up electromagnetic interference, which also translates into noise. If you must go long, look for the more expensive shielded cables.

Recording Software

For digitizing your LP records, any of the audio recording applications described in Chapter 7 will work. The main purpose of the software is to give you controls for starting and stopping the recording. There are also some editing features that are useful to use after you've captured the record. Most important is the ability to easily divide up an entire side of an LP into individual files for each track. Other useful effects include fade in and fade out — for instance, if you never liked the drum solo of a particular track, you could fade out just as it starts.

These are all pretty basic features that you'll find in midrange and high-end professional recording suites, though freeware and shareware often include these features as well. On the low end, Amadeus II from HairerSoft ($25, www.hairersoft.com) and Sound Studio from Felt Tip software ($50, www.felttip.com) will do the job. Both will record in 24 bit, 96 KHz if you wish. You can download the demo version of both to see which interface you prefer. Both are fully functional versions that expire after 15 days of use.

In the $75 to $100 range, you'll find several "lite" versions of more expensive professional software. This includes Peak LE from Berkeley Integrated Audio Software (or BIAS, at http://BIAS-inc.com/) and DigiDesign's Pro Tools LE (www.digidesign.com). These products all support VST plug-ins for expanding the feature set. (See Chapter 7 for more on VST.) Another reason to pay more for a commercial product over shareware is the technical support.

These and other recording applications are described in more detail in Chapter 7. This chapter will demonstrate the LP capture process using Peak LE ($99, shown in Figure 9-3), a popular audio tool that is a good choice for digitally recording your LP collection and burning it to CDs. Peak LE offers an easy method of dividing an album side into tracks, provides an easy way to normalize volume levels, and has a good user interface. Peak LE also lets you run noise correction applications such as VST plug-ins from within Peak. Should you ever decide to get deeper into digital audio editing and recording, Peak also offers an upgrade path to BIAS's more expensive versions. Peak DV focuses on audio recording and editing for video projects, and the full version of Peak is a midlevel ($500) professional audio-editing application.

Starting with Peak LE 4, BIAS removed a major limitation. Like the full version of Peak, Peak LE 4 can now record in DVD-quality and higher resolutions, with a sample size up to 32-bit. Earlier versions of Peak LE allowed only CD-quality, 16-bit recording. (Chapter 7 has explanations of the meanings of the sample size and sampling rates.)

Noise Reduction Software

As was mentioned in Chapter 7, there's always some sort of noise created in converting analog sound to digital audio. If you are converting music from cassette tapes, you will get a much higher level of noise than from LPs. You can use software noise reduction tools to reduce noise. However, noise reduction comes at the cost of reducing the dynamic range of your recording, so you want to use it sparingly and selectively. Fortunately, many of the software packages use nondestructive editing, which means you can apply the noise reduction and listen to the result without having to first permanently alter the file — an undo command will get you back to the original file. The basic idea is to find a good balance between removing noise and retaining audio fidelity.

If you already have a high-end digital audio workstation program such as Emagic's Logic Audio Platinum, you already have some sophisticated noise reduction tools. The noise reduction features of the shareware Amadeus and Sound Studio are fairly basic and difficult to use if you are not well versed in audio technology. Fortunately, there are two moderately priced noise reduction utilities that are easy enough for a layperson to apply and that do a good job.

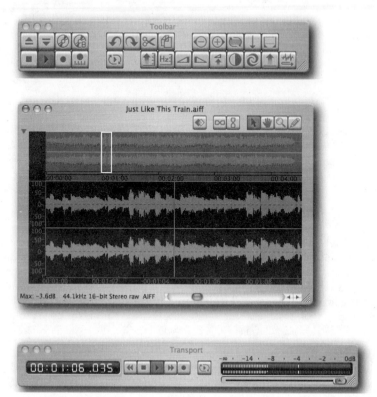

FIGURE 9-3: Peak LE has some useful tools for recording your LP collection and burning it to CDs.

BIAS's SoundSoap, $99 has the simplest user interface for correcting noise problems. Behind the on-screen knobs are advanced algorithms that figure out what needs to be done, so you don't have to. SoundSoap is good for easily eliminating broadband noise, such as the hiss that cassette tapes tend to acquire over time. For your own live recordings, SoundSoap does a great job with background noises such as wind or car traffic. It's also good for erasing fixed-frequency noise and overtones, such as the 60-cycle hum and low rumbles produced by audio equipment. The one type of noise that it does not remove is impluse noise, such as the pops and clicks that you often find on vinyl records.

To remove pops and clicks, BIAS added SoundSoap Pro ($99) to its product line at the end of 2003. SoundSoap Pro can do everything that SoundSoap can do, and more. The Pro version is aimed at professionals, however. This means that it isn't as easy to use as the original version. If you are willing to put in the time to learn it, SoundSoap Pro can is the best (affordable) noise reduction tool to use in your LP conversion process.

Another way to attack pops and clicks is with Arboretum Software's Ray Gun or Ray Gun Pro ($100 and $150, www.arboretum.com) as part of the Montage video-editing application. Ray Gun can remove the pops and clicks of vinyl, as well as the hums and other noise. Its interface is fairly simple, though not as simple as SoundSoap. Unfortunately, you can only use Ray Gun from within Montage, which supports a maximum of 16-bit, 44.1-KHz audio.

SoundSoap and SoundSoap Pro will work as standalone applications or as VST plug-ins from within Peak LE and other audio apps that support VST.

Tip

If you are interested in high-end audio restoration techniques, *Electronic Musician* magazine published an excellent article in the July, 2003 issue called "Noise Busters." You can read it at http://emusician.com/ar/emusic_noise_busters/index.htm.

Minimize Equipment Noise

Noise reduction software can be truly miraculous, but it is much better to catch the noise at the hardware sources. A few of these things have been mentioned earlier in the chapter, but they are worth saying again. There area also a few other areas you can check.

Turntables can introduce noise, which is the main reason to use a belt-driven turntable with a new belt. Other noise prevention actions include the turntable tune-up described earlier and cleaning of your LP record, described in the next section. Another thing you can do is to try to prevent a 60-cycle hum by making sure that the turntable and the amplifier are grounded to the same outlet. Turntables, particularly older models, often use grounding wires instead the three-pronged AC plug. The grounding wire can be screwed to an AC outlet.

Cables were also mentioned as a potential source of noise. If you are hearing noise from the computer side or are having volume problems with a channel, experiment with changing the cables. If that moves the problem from one channel to the other, then you need to replace the cables.

Another type of noise is clipping, which occurs when you record with the levels at too high a volume. This sounds like a distorted buzz and is very difficult to correct.

Set Up the Software

Before recording, there are three items you need to take care of:

1. Make sure that your audio capture hardware is selected as the audio input device

2. Configure the sampling rate and sample size.

3. Configure the destination drive for the recorded data.

It is very possible that all three will be automatically set for you by default. However, you can't assume that is the case.

Select Your Audio Capture Hardware

After you've installed your recording software, make sure that your audio capture hardware is selected as the input device instead of the Mac's built-in hardware. Sometimes you can do this in a Preference dialog, but if the capture hardware and the recording application both support Mac OS X's Core Audio, you can use the Sound pane of System Preferences. Under the Input and Output tabs, just click on the name of your audio hardware (see Figure 9-4).

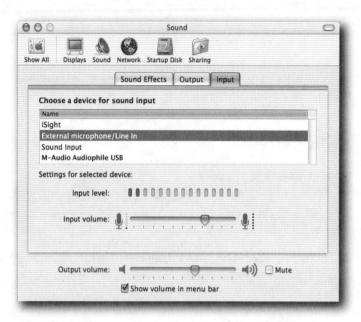

FIGURE 9-4: Select your audio hardware device in the System Preferences
Sound pane.

If your software also supports Core Audio, your sound capture hardware should be selected automatically. However, it doesn't hurt to check. In Peak LE, go to the Audio menu and select
Recording Settings. In the dialog that appears (see Figure 9-5), click the Hardware Settings button. You can use the pop-up menus for setting the input and output hardware (see Figure 9-6).

If you want to listen to your music as it is recorded, many recording applications have a monitor preference that must be set. In Peak LE, you'll need to check the Monitor check box in the
Recording Settings dialog (see Figure 9-5). If you don't, you won't hear the music as it records.

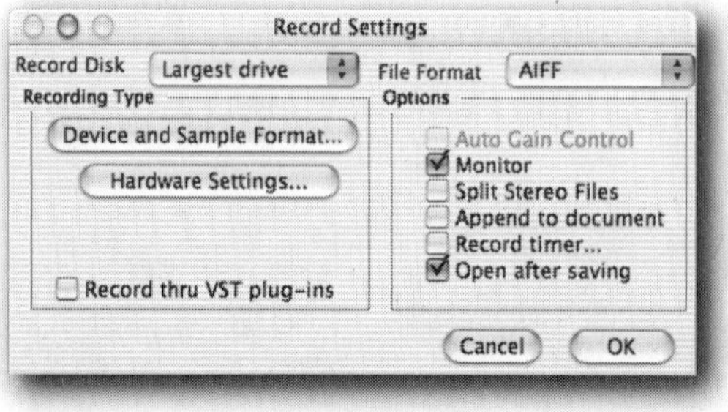

FIGURE 9-5: Peak LE Recording Settings dialog is the
main place for configuring your recording.

FIGURE 9-6: Clicking the Hardware Settings button lets you choose your audio hardware.

Set the Digital Sampling Rate and Size

Next, within your recording application, you'll need to designate the digital sample size and frequency. This is often in a Preference dialog. In Peak LE, once again choose Record Settings from the Audio menu. In the dialog that comes up, click on the Device and Sample Format button. A new dialog comes up (shown in Figure 9-7). Usually, you want to select 16-bit, 44.1-KHz for CD quality sound, or 24-bit sample size and 96-KHz sampling rate for DVD quality. If you have enough hard diskstorage, you could record at the higher bit rate and then downsize later if you need to store the files on CDs or copy to an iPod.

You might be tempted to use lower sampling rates and sample sizes to get smaller files, such as those you would use for Internet radio (as described in Chapter 2). But for digitizing your LPs, CD quality (16 bit, 24 KHz) should be the smallest resolution you capture your audio at. You can always downsize (also known as resampling) later for Internet broadcasts.

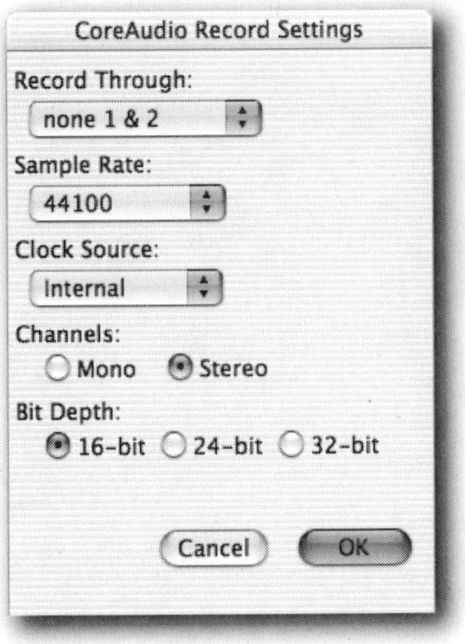

FIGURE 9-7: Setting the sample size in Peak LE.

Set File Format

When digitizing your record collection, it is best to use uncompressed AIFF as the file format. This is the format used on audio CDs. With no compression, there is no loss of sound quality.

Even if your intention is to play these songs on your iPod, it's still a good idea to have a set as uncompressed AIFF. The reason is that as compression standards keep improving, you can go back to your original AIFF files and make new files using the latest and greatest compression scheme. This would have been handy when Apple introduced AAC, a more efficient compression format than MP3, which will get you more songs on your iPod for the same sound quality.

Uncompressed AIFF does take up a lot of storage space — about 10 megabytes per minute. If you have a very large record collection, you might want to pick up a FireWire hard drive for your audio project. The large amount of hard disk space that AIFF takes up is a good motive for archiving your AIFF files onto CDs or DVDs. The optical discs also make a great backup in case of hard drive problems.

To set the file format in Peak LE, go to Record Settings from the Audio menu, and select AIFF from the File Format pop-up on the upper right (shown in Figure 9-5).

Set Destination Drive

If you have more than one hard drive or partition, you may need to designate the drive that will store the recorded data. This could be your internal hard drive or an external FireWire drive that that you are using for this project.

To set the destination drive in Peak LE, go back to the Recording Settings dialog (from the Audio menu), and click the Record Disk pop-up on the upper left (see Figure 9-8). You can choose "Largest Disk," which just chooses the drive or partition that is biggest, or you can choose a specific drive.

FIGURE 9-8: Setting the destination drive in Peak LE.

The Recording Session

Now you have all your equipment ready and connected. Your Mac is located near your stereo equipment, and both are turned on and ready to go. Your software is launched and configured, and you've just placed your first LP on the turntable. You're ready for the fun part.

However, before you hit that record button, there are a few housekeeping chores you need to do to ensure the best recording you can get.

Clean the Record

Before playing each side of a record, you should clean it. Cleaning the record will remove dust particles that can create audible pops and clicks in the recording. Dust particles that you can't see can diminish the quality of the playback of the record by interfering with the stylus as it travels through the groove.

To clean the record, you can use a velvet-covered record wiper, such as the old DiscWasher system. A fine brush made for cleaning records will also work. Using a few drops of a cleaning liquid on the brush will give you far better results than a dry rub.

If you don't have a commercial cleaning liquid, you can make your own. Start with distilled water. (Tap water has minerals that can build up on your vinyl.) Add to that a few drops of detergent — dishwashing or laundry detergent will work fine. The amount is on the order of five drops per quart of distilled water. Now shake vigorously. The mixture should foam slightly at first and become clear again after 10 seconds or so. If it doesn't foam, or if the foam disappears quickly, you can add another drop or two of detergent.

To give an extra kick to your cleaning solution, experts recommend also adding a small amount of isopropyl alcohol, no more than 5 percent. A mixture of 1 part isopropyl alcohol in 20 parts distilled water is safe. At stronger levels, isopropyl alcohol can damage certain types of vinyl. An even better mixture is 70 percent distilled water and 30 percent pure ethyl alcohol. However, ethyl alcohol is difficult to find. (In either case, include the few drops of detergent.)

Whether store-bought or homemade, always shake your cleaning solution before applying it to your cleaning brush.

The best method of cleaning a record is to hold the cleaning brush steady while rotating the turntable platter using your middle finger on the record label. Using the turntable's motor to spin the platter is not a good idea — you can can cause irregular wear on your belt if you have a belt-driven turntable, or wear out your motor if you have a direct-drive turntable.

There are also record-cleaning machines that you can find advertised in audiophile magazines. It would be an exaggeration to say that such a device is necessary for digitizing your record collection. But if you have one sitting in a closet, this is definitely the time to use it.

Clean Your Stylus

At the risk of sounding like your mother, we must mention one more cleaning task you should do. The phonograph needle can accumulate dust that will interfere with the production of the best sound. You don't have to see a clod of dust on the stylus in order to have a dirty needle.

To clean the stylus, use a small brush, either one made for the purpose or a brush used to clean the lens of a camera. Wet the brush with a few drops of the cleaning liquid you used for the LP or a liquid made for the purpose. Always wipe in the direction that is toward the end of the tone arm.

The Sound Check

Before you record your LP, you'll want to do a test recording to set the audio levels. When you do this, play the loudest section of the recording. Now, start the recording software. The object here is to set the volume of your receiver/amplifier loud enough so that even the quietest parts are louder than the noise in your system, but not so loud as to cause clipping—a distortion that will sound like a nasty buzz. Remember, you can't remove clipping later, so you want to prevent it now.

To prevent clipping in Peak LE, BIAS recommends that the optimal volume setting is one that causes the meter to be about 6 dB below zero. In most software, you can see clipping in the waveform—the two channels will be too wide for the display (as in the top of Figure 9-9). When the volume is set correctly, the loudest portions of your recording produces waveforms that don't touch the top or bottom of the display. To be safe, err on the side of a slightly lower volume.

When you stop the test recording, don't save the test recording as a file.

Record

You're now ready to capture the audio. There's usually a Record command in one of your software's menus or toolbars. Choose your Record command first. Once the software is recording, start playing the first side of the album. Don't worry about dead space before the beginning of the music—you will get rid of it later. Starting the software first ensures that you don't accidentally cut off the beginning of the first song. The easiest way to capture the album (or tape) is to record the entire side or both sides as one file. A single file is easier to work with than are multiple files in the editing phase (performing noise reduction and normalization). If your software has a pause button, you can record both sides of a record or tape as a single file, pausing while you flip the LP. For double albums, all four sides can be put in a single file. You will split the file up into individual tracks later. When the last track is over, stop the recording. Make sure that all traces of the last chords of the music have completely faded before you hit the Stop button.

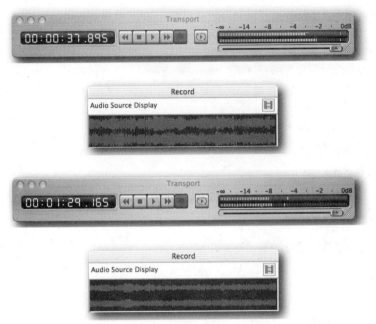

FIGURE 9-9: In the top part of the figure, clipping is occurring. At the bottom, the volume is about right for Peak LE—approximately 6 dB below zero, with the waveform not touching the top and bottom. Too low a volume setting will yield a low signal-to-noise ratio.

To record in Peak LE, you first bring up the Record dialog. There are three ways to do this: select Record from the Audio menu, click the Record button (circle icon) in the toolbar, or click the Record button in the Transport bar. Any of these actions will bring up the Record dialog, shown in Figure 9-10.

Near the bottom, Peak will display the sample size and sampling rate you've selected, as well as the file format. (For instance, if you're recording in CD quality, it should say 16 bit, 44100 Hz, and Stereo AIFF file.) Now, click the Record button (the dot) at the bottom of the Record dialog. After you start your turntable or cassette tape player, you should see the waveform of the recorded sound displayed in the top part of the Record dialog, as shown in Figure 9-10.

When the music has ended, you can click the Stop button (the square). Peak LE also has a Pause button, which you can use after the first side has ended. Turn over the LP or tape, click the Pause button again to resume recording in the same file, and then start the turntable or tape player. At the end of the last side, you can press the Stop button (the rectangle). Peak LE will bring up a Save dialog where you can name and save the file.

FIGURE 9-10: The Record dialog of Peak LE, shown here after recording has begun. You can use the Pause button (double vertical line) to temporarily suspend recording while you flip the LP or tape to side 2. Press Pause again to resume recording to the same file.

Editing the Audio File

From here on in, you're working with your music in digital form on your Mac. There are a number of editing tasks that you need to do, and others that are optional. Whichever tasks you choose to take on, doing them in the following order will yield the easiest process:

1. Remove noise if necessary.

2. Normalize (adjust the sound level).

3. Break up the file into separate tracks.

4. Remove the blank spaces

5. Add fades, if necessary

The following sections describe these tasks, and hopefully shed light on why it is important to do them in this order.

Noise Reduction

Noise reduction is one of the optional steps, though if you are converting music from cassette tapes, we recommend it. Before you start, you should listen to your recording, or to spots of it, to see where there are any problems. Be sure to check the quiet spots, where noise problems will be much more noticeable.

You might want to use a noise-filtering application such as SoundSoap or Ray Gun on the entire file or just on specific parts of a recording. Tape hiss, rumble, or a buzz might occur throughout the entire recording. Pops and clicks from a vinyl LP might occur in spots. In general, be conservative, applying only as much noise reduction as is necessary in order to preserve fidelity.

SoundSoap works as a plug-in to Mac OS X audio applications that support VST. When working as a plug-in, and the sound reduction window acts as a floating palette — it's always on top, but lets you click on the Stop and Start controls of your audio hardware. Ray Gun only works as a plug-in to the Montage application.

The next few sections will look out how you can use SoundSoap and Ray Gun to reduce noise. We also encourage you to take a look at SoundSoap Pro, which was described earlier in this chapter.

Noise Reduction with SoundSoap

As mentioned earlier, SoundSoap (www.bias-inc.com/products/soundsoap/) is the easiest way to remove noise and yields professional results, though it doesn't remove the pops and clicks found on vinyl LPs. The Learn Noise button sets the levels of the controls automatically, so that often, you don't have to fiddle with the settings.

Installing SoundSoap is simple. If you want to use SoundSoap as a standalone application, just drag it from the installation disk to your Applications folder. If you want to call up SoundSoap from within a VST-capable application such as Peak LE, run the SoundSoap VST installer. It will place files in this folder:

```
/Users/[your name]/Library/Audio/Plug-Ins/VST/
```

You can use do both types of installations if you wish.

The first step is to load your audio file. To use SoundSoap as a standalone application, you launch SoundSoap, go to the File menu, select Open Media file, and browse for and select your file. To use SoundSoap as a plug-in, you would open the audio file in the audio application, then open the SoundSoap plug-in. When you launch Peak LE, it asks you to pick an audio file. After your file opens, go to the Plug-Ins menu, choose Insert 1, then VST, then SoundSoap VST. SoundSoap opens on top of Peak (see Figure 9-11).

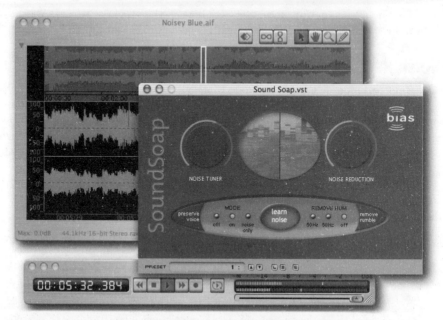

FIGURE 9-11: SoundSoap as a VST plug-in to Peak LE. Often, pressing the Learn Noise button will be the only configuration you need to do to remove noise.

Now your ready to clean your file.

1. Press the Learn Noise button in the SoundSoap window.

2. Start playing your recording. You can press the space bar or click the Play button in Peak LE or another audio app.

3. SoundSoap calculates for a few seconds, adjusts the settings, and applies the settings to the playing music, though it doesn't yet alter your file. Listen to the sound. To hear it without the proposed noise removal, click the Off button.

4. Often the Learn Noise function gets it right, and you don't need to do anything else. But you can adjust the noise reduction if you like. The Noise Tuner knob at the left adjusts the frequency range of the noise being removed. The Noise Reduction knob at the right adjusts the amount. The Remove Hum buttons remove a single frequency hum caused by equipment or cables, and the Remove Rumble button removes low-frequency (40 Hz or lower) noise that turntables can sometimes add.

5. You can save your settings if you wish. If you're using SoundSoap as a plug-in, click the small "S" button at the bottom of the window. If you're using SoundSoap as a standalone app, go to the File menu and choose Save Settings. You can also load previously saved settings.

So far, SoundSoap hasn't changed your file. When you're ready to apply your settings to your file, the changes will be made. If you're using SoundSoap as a standalone app, you can press the

Apply button in the SoundSoap window. When using it as a plug-in, there is no Apply button. Instead, you go to the host app's plug-in menu and select a command, often called *Process*. In Peak LE, this command is called *Bounce*.

Noise Reduction with Ray Gun

If you want to remove the pops and clicks of vinyl, Ray Gun is a good tool. (SoundSoap Pro can also remove pops and clips, though it is more complicated to use.) Ray Gunalso can remove some of the same types of noise as SoundSoap, though the interface is not as automatic. Unfortunately, Ray Gun was a better tool when it was available as a standalone application or VST plug-in. As part of the Montage video-editing program, it isn't quite as easy to use. Here's how you would use it:

1. Launch Montage and create a new Document.

2. Import your AIFF file using the Import command in the File menu.

3. Go to the Process menu, select the Auto Effects submenu, and select Ray Gun.

4. Go to the View menu, and select Show Plugin. The Ray Gun will appear, as shown in Figure 9-12.

5. You'll notice four tabs, each representing different types of noise. Each with sliders. You can try any of these out and click the Play button to hear the effect of your setting. On the left, is a section called Pops for removing vinyl LP clicks. Moving this slider higher will produce more of an effect. The Noise tab has two sliders that are useful for reducing tape hiss. The Rumble and Hum tabs take care of many machine-specific noises, such as the rumble caused by a turntable or a 60-cycle hum (or 50 cycle in areas outside of the United States).

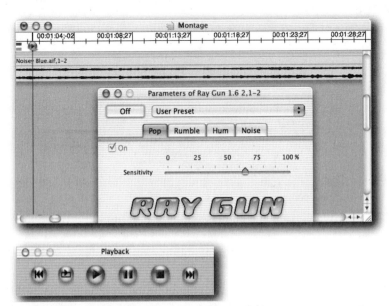

FIGURE 9-12: Ray Gun offers noise reduction presets that you can start with.

A good way to use Ray Gun is to start with listening to presets available in the pop-up menu at the top. You can then make modifications with the controls. You can listen to your settings and compare them to the original with the Play button and the Off/On toggle button — when Off is displayed selected, you'll hear the unaltered audio. Once you are satisfied with the effect of your settings, you can save your settings as a preset.

Now you have a choice of applying these settings to your entire file or going on to create different presets for different parts your recorded LP or tape. To apply the settings to the entire recording, close the Ray Gun window and click on the waveform in Montage. Now, select the entire waveform (Command-A). Open Ray Gun again (Step 3 above). Select your preset from Ray Gun's pop-up menu, and click the Apply button.

If you'd created different noise reduction presets for different parts of the music file, you'd select the part of waveform, go to Ray Gun, and apply the appropriate preset.

Manually Remove a Click

If you don't have Ray Gun or SoundSoap Pro, you can try to remove some of the worse pops and clicks manually. This is a cruder method, one that isn't practical for removing a lot of clicks, but if your records are in good condition, you might be able to get rid of the worse offenders. You can do this in any application that displays a waveform, including freeware and shareware.

The basic idea is that most pops and clicks show up as spikes in the waveform and are of short duration, a fraction of a second. First, magnify the horizontal (time) axis in your software so that the spike is wide enough for you to see and edit. One way to deal with it is to simply select the spike and delete it. However, this does shorten the music, even if only by a fraction of a second and could be noticeable.

For a subtler edit, copy a section of the waveform directly before or after the spike, and paste it over the spike. The section you copy should be the same length as the spike. For an even less noticeable result, copy a section of the waveform directly before the spike that is only half the length of the spike — paste it over the first half of the spike. Now do the same for a section directly after the spike, and paste it over the second half of the spike.

Obviously, this technique will be more effective on certain types of music than on others. Your ear will be the best judge.

Volume Correction (Normalization)

There are several reasons to correct the volume levels of your captured digital audio, a process called normalization. If you are going to listen to a mix of songs from different sources, either on a mixed CD, in iTunes, or on your iPod, you'll want all of the music in your collection to have the same approximate volume. This will save you from having to keep reaching for the volume controls whenever a new song comes up.

Another reason to normalize volume is that some or all of the music you captured came in at a low volume. This means that any noise introduced by your playback equipment or the playback environment (such as your car stereo and the road noise) could overcome these quiet volume levels. This can reduce the overall dynamic range of the recording. But if you are going to

CD-quality (16-bit) audio, you are going to a form that has less of a dynamic range than the original anyway.

If you use the normalization process to raise the volume of quiet sections, the volume of any hums and rumbles will also be raised. This is why you should do noise reduction before normalization.

Note If you've recorded with the volume too high and have caused clipping, volume normalization won't undo the buzz created by the clipping. You'll have to go back and recapture the album at lower recording levels.

The normalization process in software such as Peak LE is a complex process that is more than simply raising the volume. The software will analyze the waveform and proportionally raise volumes throughout the dynamic spectrum. Loud sections will be made louder, but not so much as to cause clipping.

Volume correction in Peak LE is very simple. Choose Normalize from the DSP menu to bring up the Normalize dialog (see Figure 9-13). Here, you can simply click the OK button. The default setting of 100 percent should be fine. It brings up the loudest sections of the music to highest volume levels without causing clipping. Once you click OK, the normalization process starts, with status displayed in Peak LE's Transport bar.

FIGURE 9-13: Normalizing in Peak LE is simple. Choose Normalize from the DSP menu, and click OK in this dialog.

Separate Your File into Tracks

There are several methods of separating your captured album file into separate tracks. The crudest method, which works with any audio-editing application, is to use cut and paste on the waveform. You'll see the waveform go flat in between songs. (see Figure 9-14.) You can simply select the waveform in between two flat sections, do a Copy (or Cut), and paste the song into a new file. Then, save it as an uncompressed AIFF file.

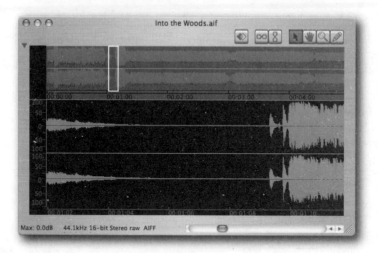

FIGURE 9-14: This flat spot in the waveform indicates a space between songs.

This process can be time-consuming and prone to errors. Some audio applications, including Peak LE, let you place markers that designate the spot where one song ends and another begins. There are two ways you can use these markers to separate your file into tracks. One way is to keep your captured file as a single file — CD players will recognize the markers that Peak LE (and some other software) creates as individual tracks. The iPod won't, however. The other method is to export each section between the markers as a separate file. Using a separate file for each track will make it easier later on to burn a CD, and is more convenient for iPod use.

Whichever approach you use, you start by creating the markers. In Peak LE, the first marker goes at the beginning of the first track. Click on the waveform before the beginning of the first track. In the Action menu, choose New Marker. (You can also click the New Marker icon, a down arrow, in the toolbar.) This will insert the first marker as a vertical line with a triangle at the bottom (shown in Figure 9-15). You can move the maker to a better position by dragging the triangle to the left or the right. It should be within one second of the first song.

In Peak LE, you can also add markers in real time while Peak plays the music. Listen for a quiet spot between tracks (but closer to the second track), and hit the Command-M keys to place the marker. You can go back later and drag the triangles left and right to adjust them.

What you do next depends if you want to keep a single file or create separate files for each track. To retain a single file, you'll need to designate regions between pairs of markers, so that CD players will recognize the tracks as separate entities. To start the process in Peak LE, hold down the Command key and click between the first two markers (in the bottom half of the window). This will highlight the first track. Now, go to the Action menu and select New Region. (You can also hit the Command-R keys.)

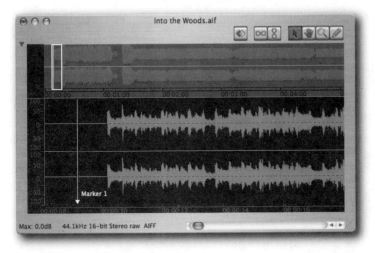

FIGURE 9-15: Placing the first marker in Peak LE to designate the beginning of the first track.

The Edit Region dialog (see Figure 9-16) will appear. In the Name field, type the name of the region — "Track 01" is appropriate. Now, hold down Command and click between the second and third makers to select the second track. When you choose the new Region command, Peak LE will now automatically name it "Track 02." Since you won't be designating the empty space before the first track and after the last track, these will be discarded.

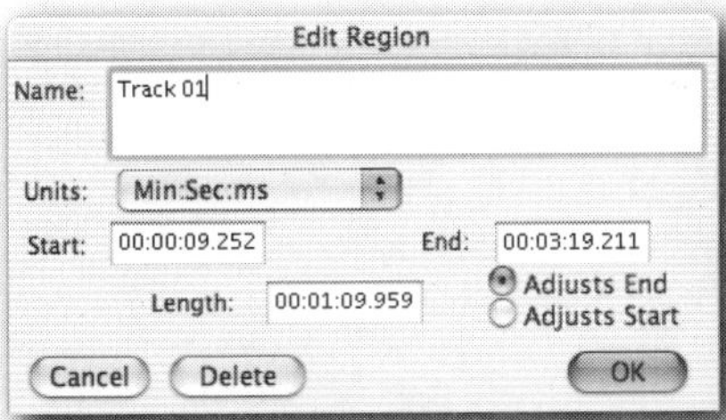

FIGURE 9-16: The Edit Region dialog of Peak LE will let you name the region so that CD players can recognize it.

To create a separate file for each track, you will export the sections between markers instead of creating regions. You start out the same way — hold down the Command key and click between the first two markers to highlight the first track. From the File menu, select and hold New. From the submenu that appears, choose "Document from Selection." Peak will create a new file and copy the contents of the first track into it. You can save this new file (also as uncompressed AIFF) with a normal music file name, such as the name of the song. If you want the tracks to stay in the order they were on the album, begin each file name with a number (such as 01 for the first song). Do this for each track in the file.

You will now have two sets of files, the files for the individual tracks that you just created, and the original single file containing the entire album. This later file you can delete at some point, after you've listened to the individual track files you created to make sure that they're okay.

Delete Spaces and Add Fades

In the previous section, the process of separating into tracks automatically deleted the empty spaces at the beginning and end of the captured file. But there may be other parts you want to get rid of. Perhaps the space between tracks on the original LP or tape was too long for your taste. Or, you may want to remove sections you don't like, such as the section of long applause at the end of a live recording, or a drum solo (with apologies to fans of Gene Krupa and Keith Moon), or sections of the music you just don't care for.

This is a simple task in just about any audio-editing application. Select the part on the waveform that you think is the part you want remove. The Play button usually will play the selected portion. Some software lets you adjust the start and endpoints of your selection. With others, you have to make your selection again to alter it. When you're sure you've got the part you want to remove, delete it.

Some of these cuts may have left an abrupt ending or beginning to a track. You can fix this with a Fade-out or Fade-in command, a fairly common feature even in low-cost audio applications. With most audio software you can select a section on the waveform to fade and choose the Fade-out command. (Make sure to select both waveforms in the left and right channels.) In Peak LE, you can select the area to fade and click the Fade-in or Fade-out button in the toolbar. Be sure you apply enough time for the fade out — at least several seconds (Figure 9-17).

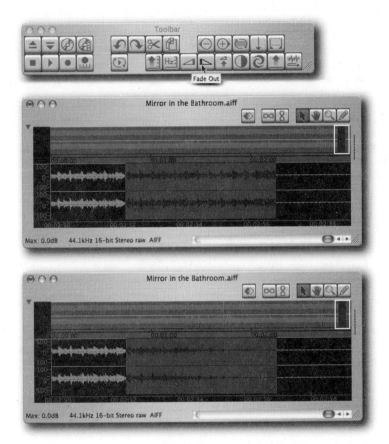

FIGURE 9-17: To set a fade-out in Peak LE, you select the section you want to fade and click the Fade-out button. Here, we have about 4 seconds selected. The resulting fade is shown at the bottom.

Moving Files to CD and iPod

You're probably aware that you can use iTunes to move your digitized AIFF files to CDs. You can also use iTunes to move your files to your iPod, though you'll want to convert the files to a compressed format. But there are other tools as well, some of which have some advantages over iTunes — one is that they don't make multiple copies of your large AIFF files the way iTunes does. Many of the audio-editing tools in the $100 range and above, including Peak LE, come with the ability to burn a CD. This section will look at using both iTunes and Peak LE for creating CDs.

Burning a CD with iTunes

One problem with using iTunes is storing the big, fat, uncompressed AIFF files that you digitized from your LPs and now want to move to CDs. When you drag files to your iTunes Library, iTunes makes a copy of all these files in the iTunes folder. This means that you will have *two* copies of these big files on your hard disk (or disks). Of course, you can always go back and delete one set, but it is an extra step.

On the other hand, if you are planning to move your tracks to your iPod, you'll have to get them into iTunes at some point, so you might as well move them in now. It makes most sense to make a third copy of the files, this time in AAC format, and then delete the AIFF files from iTunes after you've burned you CD. (See the iPod section later on for details.)

To burn a CD with iTunes, start by creating a new playlist (select New Playlist from the File menu). Give it a name — the name of the album, for instance. Now drag your AIFF files into the new playlist. (iTunes will make copies of the files, which it will place in the iTunes Music folder.) The files will appear in the iTunes Library, as well as in your new playlist.

Next, go to the iTunes menu, select Preferences, and click the Burning icon. There are two importing settings you need to make:

- Next to Disc Format, select "Audio CD" (see Figure 9-18).

- Next to Gap Between Songs, choose "none" from the pop-up menu. That's because your LP records or cassette tapes already have gaps between the songs — you don't want iTunes to add any more space between songs. Close Preferences, select your New playlist, and click the Burn button.

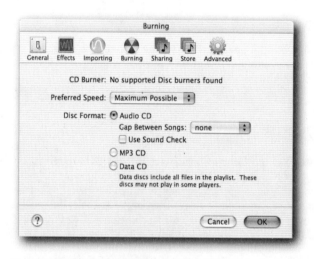

FIGURE 9-18: The iTunes Burning preferences need to be set at Audio CD and no gap between songs.

Once your AIFF files are on CDs, you can delete them from your hard disk, from both the iTunes Music folder and from the folder where you saved them when you first recorded them The CDs will act as archives. If you want to put the music on your iPod, however, don't delete them from iTunes just yet.

Burning a CD or DVD with Toast

You can avoid the issue of two sets of AIFF files by using your audio-editing application, or software that might have been bundled with it. Roxio Toast Lite is sometimes bundled with audio applications, audio hardware, and with third-party optical drives. (The full version is available from www.roxio.com for $80.) If you happen to have a copy of Toast or Toast Lite, it is very simple to burn an audio CD or DVD. It works well if you made separate files for each track.

Open Toast and select Audio. You can now drag and drop your AIFF files into the Toast Audio Window. Toast presents the amount of time between tracks. As with iTunes, set this to zero. You can then burn the CD by clicking the Record button.

If you are using Peak LE, you can use it to burn the CDs.

Burning a CD with Peak LE

Peak LE has the ability to burn a CD from the separate files you've created or from a single file with designated regions, as previously described. (The full version of Peak comes with Toast Lite. However, Peak and Peak LE both have the ability to burn CDs independently of Toast.) Unlike iTunes, Peak LE won't make duplicates of your AIFF files.

If you've created separate files for each track, you'll need to create a Peak playlist:

1. Open all of the CD-bound files with Peak LE.

2. Go to Peak's Window menu, and select Contents. A window will appear listing the tracks.

3. Open the File menu and select and hold the New item. In the submenu that appears, choose Playlist Document. An empty playlist document is created.

4. Click on the Contents window to select it. Click on the first item. Then hold the Shift key and click on the last item — this will select all the items.

5. Drag the selected items from the Contents window to the Playlist window.

6. In the Playlist window, drag the items up and down to get them in the right order.

7. Save the Playlist with a useful name (such as the name of the album).

8. Click the Burn Audio CD button in the Playlist window. (This is the CD icon with the "B," as in Figure 9-19.)

9. The Burn Audio CD dialog will open. Choose your optical burner drive, and click okay.

10. You'll be asked to insert a blank CD.

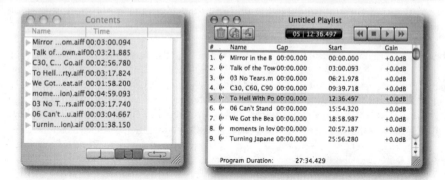

FIGURE 9-19: To burn a CD in Peak LE with multiple open files, drag their names from the Content window to a Playlist window, drag to arrange the order, and click the Burn button.

You don't have to create a playlist if you created a single file with regions (as described in the earlier section called Separate your File into Tracks). Instead, open the file with Peak LE and do the following:

1. Go to Peak's Window menu and select Contents. Check to see if you want to create any more regions or adjust the markers between them. (Markers should be close to the beginning of each song.)

2. Click the Burn Audio CD button in the toolbar. (This is the CD icon with the "B.")

3. The Burn Audio CD dialog will open. Choose your optical burner drive, and click okay.

4. You'll be asked to insert a blank CD.

You now have an audio CD copy of your vinyl LP record.

Move to iPod

If you're an iPod user, you probably know that to move music files to your iPod, you can drag them to the iTunes Library. (If you used iTunes to burn a CD, you already have the AIFF files in iTunes.) The next time you plug in your iPod, iTunes moves the files over to the iPod for you. Although the iPod can play AIFF files, it is a big waste of storage space in an iPod.

Before you plug in your iPod, you'll want to create copies of your AIFF files in the AAC format. You should then delete the AIFF files from iTunes, so that only the AAC files are left.

Note

You could use the MP3 format instead of AAC, but the AAC format that iTunes 4 and later can produce is more efficient than MP3.

To make AAC copies, go to iTunes Preferences and click the Importing button. Now, click the Import Using pop-up menu and select AAC. Click OK. Now select your AIFF files in the iTunes Library, go to the Advanced menu, and choose Convert to AAC. iTunes will create new files with the same file names. To tell which ones are the AIFF files, select a file and press the Command-I keys (for Get Info). You can now delete the AIFF files and plug in your iPod. iTunes will automatically move your new files to your iPod.

CD Labeling

Marking your CDs and DVDs is a practical matter of identifying them. If you think you can get away with marking the jewel cases, forget it. Take two or three unmarked CDs out of their cases, and you've got mystery CDs on your hands.

You can always mark your CDs with an indelible marker (provided that you can read your own handwriting). But if you really want to do it right, you can pick up CD labeling softwarethat can print out a thin label for the disc itself on your printer. You can get fancy, designing your own graphics or importing design elements of scanned album covers. But the main goal is to get a legible title and artist name for the CD, and possible even track titles. You can buy special CD labels at most office supply stores, such as Staples and Office Max, and computer stores.

One of the best label programs is Discus ($39) from Magic Mouse Software (www. magicmouse.com). It supports curved text and text at an angle to fit on a disc label. You can import photos and graphics in a number of formats. It also comes with clip art images and backgrounds, and a basic graphics editing program. You can use Discus to print inserts and folding booklets for CD and DVD cases.

Another good product is Disclabel ($30) from Smile Software (www.disclabel.com). It doesn't have as much art as Discus, but it can import playlists from iTunes (see Figure 9-20), so you don't have to type in all the song names. It also has an iPhoto button that lets you bring in your own photos from iPhoto. The user interface of Disclabel is very similar to that of iPhoto. You can edit curved text inline and create your own designs.

Demo versions of both Discus and Disclabel are available at their respective Web sites.

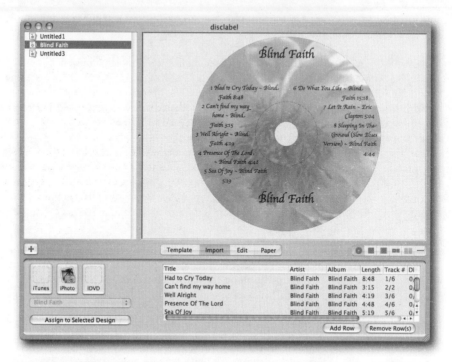

FIGURE 9-20: Disclabel lets you import iTunes playlists into templates or your own designs, to produce a CD label in minutes.

Summary

After you've digitized your first few albums, the rest will go much easier. For a summary of the entire process, see the section near the beginning of this chapter called "The Conversion Process in a Nutshell." Here, we'd like to leave you with reminders of some of the important points:

- Check your turntable to see if it needs any maintenance. Replacing the belt and the stylus will save you headaches later.

- Use good cables to prevent adding noise.

- Record your files in uncompressed AIFF format.

- Decide if you want to go DVD quality (24 bit, 96 KHz) instead of CD quality (16 bit, 44.1 KHz). Audiophiles may like this option, because it retains the dynamic range of the vinyl LPs. This does create bigger files, which you'll have to burn to DVDs (which won't play in ordinary CD players).

- If you go with DVD quality, make sure that your audio capture hardware and software support 24-bit, 96-KHz digital audio.

- Noise reduction tools can do wonders for problematic source material and are a must if you are converting cassette tapes. However, use them conservatively, because they can diminish the quality of your sound.

- Even if you aren't interested in CDs or DVDs as playback media, consider burning discs anyway, as an archive of your digitized music collection.

If this is the first chapter you've read in this book, you might want to check out some of the other digital audio projects you can do with your Mac. Chapter 2 describes creating your own Internet radio station. Chapter 4 expands your iPod horizons. Chapter 7 describes how you can turn your Mac into a digital audio workstation for creating, mixing, and playing your own music.

Convert Your Home Video and Film to DVDs

Back in 1967, *Star Trek's* Captain James T. Kirk and Science Officer Spock found themselves in a futuristic library that contained no books. The librarian pulled out a small silver disc and inserted it into a slot. Suddenly, there were moving pictures and sound. Kirk and Spock were amazed. That's because they weren't familiar with digital video discs — DVDs.

Of course, we know better. DVD discs are crowding out videocassettes in movie rental stores, and DVD players are connected to TVs in millions of living rooms. That's because DVDs have a lot of advantages. They can hold higher-quality pictures and audio, and they let you jump around to different sections instantly. The take up less room than VHS cassettes, are easy to mail to friends and relatives, and don't deteriorate with age the way tape does.

Fortunately, you don't have to buy commercial DVDs to get these features — you can convert your own videotape collection to DVD, even if it's old-fashioned analogy VHS. You can have a service do the conversion for you, but if you have a large tape collection, this will get costly. A service also can't offer that personal touch that you can add to your discs. With your Mac, you can convert as many tapes as you want, the way you want to.

Of course, Kirk and Spock may have also been amazed at VHS as well — in 1967, people shot their home movies on 8 mm or Super 8 film. If you have a box of old film reels, you can also use your Mac to copy them to DVDs. Digitizing film is a more difficult task than converting video, but it does enable people to see movies that have sat in a closet for decades.

The first part of this chapter describes digitizing your analog videotapes. We'll then move on to film. The chapter ends with creating DVDs containing your digitized footage.

Digitizing Video in a Nutshell

Converting your videotape collection to DVD is similar to converting your vinyl LPs to CDs, described in Chapter 9. In both cases, you start with an analog medium — in this case, it's VHS, Video 8, or some other format of analog videotape. As with converting LPs to CDs, this video conversion is a *capture* process that uses a piece of hardware to convert the analog signals into digital signals that computers can work with. Video usually has sound as well, which is also converted to a digital format. However, with video, you're probably not as concerned with audio fidelity as you are when digitizing an LP collection.

Converting videotape to DVD doesn't have to take a lot of time, particularly if you aren't making any changes to the material. The basic videotape-to-DVD conversion process follows these steps:

1. Plug in your VCR or analog Video 8 (analog) camcorder to your video converter box, which is connected to your Mac's FireWire port.

2. Capture the video with software such as iMovie.

3. Do some postproduction work, such as add new titles, if desired.

4. Enhance the soundtrack with noise reduction or with new music, if desired.

5. If you have a miniDV camcorder, make a copy to back to a master tape.

6. Create the user interface (menus, chapters, and so forth) of your DVD with iDVD or other software.

7. Burn the DVD. This step encodes the DV format using a compression CODEC and copies the material to the DVD.

At the end, you have a disc holding up to 90 minutes of video that can run on most off-the-shelf DVD players that connect to TVs. You can also view your disc on Macs and PCs that have DVD drives.

Let's first take a look at what hardware and software you need to collect. We'll then move on to the techniques involved with conversion.

What You'll Need for Video-to-DVD Conversion

You may already have much of what you need to copy your video collection to DVDs. If you already have a Mac with a built-in SuperDrive, all you'll need is some video capture hardware. If not, don't worry — you can enhance your Mac with new hardware and software.

Here's an overview of what you need:

■ **Video capture hardware.** This is a box that converts analog video signals to the DV format you get from digital camcorders. These connect to your Mac with a FireWire cable.

- **Hard disk space.** We're talking *serious* hard disk space. A minute of digital video takes up a quarter of a gigabyte. An external FireWire hard disk is ideal for this purpose. When you're not working on your conversion project, you can unplug it from your Mac, making it impossible for you or your family members to accidentally erase something.

- **VHS player or camcorder.** You will connect this to the video capture box.

- **Video cables.** You can use a video cable and two audio cables, or a single coaxial cable. The type of cable varies with the hardware.

- **Capture software.** You can use just about any digital video-editing application. In this chapter, we'll be using iMovie, since it is easy to use, does a great job, and is free.

- **DVD burner drive.** This can be a built-in Apple SuperDrive or an external FireWire drive.

- **DVD layout/encoding/burning software.** You'll need to create a DVD user interface, encode the digital video in MPEG-2, and burn the DVD disk. Apple's iDVD, part of the iLife suite, works great at all of these, but it only works with internal DVD burner drives. If you have an external burner drive, you'll have to use another package, such as DVD Studio Pro, Roxio Toast, or a package that came with your drive.

Figure 10-1 shows a typical setup for the videotape conversion process. The next few sections go into more detail on these items and offer some recommendations.

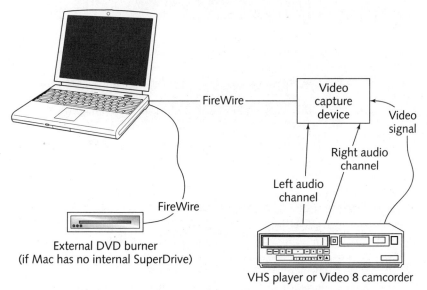

FIGURE 10-1: A typical video capture setup includes FireWire video converter. Sometimes you'll use three cables to connect the VHS player. Some devices also support a single coaxial cable.

Find a Service

If all this sounds like too much for your taste, there are plenty of services that convert videotape for you, and that will deliver a finished DVD. Locally, you'll find that many photo development shops and video equipment stores offer this service. One advantage to a local outfit is that you can ask to see a sample of a finished DVD. If you search the Internet for "video to DVD," you'll find plenty of outfits that you can mail your tape to.

Although most companies offer per-tape discounts for more volume, you should resist the temptation to hand over your box of tapes if you haven't used the service before. Start with one tape—if it doesn't come out well, you can try another company. Take a look at the DVD you got back and compare it to the original VHS tape. The quality should be as good as the original VHS tape. For an extra fee, some services offer restoration, which can try to fix the images from a tape that is deteriorating. But don't be unrealistic—a DVD created from a tape can't have better quality than the original.

Video Capture Hardware

Much like the audio capture hardware described in Chapters 8 and 10, video capture hardware takes analog electronic signals and digitizes them. In this case, it creates video in the DV format, just as you would get from a miniDV digital camcorder.

Another result of the large amounts of data with video is that video capture hardware usually connects to your Mac through FireWire, not USB, as does audio capture hardware. You can also find PCI cards for Power Macs. USB is just too slow for creating full DV video. If you see a USB video capture device, it doesn't capture in high resolution. For instance, a video capture device intended for Internet broadcasting will only give you a screen on the order of 320×240 pixels. For converting your videotapes, a resolution of 720×480 is standard. You'll need a unit that converts the signal to true DV format. These will cost over $200.

For instance, the Formac Studio DV (www.formac.com) and Director's Cut from Miglia (www.miglia.com) both go for between $200 and $300. In addition to doing a good job in creating DV files and working with Mac software, units have a full set of ports. You import video with either an S-Video cable or an RCA connector. Video capture boxes also have a video out port for connecting a TV monitor to the box, to let you see the images as they appear on a television.

You'll also find audio-in and audio-out ports on some devices. You could also use the Formac Studio DV or the Director's Cut for importing your vinyl records, as described in Chapter 10. The Studio DV and the Director's Cut provide CD-quality audio capture (though not DVD-audio quality). Formac comes with an audio-recording application called Formac's Audiomaster. Both also let you connect headphones.

Both units are powered by the Mac through the FireWire cable, which means that you don't need to use a power cord. The Formac Studio DV has the advantage of including a second FireWire port for connecting another peripheral. It also has a more interesting physical design (shown in Figure 10-2) than the plain-looking Director's Cut box. The Formac is also known as a trouble-free, Mac-compatible peripheral.

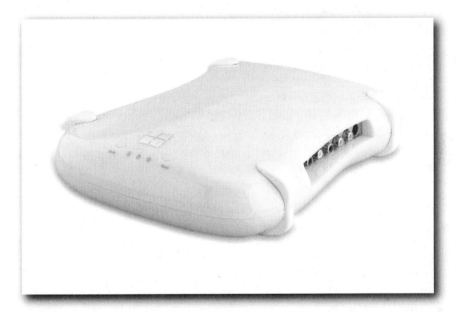

FIGURE 10-2: The Formac Studio DV offers analog video-in and -out ports, in S-Video and in RCA.
Courtesy of Formac.

You may also remember the Formac TVR from Chapter 4—it also includes everything that the Studio DV has, plus a TV tuner.

DVD Burner Drives

If your Mac came with an internal SuperDrive, you're all set to burn DVD discs. You can skip ahead to the next section. If you are buying a new Mac and are trying to decide which optical drive option order, the internal SuperDrive is the best choice. It will give you access to the easiest DVD burning solutions and will work with all of Apple's software, and probably any future video software Apple may come up with.

Don't worry if your Mac doesn't have an internal DVD burner drive, though. You can add an external FireWire drive like the one shown in Figure 10-3. Shopping for one can be a bit confusing, though, as there are several types of DVD burners available; the industry has not standardized on one type. Most of the drives available support several types of DVD burning as well as CD burning. Each type of DVD burner uses a different type of media, so you have to be careful to pick up the right type of blank discs as well.

FIGURE 10-3: Some external FireWire drives, such as EzQuest's Boa Slim DVD-RW Drive, come in this extra-slim form factor. You'll pay more for the convenience, but it is easier to carry around and store.
Courtesy of EZQuest, Inc.

The SuperDrive is a DVD-R/DVD-RW drive. The DVD-R stands for DVD write once, and is what you'll use to create your video DVDs. DVD-RW stands for DVD read-write, which means the disc can be erased and rerecorded. You can't go wrong if the drive lists DVD-R/DVD-RW in it's list of compatible formats. There are other formats as well, including DVD+R/DVD+RW. Some drives, such as the d2 DVD+/-RW from La Cie (www.lacie.com), offer these formats in addition to the DVD-R/DVD-RW used by the Apple SuperDrive. A drive that supports all four types is kind of an insurance policy against the chance that the winds might change and you might find yourself needing another format. However, you will pay more for a drive with multiple formats.

There are a few types of DVD drives that won't work for creating a video DVD. For instance, a DVD-ROM drive is a read-only version. You can play movies, but you can't burn them. Some Macs have internal DVD-ROM drives, which Apple calls a Combo drive.

Another format that won't work is DVD-RAM, found in some of the first Power Mac G4s. This format mounts on the desktop like a Zip drive, letting you drag and drop files to and from it. The DVD-RAM drive in the old Power Mac G4 did not support any other type of DVD or CD burning. However, there are external drives that include DVD-RAM with DVD-R/DVD-RW. These should work fine.

One drawback to an external drive is that Apple's iDVD software won't work with it. When shopping for an external drive, check to see that it comes with software to create the DVD user interface, encode the digital video in MPEG-2, and burn a CD. These can often be separate applications, as described in the next section.

Upgrading an Internal Optical Drive

If you'd really like to run iDVD on your Mac, but it didn't come with a SuperDrive, there is one other option—if your Mac is a PowerBook or an older Power Mac G4, or one of a few iMac models. You can replace the internal optical drive with a SuperDrive-compatible model that will enable you to use iDVD. The seller of the drive should be able to tell you that it is "iDVD-compatible." You can find these at MCE (www.mcetech.com) and Other World Computing (www.macsales.com).

The pros: You get to use the inexpensive and excellent iDVD, and internal drives are cheaper than external FireWire drives. Prices are constantly dropping, but at the time of publication, you could get an internal DVD burner for under $200.

The cons: You don't have a drive that you can move from Mac to Mac, and you only end up with only one optical drive to work with, while the old one goes in the closet. However, if this matters to you, you can overcome it by buying an external FireWire enclosure for the old drive.

Just be careful you get the right drive, one that is Mac- and iDVD-compatible. For instance, a Pioneer DVR-105 will work just fine in an older Power Mac G4. If the company runs out of stock and "upgrades" you to a Pioneer DVR-106, you won't be able to burn CDs or DVDs.

The first thing you should do after you install a new internal DVD burner is to open the Apple System Profiler utility. Go to the Devices and Volumes tab, look under the Bus section, and click the triangle next to CD-RW/DVD-R.

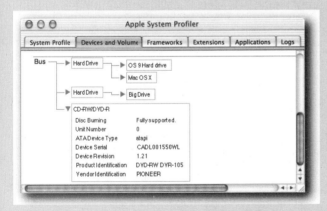

If it says Disc Burning Fully Supported, you're in like Flynn. If it says Disc Burning Not Supported, you don't have an iDVD-compatible internal drive.

Software

There are two main pieces of software you'll use in this process:

1. Video-editing software to capture the movie.

2. *DVD-authoring* software. This will accomplish three tasks:

   a. Lay out the DVD user interface

   b. Encode the video in MPEG-2 format

   c. Burn the DVD

Sometimes the DVD portion of the task will be accomplished by using more than one piece of software.

Capture Software

For capturing the video, the easiest piece of software you can use is Apple's free iMovie (www.apple.com/imovie). Usually, when you are transferring videotape to DVDs, you're not doing a lot of editing, but if you do need to edit or add titles or a soundtrack, iMovie can do it. iMovie gives you access to your iTunes music and your iPhoto images, should you decide to add a still photo. It will recognize the video converter box when it is plugged in. iMovie also lets you designate video chapters — markers that let the viewer skip ahead to another section of the movie using a menu. These chapters will be moved over to iDVD.

One thing iMovie lacks is sophisticated editing features that you might use to clean up a video, such as adjusting the color or balance. You can do some of this, but will get more editing control with Apple's top-of-the-line Final Cut Pro ($1,000), or the midlevel Final Cut Express ($300). If you are doing a lot of digital video editing, these packages might be worth your while.

A less expensive option is Montage ($150) from Arboretum Systems (www.arboretum.com/products/montage/montage_main.html). It has the benefit of coming with Ray Gun, an audio noise reduction tool that you can use to remove tape hiss or annoying recorded sounds like machinery or buzzing. If you don't have Montage, SoundSoap from BIAS ($100) will do the same thing. (Ray Gun and SoundSoap are discussed in Chapter 9.)

You have to ask yourself if your home movies really need professional-level "postproduction" done to them. There is a steeper learning curve with these more powerful video editors, and clean-up will require learning some skills. For digitizing videotape movies, most people will find that iMovie is plenty.

DVD Authoring Software

For creating the DVD user interface and encoding and burning the disc, Apple's iDVD (www.apple.com/iDVD) is your first choice. It does all three of these functions seamlessly — you don't even know you are encoding. iDVD is a no-brainer to use, with an interface similar to that of iMovie. iDVD 3 also sports a button bar similar to the one in iMovie with icons for importing photos (from your iPhoto library) and audio (from iTunes) for use in video menus.

iDVD also produces professional-quality results with little effort on your part. It contains several dozen predesigned layouts called themes that can fit any mood. Apple has been adding new themes with each new version of iDVD, so an update can get you more. If you don't like a theme, you can edit it. iDVD is also a bargain — $49 as part of the iLife suite.

The big downside to iDVD is that it only works on internal DVD burner drives, and not on external FireWire DVD-R drives. If you have an external burner drive, you'll have to use other DVD authoring software. Apple's $499 DVD Studio Pro (www.apple.com/dvdstudiopro/) has some great features, but they are features that you don't really need for converting home movies.

Formac's Devideon Authoring software (www.formac.com/p_bin/?cid=solutions_drives_devideon_soft) is another easy-to-use package, though it doesn't have the design features of iDVD. It can accept chapter markers from iMovie, and will perform encoding and disc burning after you create the interface. There is a catch here, too — you can only get Devideon Authoring when you buy Formac's Devideon DVD burner drive ($399).

Another option is La Cie's CaptyDVD authoring application; it's available with some of its DVD drives, and La Cie also offers it separately for $149. Like Apple's and Formac's software, CaptyDVD will also do the whole job, letting you create the menus and thumbnails of the user interface, and encode and burn discs.

Other drives come with combinations of DVD-authoring software. For instance, some of MCE's drives come with ImageMixer DVD from Pixela (www.imagemixer.com) for creating the user interface (www.pixela.co.jp/en/products/software/imagemixer.html) and Toast Lite from Roxio (www.roxio.com) for burning the disc. Other drives offer Charismac's Describe (www.charismac.com/Products/Discribe), which can burn DVDs. Pixela has a line of products that take care of different aspects of creating DVDs, but that are only bundled with DVD drives (http://ka.ws17.arena.ne.jp/en/products/software/). If your drive didn't come with any software, you can buy ImageMixer DVD and the full version of Toast.

The Video Capture Process

You have your hardware, you have your software — now you're ready to digitize your video and capture it to your hard disk. We will be using iMovie to demonstrate the capture process.

Bring in the Video

iMovie will place thumbnail images of the movie clips in the clips area to the right. If you have more than one segment on the tape, iMovie will separate them into separate clips. However, if your video was already finished, as a wedding video might be, you might want the whole video imported as a single clip. If this is the case, you just turn off the Automatic Scene detection feature. To turn it off, go to the iMovie menu, select Preferences, and uncheck the box called "Automatically start new clip at scene break."

To capture your video, do the following.

1. Connect your analog video capture hardware to the Mac's FireWire port. Connect the Video-Out port and the two Audio-Out ports of your VCR or camcorder to the capture hardware's input ports.

2. Turn on the VCR or analog video camcorder. The camcorder should be in VTR (or VCR) mode.

3. Launch iMovie and create a new project. By default, iMovie will capture the video to the start up drive (in the Movies folder of your home folder). If you want to capture the video to a separate hard drive, you can specify it now. Select New Project from the File menu. A dialog will slide down asking you to name the new project. Click the triangle to expand the dialog and show the file browser, and select the hard drive.

4. When the iMovie window opens, click the Camera switch in the lower left to the Camera position (see Figure 10-4).

FIGURE 10-4: iMovie's
Camera switch.

5. Click the Play button (triangle) below the screen area.

6. Start the movie playing on your VCR or camcorder.

7. Click Import *before* the movie starts to avoid cutting off the beginning. If it starts before you can import, rewind, and try again. Figure 10-5 shows what iMovie looks like during import.

8. Click the Stop button (square) after the movie stops.

FIGURE 10-5: When iMovie is capturing your video to your hard disc, it will play the movie in its screen.

You should see your movie clip (or clips) in the clips area at right.

Clean Up

You now have your digitized video on your hard drive and are ready for some basic editing. iMovie gives you lots of editing tools for creating well-mixed video pieces — we'll look at some of them in Chapter 11. For now, we'll assume that you're just interested in the transfer from analog tape to DVD. The first thing you'll want to get rid of is the empty space before and after the movie.

Start by switching iMovie to editing mode. Moving the camera switch to the scissors icon (see Figure 10-4). Now drag your clip (or clips) to the bottom section of the iMovie window. If you have multiple clips, you can arrange them in any order you'd like by dragging them left or right. Now click your first clip to select it.

To trim the dead space at the beginning of your movie, use the scrubber bar — that's the blue bar directly under the monitor window. Use the two crop markers at the beginning of the bar. Move the second one to the end of the dead space. If you drag it slowly, you'll see each frame of video displayed in the monitor pane above. You now have selected the dead space (see Figure 10-6.) Hit the delete key to remove the dead space. You can do the same for the dead space at the end of the last clip of the movie.

FIGURE 10-6: Select dead space at the beginning of the movie. You can hit the delete key.

If you like, you can delete section of the movie that you don't want. If you want to delete a large section, you're better off splitting the clip into two clips and deleting the clip you don't want.

To split a clip, click it to select it, then drag the playhead on the scrubber bar to the frame where you want to break the clip. Now go to the Edit menu and select Split Clip at Playhead. The new clip will appear in the Clips pane. You can break the clip again to get another clip.

Your video is now digitized and in good shape. There are a few more postproduction activities you can do in iMovie, such as adding titles, editing the soundtrack, and creating chapters markers for the DVD. Before we get to that, we want to explore the other type of movie medium you can digitize — movie film. The next section explains your options for capturing your really old home movies. The sections after that will show you how to use your digitized tape or film to create a DVD.

Digitizing Movie Film

Most people aren't shooting film these days, but there's a good chance one of your relatives once did. Back in the days before VCRs, it was common for people to shoot home movies on 8-mm film and on Super 8, a variant introduced in 1965 with smaller sprocket holes and bigger frames. (If you're not sure which you have, see Figure 10-7.) You may also have some 16-mm film, a higher-end film stock used in college film courses. Professional movies shown in theaters have traditionally used 32-mm film stock.

8 mm   **Super 8**

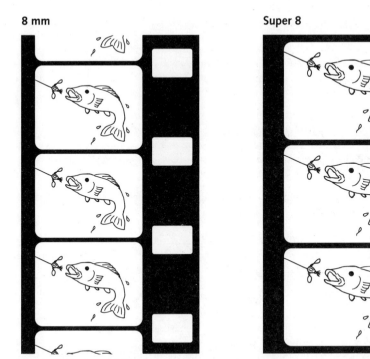

FIGURE 10-7: Super 8 film has bigger frames than 8-mm film, and smaller holes located at the center of the frames instead of at the edges. Super 8 holes are also spaced farther apart than in 8-mm film.

Digitizing film is much tougher than digitizing video, due to an extra conversion step involved — transferring a nonelectronic format to an electronic format. Home video is already electronic — you just need to convert it form analog electronic to digital. With film, you can convert light images created by a projector directly to digital electronic via a miniDV camcorder. However, there is a great deal of skill required, and the quality (and cost) of your equipment will greatly determine the quality of the result. When you digitize video yourself, you can get just as good quality as you could in paying someone to do it. With film, a professional service with a $10,000 telecine machine will give you a better result than what you can get at home.

The main issue is the flickering of the image you get when videotaping film. But if it comes to a choice of distributing your family's old movie film archives on DVD, or leaving the reels unseen in a box in the basement, most people will accept the flicker.

The good news is that DVD offers higher-quality graphics and audio than videotape, which means your old films will look better on DVD than on analog tape. For that reason, if you had films converted to tape 20 years ago, you might want to go back to the source film and convert it to digital.

The Conversion Processes

Flicker is caused by differences in frame rates between film and video. 8-mm and Super 8 film typically run at 24 frames per second (fps). Older film ran at 18 fps. However, standard NTSC video (used in North America and Japan) runs at approximately 30 fps — 29.97 fps, to be exact. Because film and video frames aren't in sync, you end up with a flicker on the videotape.

If you've ever rented movie videos, you may have noticed that there is no flicker. This is because the pros use a process that inserts one extra frame for every four frames to bring it up to 30 fps. You can have this type of processing done to your 8-mm or Super 8 movies, but it is expensive. (This is sometimes called *telecine*, though the word is also used to describe any process for converting film to video.)

There are other methods for dealing with flicker, with different degrees of success. You have three choices:

- **Tape a projection.** This involves using a digital camcorder to shoot the images created by your film projector. With this process, you can't completely eliminate flicker.

- **Buy a converter machine.** This will cost between $1,000 and $2,000.

- **Have your film professionally converted.** The results can vary, so you'll want to be sure the outfit you've selected has the proper equipment.

The next few sections will describe each of these options.

Tape a Projection

This is the cheapest and easiest way to get movie film onto video. The result isn't as good as when done with a telecine machine, but you can experiment completely without risk.

You will need a film projector, a digital camcorder (such as the popular and high-quality miniDV format) mounted on a tripod, and a television monitor connected to the camcorder. Figure 10-8 illustrates the setup. The television monitor should be located behind the camcorder, but in a place where you can see it as you make adjustments You'll want to feed the video (without recording) to the monitor while you make adjustments to the projector and camcorder. The camcorder's LCD screen is too small for this purpose.

Note
You could use an analog camcorder, such as the Video 8 format, if that's what you have. However, you'd then have to digitize the video, as described earlier in the chapter, in order to get it onto your Mac.

Since it takes some trial and error to get everything positioned correctly, you might want to record all of your film in one session. This is especially important if you plan to edit the video with clips from different reels — in that case, you'll want the framing and size of the image, and the other attributes to be similar for all the captured reels.

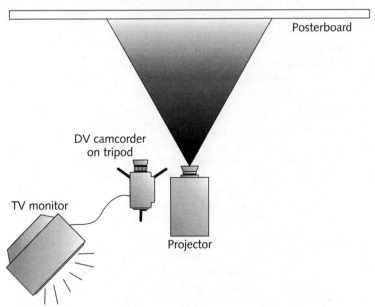

FIGURE 10-8: When taping film, the camera should be as close to the projector as possible, and at the same height as the projector's lens.

Position the Projector and Camera

Project the movie image on a white poster board or white paper mounted on a wall, or other matt white surface, such as a spray-painted board. Don't use a movie screen—these are designed to reflect light at wide angles for viewing by multiple people; you want the light to directly enter your camcorder lens.

Adjust the distance between the projector and surface so that you create an image that is between 1 and 2 feet wide. In general, smaller projections will give you cleaner, sharper results, but if you go too small, the white areas of the image will get too bright for your camcorder. In the terminology of color balance, the white point will be too hot, which will affect all of your colors. If you are familiar with your camera's white balance settings, you might want to experiment with them while watching the monitor.

Place the camcorder as close to the projector as possible. This will give you a taped screen that looks rectangular, not distorted by perspective. The camcorder's lens should also be at the same height as the projector's lens, and as far away from the image surface as the projector's lens.

Now you'll want to adjust the camcorder for framing of the images using your optical zoom. There is a slight difference in aspect ratio between video and film, in that the film is slightly wider. If you zoom in too close, you'll crop some of the image. You should instead consider going a little big on the framing to include black area on the edges. If you put the video on DVD, you can always use a frame around the image.

Focus and Flicker

Using your camcorder's automatic focus can be tricky, because the variations in light and the motion will confuse the autofocus. The camera needs to focus on the flat surface that is a few feet away. One way to go is to manually focus while you watch the images in the television monitor connected to the camcorder. If that is too difficult, tape a printed image to the poster board. With the projector turned off, have the camera autofocus on the printed material. Then, turn autofocus off, and don't mess with the focus during the taping.

Now you can decide if you want to try to reduce flicker. You can experiment with some options while the camera is producing an image in the monitor, but not recording. If you have a variable speed projector, you can try slowing down or speeding up the film. If the film was shot at 24 fps, you can speed it up to 30 fps. The drawback speeding up the film is that it could make the action look unnatural, particularly if there are people in the shots. Slowing the projector down to 20 fps might be more acceptable and will greatly reduce flicker, because more frames will be in sync. If you have 8-mm film shot at 18 fps moving up to 20 will have even less affect on the action.

Don't worry about the numbers — keep your eye on the TV monitor as you adjust the projector speed. It's a judgment call on which is more acceptable, the change in speed or the flicker.

Note   Some high-end (and expensive) digital camcorders, such as the Panasonic AG-DVX100, can shoot at 24 frames per second in what is called 24 progressive mode. However, televisions only display video at 29.97 fps, so the camera will do telecine process known as 3:2 pulldown to convert the picture to 29.97 fps, resulting in flicker. The only way to view the flicker-free 24 fps is to convert the images to a QuickTime movie to view on your Mac. As soon as you convert it for TV viewing, you get flicker.

Buy a Telecine Machine

If you are transferring a lot of film to video, you might be interested in getting your own telecine machine. These will give you better results than shooting the projected movie. However, the results can vary with the different machines. Hollywood converts films to VHS using a machine called a flying spot scanner. Although several companies now make these, they are often referred to as "Rank" machines after the Rank-Cintel company that perfected the technology for the film industry in the 1980s. You can't afford one of these, unless you're ready to drop $60,000 for a used system. However, if you are searching for a service to do a transfer for you, one with a Rank machine is at the top of the line.

What you can get are machines in the $1,000 to $2,000 range. These are often used units that you can find for sale on the Internet or through photo supply outfits. The most common models are the Goko TC-20 and the Elmo TRV series. Using a revolving prism mechanism, these devices were designed in the early 1980s for photo shops doing film-to-video conversion. However, this old technology has limitations. For instance, the Elmo TRV series can only give you 240 lines of horizontal resolution — compare that to the more than 500 lines that DVD supports. These early machines also tend to crop the images. Other, less common, but possibly newer units in this category include the Fumeo 9131, Panasonic WV-J20N, and Sony BM2100. Machines by Laird Telemedia and Buhl are more recent and give better results.

Video Transfer Boxes

Another way of taping a movie film projection is to use a video transfer box. These were invented when video first hit the big time, replacing Super 8 as the home movie medium of choice. You can still find such a transfer box at some photo supply stores. The projector and the cameras both point into the box. Mirrors are sometime used. With a video transfer box it is easier to get a true square image than with a wall projection. The problem with transfer boxes is that the projected image is often small, just a few inches wide, which can give you the problem mentioned earlier of having a very "hot" white point balance. This gives you very bright white spots and washed-out color. If the film footage that was shot was on the dark side, you might not have this problem and will be able to get good results.

In addition to any questions of quality, there is a risk to plunking down a big chunk of money for a used piece of equipment that is no longer built. If it breaks down, you may find it difficult to get repaired or find replacement parts. There is one small company, MovieStuff, that will sell you a brand-new, handmade telecine in this same price range. The machine is the Video WorkPrinter

The Video WorkPrinter

In 2001, a commercial filmmaker and photographer named Roger Evans was wrestling with the idea of buying a used telecine machine. "I was looking to transfer my own film to video, and the latest unit I could find was built in 1980, and the quality wasn't all that good."

Evans, who also has a background in optics and electronics, decided to build his own telecine machine. A few people he knew were impressed with the results, and asked Evans to build them one as well. Word spread, favorable reviews on the Internet popped up, and now Evans is building 400 telecine machines a year from his Web site MovieStuff (www.moviestuff.tv). Every unit is hand built.

Evan's most popular model is the Video WorkPrinter (see Figure 10-9), which starts at $1,200. It's also popular with film hobbiests. A poll of Super 8 users at the Shooting 8mm Web site (www.8mm.filmshooting.com) showed that the Video WorkPrinter most readers' favorite machine for transferring film to video.

The reason for the WorkPrinter's popularity is the high-quality, flicker-free transfers it produces. The WorkPrinter captures every frame, one frame at a time. Every frame is sharp and accurate. Connected to your Mac and a special mouse that comes with the system, the WorkPrinter acts as an optical scanner. A custom-built projector shoots the movie image through a condenser lens assembly that aims the image directly at your digital camera's CCD (charge-coupled device). The CCD converts light images into electronic signals. Using special software, the WorkPrinter creates a digital video file directly on your Mac through the camera connected via FireWire.

FIGURE 10-9: The Video WorkPrinter from MovieStuff scans in your movie one frame at a time.
Photo by Roger Evans/MovieStuff.

The role of the special mouse is to trigger the capture of each frame. One cable plugs into the USB port of your Mac and another connects to the projector. The mouse sends a mouse click signal at between 1 and 6 frames per second. With each click signal, the WorkPrinter captures a frame and advances the film to the next frame.

To move the film, the WorkPrinter doesn't use sprockets, which can sometimes rip or crumple film. Instead, the take-up reel moves the film, which is handled on the edges by spring-loaded dampers.

Software for Video WorkPrinter

Roger Evans doesn't sell the software necessary to operate the Video WorkPrinter, but he does recommend software created specially for the purpose. For the Mac, there's CaptureMate ($40, www.bensoftware.com/capturemate/), by software developer Ben Bird.

Figure 10-10 shows the CaptureMate setup window, which is what you see when your Mac is connected to the Video WorkPrinter but before you start capture. You use the Options button to define the parameters of your setup. The image is a video preview. Once you have things set, press the Start button to start the process. If you have the Preview during Capture check box selected, you'll see each frame displayed as it is captured.

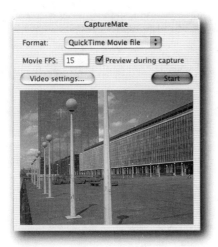

FIGURE 10-10: CaptureMate works with the Video WorkPrinter
from MovieStuff. Press the Start button to begin the capture.

Once you press the Start button, you can go to the beach, or to work, because the process can take awhile. If you have the 1-fps WorkPrinter Jr., a 400-foot role of film could take about 9 hours to capture. At 6 frames per second capture rate, the time is reduced to 90 minutes. You'll need a faster Mac for the higher-speed Video WorkPrinters, however.

If you're planning to view the captured movie on a television monitor, you'll have to use another piece of software to process the frame rate of the movie. The process, called 3:2 pull down, converts the 24 frames per second of your film to the 30 frames per second of the NTSC television standards. Unfortunately, the software to do this tends to be fairly expensive. Apple's $1,000 Final Cut Pro does a great job, but the $300 Final Cut Express doesn't have this ability. Adobe Premier can also do this, but doesn't do as good a job.

Twixter from RE:Vision Effects, Inc. ($330, www.revisionfx.com/rstwixtor.htm) does a very good job as an After Effects plug in inside of Adobe Premier, Final Cut Pro, and other video-editing applications.

Another option is a program called Dodcap ($70, www.alternaware.com). Dodcap is another capture program for the Video WorkPrinter, but it also does the frame rate conversion, something that CaptureMate doesn't do. That catch is that Dodcap is Windows-only software. You can run it on the Mac with Virtual PC, the emulation program from Microsoft (formerly from Connectix). However, Virtual PC is very processor-intensive, so your Mac may not be able to capture at higher frame rates.

Importing into iMovie

With your film in digital format, the hard part is over. Now you'll need to bring the digital file into iMovie for some postproduction, to get it ready for the DVD.

If the digital video is on a Mini DV 8 cartridge, importing it into iMovie is easy. Connect the digital camcorder to your Mac's FireWire port and open iMovie. Switch iMovie to Camera mode. You can now use iMovie's Import button. The process is almost the same as importing analog video through a video capture device, as described earlier in the section called The Video Capture Process. The difference is that with a digital camcorder connected via FireWire, you can use iMovie's motion controls (Play, Stop, Rewind, and so on) to control the camera.

If the digital video is already on your hard drive, go to iMovie's File menu and select Import. In the file browser dialog that appears, locate the digital video file, select it, and click the Open button. The file will appear as a clip.

Shopping for a Film Transfer Service

If all this sounds like more than you're willing to take on, you always can use a telecine service. A service might also give you better quality than you can get yourself. There are a range of businesses that offer film-to-digital transfers, from local camera shops, film developers, and video stores to national companies that specialize in telecine. The cost also ranges widely, depending on the quality of the equipment. Some businesses charge per foot, others charge per hour. A per-foot charge gives you a more definite idea of what the cost will be.

After you ask about the cost, you should ask what type of equipment they use. Ask for specifics: Is it Rank, Moviestuff, Buhl, or Goko? If they use a digital camera, ask if it has three CCDs, which will give better results than a one-CCD camera. More expensive services will clean the film before transferring it. For an extra fee, some services offer color correction to restore film that may have faded with time.

You don't necessarily need the best processing. A Rank lab, the type used by Hollywood, is probably more than you need. You can find services using older equipment referred to as multiplexers, such as a Buhl machine, which can charge 10 cents a foot. Services that use the old Goko and Elmo won't give you best quality—use these only if the price is right. At the bottom end are people who are not using a telecine machines, but are shooting projects off of the wall or with a video transfer box. These will give you flicker. If you go with a service like this don't pay anywhere near 10 cents a foot.

Some shops use equipment built by Roger Evans' MovieStuff (www.moviestuff.tv). Moviestuff itself does transfers on Evan's $10,000, three-CCD DV8 Professional Telecine Machine, the most complex model that Evans builds. At press time, Moviestuff was converting film for a rate of $20 per 50 feet. Moviestuff cleans your film and offers color correction for extra fees. One very nice feature is that Moviestuff offers a free test—it will convert 1 minute of film for free.

Ask about what media the movie comes back on. Some services offer DVDs. If you want to create your own DVD, ask for MiniDV tape. Just make sure that it's digital. If your movie comes back on analog videotape, you'll have to run the signal through a video capture device, as described earlier in the chapter.

There is good reason to find a local telecine service—you can personally hand deliver your precious old family films, without risking shipping them. However, that isn't always possible, and you might not find the best deal locally. There are many services that get most of their business through the Web. You can find some of them by searching the Internet for "film to DVD" or "digitize film."

If you do have to ship your file, ship it overnight with a service that tracks your packages, such as Federal Express or the Postal Service's Express Mail. (Other Postal Service options are not tracked.) You don't want your film sitting all day in some hot warehouse, or going for an un-air-conditioned cross-country truck ride. You should also insure it, though it's tough to put a monetary value on something as priceless as old home movies.

Postproduction

At this point, you have a digitized movie. It doesn't matter whether it originated on videotape or Super 8 film—to iMovie, it's the same. Before you place it on a DVD, there are a few optional editing tasks you might want to do first. In the film industry, *postproduction* is a general term that describes everything that occurs after filming, including editing. In this chapter, we're using the term to mean four procedures, which should be done in this order:

1. Adjust the color and brightness.

2. Add titles.

3. Enhance the soundtrack.

4. Add chapter markers for use on the DVD.

Of course, iMovie and other video editors offer much more in terms of editing tools. And, of course, you can still cut out scenes that are dull, too long, or badly shot. However, in this chapter, we're assuming that you started with movies that are finished. If you are interested in the fancy transitions and effects, knock yourself out. However, these four postproduction items are the main areas to consider before going to DVD. We'll also look at archiving to digital tape, which is a good idea for safeguarding your work.

 Note Once you have a library of old videos or movies in digital form, you have the ability to make a brand-new movie by using segments from different old home movies—your own Ken Burns documentary on your family history. Some of the editing techniques you might use for those projects are described in Chapter 11.

Adjust the Color and Brightness

You should think of the color and brightness controls as repair mechanisms for problem spots in a movie, an attempt to restore faded colors or to make a dark scene more visible. You will probably not need to apply color and brightness for the entire movie. You may not need to apply color and brightness changes at all.

iMovie does not give you a high degree of color and brightness adjustments—you can get far more control in Final Cut Express, Apple's midlevel video editor. The problem is, that you really have to know what you are doing with the more advanced tools. If you are a novice video editor, iMovie doesn't require that you become an expert. If you are a video-editing expert, iMovie's controls won't satisfy you.

In iMovie, the color and brightness controls are applied as effects. You select the frames you want to alter, choose an effect, make adjustments, and view the results. If you think there's an improvement, then you add the effect. You can also view the movie with the effect before making it permanent.

To start, click the Effects button on the right. The clips pane will turn into the Effects pane, shown in Figure 10-11. There are two effects we're interested in now, Adjust Colors and Brightness & Contrast. Here's how to apply them:

1. Select the clip you want to tweak.

2. Use the crop markers on the scrubber bar to choose the frames of the movie you want to tweak.

3. In the effects pane, click on an effect and use the sliders to make adjustments. The Adjust Colors effect gives you slider controls for Hue Shift, Color, and Lightness. The Brightness & Contrast effect gives you one slider for each.

4. Click the Preview button to view your changes in the big monitor window to the left.

5. When you are satisfied with your adjustments, click the Apply button.

There are also third-party plug-in effects that you can add to iMovie. These will appear in the effects pane.

Add Titles

Titles can add a lot to a movie. They announce the subject matter and the start of the piece. Credits at the end can announce the end. You can also insert titles in the middle of a long movie to break it up and to transition between contrasting sections or subjects. You can also add identification text as commentary in a corner (as with iMovie's Music Video title style) or at the bottom (the Subtitle style). If your digitized movie has primitive titles, such as those added with an old video camera, you may want to replace them with new titles you create in iMovie.

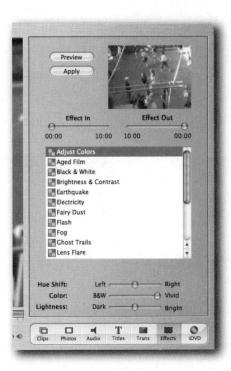

FIGURE **10-11:** iMovie's Effects pane gives you different controls for each selected effect.

Titles should be easy to read — if the audience can't read them, the titles have failed. In general, simpler is easier to read. There are several things you can do to increase legibility:

- Use white letters on a black or dark background. Resist iMovie's offer to let you use colored text.

- Use a still (nonmoving) background. iMovie lets you put titles over a movie, but if there's a lot of panning and zooming or action on the screen, the titles won't be noticed. You can use a frame from the movie, but importing an old photo to the beginning of a movie can be a nice touch. Just don't use a shot of people looking into the camera. Use a landscape, a building, flowers, or an abstract subject. Woody Allen often starts his movies with white letters on a black background. That's still an effective way to go, and is *really* easy in iMovie.

- Use large letters. In iMovie, you set the text size with a slider bar next to the font pop-up menu (see Figure 10-12).

- A simple, sans serif font, such as Arial or Helvetica, works best. You choose these from the font pop-up menu.

- Titles at the beginning of a movie should be short. If you have a lot of words, include them as credits at the end of the movie.

- The titles should be on-screen long enough to be read. iMovie's Speed and Pause sliders let you set how fast the text moves and how long it pauses.

- Use a drop shadow. (iMovie uses a drop shadow by default.)

FIGURE 10-12: iMovie's Title pane lets you put a title over a still photo, shown here. The movie here starts with a title over a black background.

To create titles in iMovie, you first work with the text. iMovie offers various title styles which animate the text in different ways. After you decide on all aspects of the text, you then place the title in the movie.

1. If you are using a still photo, bring it into the movie. You can drag it to the Clip Viewer from the Finder, or use the iPhoto button and drag down a photo from your iPhoto collection.

2. Click the Titles button to bring up the Titles pane.

3. If you want to use a black background, click Over Black.

4. Type your text in the fields provided.

5. Scroll through the list of title styles in the center of the pane. When you click a style, your text will appear in the small sample box in the upper right.

6. You can change the direction of motion of the text with the arrow buttons.

7. Adjust the Speed and Pause sliders to set the time the titles appear on screen.

8. Change the font and text size if necessary.

9. Click the preview button to see your titles.

Now drag the title style name to the Clip Viewer, dropping it in front of the clip or photo you want it to appear on. If you choose a black background, iMovie will add a new clip with the title.

Enhancing the Soundtrack

You can consider the soundtrack after you completely finished the video and titles. Otherwise, your soundtrack might not be in sync with the video. There are a number of things you can do with iMovie to spruce up the soundtrack to improve the movie. First you can add audio content that isn't there. For instance:

- Add music to titles and other areas where there is no dialog. iMovie gives you direct access to your iTunes music library and to any audio CDs in your Mac's drive.

- Add a soundtrack of music and/or voice. If your movie originally came from 8-mm or Super 8 film, you may have a silent movie. Using popular music from the year the movie was shot can be an effective device.

- If your videotape already has a music soundtrack, consider rerecording it with iMovie. DVD can hold better quality sound than videotape, which may have degraded and acquired a hiss over time.

- Record a vocal commentary — either your voice or those of people in the movie. To record your voice, you use the Record button in the Audio pane.

iMovie supports multiple audio tracks so you can have music and spoken words at the same time. Just lower the volume of the music when people are speaking.

You can also touch up the existing sounds in the movie:

- Adjust the volume or portions of the soundtrack. Maybe you were talking too loudly behind the camera while the four-year-old was speaking too quietly in front of it. With iMovie, you can fix this.

- Remove parts of the original soundtrack. Remember that unbelievably stupid thing you said from behind the camera? Now's your chance to get rid of it.

- Have dialogue or music fade in and out. Fading dialogue in or out is a great way to smooth what otherwise might be a rough transition.

- Use a part of the soundtrack in a different part of the movie. You do this by splitting the section of soundtrack from the main movie with a command called Extract Audio.

iMovie has also sound effects — things like applause, trains, and thunder. Use these sparingly, if at all.

Adjusting Volume in iMovie

To work with sound in iMovie, you use the Timeline Viewer. Click the clock icon on the lower left, and the Clip Viewer is replaced by the TimelineViewer (see Figure 10-13).

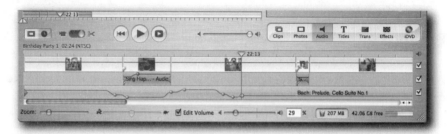

FIGURE 10-13: When working with sound in iMovie, the timeline view lets you control the volume of two tracks of sound, in addition the soundtrack on the video. The line in the middle of each track represents the volume.

On the timeline, you'll see three horizontal tracks. The top is the video track. The second is an audio track that you extract from the video. The bottom is for audio that you add.

To adjust the volume of any portion of the movie soundtrack, including the fade in and fade out, click the check box labeled Edit Volume. When you do, you'll see a line appear in the middle of each track. You can edit the volume at any place by clicking at a spot and dragging the volume line up or down.

Extracting the Audio Track from a Video Clip

To separate the sound from the soundtrack, click on a video clip to select it. Now choose Extract Audio from the Advanced menu. The audio appears in the first track under the video track, as before. However, it will be locked to the video, as indicated by a little drawing of a pin. To unlock the audio clip from the video, select the audio clip and choose Unlock Audio Clip from the Advanced menu. Now you can copy or move this soundtrack around the timeline.

Adding Audio to your Movie

You add sound to the timeline using the Audio pane, shown in Figure 10-14. Press the Audio button to bring up the Audio pane. The Audio pane lets you add four types of audio:

- Audio from your iTunes library and playlists

- Audio from a CD in your Mac

- Sound effects that come with iMovie

- Voice that you record with the Audio pane

You can access the first three from the pop-up menu at the top. You can also search your iTunes library with the Search field.

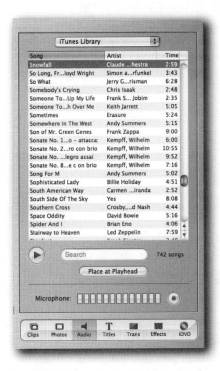

FIGURE 10-14: The Audio pane lets you choose a song from iTunes or an audio CD in your movie. You can also record narration here.

Tip   You can sort the list of songs by clicking on the column heads in the Audio pane. Clicking on the Time column head will help you find a song that best fits a scene.

To place a song or sound effect in the timeline, select it from the Audio pane. Move the play-head along the scrubber bar (under the monitor window) to the exact frame you want the music to start. Now click the Place at Playhead button. Your song or sound effect will appear in the bottom track of the timeline.

Shortening Audio Clips

You don't have to use an entire song, as iMovie lets you clip a song and then fade it in and out using the volume controls. There are two ways to shorten a piece of music. The first is to split the audio clip just as you would split a video clip and delete the part you don't want. To cut an audio clip:

1. Click on the audio clip in the timeline to select it.

2. Drag the playhead to the spot where you want to split the audio clip.

3. Go to the Edit menu and select Split Selected Audio Clip at playhead.

4. Click on the part of the clip you don't want and hit the Delete key.

The other way to shorten a piece of music is to keep the whole clip, but tell iMovie to only play a portion of it. This method has the advantage of letting you readjust the portion to be played in case you change your mind. Volume editing must be turned off to do this.

1. Make sure the Edit Volume box is unchecked.

2. Click on the audio clip in the timeline to select it.

3. Drag the triangle crop markers at either end of the clip to shorten the clip.

The muted portions of the audio clip will be a lighter color (as shown in Figure 10-15.)

FIGURE 10-15: Cropping an audio clip in iMovie retains the music, but mutes the portions not within the crop marks.

You can now fade in using the Edit volume lines, as described in the previous section.

Using Noise Reduction Software

You may remember from Chapters 7 and 9 that you can use noise reduction software on digital video sound soundtracks as well as on audio files. This software also works well for removing constant noise from video soundtracks, such as wind blowing into a camera's microphone, free-way noise, or the hum from recording equipment.

To use noise reduction software, you have to split the soundtrack from a clip. Click on a clip to select it. Now choose Extract Audio from the Advanced menu. The audio appears in the first track under the video track, as before. What iMovie has done is to create a new audio file containing the soundtrack. (The soundtrack is still in the imbedded file—it's just muted.) All you need to do now is to go to the new audio file and open it with your noise reduction software.

Open the "Media" folder for the iMovie project you are working on. The default location is in your home folder:

/Users/[yourname]/Movies/[project name]/Media

If you told iMovie to create the project on a separate hard disk, it will be there. The first file you extract is called Voice 01. The second is Voice 02, and so on. Now launch your audio software, and open the Voice file. You can use Ray Gun, SoundSoap, or an audio-editing application such as Peak LE running SoundSoap as a plug in. You can make changes to this file. iMovie will continue to use it, just as long as you keep it where it is and don't rename it.

Add Chapter Markers for iDVD 3

Remember in Chapter 9 how we broke up a recorded album into separate tracks? You can do a similar task in digital video when you create chapter markers. iMovie 3 and later lets you add up to 36 chapters that will be moved over to iDVD, complete with identifying thumbnails. (You need iDVD 3 or later.) Chapters let the viewer of a DVD jump to a section without having to fast forward. If you've rented DVD movies, you've probably seen chapters in the video menu.

Use chapters to mark the beginning of new scenes, or to indicate the beginning of a change in the action. Chapters that start randomly or in the middle of some action just aren't useful. Create chapter titles that describe how the scene begins or what transpires. Titles such as "Chapter 5" or "Sue and Dad" aren't descriptive, but "The Bride Enters the Church" is. Section titles that you inserted into the middle of a movie are perfect spots for chapter markers.

To set a chapter in iMovie, do the following:

1. Bring the timeline view up by clicking the clock icon on the lower left.
2. Drag the timeline cursor to the spot where you want a chapter to begin.
3. Click the iDVD button on the right side.
4. Click the Add Chapter button. A thumbnail will appear in the list at right. (See Figure 10-16,)
5. Type a name for the chapter to the right of the thumbnail.

You can keep on adding chapters this way until you have enough.

FIGURE 10-16: Chapters you add in iMovie will move to iDVD.

Archive to Digital Tape

If you have a digital camcorder, it's a good idea to archive the completed movie to digital tape, such as the miniDV. Use a brand-new tape. This will be the master version of your completed movie. In the long term, you don't want to keep your movies on your hard disk. In addition to taking up a lot of storage space, hard disk are prone to problems that can result in the loss of data.

DVD is a good distribution method and is estimated to last 100 years, but a serious scratch in the right place can make a DVD unplayable. With the project archived to miniDV tape, you can create new DVDs or go back to use portions of the movie for another project.

To archive your movie to miniDV tape in iMovie, connect your digital camcorder to the Mac's FireWire port. Go to iMovie's File menu, and pick Export. A dialog appears (see Figure 10-17). Select To Camera in the Export menu. Change the amount of black before and after the movie to 30 seconds. This will give you a safe cushion should you need to use this tape again.

Remember, this is a backup tape—don't use it to watch the movie. It will be safest kept in a cool, dark, dry place with your other master tapes.

FIGURE 10-17: iMovie's Export dialog.

Move the Movie to iDVD

When you are finished making any changes, you can export the movie from iMovie 3.0 and later to iDVD. To do this, you need to have the iDVD pane displayed (see Figure 10-16). Click the Create iDVD Project button. Your Mac will think for a bit, and then iDVD will open.

Creating a DVD

There is a lot you can do with DVD video. You are moving the movie to DVD because it is an easy distribution media, and lets you jump around the movie while you play it. DVD can hold 90 minutes of video—a pretty long home movie, but you are not obligated to fill it up. You can add "bonus features"—as on professional movie DVDs. For instance, iDVD makes it easy to add a slide show of some of the photos you took on the vacation along with the video. Or, if this is an old movie, you can shoot some new footage of family members reflecting on the events of the original.

This section is going to take you through the basics of moving the main movie to DVD. We are going to demonstrate using iDVD, but the concepts can be applied to other DVD authoring tools. The first step is designing the interface that will greet your viewers when they slip the disc into a DVD player and turn on their TV.

Designing a User Interface

Unlike an audio CD, a DVD has a user interface that appears on screen. If you've never rented DVD movies before, do so before you start your project. You'll see some of the elements. In Hollywood movie DVDs, you get a sort of pre-movie title page that shows some action or animation and often takes you to the video menu. The video menu is where the user chooses to play one or more movies, or to go to an "extras" area (called a folder in iDVD). The video menu can also offer a scene selection item that brings up another screen for jumping to different places in the movie. (These are the *chapters* you may have created in iMovie.)

iDVD doesn't give you the pre-movie action, but it does let you have a video/audio preview in a big window on the video menu. Figure 10-18 shows iDVD with a big picture along side of the video menu selections. The big picture is actually a preview area, a short loop of video (perhaps 15 seconds long with some music playing behind it. This could also be a still photo with or without music, or a slide show (a succession of still images). The preview area (or Drop Zone, as it is called in iDVD) gives the viewer an impression of what's in the movie, but is not a menu item. The menu items are text only in this design.

FIGURE 10-18: This iDVD theme has a big preview window for a short loop of video, while the menu items are text.

iDVD has several dozen other design templates, called themes. Figure 10-19 shows another theme that doesn't have a Drop Zone preview area. Instead, the menu items are video instead of plain text. This type of design works better if you have several short movies (or slide shows).

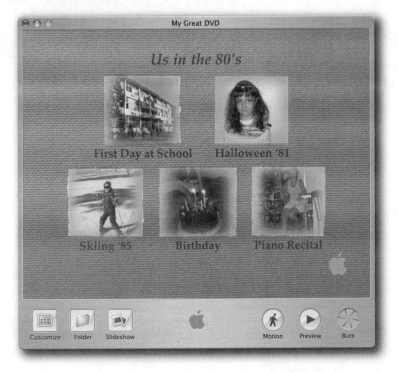

FIGURE 10-19: This iDVD theme uses video in the menu selection items.

Choose a Theme in iDVD

In iDVD, the first step in designing a DVD user interface is to choose a theme. Each theme defines the location of items, the color scheme and decorative art, as well as fonts. (You can change them if you like.) To choose a theme in iDVD, do the following:

1. Click the Customize button at the bottom of the iDVD window. A drawer will slide out (see Figure 10-20).

2. At the top of the drawer, you'll see a button bar similar to the one in iMovie. Click the Themes button.

3. Choose All from the pop-up menu near the top of the drawer.

4. As you click on different themes in the drawer, you'll see the main screen change. Click the Motion button (see Figure 10-21) on the main window to see the animation in the themes. The Motion button toggles the motion on and off.

5. Pick a theme now—you can select another later if you change your mind.

FIGURE 10-20: The iDVD drawer is where you choose your theme. Clicking one of the buttons at the top of the drawer lets you change other aspects of the DVD project.

FIGURE 10-21: The Motion button.

Filling a Drop Zone

Your project windows start with either a title and a Drop Zone, or just a title. There are no buttons yet.

If your theme has a Drop Zone (the area that shows a video preview), it will say "Drag your movies or photos here" (see Figure 10-22). You can drag and drop a movie there. To do that, click the Movie button on top. Drag a movie from the movie pane into the Drop Zone. If you'd rather have a still image, click the Photos button (see Figure 10-22) and drag a photo to the Drop Zone. If you'd rather have a slide show, drag a photo album. To have accompanying music, click the Music button to get access to your iTunes library. Drag a song over to the Drop Zone. (You can also drag any of this content from the Finder instead of using the buttons.) If you decide you want a different movie or photo, just click and drag the image to outside of the iDVD window.

FIGURE 10-22: This theme has a Drop Zone, so the buttons will be text only. The Photos button will let you drag your iPhoto pictures into the Drop Zone.

Once you have an image in the Drop Zone, you can arrange its position. Click the Motion button to stop the movie. Move the cursor over the image in the Drop Zone, and drag the image around until it is in the right place. Click the Motion button to start the movie and the music. This preview area won't play the entire movie, just the beginning of it.

You'll notice that the theme in Figure 10-22 comes with a rose petal background around the Drop Zone. If you don't like it, you can drag your own photo to the background.

Note that you haven't added the full movie to the DVD yet. For that, you need to create a button.

Add Buttons and Movies

You add an actual movie to the DVD project by dragging it to the menu area of screen. This also creates a menu item called a button.

In Figure 10-23, we've created three menu items on our Wedding menu. These are text only buttons because we are using a theme with a Drop Zone. (You could change these to graphic buttons if you want with the Settings button in the drawer.)

First, we dragged over the actual wedding video from the Movies pane to create the first item. You can drag in other movies if you like, but we're going to stick with one. The movie file had a funky file name, so we clicked on the name and renamed it to a simple "The Wedding Movie." When a user selects this option, the movie will play.

FIGURE 10-23: Dragging in a movie created the first two menu items (buttons). The third was created by dragging in an iPhoto album. A movie is running in the heart-shaped Drop Zone to the right.

Because our movie already had chapter markers in it from iMovie, iDVD automatically created the Scene Selection button, which links to a Scene submenu. Double-click the Scene Selection button, and you'll see a new video menu containing the first six chapters of the movie. A Next button brings the viewer to the next six chapters. There's also a Back button.

Finally, we dragged over an iPhoto picture album with some still photos of the wedding. This is our "bonus content." The iPhoto album originally had the same name as the movie — we renamed the menu item to make it more identifiable for the viewer.

To take a look at how the DVD might work, click the Preview button. A remote control panel (see Figure 10-24) appears to let us control the screen. It all works, except for the scene selection, which we haven't added yet.

FIGURE 10-24: iDVD's Preview button brings this remote control module up, to let you test out how the video menu will work.

Burn a DVD with iDVD

Once you are finished with importing your content and designing your user interface, you can burn the DVD. (There isn't actually anything being burned in the process, by the way. The term refers to the fact that a laser is used to heat the surface, which changes the reflectivity to represent either a 1 or a 0.)

If you've ever burned a CD in iTunes, then you know how to burn a DVD in iDVD. Click the Burn button. A little door opens on the button revealing a flashing icon. Click it. iDVD will check to see if your project has the required elements, then ask you to insert a blank DVD-R disc, as in Figure 10-25.

iDVD will first encode the movie in MPEG-2 format. This should take several minutes, depending on the speed of your Mac. It will then write the data to the disc — burn the DVD. This usually takes a minute or so, but doesn't take as long as the encoding.

Once you're done, you can burn additional copies if you like.

FIGURE 10-25: Click the Burn button twice, and the iDVD window goes blank.

Label Your DVD Disc

Imagine a shoebox full of unmarked silver discs. The only way you could locate anything would be to stick disc after disc into the DVD player. The answer is to label the disc and the jewel case you keep it. The jewel case gives you a little more room to list what's on the disc. If you're organized, you can mark a number on the disc with indelible ink and keep a log sheet that lists each number with a description of what's on each DVD. This only works if you keep the log sheet with the DVD collection.

However, it's far more fun to print labels for the DVD and the jewel case, especially if you're giving out copies of the DVD. You can do this with inexpensive software for your Mac and labels you can buy in an office supply store. Labeling a DVD is exactly the same as labeling a CD. Check the end of Chapter 9 for details.

Summary

Converting analog videotape to DVDs is a little like converting your vinyl LPs to CDs, as described in Chapter 9. In both cases, you connect your analog hardware to your Mac through an analog-to-digital converter, use software to capture the digitized signal, then save to an optical disc. In the case of video, you use a video capture box connected to a FireWire port. For software, you can use Apple's free iMovie, which does a great job.

Movie film, such as 8 mm and Super 8, brings a whole other level of complexity to the process. It's not so easy to get great results. The more you spend on equipment, the better results you can get. The same is true for a film conversion service you might use — the better equipment they have, the better results you will get. Just make sure you get digital video back,.

When your video or film is in digital form, you can perform some postproduction tasks to clean it up. iMovie is a good tool to add titles, clean up a soundtrack, and prepare the movie for the DVD.

You'll need a DVD burner drive. If you have an internal SuperDrive, you can use Apple's iDVD, which is the easiest DVD-authoring software to use and gives you better results than many packages that cost more. If you have an external FireWire DVD burner, you'll have to use another package.

This chapter focused on movies you or your older relatives have already made using older media. The next chapter focuses on digital movies that you haven't made yet.

Make a Killer Video

Making a digital video is easy. Whether it's a home movie or a short film that you might want to use in a business or school presentation, with today's equipment and your Mac, it just isn't that hard to do. Shoot on your digital camcorder. Plug it into your Mac via FireWire. Import it into iMovie.

The problem is, it's also easy to make a *bad* movie, one that is dull, pointless, repetitive, and fails to convey a message. The ease of use of the technology hasn't given us knowledge of how to make a *good* video, let alone a killer video.

Part of the trick is knowing what a killer video is. It's video that people want to watch. It's video that has a structure, that goes somewhere. It's video that gets a point across.

Getting there takes a little knowledge, some practice, some variety in shooting and editing. It doesn't take a lot of money — you can do a fine job with iMovie. Sure, you could better with Final Cut Express or Final Cut Pro, but only if you know what you're doing.

What Makes a Killer Video

A killer video can be fun and entertaining, or business-like and informative, but it is always interesting. A killer video is not an archival record of an event or a vacation. You can recall some of the fun aspects, or capture the feel, but you can't recreate a vacation in a video. And if a video is dull, you'll never watch it.

When you create a killer video, shoot with the idea that you will be editing. Edit with the idea of creating something interesting. You will create something interesting not with high-tech gadgets and fancy effects, but with the footage you shot.

This chapter gives you tips and techniques to help you put it together. Throughout this, keep in mind a balance of three directives you should follow:

Keep it short, keep it simple, and keep it moving.

- **Keep it short.** We're talking about a finished movie that is 10 minutes long, 15 minutes tops. A 10 minute-long home movie doesn't have room for dull segments that go on and on. A short movie is also something you can actually show to friends and family without monopolizing an entire evening.

  If you're creating a video for a presentation, go even shorter — think music video. When used in a business or school presentation, a short video breaks up a talk and highlights ideas. The video should not *be* the presentation.

  There is also a more practical reason to keep it short — you'll finish the project. If you have 8 hours of footage that you're trying to cut down to 90 minutes, the project will sit on your Mac for months. You'll learn a lot more by completing a bunch of short projects than by trying to tackle one *Lawrence of Arabia* that you won't finish.

  Yes, some videos have to be long — a wedding for example. But you won't be able to make a *killer* wedding video until you've made some killer 10-minute videos first.

- **Keep it simple.** Basically, don't go nuts with tricks. Don't use a lot of fancy special effects and transitions, or fancy fonts with long titles, or colored text. These things don't make a killer video; they make a confusing video. When you edit, use shots where the camera is still. In a business video for a presentation, don't try to jam in too much information or facts. This also applies to your equipment and your software — you don't need a bag of magic tricks. When shooting, some basic techniques will take you a long way.

- **Keep it moving.** Here's where the balancing comes in: Simple doesn't mean static. A movie should go somewhere. You can keep a movie moving with different camera angels and shots of different items, and good editing. It helps to have your subjects moving in certain shots. You should not have the camera moving, however.

What You Need

To create a killer video, you only need two basic ingredients: a digital camcorder (also known as a digital video camera) and a piece of digital-editing software. The digital camcorder doesn't come cheap, as you can spend $500 to $1,000 for a consumer model, and up to several thousand for a beefier camera. To balance it out, however, you can use a great piece of free software — iMovie. And, as with all *Mac Toys* projects, you'll need a Mac.

Hardware — Choosing a Digital Camcorder

The main piece of hardware is your digital video camera. If you don't have one yet, there are a few things to look for. First, look for a camera that fits your hand comfortably. Don't buy a digital camcorder without going to a store and physically handling it. Digital camcorders come in a variety of shapes and form factors — some are long and thin, others are more upright shaped. Check out which is comfortable for you. Look at the controls and see if you can easily reach them. You should be able to easily start and stop recording, zoom, or set various levels while you use the camera. Some camcorders offer touch screen controls on the LCD — this can smudge the LCD, but can be convenient.

As for features, you want a digital camera that connects to your Mac with FireWire, is Mac-compatible, and shoots to MiniDV tape.

There are lots of connectors and ports on digital video cameras that can connect directly to TVs, or to VCRs or other things. That's all fine, as long as you have a FireWire port. FireWire is common, but has different names. Sony uses the name iLink for its FireWire port, which is 4-pin FireWire instead of the standard 6-pin. This works just fine. Other manufactures use the term IEEE 1394. That's also just fine. Some cameras support wireless Bluetooth, which is built into Mac OS X 10.2 and later versions. However, at press time, there were no digital camcorders that could transfer video to Macs via Bluetooth. At this point, you need to stick with FireWire as the method of moving video into your Mac.

There are over a hundred Mac-compatible digital camcorder models. Cannon, JVC, Panasonic, and Sony all have many cameras that work with Macs. Some have features that only work using software for Windows. Don't fret too much — many of these features are there to make up for abilities that the Mac already has. Basically, the camera needs to be able to communicate with Macs. You can always ask the manufacturer or check its Web site, but Apple keeps a list of camcorder models that it has tested and certified as working with Mac OS X. You can see it at `www.apple.com/macosx/upgrade/camcorders.html`. However, even this page isn't the final word, because the list isn't always current — brand-new camcorders often take a few months to make it onto Apple's certification page.

MiniDV is a standard digital video camcorder format that describes both the tape and the recording format. The tape (shown in Figure 11-1) provides high quality at reasonable cost. A MiniDV cassette measures a mere 2.6" × 1.9", with tape that is $1/4$" wide. (You can find MiniDV tapes from Fuji, Maxell, Panasonic, and Sony, among others.) The DV format is used by iMovie, Final Cut Express, and Final Cut Pro. It provides better quality than the older analog formats, with up to 500 lines per inch resolution. MiniDV also provides excellent audio quality, providing two channels of up to 16-bit, 44-KHz stereo sound, or four channels of up to 12-bit, 32-KHz sound. However, lower-priced cameras have been known to pick up noise from camera's zoom motors. Some of Sony's entry-level digital camcorders put the DV format on the Hi8 tapes, a larger tape used in analog camcorders. There is no particular benefit to putting DV on Hi8, a practice that is likely to disappear over time.

The MiniDV format is big — 11 GB an hour. Several digital video cameras offer recording in a lower-quality, more compressed format for use on the Internet. These include MPEG-2, MPEG-4, and Motion-JPEG, which are often promoted as being used for emailing, or in the case of MPEG-4, for streaming on the Web. (QuickTime 6 and the QuickTime Streaming Server supports MPEG-4.) However, Mac users don't actually need the camcorder to support these formats, because iMovie 3 and Final Cut Pro can export in MPEG-4 format. It's best to shoot in straight DV format. Compression will occur later if you create a DVD.

Beyond the basics, there are a few other features to consider. Look at the LCD display, the flip-out panel that shows the image you're shooting. You'll want to check if the display is big and bright enough. More expensive digital camcorder often come with bigger displays (usually topping out at 4 inches maximum) or displays with higher pixel resolution. Bigger displays let you see the display when the camera is not next to your face, which is handy for getting shots from above or below your head. The tradeoff is that bigger displays can mean bigger cameras.

FIGURE 11-1: MiniDV tape, also called digital video cassette (DVC), is high quality and high capacity.

When looking at zoom specifications, you can pretty much ignore digital zoom — optical zoom is what counts. Optical zoom, produced by the lens, produces higher quality images than digital zoom, which is an interpolation of the image. Optical zoom gives you the same quality image at any zoom seating — digital zoom decreases image quality as the zoom setting increases.

Another feature where optical beats digital is *image stabilization*, which helps keeps the image from blurring as the camera moves. Blurring from motion is more of a problem at higher zoom levels. Digital stabilization degrades the image quality, while optical does not.

If you are interested in shooting low light conditions or fast moving objects without blurring, look for a camcorder with a large maximum aperture, which lets in more light. Larger apertures are indicated by a *smaller* f-stop number. Typical large-aperture camcorders come with an f1.4-to-f1.6 (where f1.4 is the larger aperture).

Tripods and Unipods

Getting a steady picture is always a concern when shooting video. A tripod can work wonders in getting good images and lets you walk over and be in the picture. However, you may find yourself leaving the tripod at home when traveling, because a full-sized collapsing tripod weighing several pounds just isn't a necessity. The cost also goes up as the tripod gets lighter.

Instead of full-sized tripod, think about getting a mini-tripod that doesn't expand to eye-level. To use, you can prop up on a table, wall or other object. Another option is a unipod (also called a monopod). Twenty dollars will buy you a full-sized unit that collapses into a small stick, though you can also spend much more. Because they only have one leg, you can't use unipods to get into the action yourself, but they will greatly stabilize your image. You can find mini-tripods and unipods in camera stores.

Editing Software

The first word in editing software is iMovie (`www.apple.com/imovie/`). It's free, it gets you editing immediately, and is the easiest way to import digital video. In order to become easy, iMovie did away with some of the options that higher-end editing programs have. (iMovie doesn't let you work with time codes, for instance.) But it lets you produce great results.

A good approach is to start with iMovie and get some killer videos under your belt. If you discover that you wish you had some other feature, then it might be time to spend some money. You can expand iMovie's functionality by adding plug-ins. (For instance, see `www.ezedia.com` and `www.imovieplugins.com`.) Or, if you want more options to tweak, you could move up to Apple's Final Cut Express ($300). It does things the way the high-end Final Cut Express does, but has fewer options.

Shooting Digital Video

This section will cover several basic techniques in shooting video for your killer video. They all have one thing in common — they strive for variety.

Shooting is the just the first part of making a killer video. Editing is equally important. But when you are shooting with the intention of editing, it changes how you shoot. You don't have to worry about what order you take shots. You might shoot your ending shot first, and your beginning next, followed by the middle. Editing also gives you the freedom to experiment with shooting the same subject several times from different angles or holding the camera at different levels. When you get back to your Mac, you can pick the shot that works best. If you're not sure you've got a shot, shoot some more footage. Keep in mind that you are collecting footage, most of which you won't use.

But don't collect too much. For your 10-minute movie, an hour's worth is enough.

Planning Your Video Shoot

Before you start shooting, think a little about what you are going to shoot, or even make a list of the shots you want to try to get. To start planning, consider that a killer video has structure: a beginning, a middle, and an end. The beginning of a movie often has one or more establishing shots that convey a sense of place or activity. It could be a landscape or a shot of a building, or action, such as a car driving up to (or away from) a house, or a person getting ready to go out. The beginning shots should build on each other, providing more information as to what will happen.

The middle is the main action of the movie. These shots are the easiest to plan for, because they are the reason you are doing the movie. Here, you want a variety of different shots, as described a little later on.

The ending shots of your movie let viewers know that it's over. Your last shot could be of people walking into the distance, or even out of the frame, leaving an empty scene. (See Figure 11-2.) You can have people wave goodbye, get in a car, and drive off. You could end with a joke or something funny, or with a closeup of some meaningful objects such as empty champagne glasses. With some of these shots—such as people walking out of a scene or the closing of a door—you can later add rolling credits right on top of the shot. Not that credits are necessary, but they signal the end, and let you add some fun text. If this is what you're after, be sure to shoot enough footage to give you time for credits.

Throughout the video, think about inserting little shots to help with the mood—a child's untied shoe, a closeup of a toy a baby is holding, a flower, dirty dishes in the sink after a party, the pile of wrapping paper on Christmas morning. These are short shots that can help break up a longer segment or provide a transition to another segment. They also keep the movie moving.

Another way to plan for the shots you want to take is to ask yourself why you are shooting the movie. Most home movies are time capsules—a record of the kids and family at one period of time. You will marvel at how cute Cindy was when she was 7, or how different Uncle Frank looked when he had hair. If your motivation is to create a time capsule, take some shots that reflect when the video was shot. Include things that will change—the inside of different rooms in your house, magazines on a coffee table, a home office with your brand-new Mac, a street scene with cars, a scene that shows how people are dressed.

Five or ten years from now, you won't care what Disneyland or the Tower of London looked like in 2004. These kinds of tourist attractions don't change much and should not be the focus of a time capsule movie. If, however, your motivation is to remember a good vacation, you'll want more footage of the attractions. Just remember to include lots of people (see the section called "Shooting People" a bit later).

Another motivation is to record an event for posterity, such as a wedding video or childs birthday party. These are like time capsules, but are more restrictive because there are required activities you must record—the throwing of the rice, the cutting of the cake, the first dance.

Or, maybe you just want to create something entertaining or artistic. If that's the case, you might want to create a storyboard (see sidebar).

FIGURE 11-2: The cowboys and girls ride off into the sunset, signaling the end of the movie. Here, keep the camera still as the horses walk out of the frame.

Storyboarding for Killer Business Videos

In a home movie, it's likely you don't know what you will be shooting beforehand. But with a movie for business or presentation, a bit more planning will help focus your movie on the topic at hand and save time during the shooting phase. A tool that professionals use for planning is the storyboard—a cartoon strip with rough drawings of what you think should be the shots for the beginning, ending, and for the key scenes. A storyboard is a kind of like a graphical list. Each frame of the "comic strip" contains a rough drawing of the type of shot (wide, closeup, person, building, object, who's in the scene, what they are doing). Under each frame, you can have notes about the scene. Don't worry too much about how the art looks. The final look of the storyboard isn't important—it's the process of getting you to think about the movie's structure that counts.

If you are working with a group, you might want to get more serious about storyboarding using software. StoryBoard Quick (www.storyboardartist.com, PowerProduction Software) lets you build and manipulate drawings with people doing different activities in different locations and with props. PowerProduction Software offers add-on libraries of situations and props to expand. You can specify different types of shots, such as closeups, wide shots, and over-the-shoulder shots.

Holding Your Camera

When you are collecting your video, try pulling the camera away from your face once in a while and shoot from different levels and angles. You won't use all of these shots, but you may find some that work. The camera's rotating LCD screen makes these types of shots possible. If you flip the screen up, you can shoot while holding the camera at chest or waist level. Flip it down to get a shot with the camera over your head pointing down. To get a shot of yourself, point the lens at yourself and flip the screen 180 degrees (shown in Figure 11-3) — the image might be upside down, but some cameras will flip the image when you do this.

FIGURE 11-3: The LCD screen on most digital camcorders tilts up and down, and can flip around like this one, letting you hold the camera in different positions away from your face.

Today's digital camcorders have image stabilization mechanisms that help prevent shaky images, but you still need to take care you hold the camera still, especially when the lens is at full zoom. Often a comfortable position is a solid position. For a waist-level shot, shooting from the hip works for some people; others do better holding the camera away from the body. With most camera positions, having your feet spread apart is helpful. If you can stabilize yourself by leaning on a building or tree, go for it.

Shooting People

For most movies, home or otherwise, people are the main subject matter. Or rather, people *should be* the main subject matter. (In nature documentaries, animals substitute for people.) Scenery is nice, but it is the stuff that fills in between the action. It is not the action. Too many home movies show scads of scenery, buildings, and amusements. It's dull.

Not convinced? PBS sometimes run a series called *Rick Steves' Europe.* The travel writer takes you to the most spectacular places in Europe. The next time you watch this show, pay attention to the shots — they are mostly of Steves or of people enjoying themselves in beautiful settings. There are short shots of pure scenery, but then the video goes right back to people. People are the action. (There's more about how to convey action in the section on composition a little later.)

There are also small shots you should add to use in between — a funny-looking duck, twisted tree limbs, a closeup of an architecture detail. They help establish a sense of place as much as the wide shots of scenery, but on a different scale.

Having your family pose in front of attractions gets dull pretty fast. Your family members don't have to be the only people you shoot. You can use short shots of a crowd to set the scene, to establish where you are. For instance, if you're at a playground, include a few seconds of random kids running by. You can use a shot of a businessman in a suit hurrying through your frame to demonstrate the frenetic pace of midtown Manhattan. Shots of street vendors can add color to your travel video. The polite thing is to first ask if it's okay to shoot them, though.

Closeups, Medium Shots, and Wide Shots

A killer video should include people shots at three levels of intimacy: closeups, medium shots, and wide shots. Not that your finished movie will be a random assortment of shots — most of your people shots should be from the waist or chest up. These are medium shots, which, on a television screen, make people appear to be a natural size. Medium shots can take a little time to set up because you must adjust the zoom to somewhere in the middle range.

Your scenes should also have some closeups — just the head or even part of the head. Don't be afraid to fill up the screen with the face. Try to get the eyes one-third of the way from the top of the screen, as shown in Figure 11-4, even if this chops off the top of the head. (This is part of photography's rule of thirds, which is discussed in the section on composition a little later.) Use closeups as highlights to break up the medium shots. Too many closeups can be uncomfortable, because they show a face closer than the distance at which people are used to relating.

A wide shot fits a person's entire body, from head to toe or more. Some people shoot too many wide shots in an effort to get all of the scenery in. The problem here is that there is a lot going on in a wide shot, and the action is too far away to enable the viewer to relate to the people in the shot. Still, you need wide shots in your video to establish the setting of a scene, or at the beginning or end of the movie. You can also use wide shots to briefly remind the viewer of where you are. You should use wide shots in place of moving the camera to capture a scene. As is discussed later, it is much better to keep the camera still than to move it.

FIGURE 11-4: It's okay to cut off part of the head in a closeup.
The rule of thirds suggests the eyes be about one-third of
the way down from the top of the screen.

Candid Shots

Another way to vary your people shots is to not have your subjects looking straight into the camera lens all the time. Instead, shoot subjects as they do something other than talk to you. Simple actions such as walking or picking up something or talking to someone else are preferable. These shots are harder to get, because people have been trained to look at the lens when someone points a camera at them. But candid shots are more valuable — they tend to look better and are easier to edit into your movie.

People being interviewed on TV almost never look into the lens. That's because the cameraman isn't askng the questions — the interviewer is usually sitting off to one side of the camera. When you are interviewing someone, try putting the camera on a tripod and standing next to it. Or, hold the camera at your side or above or below eye-level. The idea is to have the subject look at you, not the camera.

One type of candid shot that is easy to edit is a shot taken when your subject is watching something. For this type of shot, you can also add some shots from the subject's point of view.

Points of View Shots

Including shots of your subject's point of view is another way to get movement into your movie. That is, shoot what they are looking at. This is handy when you are on vacation and want to get some of the scenery in the movie. Instead of telling your subjects to "go stand over there" all the time, shoot them as they look at something. Then, move to where they are and shoot what they were looking at.

If you're shooting two people interacting with each other, shoot over one person's shoulder toward the other. You'll see the back of one person's head and a shoulder, and the front of the other. Then go to the other person and shot from behind their back at the first person. This is called an over-the-shoulder shot.

Don't worry about capturing all of the dialog while you move from one position to another. It's not important to capture unscripted conversation, which often doesn't hold up well in a movie. Remember, you're striving to capture the essence of the occasion, not creating a literal record of events.

Point-of-view shots don't have to be of people. If a subject is doing something odd or funny, add a shot of the family dog looking up quizzically, followed by what the dog might see — that is, hold the camera at the dog's level and shoot up. If a kid is playing with a pet, take an over-the-shoulder shot from the pet's point of view looking up at the kid, and another of the pet from behind the kid.

Composition and Framing

Composition and framing are techniques to set up what is in the viewfinder. This involves using the zoom and moving the camera until you get a sense of balance in your shots that makes them more interesting. Composition and framing techniques can also establish motion, or the illusion of motion.

The framing technique that most amateurs use is to shoot every subject at the center of the frame. You will sometimes center your subject, but these shots are often dull and can be unbalanced.

The first basic technique to framing is called the rule of thirds. The rule of thirds says that the best place for the focal point of a shot is not dead center, but one third of the way from the sides or top or bottom of the frame. The rule of thirds is more of a guideline than an absolute rule, but is about balance. A shot of a person with the eyes in the center of the frame is unbalanced — there's a big space above the subject's head, and not enough below the chin.

FIGURE **11-5**: This shot follows the rule of thirds: the eye is about one-third of the way down from the top, and one-third of the way from the left side.
Photo by Adriana Rizzo.

Eyes are often the focal point, as shown in Figure 11-4, a closeup, and Figure 11-5, a medium shot. It also applies to wide shots. A shot of sky and land looks better with the horizon one-third of the way from the bottom or one-third of the way from the top, as shown in Figure 11-6.

This figure also illustrates another composition technique — have your subject look or move into the two-thirds of the frame, not the other way around. The woman, one-third of the way from the right edge, is facing left.

In a video, your subject isn't likely to stay still. Does that mean that you should move the camera to keep the subject one-third of the way from the edge? The answer is no — let the subject move into the frame while holding the camera still.

FIGURE 11-6: This shot also follows the rule of thirds with the horizon and the woman. It is also balanced, because she is looking into the frame.

Keep the Camera Still: Panning and Zooming

Panning and zooming are great tools for collecting a variety of shots that you can use in the editing process. For instance, you zoom to go from a wide shot to a closeup, or move the camera to get a different angle. You shouldn't, however, use the panning and zooming shots themselves — use only the shots before and after. Think of these as transition footage, helping you to find new views. For the shots you are going to use in the finished movie, keep the camera still and the lens at one zoom setting.

There are several reasons for this. For one thing, you can more effectively convey a sense of motion if you let your subjects enter and exit the frame. This also helps you with editing. A person walks out of the frame, it's obvious that he or she is gone, and you can start the next scene with something else. If your subject is moving around too fast to stay in the frame for long, try zooming out a bit. Don't move the camera around to keep the subject in the center of the frame. It's okay for the subject to be on one side of the frame or the other, and is more convincing in conveying motion. It's even okay if the subject leaves the frame and returns.

If you follow your subject around with the camera, the person will still be in the frame when you stop shooting. This makes it much more difficult to create a smooth transition. It's also easier to watch a movie that consists of a series of fixed camera shots than one in which the reference frame is constantly changing.

Yes, you will see panning and zooming in professional movies, but with your camcoder, still shots look better. When you move the camera, much of the footage will be blurry — a blurry moving background is tough to watch. Lighting conditions will change as you pan and zoom. Your camera can't adjust fast enough and will capture some pretty unattractive footage. Also, when you move the camera, it won't be a completely smooth move — you'll probably get some bumpiness that will make viewing less pleasant. Instead of panning, try a wide shot, like the one in Figure 11-7. In this example, you don't have to capture the entire rocket — having large objects extend outside of the frame conveys a sense of size.

FIGURE 11-7: A still, wide shot like this is better than panning up at the rockets, which will change lighting conditions.

Now, occasionally you have to pan to capture something — you really want that grand canyon pan or *really* need to follow a subject. When you must pan, use a tripod or monopod or keep your body firmly positioned to minimize bumping. And pan *slowly* — this is easier for the viewer and gives the camera more time to adjust to changing conditions. There's even less reason to use zoom in your movie, but if you must, zoom slowly and use a short zoom — not the full 1× to 12× on a 12× camera. When you edit, use these scenes sparingly, as often as you might use a special effect. But also try the same shot as a still shot — when you edit, you may find that the still shot looks better.

Tip Whenever you zoom, use only the optical zoom on your camera. Never use the digital zoom, which really isn't zoom at all — it's just enlarging the picture and the pixels, like using the magnifying glass tool in Photoshop or other painting programs. With digital zoom, the image gets grainy and less realistic.

Lighting

The most common lighting mistake most people make is shooting a subject that is backlit — a condition in which there is more light behind the subject than in front of him or her. For instance, if you're shooting a person in the shade with a sunny background or shooting into the direction of the sun, the subject is backlit. Backlit subjects will come out dark (see Figure 11-8), because your camera's aperture adjusts for the backlight, not for the light bouncing off of your subject. The pros add photographers' lighting to the front of the subject, but this requires that you acquire and store a new set of equipment. Usually it's easier to just move the person you are shooting or come back at a different time of day. Overcast days make for good outdoor shooting, because everything tends to be evenly lit.

FIGURE 11-8: A subject that has light behind it will come out dark.

Occasionally, you might want to shoot into the sun to create a special effect — the old palm tree silhouette at sunset, for instance. These kinds of shots can occasionally work. However, if want to your viewers to *see* the subject, don't shoot into the light.

Direct sunlight streaming into the lens can also cause a phenomenon called lens flare, caused by light refraction inside the camera lens itself. Lens flare can show up in the video as bright streaks, as a series of bright spots, or as a washed-out, low-contrast image. One way to prevent lens flare is to use a lens hood on the camera. A lens hood is a kind of collar that fits on the end of a lens. You can also try going back to the spot at a different time of day when the sun is in a different position.

Switching between different light sources can affect the way your camcorder interprets color, so can using multiple different light sources. For instance, the camera can tint shaded scenes blue if sunshine is the light source and can make the scene look green in florescent light. For each shot, try using as few light sources as possible — shut off the florescent lights, or use the fluorescents and pull the blinds down. Then, adjust your camcorders white balance setting while it's pointing at the main light source. Or, just look for another room or building to shoot in.

A polarizing filter can help with some situations where there's bright sunlight. It's also a good way to keep your lens from getting scratched.

Shooting Sound

You don't have to use the sound you record with the video footage you collected. This means that you can shoot some shots just for the video and others just for the sound. For instance, you might envision a shot of kids reacting to the sound of an ice cream truck. You then see the ice cream truck pulling over, and the kids running over to it. Trouble is, when the camera is pointed at the kids, the microphone doesn't pick up the truck behind you. No problem — take some footage of the truck, sitting there doing nothing, but playing its jingle. During editing, you'll copy the sound to the section of video of the kids first hearing it.

Another example is a situation where you get some great video but have an annoying sound-track — a fire truck, car alarm, or the annoying noise of wind blowing against a microphone. To fix this, go somewhere that has the same type of ambient sound — street noise, birds, waves at the beach — and shoot some video in order to collect the sound.

Tip If high-quality sound is important, get a separate microphone that you plug into your camera's mic jack.

Another sound tip — try not to speak from behind the camera unless you're conducting an interview. When you do, speak softly. You are closer to the microphone than the subject, and your voice will boom otherwise. For other scenes, try to capture the scene as it is, with people saying and doing what comes naturally. The sound of you telling people where to stand or move is not particularly interesting. Neither are spur-of-the-moment narrations. If you want to do a voice narration, add it while you are editing the footage. If you are planning to replace the soundtrack with music or with a more planned narration, then you can speak during shooting to record verbal notes.

Time Code

The time code on a digital camcorder is a record of the relative time of your shooting. When you start shooting, the time code is 00:00. At 5 minutes, the time code is 5:00. (Sometimes the number of frames in each minute is recorded, so a time code of 25:06:16 means 25 minutes, 6 seconds, and 16 frames of recorded video.) The current time code is displayed in the camera's view and is recorded (invisibly) on the MiniDV tape.

iMovie doesn't do much with the time code, but other video-editing applications rely on the time code to determine where in the tape you are. Because there is always a possibility that you might move to another video editor at some point (or that a new version of iMovie will start using time codes), you should try to prevent any two frames from having the same time code — every frame on a tape should have a different time code.

Here's how to do this: Don't start shooting if you see blue in the camera. Shoot only when you see black. You make this possible by adding black space before each clip. When you put in a brand new tape, shoot 10 or 20 seconds with the lens cap on. Shoot your scene, then put the lens cap back on, and shoot 5 more seconds of black. This will also help iMovie separate the tape into individual clips, making editing easier.

If you don't do this, a problem can occur if you rewind to look at something, then fast forward into a blue-screen section. When you do, you will confuse the camcorder into thinking it has a new tape, and it will set the time code to 00:00. So, now you have two 00:00 points, one at the beginning and another in the middle, which will confuse some video-editing software.

Remember — a black screen is tape with a time code, and is good for beginning to shoot. A blue field is tape without a time code and means that you've fast forwarded too far.

Editing Your Movie

Editing is where you sculpt your movie out of the raw footage. You create a structure (beginning, middle, end), arranging shots in an order that conveys a sense that something has happened. You can take scenes shot out of order and arrange them in a sequence that makes sense. You can create a soundtrack consisting of the original recorded sound or new music or voice. You can also add still photos to good effect. Add titles to give the movie a finished quality, sprinkle it lightly with a special effect or transition, and you have your movie.

With editing, you want to create something that moves along from scene to scene, is always fresh, and is not repetitive. Given this, you may not use $4/5$ of the footage you shoot. Some of the $4/5$ will be bad — poorly lit, poorly framed, or something that just won't work in the movie. Some of this unused footage will be good, however. The tough part of editing is deciding which of the good footage you're not going to use.

Don't waste a lot of time adjusting color and brightness controls (as you might when importing old movies). Unless it's a really critical shot that can't be replaced (the bride cuts the cake), just use some of the other $4/5$ of footage that looks good.

The rest of this section describes the video-editing process using iMovie. When using other video-editing applications, some of the techniques will be different, but the advice on how to edit a killer video applies to any video editing app. When you boil it down, editing is about making good transitions between shots and then good transitions between scenes.

Import Your Video into iMovie

Moving your video from your digital camcorder to your editing software is pretty easy, especially with iMovie. It's much the same as the procedure described in Chapter 10 for importing analog video, except that you can control the digital camcorder from within iMovie.

Before you import your video, decide if you want iMovie to create a single big clip or multiple smaller clips. The latter is easier to work with, but you can always break up a bigger clip yourself. If you have Automatic Scene Detection turned on, iMovie can sometimes detect where in the tape the camcorder switched from standby to record mode. To turn this feature on, go to the iMovie menu, select Preferences, and check the box next to "Automatically create new clip at scene break."

To import your movie, do the following:

1. Connect your digital video camera to the Mac's FireWire port.

2. Launch iMovie.

3. Create a new iMovie project from the File menu.

4. Make sure the switch at the lower left is switched to the camera icon. iMovie will then tell you that it recognizes the camera (see Figure 11-9).

5. Click the Import button.

6. Click the arrow button. This will start the camcorder playing.

If you'd rather break the move into clips yourself, you can break it up after it is imported, or break it up as you import it. To do the latter, use the Stop button (the square) to stop the camera when you get to one of the black parts that you filmed in between shots. (See the previous section called "Time Code.") Then press the Import button. When you press Import and Start again, iMovie will start the capture with a new clip.

It's a good a idea to watch your movie as it is imported. This will give you your first impression of what's on the tape. Take some notes as to what appear to be particularly good or bad scenes. Note which clip they are in and approximately when in the clip they start.

FIGURE 11-9: When you start a new project and start iMovie, it will recognize the camcorder.

First Pass Edit

When you're done with your import, you'll have one or more clips in the clip shelf at right and nothing in the area below. Move the mode switch to Edit mode, and you can start viewing the imported footage. To view a clip, click on it and press the play button (see Figure 11-10). You can move to a specific frame by dragging the *playhead,* the triangle pointing down on the *scrub bar,* which is the horizontal blue bar under the viewing are. Figure 11-10 shows the playhead near the end of a clip.

FIGURE 11-10: iMovie with newly imported footage, in Edit mode.

Now it's time to do a first pass edit. This involves breaking up your clips into smaller clips, deleting truly unusable material, and renaming the clips.

To break up a clip at a specific frame, click it to select it. Next, drag the playhead to the exact frame you would like to set the break at. iMovie will display the frame. Finally, go to the Edit menu and select Split Video Clip at Playhead. You'll now have an additional clip in the clip shelf.

Tip Most video-editing software and camcorders designate time with the frame number displayed last. The time 9:07:18 signifies the 18th frame in the 7th second of the 9th minute.

To delete a clip, just select it and press the Delete key. (You can also drag it to the Trash icon at the bottom of the iMovie window.) If you're not sure about deleting it, don't. Here, you're deleting unusable clips — footage that is too dark or too washed out, or footage where you put the camera down without remembering to turn record off. (Just admit it — you've done this before.) Other things to delete are long black spaces at the beginning and end of the movie. Don't, however, worry about the black spaces in between the clips just yet. If some footage has some good audio that you think you could use, keep it.

Deleting doesn't become permanent until you empty iMovie's Trash. The Trash icon displays how much is in the Trash in terms of disk space (as shown in Figure 11-11). To empty iMovie's Trash, click it once.

FIGURE 11-11: iMovie's Trash.

Find the Golden Clips

A big part of the editing process is one of winnowing down — here, your hour's worth of footage will become 10 minutes. To start, watch the footage a few times. Locate the golden shots — the really great moments that you will build your scenes around. Note where they are. Think about which scenes could be used for the beginning and end of the movie. Also listen to the soundtrack. Some of your editing will be focused on what is being said rather than what is being done.

Separate Shots into Clips

You will need to further cut the footage into separate clips. You want each separate shot that you might use to exist as it's own clip. This will enable you to use the clips in different places in the movie. Remember, in editing, it doesn't matter in what order you shoot the footage. In any one scene, you might have wide shots, point-of-view shots, and closeups. These should all be separate clips.

Figure 11-12 shows imported video that was originally two clips now broken up into a bunch of clips. The clips that originated from the first original clip have a number that starts with "01/" as in "01/12," the twelfth clip from the first original. Clips from the second original clip begin with "02/."

Rename the clips to something useful. Right now the clips have names such as Clip 01 and Clip 02. More useful names might be "beach, wide," or "train leaving." To rename a clip, double-click it. Type a new name in the Clip Info window that appears (see Figure 11-13).

FIGURE 11-12: The imported movie broken up into multiple clips.

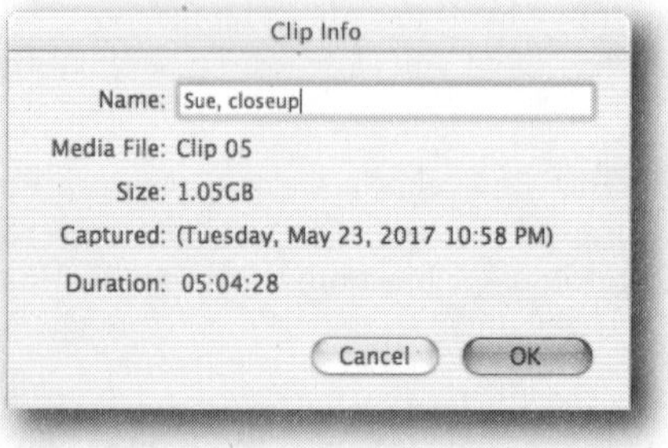

FIGURE 11-13: iMovie's clip info window lets you rename a clip.

Interviews with people may be some of your longest clips. You might want to break them up later with other shots, but for now, keep them intact.

Trimming Clips

Now find some of your best shots and trim them down. You might have some of the black space that preceded the shot, or the shot might start out of focus. Maybe there's an interesting bit in the middle surrounded by the mundane. If you're not sure, leave it in for now.

iMovie gives you several ways to trim clips. First, select a clip from the clip shelf. You next set the crop markers on the scrubber bar — the blue bar directly under the monitor window. (See Figure 11-14.) You then use the Cut, Clear, or the Crop commands in the Edit menu.

Tip   An easy way to adjust the crop markers is to drag the playhead to the frame you want the crop mark to be in. Now, click directly under the playhead — the crop mark will move to the spot where you just clicked.

FIGURE 11-14: Setting the crop markers on iMovie's scrub bar below the monitor.

The Cut command cuts the selected area between the crop marks, and places this section in the Mac's Clipboard — which means that you can paste it somewhere else. If you don't need to paste it elsewhere, use the Clear command, which simply removes the section. (You can also hit the Delete key.) The Crop command does the opposite — it removes the area outside of the selected area.

Not all shots will be the same length. Wide shots should be longer than closeups. Interviews will probably be your longest shots. With interviews, listen to the soundtrack to determine what is valuable. Don't cut out the middle sections of an interview just yet.

Where to cut is something else to think about. It's easiest to make a cut when nothing is moving and no one is talking. But if something is moving when the clip ends, it's a bit tougher. One trick you can try is to follow a moving clip with another clip with similar motion, or motion in the same direction. The continued direction of motion in two clips makes the cut less noticeable.

Build a Scene

Now you have an assortment of clips that you can use to build a scene. It's probably easiest to start with a scene in the middle. Find one of your golden clips and drag it down to the Clip Viewer along the bottom of the iMovie. Now drag down some of the clips that are related to this main shot — closeups, wide shots, point-of-view shots, shots of small items. You'll integrate these other shots into the main shot. Scenes often start with a wide shot to establish the setting. However, you can also start a scene with a closeup. For instance, a scene could start with a closeup of flowers in someone's hand, then cut to a shot of a person arranging flowers.

In this example, we're going to build a simple scene for our movie's climax — kids singing "Happy Birthday." In Figure 11-15 we have three shots in the Clip Viewer. The first clip is the main shot for the scene, a wide shot of kids at a table singing Happy Birthday. We've edited the shot so that it starts a couple of seconds before the singing, thus establishing the setting. This clip only takes about a minute, a good length for our 10-minute movie. However, a minute of the same shot can be dull, so we're going to break it up with a closeup of the cake and a close-to-medium shot of the birthday girl. First, we look at the length of the clips. We find that the two closeups are too long, at 42 and 20 seconds, respectively. All we need here is about 4 seconds of each closeup. We could do another Crop of the best 4 seconds of each or do a Copy to keep the original clips intact.

FIGURE 11-15: Here we've dragged a main clip and two closeups to insert into the main clip.

If we didn't care about the soundtrack (for instance, we were adding a music soundtrack or voice-over), this would be easy. We could break the main clip in two places, and drag our two 4-second closeups to where the breaks are. To play the whole scene, Shift-click all the clips and click the Play button.

The problem is that we *do* care about the recorded soundtrack — the kids are singing a song we all know, and we don't want to break it up. In order to keep the original audio, you can *paste* in video only. Here's how:

1. Go to iMovie Preferences and make sure "Extract audio in paste over" is selected.

2. Go to your closeup clip and select a short bit using the crop makers on the scrubber bar. (Here, we'll select 4 seconds of cake and candles.)

3. Choose Copy from the Edit menu.

4. On the main clip, move the playhead to the first frame to be replaced.

5. Go to the Advanced menu and select "Paste Over at Playhead."

You will notice that iMovie automatically switches you to time-line view to show you what happened. Figure 11-16 shows that iMovie has automatically extracted the original audio for the two video paste-overs and placed it in audio track 1.

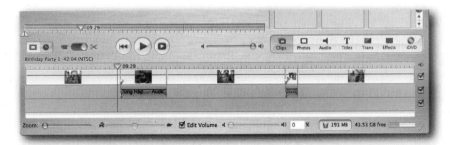

FIGURE 11-16: The "Extract audio in paste over" command takes the original audio and puts it in a separate audio track. This retains the continuity of the original audio while letting you paste in video.

Pasting the video-only while retaining the original audio is an incredible powerful feature that makes a variety of editing solutions possible. It's great for interviews. If you watch an interview or someone talking on TV, you'll notice that the camera doesn't stay on the subject during the entire talk. The shot of the subject is interrupted by a quick shot of the person listening, another shot of both people talking, closeups of the people involved, or photos of other objects. You can do the same with your video using iMovie.

One word about transitioning between shots within a scene — don't use any special effects. Save any transition effects for use in between different scenes. Even then most professionals use effects very sparingly. Instead, they create transitions by using cuts—which is to say, the putting together of two shots *is* the transition.

Using Still Images Effectively

You can also use still images in your video to make it more effective. These can be photographs that you've digitized with a scanner, shot with a digital camera, or created from your video. For instance, a wedding video can include some of the photographer's shots. You can also use the techniques of documentary makers and use photo's of long-gone relatives in an interview where they are mentioned. You can also use still images as transitions between shots.

Create a Still Frame from Your Video

If you have a shot with no motion in it, you can make it into a still frame in most video-editing software, including iMovie. Using a single frame for several seconds will give you a rock-steady image, something that you can't get from a hand-held camera.

To create a still frame, select the clip you want to use and move the playhead to the frame you want. Now, select Create Still Frame from the Edit menu. This will give you a new 5-second clip that is a still frame. To change the duration, double-click the clip and type in the amount of time. If you're using the still frame as a transition between shots, then you'll want a duration that is shorter than 5 seconds. If you are using it to put titles over at the beginning or end of a movie (another great use for still images), you might want to lengthen the time on-screen.

Using Images from iPhoto

In iMovie, you can use photographs stored in iPhoto in your movies. iMovie's Ken Burns effect literally adds motion to still photos as slow panning and zooming, which you can adjust.

To insert a photo, do the following:

1. Click the Photos button in the toolbar on the lower right. The clip shelf turns into the iPhoto area of Figure 11-17.

2. In the pop-up menu, select Library (to select from all of your iPhoto images) or choose one of the iPhoto Albums listed here.

3. Scroll through the list, and click on an image you want to use.

4. If you want the Ken Burns effect, make sure the check box at the top is selected.

5. Set the controls for the Ken Burns effect. The Start button is where you want the pan/zoom to start. The Finish button is where you set the action to end. You can click and drag the image in the small sample window at top right. The Zoom slider lets you zoom in on one spot of the image. Usually, the finish is at a higher zoom level than the start.

6. Drag a photo down to the clip bar or time line. iMovie will take a few moments to render it.

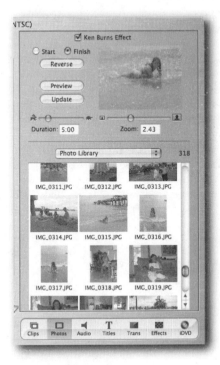

FIGURE 11-17: iMovie can insert images directly from iPhoto.

Tightening Edit

Now, view and listen to the movie again and look for places to tighten it. Look for shots that just don't work and can be deleted. Look for shots that can be shortened at the edges or that can have parts in the middle that you don't need. Removing material usually makes for a better movie.

Putting Multiple Scenes Together

After you've built a few scenes like this, including a beginning and ending, you can start to think about how you will make a transition from one to the other. One way is to add a transition effect. (In iMovie, you click the Trans button.) Common transitions are fade in and fade out, which fades the image from or to black, and the cross dissolve, where one shot fades out as another fades in. These transition effects can add a few seconds to your movie. Fade ins and fade outs are good to use at the beginning and end of your movie, particularly if you are using titles on a black background.

You don't have to use transition effects between every scene. Rent a movie, and you'll see that most scenes simply go from one to the other without a special effect. Sometimes the cuts are abrupt, other times they are smooth. Smooth transitions use cuts that have similar motion. For instance, in *2001: A Space Odyssey*, a shot of a spinning bone thrown in the air suddenly changes to a spinning space station. Not only is this transition smooth, but it implies a meaning (human evolution from ape to space traveller).

Other Effects

iMovie and other video-editing apps have other special effects — iMovie has Aged Film and Sepia Tone for that old look, Earthquake for a sort of music-video shaky-blurry look, as well as some color correction effects. These are interesting looking at the first viewing, but they get old *very* quickly. Use them very infrequently, and for very short durations. These kinds of effects don't help you make killer videos.

To apply an effect, do the following:

1. Drag a clip down to the Clip Viewer, and click to select it.
2. Click the Effects icon in the bar at the lower right.
3. Click an effect in the list on the right. Click the Preview button to see how it looks with your clip.
4. You can experiment with the various controls for duration and magnitude. These controls vary with each different effect.
5. When you are satisfied with the effect and the settings, click the Apply button.

Mac OS X will take a minute or so to process the effect, depending on how long the clip is.

Titles

Titles are great. They add a touch of class or a touch of fun and announce the beginning and end of a movie. Here, simplicity works best — black background or a dark still image with sans serif white text. iMovie's Titles button enables you to do several different styles of titles, including rolling credits for the end of your killer video.

For more on titles, see Chapter 10.

Adding a Movie Soundtrack

As was mentioned in Chapter 10, iMovie lets you add music directly from iTunes or record a narration. Music adds a lot to a video. iMovie lets you control the volume of the music, so you can lower it or fade it out when the dialog appears. If you are adding music, it's best to add it at the end of the project, after you've finished editing the video.

We also mentioned earlier that you can separate the recorded sound from the video and use it with other video shots. To separate the sound from the soundtrack in iMovie, click on a video clip to select it. Now choose Extract Audio from the Advanced menu. The audio appears in the first track under the video track, as before. However, it will be locked to the video, as indicated by a little drawing of a pin. To unlock the audio clip from the video, select the audio clip and choose Unlock Audio Clip from the Advanced menu. Now you can copy or move this soundtrack around the time line.

Chapter 10 has more on soundtracks.

Save Your Work

When you are finished editing your movie, you should save it to a master MiniDV tape using the Export command in the File menu. You can also put it on a DVD, as described in Chapter 10.

Summary

This chapter started with three pieces of advice for creating a killer video — keep it simple, keep it short, and keep it moving. This applies to both the shooting and editing of the movie. With both, variety will keep your video moving.

For shooting, there are several things to remember:

- Your movie has a beginning, middle, and end. Think about footage for all of these parts. If you are doing a video for business or a presentation, try planning your movie with a storyboard.

- People should be the focus of your movie.

- When shooting people, add some variety — different angles, some point-of-view shots.

- Most of your people shots should be from the waist or chest up, but also include closeups (the face filling the entire screen) and wide shots (full body).

- Applying the rule of thirds to frame your shots makes them more interesting than centering everything.

- Watch your lighting conditions. Don't shoot a backlit subject.

- Keep the camera still — let your subjects move in a still frame.

- Shoot for sound as well as video. If you can't get the sound you want with the video you want, shoot each separately, and join them during editing.

Editing is equally important to shooting. Here are some key points about editing to remember:

- Edit your video so that it is always moving.

- *Don't* fall in love with your footage. Be prepared to not use $^4/_5$ of it.

- Watch and listen to your raw footage a few times. Take notes on which shots are gold and which are gone.

- Divide your imported footage into clips of different shots.

- Integrate short shots of different views into your main clips to create scenes.

- Still images can be very effective in your videos.

- *Don't* use a lot of fancy transitions and special effects. They get old fast.

- *Do* use titles. They are easy to do and add a great deal to your killer video.

Video photography and editing are acquired skills. Like playing the piano, it takes some talent, but practice is key. For more information on video photography, there are a number of books on the subject. The *Little Digital Video Book* (Peachpit Press, 2001) by Michael Rubin is a good one, as is the *Digital Video Pocket Guide* (O'Reilly, 2003) by Derrick Story. On the Web, there are some good tips at O'Reilly's Mac Development Center, www.macdevcenter.com/pub/a/mac/collections/iphoto. If you're shopping for a digital video camera, check CNET.com, Macworld.com, and MacUser.uk for the recent reviews and information.

For samples of some of the suggestions mentioned in this chapter, watch TV and movies. You can learn some great techniques from the pros.

Use Your Mac as a Wireless Jukebox

In this chapter, we'll discuss another musical project designed to keep your Mac at the heart of your home entertainment.

Of all Apple's digital hub ventures — including photos and movies — managing your music is the most advanced, and probably the most successful. We'll focus on getting your music into iTunes and describe how you can use your Mac and wireless network to play your tunes anywhere in the house, without CDs or wires.

Overview

The recording industry has been much in the news lately because of the controversial convergence of music and computers, which has led to the phenomenon of file sharing and music downloading. Digitizing music and putting it on your computer is an incredibly popular pastime. In fact, it's gotten a little too popular for many recording executives and artists, who now see their music traded and freely downloaded on the Internet.

As usual, Apple has taken a "think different" approach to this problem. iTunes software lets you keep track of and play your music, iPod offers a portable music player, and the iTunes Music Store is a place to legitimately buy music online. And when you add an 802.11 wireless network, you have everything you need to play music from your computers without wires.

While you're reading up on the music information in this chapter, you might also want to check out several other chapters for useful information. Chapter 6 is all about putting together a wireless network, Chapter 9 describes how to digitize your vinyl LPs and get them into your Mac, and Chapter 4 tells how to get the most from your iPod.

To learn a lot more about music and copyrights, see the Chapter 2 sections entitled "An Internet Radio Primer" and "Digital Copyright Issues."

What You Need

Putting together your wireless jukebox is very simple, and Apple provides almost everything you need. You'll need at least two computers: one is the jukebox itself, storing all your music, and the other(s) act as music players, getting access to the source via iTunes. Of course, you can also play music directly from the jukebox computer — you only need another Mac if you want to fulfill the "wireless jukebox" dream. All Macs have to run iTunes 4, the version with music sharing, which requires Mac OS X version 10.1.5 or later.

Here are the basic steps you'll follow to put everything together:

1. Set up a wireless network for your wireless jukebox (see Chapter 6). Of course, everything in this chapter works with a wired network as well, but wireless is so much more convenient and versatile.

2. Download and install the latest version of iTunes, if you don't already have it running on your Mac.

3. Use iTunes to transfer music from your CDs to your Mac. (See Chapter 9 to learn how to import your vinyl music as well). You can also buy music at the iTunes Music Store.

4. Create iTunes playlists to organize your music just the way you want.

5. For the best sound quality, connect your Mac's audio output to a stereo system, external speakers, or headphones. Using iTunes, you can share your music with other computers and play your tunes over a wireless network.

Successful Networking

Here are some additional things to keep in mind as you set up your wireless jukebox. First, as described in Chapter 6, your wireless network should have encryption turned on. This won't affect the ability of computers on your network to access and play music.

Second, you'll have to do some fancy footwork if you have the Mac OS X firewall turned on. In this case, you have to open an additional port to get music sharing to work. Here are the steps:

1. Open System Preferences and choose View→Sharing.

2. Click Firewall, then click the New button.

3. Click the Port Name pop-up menu and choose Other.

4. Enter 3689 in the Port Number, Range, or Series field. That's the magic number iTunes uses as a sharing port.

5. Enter iTunes Sharing in the Description field, and click OK.

Speakers and Other Music Hardware

A jukebox includes speakers, as your Mac does, but you greatly improve the sounds you get from your Mac by connecting it to external speakers or a stereo amplifier. Macs have a sound output port that's usually used for connecting headphones. You can use this port for connecting to virtually any powered external speakers, from a $10 pair you can buy at RadioShack to fancier models costing hundreds of dollars. Apple carries a wide range of external speakers at its online store and retail locations.

In addition to the standard headphone sound output port, many recent Macs include a digital sound connector officially called the Apple Speaker sound output port. This port is found on PowerMac G4 models greater than 500 Mhz and iMacs with flat panel displays. Use this port to hook up to Apple Pro Speakers, which are made in conjunction with stereo giant Harman/Kardon. You can learn more about the Apple Pro Speakers at `www.apple.com/speakers/`.

Another neat trick you can do with the Apple Speaker port is connect to unpowered speakers, the kind you usually hook up to your stereo. This takes a special cable, made by Griffin Technology, that costs about $25. With this cable, you can use virtually any standard stereo speakers directly with your Mac jukebox, with no amplifier required. See the cable at `www.griffintechnology.com/products/cables_accessories/prospeaker_breakout.html` to find out more. This cable is also available at Apple stores.

USB provides another option for connecting speakers. For about $35, you can get the Griffin iMic, previously described in Chapter 9, which adds both high-quality input and output capabilities to your Mac. From the iMac or from your Mac's headphone jack, you can connect to an amplifier using standard RCA cables. You can plug into any unused audio-in connection except one reserved for a turntable, usually marked Phono. For much more on connecting your Mac to a stereo, see Chapter 9.

Remote Control

Remote control is a great feature of traditional stereos (that is, stereos that aren't also computers). You don't have to give up this wonderful convenience when you start playing music through your Mac. The Keyspan Digital Media Remote gives you wireless access to iTunes so you don't have to remove yourself from your chair in order to fool with the sound. This remote costs about $50 and includes an infrared receiver that connects to a USB port on your computer. You can use it to quickly pause, play, mute, skip to the next song, and perform other functions. Figure 12-1 shows you what it looks like, and you can go to `www.keyspan.com/products/usb/remote/` for more information.

FIGURE 12-1: Keyspan Digital
Media Remote.
Courtesy of Keyspan.

Installing and Using iTunes

Apple introduced version 4 of iTunes in April 2003, and that's the minimum version you'll need for your jukebox. Earlier versions provided some of the same basic features, but version 4 added support for music sharing, which is essential for our project. You also need version 4 to do business with the iTunes Music Store and to import songs in the AAC format, which gives you good sound quality and smaller file sizes.

Since the introduction of iTunes 4, it has been included with all new Macs. If you have an older version of iTunes, or if you, for some reason, don't have a copy at all, you can acquire one for a great price: nothing. Just download a copy at www.apple.com/itunes/download. If you have an earlier version, you can update it by using the Software Update feature in System Preferences.

Note

If you prefer to get your copy of iTunes 4 on a good old-fashioned CD and you don't mind paying for it, you can buy iLife, Apple's bundle of digital hub applications. The CD includes iTunes, iPhoto, iDVD, and iMovie. It's available from Apple's retail and online stores for $49.

Once again, be sure that you get iTunes 4, which is a significant advance from prior versions. Without version 4, you won't be able to take advantage of the effortless sharing feature that's essential to using your Mac as a wireless jukebox.

Adding Music to the iTunes Library

Once you have iTunes 4 running, you can start getting your music collection onto your Mac. When you first start iTunes, it will offer to look for music on your hard disk and add it to the iTunes library. In general, you'll probably want to decline this kind offer, because iTunes might find files that you don't really want as part of your music collection, such as random sound effects that belong to games and other software. By skipping this option, you can retain greater control over what music you add to your library.

The source list on the left of the iTunes screen (see Figure 12-2) includes entries for various places that hold your music:

- Library consists of all the music on your computer that iTunes knows about.

- Radio lets you tune into streaming Internet radio stations.

- Music Store provides access to songs you can buy at the iTunes Music Store, and Purchased Music contains all the songs you've bought.

- If there's an audio CD inserted in any drive connected to the Mac, it appears next in the source list.

- If you have an iPod connected to your Mac, it will show up in the source list.

- Last in the source list are any playlists you've set up. If you've never used iTunes before, you'll see that it comes preconfigured with several playlists. These are smart playlists, which we'll talk smartly about later in this chapter.

FIGURE 12-2: iTunes window.
Courtesy of Apple.

You can easily get your beloved music from CDs to the iTunes library. Here are the steps:

1. Gather some of your favorite audio CDs. If you don't have any favorite audio CDs, you probably won't be very interested in the rest of this chapter.

2. Put a CD into your Mac's CD or DVD drive. This should start iTunes and bring it to the front. You'll see the CD in the source list at the left. If this doesn't happen automatically, you can start iTunes manually.

3. Make sure that the CD is selected in the source list.

4. Click Import (at the upper right) to start copying songs into the iTunes library. You can watch the progress in the iTunes display area.

The process of getting music from CDs into your Mac is called "ripping," as in "tear the music from the CD as you would a coupon from a magazine" and not "rip off," as in steal. When iTunes rips a song from a CD, it converts the audio into a compressed format, such as MP3 or AAC, which takes up a fraction of the space of the full song.

Settings

iTunes has a set of preferences you can play with to customize the ripping process. You'll find them by choosing Preferences in the iTunes menu, then clicking the Importing panel, as shown in Figure 12-3.

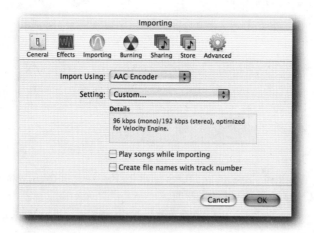

FIGURE 12-3: iTunes Importing preferences.
Courtesy of Apple.

The settings in this panel control just how the songs will be converted from audio on the CD to storage on your hard disk. The first pop-up menu lets you specify the format that songs will be converted to when you import them. You should choose AAC for your digital jukebox. As described in earlier chapters, AAC provides the highest quality for the smallest file size. If you want to be able to move your music among various computers and portable players, including those running Windows, you might consider MP3, because AAC players are still rare.

Another preferences panel, the General settings, gives you more control over how iTunes behaves when you're importing your CD collection. This panel has an "On CD Insert" setting that lets you decide what should happen when you put an audio CD into the drive. If you're going to be ripping a bunch of CDs in a row, choose the setting "Import Songs and Eject." When you use that setting, iTunes will automatically start ripping music when you insert a CD, and then, when it's done, it ejects the CD from the drive so you can insert the next one. Handy!

When you insert a CD, iTunes thinks for a moment and then determines the name of the CD and its tracks. You might guess that that information is encoded on the CD itself, but not so—iTunes actually grabs it from an Internet database maintained by a company called Gracenote. A setting in the General panel ("Connect to Internet when needed") controls whether iTunes automatically connects to the Internet to get this information. You should make sure this setting is on, as it is by default.

Tip The Shuffle setting in the Controls menu is great for a jukebox. When you turn Shuffle on for your library or playlist, iTunes randomly selects the next track to play instead of just going in order. This makes your Mac work like an amazingly versatile radio station, and you'll be constantly surprised at what comes up.

Playlists Smart and Dumb

iTunes lets you create playlists of songs you like to hear together. For example, you can make a playlist of superenergetic tunes you love to hear when you're exercising, or a quieter selection of nonvocal music that's great to listen to while reading.

All playlists are divided into two kinds: regular and smart. A regular playlist is simply a list of songs that you create by dragging and dropping. A smart playlist is a really cool thing: iTunes constructs it based on criteria that you specify. We'll discuss making each kind of playlist.

First, to create a regular playlist:

1. Choose File→New Playlist. A fresh playlist appears in the source list.

2. Your playlist is called "Untitled Playlist", and that's terrible. The name of the new playlist should be selected, so you can type a better name.

3. Click the item in the source list, such as Library, that holds the music you want to add to your playlist.

4. Click a song and drag it to your new playlist icon to add it to the playlist.

5. You can add more songs, and you don't have to do so one at a time. To select a bunch of songs that are next to each other, click the first one, then hold down the shift key while you click the song at the other end of the range. To select multiple songs that aren't adjacent, hold down the command key while clicking tunes. When you have multiple songs selected, you can drag the whole mess to your playlist icon.

What's Really There?

You can remove a song from a playlist by selecting it and pressing delete. But does that delete the song from your hard disk? No. A playlist is just that, a list of songs. When you delete a song from a playlist, it's just like crossing an item off your grocery list — it doesn't make the item itself go away, it just takes it off the list. Note that it's different if you have Library selected instead of a playlist. In that case, you'll get the option of actually sending a file to the trash when you press delete.

Regular playlists are handy, but smart playlists are practically magical. You can create a smart playlist that includes the songs you listen to the most, those that you haven't heard for a while, or the ones you've ripped this month. You can make a list of only your highest-rated songs, or all the songs by The Beatles or They Might Be Giants.

Here are the steps for making a smart playlist:

1. Choose File→New Smart Playlist to start your first smart playlist adventure. You'll see the dialog shown in Figure 12-4.

FIGURE 12-4: Smart Playlist creation dialog.
Courtesy of Apple.

2. Use the first area in the dialog to set up the criteria you want for songs in your playlist. For example, to build that Beatles playlist, you can choose "Artist is The Beatles" from the pop-ups; select "Song Name contains jungle" to find all the songs with the word "jungle" in the title. To pick your most recently ripped music, choose "Date Added is in the last 30 days."

3. To get really fancy and set up more than one criterion, click the plus sign at the right. You can use this to create a playlist of your favorite band ("Artist is They Might Be Giants") that includes songs you haven't played recently ("Last Played is not in the last 60 days").

4. The second set of pop-ups lets you limit how much music gets into the playlist. You can set a limit based on the number of songs, their total duration, or the amount of storage they take up. The last criterion is especially useful if you're going to put the playlist on an iPod.

5. Every song in your iTunes library has a check mark that sort of lets you turn the song into a second-class citizen. When a song is unchecked, it won't be played when its turn comes up. It's like saying yes, you want to keep the song around, but no, you don't really want to play it much. You can check "Match only checked songs" to prevent these unloved songs from getting into your playlist in the first place.

6. The "Live updating" item tells iTunes to keep watching for new songs to see if they fit into the criteria set by the smart playlist, and add them if so. That way, your Neil Young smart playlist will continue to grow automatically as you add new Neil Young music.

Sharing

When iTunes 4 appeared in 2003, Apple unexpectedly included a nifty sharing feature: it lets you play music from iTunes libraries and playlists on other people's computers in your local network. That sounds a lot like file sharing that has the record companies so worked up, but it has a crucial difference: you don't get to download the music onto your computer. Instead, you're streaming it from the source. When you (or the source computer) disconnect from the network, the tunes are gone. (See Chapter 2 for more on digital rights and the record industry.)

Within a few days of the release of iTunes 4, clever music lovers discovered a way around one of Apple's limitations: instead of just playing music from local computers, you could share music located in iTunes playlists on any Internet-connected Mac that had the sharing feature turned on. This was too much, Apple decreed. Soon thereafter, a new version of iTunes appeared (version 4.0.1) that clamped down and made sure you could only share music with your local network family or coworkers.

The sharing feature in iTunes is the key to making your wireless jukebox work. To play music throughout your house without wires, you need at least two Macs running iTunes 4, one to hold the music and the other connected via an 802.11 wireless network (as described in Chapter 6). The second computer is your music player, getting access to the tunes via the network and iTunes sharing. If this computer is a laptop, you can play music anywhere you can take the laptop and still get local network access.

To turn on and use sharing in iTunes:

1. Make sure that you're connected to your wireless network.

2. On the computer that holds all the music (the jukebox itself), choose iTunes→ Preferences and click Sharing. You'll see the sharing preferences panel (Figure 12-5).

3. To make sure the music from this computer is shared, turn on "Share my music." You can choose to share your whole library or only certain playlists. Usually, you'll want to share the whole library. This will make your songs show up in the source list of anybody else looking for music on your local network.

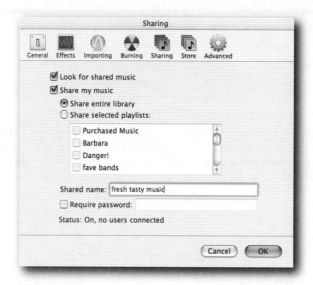

FIGURE 12-5: Sharing pane of iTunes preferences.
Courtesy of Apple.

On every computer that will have access to the jukebox (the "player" computers), choose iTunes→Preferences and click Sharing. Make sure that "Look for shared music" is checked. Once you've turned on these sharing settings, you'll see a "Shared music" item in the iTunes source list on the "player" computer, with the shared playlist from the juke- box computer appearing there. Now you're ready to rock and roll—literally.

Go ahead and test out playing music from the jukebox. On the player computer, choose one of the jukebox playlists in the source list. After a moment to make the connection, you should see the songs from the playlist, just as if they were right there on the player machine. Select one of the songs, and click the iTunes play button. iTunes should make the connection and start playing your song.

Like a Version

When Apple released iTunes 4.0.1, the version that cut off sharing via the Internet and restricted it to the local network only, it added few new features, which reduced the incentive for users to update. There is one strong incentive, however: computers running 4.0 can't share at all with those running 4.0.1 or later. For maximum sharing goodness, it's easiest to make sure that all sharing computers on your network are running 4.0.1 or later, even though you'll have to give up the little-used Internet sharing feature from 4.0.

Sharing and iTunes Music Store

Apple's famous iTunes Music Store lets you choose from tens of thousands of songs that you can buy and download, most for 99 cents each. Songs that you buy from the iTunes Music Store have some restrictions, though. For example, you can only play them on three different Macs, and unfortunately, you can't play them from a shared computer with the iTunes sharing feature, even if the shared computer is one of the three authorized to play the song.

There is a way around this restriction, however. You can convert the rights-restricted Music Store files to unrestricted MP3 files by burning them to CD, then ripping the CD back into iTunes. When you do this, the newly ripped files are MP3s that can be played anywhere, although the quality is lessened by the ripping process. Even with this workaround, it's a good idea to respect the rights set up by the Music Store.

Tip

Sharing music over a wireless network sends a lot of data flying through the air, using plenty of bandwidth. For best performance, you should have a network that uses AirPort Extreme (802.11g) components.

AppleScript

You can use AppleScript to help you automate and customize your digital jukebox experience. For example, there are scripts to help you clean up track listings and to assist in constructing smart playlists with fancy settings. You'll find a vast treasure of scripts for iTunes at Doug's AppleScripts for iTunes site (www.malcolmadams.com/itunes/).

To use the scripts, you download the ones you want, then install them inside your home directory, in the Library/iTunes/Scripts folder. When you quit and restart iTunes, the scripts will show up in the AppleScript menu, just to the left of the Help menu. To use one, you just select it from the AppleScript menu.

Here are some of the most popular and useful scripts:

- Append To Comments lets you add text to the comment field of many tracks at once. This is useful for building smart playlists that look for specific words in the comments field, such as "Bob's favorites" or "music to read by."

- Super Remove Dead Tracks cleans up your library by taking out entries to songs that aren't on your hard disk any more.

- Wrangle Same-Named Tracks helps you find and clean up duplicate songs.

- iTunes Music Store Player lets you select a bunch of songs in the Music Store, then play their free 30-second samples automatically, one after the other.

Summary

Creating a Mac-flavored wireless jukebox consists of setting up an 802.11 network, getting iTunes 4 running on two or more Macs, and setting up music sharing so the Macs can see each other's libraries and playlists. Make sure that your jukebox is the best it can be by following these tips:

- For the best combination of quality and storage efficiency, encode in the AAC format.

- Playlists are your friends. If you spend a little time organizing your music into playlists and setting up a few smart playlists, you'll have a better chance of finding just the music you want to hear.

- Use AppleScripts to help you maintain your library and playlists.

- Don't forget about your favorite LPs. Instead, use Chapter 9 to get them into iTunes so you can enjoy them all over again.

Happy listening!

Index

Continued